Voldofte

Woedke

Handewitt

Obliwitz

Westerohrstedt

Norddorf

Hamburg-Boberg

Feddersen-Wierde

Biskupin

Brzek Kujawski

Ezinge

Einswarden

Hatzum

Perleberg

Hijken

Jemgum

Konin

Biskupice

Elp

Ripdorf

Berlin

Angelsloo

Buch

Burg

Vaassen

Wallwitz

Ksiacek

Cracovie

Albersloh

Senftenberg

Haps

Soest

Ludwigsdorf

Niederzier

Altburg-Niedenstein

Bedburg

Postoloprty

Libenice

Heidetränk

Steinsburg

Stradonice

Zavist

Stare Hradisko

Spissky Strvrtok

Titelberg

Bundenbach

Finsterlohr

Jaispitz

Lovcicky

efon

Donnersberg

Trisov

Hohlandsberg

Devin

Hatvan

Goldberg

Künzing

Braunsberg

Hochdorf

Kelheim

Hradok

Sainte-Odile

Entringen

Manching

Nitriansk

Kyberg

Salzburg

Sopron

Gellérthegy

Hohenasperg

Breisach-Hochstetten

Holzhausen

Lovasberény

Britzyberg

Wittnauer Horn

Hallstatt

Velemczentvid

Toszeg

lte des Planches

Montlingerberg

Hallein

Sarbogard

Baldeg

Zürich-Uetliberg

Salins

Auvernier

Zug-Sumpf

Regöly

levaix

Cortaillod

Szalacska

Bàta

Clairvaux

Châtillon-sur-Glâne

Mottata

TOWNS, VILLAGES

AND COUNTRYSIDE

OF CELTIC EUROPE

From the beginning of the second millennium to
the end of the first century BC

Françoise Audouze and Olivier Büchsenschütz

Translated by Henry Cleere

B.T. Batsford Ltd, London

© 1989 Hachette, France
First published in French, 1989, as *Villes, Villages et Campagnes de l'Europe Celtique*

English translation © B.T. Batsford 1991
First published in English 1992

All rights reserved. No part of this publication may be reproduced, in any form or by any means, without permission from the Publisher

Typeset by Servis Filmsetting Ltd, Manchester and printed in Great Britain by Butler and Tanner, Frome, Somerset

Published by B.T. Batsford Ltd
4 Fitzhardinge Street, London W1H 0AH

A catalogue record for this book is available from the British Library

ISBN 0 7134 6523 9

Contents

Illustrations

Foreword

The publication of the original version of this book by Hachette in 1989 represented the first broad-scale 'settlement archaeology' of later European prehistory. 'Settlement archaeology' is used here primarily in its literal, rather than its figurative, sense; for this is a book anchored in the physical remains recovered by excavation and field survey from a great swathe of the Continent, stretching eastward from the Pyrenees to the confines of European Russia, and north to Great Britain and southern Scandinavia. Its concern with such matters as inter-site patterning is altogether secondary.

The original Introduction to the volume addressed itself primarily to a French-speaking audience; and especially to the authors' compatriots. In redrafting, I have retained the issues that concerned them, but have attempted to refocus these in order to explain to an English-language readership why this book takes the form it does.

Audouze and Büchsenschütz selected a quotation from the last work of the distinguished French historian, Fernand Braudel, to introduce their theme:

> . . . such units as villages, hamlets, bourgs, isolated farms, are ancient creations, belonging to history in its fullest sense, that is going back beyond the historical into the centuries and millennia of prehistory. Peering this far back in time, we cannot see clearly. We are reduced to hypotheses.'[1]

In so doing, they firmly established that one of their principal concerns was to provide the foundations that only archaeological data can supply for historical approaches to the settlement record of France in post-Roman times. As elsewhere, of course, written sources do not adequately cover the timespan of much of the development of the European countryside. Since significant modifications through human impact began at the time of the first villages, in the Neolithic, only archaeological means are available to illuminate the initial steps in man's shaping of the landscapes of the Continent. French scholarship has for long identified the succeeding Ages – of Bronze and of Iron – as a unit of study; and it is the two-thousand-year span of these 'Ages des Métaux', ending with the Roman Conquest, which form the core of this study. It is certainly arguable that this long period was marked by the first substantial human colonization of much of Europe's diverse terrain; the extent and the complexity of the resultant exploitation of the Continent's landscapes far exceeding most non-specialists' perceptions.

In France itself, the Bronze and Iron Ages were until recently little studied, in contrast to many temperate European countries where the archaeology of these periods has been a major interest for decades. Both school textbooks and introductory volumes on French archaeology began, promisingly enough, with discussions of the Palaeolithic record of the country, well-known from the study of the gravels of the Somme and the caves of the Dordogne. But, thereafter, they focused on such achievements as the civilization of Egypt. France itself only re-entered the story at the

[1] Braudel, F. (1988) *The Identity of France. I – History and Environment*. Translated by S Reynolds; London, Collins. (p.138).

dawn of the Roman period, with brief mentions of the mustachioed Gauls and their huts given to provide 'native colour', a backdrop to a discussion of the Roman Conquest. The activities of Vercingetorix, the Gallic war leader around whom resistance to Rome developed, allowed the first chapter of history from a nationalist perspective to be written: but readers were never left in any doubt that true civilization reached France with the Roman legions.

Such a view, rooted in nineteenth-century models, is still prevalent in a number of introductory texts on French archaeology written for schools. Of course, individual teachers, many of whom have taken part in excavations as volunteers, are well able to redress this. As in Britain, the expansion of 'rescue archaeology', occurring a little later than on the British side of the Channel, initially relied heavily on volunteer labour, thereby contributing to the popularization of the subject.

In France, protohistoric archaeology – a term used in French to embrace the archaeological record of periods contemporary with surviving written sources (and thus with 'history' in this narrow sense) – has equally had a rather different relationship with

written sources than that which has prevailed in Britain, throughout this century at least. Since the development of the study of antiquity, it has become increasingly clear that the evidence conveyed by the Classical authors and that recoverable from the field by archaeological means are sometimes in conflict. Faced with this dilemma, authors have argued in favour of one or other set of evidence. In Britain, as in Germany and neighbouring countries, the balance was firmly tilting in favour of archaeological evidence before the end of the nineteenth century, not least, Audouze and Büchsenschütz propose, because these are countries where the amount of evidence that can be gleaned from Greek and Latin sources is sparse. But in France it was still possible in the 1960s for writers to devote a hundred pages to its late Iron Age inhabitants, the Gauls, framed exclusively around the information contained in the Classical authors; and to search for the site of Julius Caesar's last great siege in Gaul, at Alesia, with only his *De Bello Gallico* and the equivalent of the Ordnance Survey maps to hand. It still remained acceptable to discount the results of a century and a quarter of archaeological enquiry.

To appreciate the contributions of the inhabitants

1
Barbarian fighting a Roman legionary. Paris, Musée du Louvre. This relief is often used in school textbooks to illustrate a Gaulish house before the conquest, whereas it shows a Dacian from Romania and was carved around AD 100. This example well illustrates the way in which textbooks perpetuate fallacious ideas that are solidly fixed in the collective memory. (M. Vincent et al., 1977. Photograph: Lauros-Giraudon.)

of temperate Europe during the last two millennia BC to the historical development of the Continent requires us to take on board the strengths and weaknesses of the archaeological record of these periods. Audouze and Büchsenschütz implored their French readers to forget the Greeks and the Romans, writing and elaborate stone architecture – all elements which have traditionally played a major role in the definition of European civilization. Also to be set aside are standard views of barbarians (Fig.1) – so powerful when composed by the likes of Caesar or Tacitus. Barbarians remote from the power of Rome are normally presented as true savages, formidable in battle, but simple and direct in their customs; the speeches purportedly made before the battle of Mons Graupius in Tacitus' *Agricola* are celebrated examples of this view. Contrastingly, barbarians affected by Roman influences are portrayed as having begun to modify their internal political arrangements and to construct towns, but as having lost their vigour as a result of contact with civilization. Such statements are nothing more than clichés. They have more to tell us about the mentality of the Romans than about the peoples to the north of the Alps; but, until recently, many historians have taken such remarks at face value.

It may equally be contended that our perceptions of protohistoric architecture are similarly coloured by immersion in a tradition that was initially expressed by Vitruvius in his *De Architectura*, written at the end of the first century BC. In this, architecture in stone only is seen as worthy of consideration. In one sentence, all house-building styles that are not dependent on stone are dismissed: 'Some peoples make roofs out of leaves; others dig artificial caves beneath mountains; and some, copying the nest of the swallow, shelter in structures made of mud and twigs.' A civilized man can only live in a stone building: everything else is but a shack or hovel, fit only for creatures not far removed from beasts. Such a viewpoint remains so firmly embedded in contemporary French culture, Audouze and Büchsenschütz explain, that recent texts have often devoted only a few lines to that fundamental element of material culture, the house and its accompanying outbuildings. It may also be argued that this perspective depressed the expectations of French archaeologists, especially those working before the 1960s, as to what might be recoverable by careful on-site dissection, in terms of the remains of structures. Again, the contrast with Britain and indeed other countries around the North Sea is significant; for in these islands, the examination of timber buildings as part of the routine of excavation

is a standard element of field programmes from the period between the two World Wars on.

For some parts of continental Europe, it has to be conceded that knowledge of protohistoric structures and settlement plans is still very partial. However, the risk of leaving the results of a century of archaeological work on this evidence in the hands of the specialists concerned, and of not presenting current debates on how it should be interpreted to the public, is that the grip of the Classical authors will not be broken: the general view of European protohistory will continue to be mediated by these scattered textual sources. Audouze and Büchsenschütz believe this state of affairs to be indefensible. The task they set themselves is to outline the archaeological evidence that has accumulated for protohistoric settlement in non-Mediterranean Europe. The reader will thus be provided with a number of starting points on a research programme that still has a long way to go. This large sector of Europe, in later prehistory in substantial measure under Celtic and Germanic influences, is characterized by its heavy reliance on wood as the principal building material. It includes both the temperate and nordic zones of the Continent. The immediate hinterland of the Mediterranean Basin, which was rapidly affected by traits from that area, more particularly the tradition of building rectilinear structures in stone, is not considered in this study.

Developing their historical perspective, Audouze and Büchsenschütz focus on some of the distinguished – and justifiably popular – research conducted by French historians in recent years. They note, as evidenced by certain case studies on Medieval France, the emphasis placed on detail when considering the organization of settlements, and of life therein. But the achievement represented by such writing needs to be set in context: there are still huge gaps in our understanding of the general pattern of the evolution of everyday rural living standards. In re-reading the contributions of scholars on the medieval period, Audouze and Büchsenschütz were forcibly struck by the fact that, although focused on the same issues and rooted in the same methods as those that interested archaeologists concerned with the Bronze and Iron Ages, the medievalists often arrived at conclusions very different from those reached by protohistorians. It is debatable whether medievalists do not regularly underestimate the achievements of the Bronze and Iron Ages in terms of the development of rural-based societies, by underplaying both the technical skills apparent for example in their surviving structural records and the evidence that such societies had already set in place complex systems of land use. On

*2
Butser Ancient Farm,
Hampshire.
Experimental
reconstruction of an
Iron Age farm. (P.J.
Reynolds.)*

the other hand, it may be contended that protohistorians are over-optimistic in the reading of their evidence: they may be too ready to attribute to that nebulous group, 'the Celts', as a single job-lot all the inventions which gradually helped shape the European countryside. It is clear that half a century of sustained research on the countryside, in which there have been significant contributions from a number of disciplines, means that many traditional views now look distinctly outmoded. The dating of the establishment of certain land-use patterns also demands fresh assessment.

However, Audouze and Büchsenschütz entirely go along with historians of later periods in wishing to discard 'the long-held illusion of the Ancient Economy as being town- and money-based'[2]. To say this, they argue, is not to downgrade the role of Romanization in the development of European culture and society. Rather this viewpoint lays stress on the development of the rural sector, the dominant one in both spatial and population terms until recent times. Elements of continuity are detectable in rural life from the first farmers of the Neolithic until the modern era. The Roman achievement, couched in terms of an urban-based civilization, was indeed remarkable, but it did not fundamentally modify conditions in the countryside. Recent archaeological research in both the Low Countries and Denmark, they point out, demonstrates that certain land units went on in use for very long

periods. Whilst such areas were touched by both political changes and technical progress, discernable reactions there are marked by their slow, cautious implementation; technological innovations and changing political circumstances are both accommodated, but without flying in the face of the opportunities and constraints afforded by local resources, nor by negating local customs.

In France, the revival of interest in the rural dimension of its history is identified as being attributable to the work of the *Annales* school of historians; and to more general preoccupations with 'green' matters. The relevant section of the book is slanted more to the formation of rural landscapes in France than more widely in Europe, although broader concerns are not omitted. It is thus worth rehearsing the major lines of French scholarship that contributed to Audouze and Büchsenschütz's perspective.

Issues that were major concerns (as witnessed by the writings of Marc Bloch and Gaston Roupnel) in the inter-War years — when historians began to consider the patterning inherent in field systems and geographers tackled the identification of the chronological stages perceptible in the development of landscapes — are again coming to the fore. From the 1930s, both Roupnel and the distinguished Celtic scholar Henri Hubert posed the question of the origins of France's rural landscapes: for the first, their origins could be traced back to the activities of Neolithic and Bronze

[2] Chapelot, J. and Fossier, R. (1980) *Le Village et la Maison au Moyen Age*. (p. 17).

Age farmers; Hubert contrastingly attributed the different field systems visible in the country to successive waves of Celtic immigrants. Since that time, a wealth of new data produced by archaeology, and by aerial photography in particular, has modified the picture substantially. With the benefits of both this vastly enlarged database and of much finer chronological precision than was available half a century ago, the tendency now is to play down the role of peoples whose names have come down to us by chance. There is no sound basis for identifying a Bronze Age population as 'Celtic'; and no *a priori* reason to link place-names with the origin of field systems with which they now happen to coincide in spatial terms. Leaving aside the detail of their differences of opinion, the crux of the matter is that Roupnel and Hubert shared the view that the key to the organization of the rural landscapes of France lay in the pre-Roman world. And if the debate between these authors is framed in terms which would now be treated rather sceptically, it represented an attempt to address questions to which present-day authors would like in the long term to furnish answers.

'There is often a tendency to attribute the shaping of a rural landscape to the Gallo-Romans, when they were only its later inheritors', wrote Roupnel in 1932. It is questionable whether, nearly sixty years later, the desire mistakenly to mark the development of the French countryside down as a Gallo-Roman achievement has entirely disappeared. The impact of Marc Bloch's study, *Les Caractères originaux de l'histoire rurale française*, published in 1929, may lie behind more recent historians' ignorance of the distant origins of the rural landscapes of Europe; for that work is silent on the early period. The major study, edited by Duby and Wallon in 1975, and published as the first volume of the *Histoire de la France rurale*[3], directed attention to the development of agriculture in the Neolithic period, by then much better known in France as the result of intensive archaeological research on that period. In contrast with Britain, where the results of excavation and post-excavation work were beginning to be complemented by data from experimentation (Fig. 2), knowledge of the Bronze and Iron Ages had made less rapid headway, as is highlighted by its brief treatment in Duby and Wallon's synthesis; this may in part be due, the authors suggest, to the absence of these periods in the archaeological curricula of French universities. But there is, they contend, enough evidence to begin to dispel the 'still hazy' – the phrase is E. Le Roy Ladurie's – origins of French rural life. The aim of this book is thus, without attempting to overstate the hypothesis or the evidence on which it is based, to demonstrate that the last two millennia BC are of fundamental significance in any understanding of the making of Europe's rural environments.

The present text is very substantially a direct translation by Henry Cleere from the French edition. In general, radiocarbon-based dates or periods are quoted without calibration. In Chapter 11, the opportunity has been taken to begin to reassess the evidence that has accumulated since the French text was completed for isolated settlement in the continental Bronze Age. Minor corrigenda have been incorporated, in particular in a number of the illustration captions.

Ian Ralston
University of Edinburgh
March 1991

---

[3] Duby, G. and Wallon, A. eds. (1975) *Histoire de la France rurale. I – la formation des campagnes françaises des origines au XIVe siècle* by Bertrand, G., Bertrand, C., Bailloud, G., Le Glay, M. and Fourquin, G.; Paris, Editions du Seuil.

1 From primitive society to the birth of the European countryside

What is the reality underlying the Bronze and Iron Ages? The introduction of copper, followed by bronze and finally iron, represents only one aspect of the evolution that these two millennia witnessed. The Neolithic farmer, tenuously bound to the soil by the exploitation of fields that were restricted to the best lands and integrated into his community for the whole of his life, tended to become increasingly sedentary – a peasant clinging to a piece of land whose resources he exploited to the full. Another two thousand years were to pass before a Europe that was hardly deforested became a mosaic of small holdings of land; to all appearances these were self-sufficient with their fields, their flocks and herds, their poultry, their pigs and their craft activities, but linked one with another by multiple short-, medium-, and long-range exchange mechanisms. This dynamic rural society was well established north of the Alps by the fifth century BC. It was in many respects closer to French peasant society of the eighteenth century than it was to the groupings of the Early Bronze Age.

It is, however, a different aspect of this evolution which has attracted the attention of specialists. They use the term 'protohistory' for this period without always reaching agreement on its definition or on its spatial and temporal extent. Did Europe enter protohistory with agriculture, with metals, or with the earliest Greek and Latin texts which provide 'historical' evidence about these otherwise mute peoples? C.-A. Moberg has admirably demonstrated how the different technological and other acquisitions which brought these primitive peoples into the historical world, such as urbanization, coinage and writing, spread progressively across Europe from the Mediterranean to Scandinavia in a series of waves. The reason why the Romans were so successful in the northerly extension of their Empire is that they came into contact with peoples there who were fully equipped to enter history.

The Bronze Age

The East and the Mediterranean were always several decades, if not several centuries, ahead of the rest of Europe in that march towards a civilized state that we call progress. Although relations with the Mediterranean played their part, it was above all the local development of peoples and exchanges between the various regions of the continent that shaped Europe during these two millennia. Technological innovations and the economic and social changes that resulted from them needed centuries to take effect and never violently disturbed everyday life. Thus, Neolithic long houses of the *Linearbandkeramik* culture covered the loess plains of central Europe for nearly two thousand years, and the three-aisled byre-houses of northern Europe, which first appeared during the Iron Age, survived for 1500 years.

European protohistory is traditionally divided into two periods, the Bronze Age and the Iron Age. Within the former several major cultural areas are distinguished which spread over one or more of the Early, Middle, and Late Bronze Age phases. The first Iron Age takes its name from the cemetery at Hallstatt in Austria and the second from the site of La Tène on Lake Neuchâtel. The dates shown in Figure 7 refer to innovatory regions: they are not yet accurate even to the quarter-century. It should not be forgotten that these sub-divisions are sometimes based only on the appearance of new materials, more often on a change in funerary practices, and only rarely on true culture

3

Hoard of axes found at Henon (Côtes-du-Nord). Thousands of hoards of weapons, tools or jewellery were buried during the Bronze Age. Some consist of worn or broken objects intended for remelting, others are founders' hoards of new artefacts, whilst others testify to phenomena relating to the hoarding of precious objects and religious offerings that are as yet not understood. (J. Briard.)

change. It is not yet possible for the significant cultural developments, which we are about to discuss, to be related closely to typological changes in the material culture record.

The arts of fire

The discovery of metals in reality dates back to the end of the Middle Neolithic. It is between 4500 and 3500 BC that we begin to find rings, awls and small personal ornaments made of worked copper in eastern Europe. A few centuries later the recognition of the properties of arsenical copper, which is harder than the pure metal, led to the development of metallurgy proper. As a result of mastering the technique of handling heat in hearths and kilns it became possible to melt copper and cast it into artefacts in simple moulds. The use of the copper-tin alloy known as bronze did not become general until around 1850 BC in central Europe. Throughout this period continuous technological improvements, both qualitative and quantitative, were being introduced: native arsenical copper was succeeded by increasingly complex alloys in which the copper content varied between 95 per cent and 85 per cent. Alongside tin, which conferred hardness on the alloy, came antimony and nickel, and then, in the Late Bronze Age, lead, which lowered the melting temperature, but at the same time reduced the strength of the metal. The presence of trace elements in ore compositions makes it possible to determine the provenances of metal objects. Cold working was followed by the techniques of hot working and annealing and, above all, of casting in sand, stone, or metal moulds. Two-part moulds were introduced early, and the lost-wax casting process is known from the Late Bronze Age.

Mines, trade, and founders' hoards

The search for raw materials, which are not available evenly across Europe, their distribution, and the struggle to possess them resulted in inevitable changes in society, although these can only be detected indirectly. Copper ores, often exploited from alluvial deposits, are abundant in Spain, in Britain, and in the mountainous regions of central Europe; they are less common in France and completely absent in the north European plain and in Scandinavia. Tin ores are even more concentrated: in Galicia, in Brittany, and in the south-west of Britain, in those regions known to the Greeks and Phoenicians as the Cassiterides, in the ore-bearing mountains of Bohemia, and in north-western Italy. These metals were the object of long-distance trade, as evidenced by the numerous ingots in the form of bars, cakes or torcs that have been found all over Europe. Copper and tin were traded independently, being alloyed at manufacturing sites.

Many thousands of artefacts are known as a result of frequent discoveries of 'founders' hoards'. These are concentrations of perhaps as many as several hundred weapons and tools, which may be unused, worn, or broken, collected together in a pot, between stones, or simply buried in the ground (Fig. 3). They become more numerous in the Late Bronze Age: some deposits, such as that of Vénat in the Charente, contain several thousand pieces. How should these be interpreted? For a long time they were seen as testifying to the insecurity of the countryside in this period. Nowadays, however, this phenomenon is related to the process of controlling and distributing metal products among different population groups. On the basis of an analysis of material from Middle Bronze Age hoards in Britain, M. Rowlands believes that the manufacture of artefacts was carried out by sedentary craftsmen working for a local clientele; he calculates the radius of distribution to have been around 20km (12 miles) in the Thames Valley. The stocking of material in permanent deposits would permit those craftsmen who worked only part-time to respond to demand throughout the whole year. The increase in the number of hoards and the high proportion of objects removed from circulation in the Late Bronze Age would correspond to a control over supplies, either by the craftsmen themselves or by the political power that employed them. Certain weapons, such as swords, which are more complex to manufacture, are more widely distributed geographically. It would appear that they came from specialist centres and were produced for a more restricted clientele.

More recently, K. Kristiansen and M. Rowlands have stressed the social significance of bronze weapons and jewellery, which express the status of their owners. Hoards can thus be interpreted as accumulations of wealth, foreshadowing the colossal fortunes in gold amassed by the Celts in their sanctuaries at a period when coinage was already in use.

In any case, it is clear that long-distance trade was a feature of society. As early as the late Neolithic, flint mines such as that at Grand-Pressigny (Indre-et-Loire) were exporting their products over several hundred kilometres. Irish gold and Baltic amber were reaching France, and soon the routes had become so complex and the imitations so numerous that it is no longer possible to disentangle the directions of the flow of material goods.

The whole of Europe testifies to a surprising uniformity in the development of technology and production: although there are regional variations, the same forms are to be found from one end of the continent to the other. Early Bronze Age triangular daggers were followed in the Middle Bronze Age by short swords with trapezoidal hilt-plates, long pins with ribbed heads, and the flanged axes; in the Late Bronze Age these in turn gave way to a range of sword types characterized by tripartite hilts, to small vase-headed pins and socketed axes. Even though it was manufactured locally, pottery did not escape this tendency towards uniformity, and a stylistic family resemblance can be observed within each major phase. Agriculture and domestic economy also made substantial progress, although this is difficult to detect before the Late Bronze Age owing to the lack of data.

Ards, byres and horses

Animal bones collected from settlement sites show a progressive reduction in the number of species being hunted. In parallel with this, pollen analysis has shown the area under grass increasing at the expense of woodland, which can be explained by the growth in the raising of cattle, sheep, goats, and pigs. The enclosures of the Fenland of eastern England with their staggered entrances attest to the existence of pastures in enclosed fields. The distribution of sites in the Pyrenees suggests, by contrast, that transhumance was being practised. It was above all the discovery of true byres in the Netherlands and northern Germany which confirmed the existence of systematic animal husbandry, controlled by man and rigorously defined spatially so as not to interfere with arable farming.

There was an undeniable evolution in agricultural implements: axes with different forms of hafting and curved bronze sickles replacing the straight wooden sickles with flint cutting edges are evidence of the continuous search for greater efficiency. But did metal artefacts reach farmers everywhere and were wood and flint tools not competitive?

In fact, the most profound change in agricultural practice resulted from the introduction of the ard in the Late Bronze Age. It appeared at almost the same time all over Europe, as evidenced by the rock carvings of Scandinavia and the Alpes-Maritimes in southern France, and by the ploughs themselves, which have been discovered in peat bogs in Great Britain, the Netherlands, and northern Europe. Whilst differing in construction, they were still quite simple. They had wooden shares and were drawn by oxen harnessed to a collar yoke (see Fig. 93). Traces of furrows have been found, preserved under burial mounds or associated with settlements engulfed by sand dunes in Scotland.

The cart (Fig. 4) made its first appearance, with solid wooden wheels, in central Europe in the Early Bronze Age. Spoked wheels with hubs encased in bronze, vehicles with two, four, or even three wheels, rock carvings and pottery models testify to the various

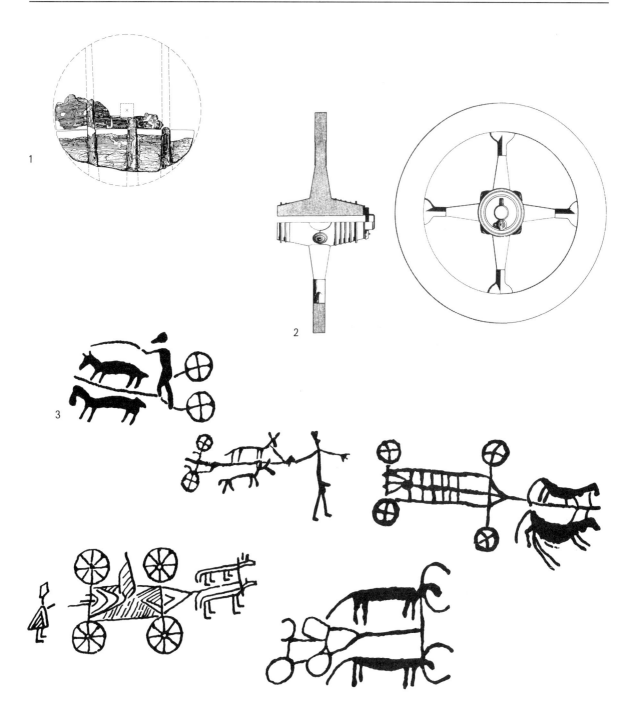

4

The wheel in the Bronze and Iron Ages. 1: Late Neolithic wooden wheel found at the lake settlement of Zürich-Pressehaus (drawing: U. Ruoff). 2: Bronze wheel from the Urnfield burial at Hart-an-der-Alz, Bavaria (Munich, Museum für Vor- und Frühgeschichte). 3: Representations of protohistoric wheeled vehicles (G. Cordier 1975). Wagons and carts played an important role in the societies of temperate Europe and various types have been found in settlements and burials; they are also represented on pots and rocks.

purposes to which these vehicles were put: war chariots, transportation wagons, ceremonial vehicles or those for ritual purposes, in the latter case linked with the sun cult. In the Iron Age a ceremonial vehicle would accompany deceased wealthy members of a community to their tombs, and the Romans borrowed not only the technology of wagon building from the Celts, but also the names of the different types of vehicle.

Horses had been domesticated in the steppes of eastern Europe from the early Chalcolithic, but their use as draught animals and then for riding increased slowly. The gradual appearance of horse bits and other pieces of harness equipment can be followed in their passage from east to west throughout the whole of the second millennium BC; they did not reach western Europe until the Late Bronze Age.

Inequality in death

Modern economic concepts suggest that the appearance of an evolved set of implements and the hoarding of durable assets result in social differentiation between rich and poor and between producers and consumers. However, our knowledge of the nature and method of operation of societies in the Bronze Age and the Hallstatt period (Fig. 5) is largely based on hypothesis. It is only possible to advance certain theories on the basis of information about funerary rites, the circulation of precious materials, and, to a lesser extent, settlement remains.

In the Late Neolithic and the whole of the Chalcolithic burials took the form of collective inhumations in western Europe and individual interments in central Europe, and there was little differentiation in grave goods. In the Early Bronze Age flat burials took over, often grouped into cemeteries. In addition to skeletons these contain pottery vessels and a few metal objects. The deceased left for the other world alone, but the provisions for the journey were the same for all. In Brittany, Wessex and Saxony, however, some richer tombs are found covered with a mound or barrow. These earth and stone mounds, which vary in diameter between 5 and 20m (16 and 66ft), can be several metres high. They are often delimited by a circular kerb of stones, a ditch or a palisade and they cover a mortuary chamber of timber construction or of stone. Such burials are distinguished by the richness of their grave goods and frequently by the presence of gold objects. The end of the Early Bronze Age saw the spread of the practice of secondary interments, often dug into the mound, either to accompany the original deceased or to take advantage of a privileged site.

The use of funerary mounds spread over practically the whole of Europe in the Middle Bronze Age: inhumation in sepulchral caves seems to have persisted only in southern France. An overwhelming majority of humble burials continued alongside a small number of exceptionally rich graves. The nature of the grave goods makes it possible to distinguish between the sexes: pins, bracelets, anklets, ear-rings, and knives are found alongside the pots in women's graves, whilst men's graves are characterized by daggers, swords, belt-hooks, and different types of pin. In addition to the artefacts that are typical of each region, certain types of jewellery and gold and amber ornament circulated widely over the whole of Europe.

Whatever the cause and nature of the upheavals of the Late Bronze Age they are illustrated by the appearance and rapid spread of a completely different funerary ritual. The peoples of the Urnfield Culture cremated their dead and collected the ashes and calcined bones in an urn which was then buried in a cist formed of stone slabs or directly in the ground. These large cremation cemeteries can be distinguished from those of the previous period both by the funerary ritual employed and by the appearance of an entirely new form of pottery, black, burnished and decorated with characteristic rilled decoration.

The birth of warfare and the emergence of nations

Neither archaeology nor place-name studies is yet capable of reconstructing with any authenticity the routes followed by the peoples who brought the Urnfield Culture. It is becoming increasingly difficult to assert that these changes were due to invasions of new groups of peoples. We have, however, no reason to believe that the evolution was brought about by simple acculturation, that is to say, progressive impacts on static peoples, without conflict or clashes with their neighbours. The most recent theories are turning towards the displacement of very small groups of people during periods of crisis, leading to the destabilization of neighbouring groups, a movement which could gradually extend over entire regions.

At the same period in the eastern Mediterranean the Mycenaean civilization was extinguished just as it was beginning to develop the use of iron artefacts. A relatively large number of graves and hoards all over Europe have produced helmets, breastplates, and greaves, as well as several thousand bronze swords. Confronted with such heavy equipment one's thoughts are irresistibly drawn to the image of the

5
The main Bronze Age cultural regions. 1: Around 1650 BC. 2: Around 1000 BC. (F. Audouze and O. Büchsenschütz.)

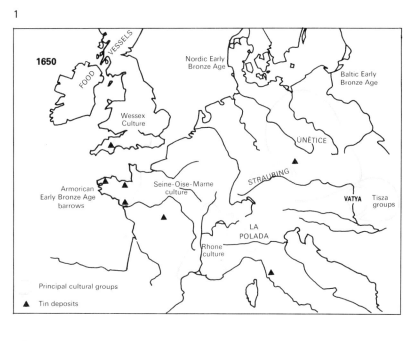

1

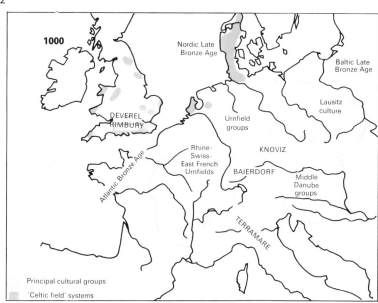

2

Homeric hero. This evidence of heavily-armed warriors presupposes the existence of political power, of rival peoples, and of the first conflicts in order to define frontiers or to control a commercial artery.

Europe exploded into a multitude of petty 'kingdoms' (Fig. 6), the most fortunate of whose princes were given sumptuous burials during the whole of the first Iron Age, the Hallstatt period.

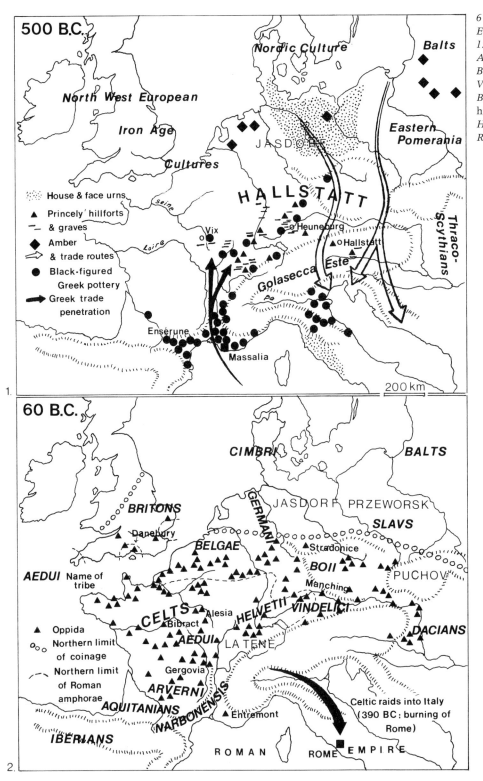

6
Europe in the Iron Age. 1: Around 500 BC. 2: Around 52 BC. (O. Büchsenschütz in P. Vidal-Naquet and J. Bertin, Atlas historique, *Paris, Hachette 1986. Redrawn by G. Searle.)*

Iron Age peasants, plunderers and craftsmen

Increasing contact with eastern Europe and the Mediterranean favoured the development of this aristocracy. Graves of the eighth century BC have yielded horse trappings, bits, and the earliest iron swords. This must be an indication of the prestige of the first horsemen (up till then the horse had only been used as a draught animal) and the superior qualities of iron swords. Should these innovations be related to the movements that were affecting the Thraco-Cimmerian peoples from the region to the north of the Black Sea, under pressure from the Scythians? There is no doubt that at this time Europe was experiencing pressure from the east, while at the same time it was being penetrated by Mediterranean influences coming from the south, along the trade routes. Although the political events that brought these contacts about are unknown to us, their consequences are very apparent in the progress of technology.

Iron and the coming of metal into everyday use

Iron was introduced gradually, but the changes that it brought with it were decisive ones. Unlike copper and tin, iron ore is widely available throughout Europe, it can in places be gathered on the surface. Iron is stronger than bronze, and a better cutting edge can be obtained by forging and whetting. The technological problems posed by the high temperatures needed for smelting iron ores and the processes of quenching and forging were gradually solved by smiths. The Celts were renowned in antiquity for their skill in combining hard steel and soft iron in a single implement or weapon and by so doing producing a ductile blade with a hard cutting edge. Iron tools, such as axes, chisels, gouges and dies, and saws and augers towards the end of this period, became increasingly diversified and specialized. Productivity rose markedly in the second century BC: iron was common enough for nails to replace wooden pegs and ties in building, and excavated settlements produce tens of kilograms of slag. Europe did not always know such abundance subsequently.

From DIY to craftsman

Technological progress brought with it specialization in tasks. Domestic products such as pottery began to experience competition from high-quality products made by specialist craftsmen. These latter had greater mastery over high-temperature firing, which produced more durable vessels with more accomplished decoration. The addition of rotary motion with the potter's wheel, the lathe and compasses to the craftsman's equipment also required the touch of the specialist: vessels of turned wood and wheel-thrown pottery began to multiply. The primitive saddle quern was replaced by the much faster rotary quern. All-purpose tools were replaced by batteries of specialized tools appropriate for each group of craftsmen. J.-P. Guillaumet has been able to demonstrate, by comparing them with a plate from Diderot's *Encyclopédie*, that the objects from the burial mound of Celles (Cantal) were the toolkit of a worker of inlays in bone and horn. This period is characterized by specialization and increase in productivity in the spheres of both craft production and agriculture.

Intensive farming and stabilization of boundaries

Iron shares and coulters are the main elements of the true plough, the precise definition of which is the subject of disagreement among specialists but the Latin name of which is Gaulish in origin. It is well known that from the fifth century BC onwards the Celts had the capability to cultivate the heavy or poor soils that had been avoided by their predecessors, thanks to their improved ards and to the soil-improvement techniques described by Roman writers. Many hectares of 'Celtic fields' were worked in Europe in order to increase agricultural productivity. The experimental work of P.J. Reynolds has shown that the Celts succeeded, by 'gardening' their fields, in producing high crop yields. Rye was added to the range of cereals available, along with hard and soft wheats and naked or hulled barley for brewing beer. There was similar diversification of livestock: domestic poultry began to develop in the Hallstatt period and pigs, in some ways the symbol of settled intensive agriculture, represent as much as 40 per cent of the animal bones from late La Tène farms. We shall see later on how the organization of settlements and land-holdings also reflects intelligent exploitation of all the available resources. We shall endeavour to show that the distinctive characteristics of the European countryside first appeared with these Celtic peasants, who created a landscape the broad outlines of which are still in place today.

	Periods	Western Europe		Central Europe		Eastern Europe	
		Cultures	Sites	Cultures	Sites	Cultures	Sites
1850	Early Bronze Age	Armorica / Wessex / cordoned urns	Skara Brae / St Adrien / Stonehenge / Gwithian	Straubing / Rhône Culture	Clairvaux / Baldegg	Únětice / Hatvan / Otománi	Postoloprty / Tószeg / Hatvan / Březno
1500	Middle Bronze Age	Atlantic Bronze Age / Deverel-Rimbury	Dartmoor / Fort-Harrouard	Tumulus Culture	Padnal / Bavois	Tumulus Culture	Tószeg / Várdomb
1250	Late Bronze Age I-IIa	Late Atlantic Bronze Age	Dartmoor / Rams Hill / Mam Tor	Early Urnfield	Zug / Greifensee / Buchau	Piliny / Mad'arovce / Knoviz / Lausitz	Nitriansky Hrádok / Lovčičky
1000	Late Bronze Age IIb-IIIa		Flag Fen / Black Patch / Itford Hill	Urnfield / Rhine-Swiss / Eastern France	Dampierre / Hohlandsberg / Buchau / Cortaillod / Auvernier		Künzing / Vikletice / Perleberg
850	IIIb / Early Hallstatt	Early Iron Age	Jarlshof / Pimperne / Coulon / Moel-y-Gaer / Camp Allaric / Crickley Hill / Staple Howe / Choisy au Bac / Gussage All Sts	Hallstatt	Wittnauer Horn / Goldberg / Senftenberg / Heuneburg / Befort / Vix / Salins	Hallstatt	Biskupin / Sopron / Hallstatt / Závist
650	Late Hallstatt						
500	Early La Tène	Middle Iron Age	Danebury	La Tène	Suippes / Otzenhausen / Markvartice / Preist / La Tène	La Tène	Hallein
400			Little Woodbury				
300	Middle La Tène		Glastonbury		Bundenbach / Verberie		Libenice / Stradonice / Třísov / Závist / Velem-Szent-Vid / Gellérthegy / Magdalensberg
100	Late La Tène	Late Iron Age	Hengistbury Head / Tollard Royal / Jarlshof / Maiden Castle		Aulnat / Hochstetten / Bâle Levroux / Manching / Titelberg / Bibracte		
0							

Northern Europe		
Cultures	Sites	
		1850
	Handewitt	
		1600
Bronze I	Norddorf	
	Myrhøj	
Bronze II		1400
Hilversum		
	Nijnsel	1250
	Zijderveld	
Bronze III	Angelsloo	
	Elp	
	Boverkarspel	
Bronze IV	Ristorf	
	Trappendal	900
	Fragtrup	
	Bjerg	850
Bronze V	Spjald	
Bronze VI		
	Hijken	
		500
	Grøntoft	
	Borremose	
	Zeijen	
	Ezinge	
Iron		300
Age		
	Haps	
	Hodde	
		0

7
Chronology. The principal sites are shown in relation to the cultures to which they belong and at a date corresponding with their main occupation layer. (F. Audouze and O. Büchsenschütz.)

Demographic pressure, pillage and migration

Despite progress in agriculture and craftsmanship Iron Age peoples seem to have undergone a demographic expansion during the whole of the first millennium BC such that their original lands were no longer large enough for their needs. Their relationships with the peoples of the Mediterranean, the nature of which is still for the most part unknown to us, all tended towards the search for an equilibrium which seems not to have been reached before the imposition of the *pax romana*. It may be assumed that, in exchange for wine, luxury ornaments and Greek or Etruscan bronze vessels, the Hallstatt peoples supplied not only ores, salt and amber but also slaves: this is a likely hypothesis but the proofs are slight. Celtic incursions into Italy, Greece and as far as Asia Minor are, on the other hand, well attested. The *tumultus gallicus* of the Romans ranks Gallic raids with natural catastrophes – intermittent, unpredictable and inevitable.

In reality these Celtic migrations took several forms simultaneously – the displacement of an entire people (for example, that of the Helvetii described by Caesar); the departure of the younger members of a group, warriors accompanied by their wives and children, as reported by Livy in describing how the old King Ambigatus 'wished to relieve his kingdom of the crowd that overburdened it' (*Hist.*, 5.34); or pillage by armed bands, such as the sack of the sanctuary of Delphi in 279 BC. These incursions sometimes resulted in the establishment of permanent settlements, as in northern Italy or Asia Minor, or resulted in their devastating power being deflected, as when Celtic warriors were enlisted as mercenaries into the Hellenistic armies. The characteristic cultural equipment of the Middle and Late La Tène occurs along the length of the Danube, right up to its mouth, but this is a case of cultural influence rather than colonization.

Is it possible to write the history of a people such as this without committing grave errors due to incomplete documentation or doubtful comparisons? It is necessary to find words and concepts from our own history in order to express what their sumptuous tombs or imposing defensive works so strongly evoke. The scenario that we are sketching here should be treated only as a metaphor. Or perhaps rather it should be considered as the transcription, by comparison with our history, of a reality which must always unfortunately escape us.

Halstatt princes

The Hallstatt culture that covered most of Europe can be divided into a number of regional groups. The south-eastern group, centred on Austria and Yugoslavia, is characterized by situla art, which takes the form of a bronze vessel decorated with animals and people; the central group includes the Hallstatt salt mine and cemetery, western Hungary and southern Bohemia; the northern and western groups, the boundaries of which are less clearly defined but within which the Rhine-Rhône-Saône axis played an important role in trade.

The most original characteristics of this culture manifested themselves in the seventh century BC, when fortified settlements associated with 'princely' graves grew up on the major trade routes. It is impossible not to conjure up the image of an aristocratic society when confronted with the luxury of the Vix tomb in Burgundy or that of a tomb at Hochdorf, recently discovered in Germany (Fig. 8) – a ritual cart and a complete service in gold and bronze for serving wine accompanied the richly dressed dead man lying on a bronze couch. These rich burials, protected by funerary mounds and disposed in small groups, evoke the idea of dynastic links between royal houses. Nearby there is a fortified enclosure, usually small in size, which could house a garrison, a court and some craftsmen, but not the main body of the people and their animals.

Recent research has proposed, in place of the model of a feudal society which was originally favoured, the adoption of an explanation based on the control of trade through prestige objects. According to this hypothesis the relative wealth of the material imported from the Mediterranean makes it possible to distinguish a hierarchy of social groups, defined according to their degree of direct access to material of this kind, which serves to symbolize social relationships. H. Härke has shown the geographical boundaries of this phenomenon, which is to be observed principally in eastern France and southern Germany, and he has laid stress on the many gaps that still exist in our knowledge. The reasons for the appearance and abrupt disappearance of this society are still unexplained. Was the power of these 'princes' based on control of tin mining or trade? Is it a case of stock rearers who gradually assumed control of the trade routes over the Alps? Their 'castles' were deserted in the fifth century BC when the first sites of the La Tène culture were created on the Marne and the Rhine.

8

Hallstatt wagon burial at Hochdorf (Baden-Württemberg). The dead man is wearing a birch-bark cap and is laid out on a bronze couch (see Fig. 66), accompanied by his weapons, drinking vessels and a parade wagon. (J. Biel, 1987.)

Celtic warriors and peasants

The trade routes changed, as did the materials being imported; these were still associated with wine drinking, but they were both simpler and more abundant. They were intended for graves in the enormous cemeteries spread over the countryside. From now on the richer graves were only distinguishable by virtue of the presence of a few imported materials, the presence of a two-wheeled cart or precious metal ornaments. Grave mounds were smaller or dispensed with entirely. Bodies were buried with a garment of some kind, bronze or iron ornaments and weapons in the case of warriors. Food offerings were deposited in pots. Gradually the spatial separation according to sex was replaced by family groupings. The peasant society, which reached its apogee at this time, seemed to have restrained or marginalized the aristocracy whose great wealth had been displayed in the burials of the Hallstatt period.

This was in fact the period of full Celtic expansion, military in character towards the south, as we have seen, but also agricultural, into lands that had until then not been exploited. Farms, hamlets and small villages were dotted all over the European landscape, and wherever they have the opportunity to study large areas, archaeologists are astonished by the density of occupation of the land.

This social evolution can be observed in Celtic art. Objects from the earlier period are unique, small masterpieces intended for a clientele with refined tastes, ornaments which combined a traditional format with motifs borrowed from the art of the steppes or of Greece. This art then began to become more widespread and simplified in order to adapt to a wider clientele: the various motifs were combined into continuous patterns or in clever symmetry. A mannerist art, the plastic style, characterized by designs in high relief heightened by coloured enamels, developed during the third century BC, 'an art of parvenus enriched by conquest' according to M. Szabó.

The civilization of the *oppida*

The Celts brought new technologies back from their Mediterranean incursions – the fast potter's wheel and rotary quern, to cite the most obvious – and new economic practices, such as the use of coinage. Was this an internal evolution; colonization by Greek and then Roman merchants; or lessons that were well learned in a receptive region? The causes of these transformations are debatable but not their existence. The second century BC saw the emergence of specialized craftsmen making series of artefacts that were traded over the whole of Europe: bronze ornaments of a rather austere style and pottery that was painted or enhanced with graphite or mica. The workshops where these artefacts were manufactured, tools were forged, wool was woven and coins were minted came to be grouped together in large agglomerations. These large villages came more and more to resemble towns, most of the functions of which they were carrying out by the end of the second century BC. It is when there was a general movement to transfer these settlements to higher ground that their level of development can best be appreciated by archaeologists. These *oppida* covered very large areas, between 20 and several hundred hectares. Their fortifications were intended less for effective defence than to express prestige by their monumentality. Excavations have brought to light streets, organized districts for specialized activities and sanctuaries. To these productive, commercial and religious functions was added a political role, which Caesar stresses in *De Bello Gallico*. The conqueror's account suddenly illuminates the complex reality of a society in a state of complete change in which he had an excellent opportunity to play off against each other peasants, craftsmen and nobility. The nobles seem to have led the resistance to the Roman armies, but the economic pressure towards fusion had been so strong for a century that there is no evidence of the war in the contemporary settlements, to the despair of those who want to identify the battlefields of the war.

The Roman conquest produced profound changes in the geography of the continent. Although for more than a thousand years temperate Europe from east to west had evolved as a single entity between the Mediterranean world and northern peoples, the division invented from nothing by Caesar between the peoples separated by the Rhine, quickly given physical form with the building of the *Limes*, was to transform the development of material cultures and at the same time the perceived geopolitical representation of Europe. We, too, are conditioned by this division, which was adopted by subsequent empires by basing themselves precisely on the Roman Empire. 'Temperate Europe', which developed from the Tumulus Culture of the continental Middle Bronze Age into the Celtic nation, no longer evokes any human community in our minds.

2

The history of protohistoric studies

The archaeological study of protohistoric settlements began in the mid nineteenth century with the discovery of the first submerged settlements in the Swiss lakes, the 'lake dwellings', and the development of research into 'Caesar's camps', the hillforts of France, at the instigation of the Emperor Napoléon III. Nevertheless, 125 years later the public still retains the traditional image of the Gaulish hut that has come down to us from the classical writers. The considerable variations in form and size, in materials of construction and building design, revealed by archaeologists over large areas and long periods remain nothing more than the subtleties of specialists. Protohistorians themselves are more interested in the problems of the typology and classification of rich grave goods than in the modest traces of unspectacular settlements. This branch of research has therefore developed in a marginal way, thanks to exceptional discoveries or isolated individual researchers. Study of the dates of discoveries and publications makes it clear that adherence to outdated concepts and work of a high standard for its time have long co-existed. We can nevertheless identify five stages in research which, although they may overlap chronologically, progress towards a more coherent and wide-ranging approach to settlement.

The Second Empire in the footsteps of Caesar

Settlement studies began with the Second Empire in France. Research on the Bronze and Iron Ages was confused at that time, since the distinction between the two periods had not yet been clarified, and the Iron Age was considered to have followed on directly after the Neolithic. The controversy between partisans of a Bronze Age and those who adhered to the idea of a direct transition from Neolithic to Iron Age raged during the 1850s. An echo of this debate, together with its conclusion, is to be found in the monumental discussion by Ernest Chantre, who needed three octavo volumes on *Études palethnologiques dans le bassin du Rhône*, published in 1875 and 1876, to bring it to a definitive end. Napoléon III's research into Caesar's conquest of Gaul encouraged the earliest studies in protohistory. The Emperor was basically interested in remains of the military campaigns, and the identifications made by his excavators were sometimes rather hasty ones. However, this work did focus attention on the archaeology of France. It quickly became apparent that there were many defensive earthworks, of all kinds and from all periods, scattered over the whole country. Learned societies began to record them and large-scale excavations were carried out. In this way the first Bronze Age settlement was excavated, under the mistaken impression that it was a Gaulish *oppidum*. Napoléon III, who was staying at the Château de Compiègne and at Pierrefonds, then being restored under the direction of Viollet-le-Duc, instructed his favourite architect to carry out excavations at a so-called 'Camp de César' at Vieux-Moulin in Saint-Pierre-en-Chastre commune (dept. Oise). Viollet-le-Duc carried out the excavation with his customary gusto and found the remains of fortifications. He had no hesitation in restoring the site according to his own principles and recreating the original appearance of the monument, which was, in his opinion, a Roman fort. He accordingly dug a double ditch and introduced staggered gateways, using an infantry regiment from Compiègne. Examination of the material that Viollet-le-Duc discovered shows that this was in reality a Late Bronze Age fortified village, briefly reoccupied in the late La Tène period, and considerably altered by the building of a priory in the Middle Ages.

The first systematic excavations

Not all the excavations of that period were so casual: some large-scale projects were being carried out which still command respect today. The first identification of a *murus gallicus* at Murcens by Castagné, the study of the pits in the settlement at Sainte-Geneviève, near Nancy, and above all the excavation of Mont Beuvray, Caesar's Bibracte, initiated by J.-G. Bulliot in 1867 and resumed by his nephew J. Déchelette between 1897 and 1901, are better representative of the archaeology of the period. Excavators were interested above all else in the structures of ramparts: the occupation of a site was more often than not dated by material collected within the enclosure.

The period of large surveys

In 1906 the Société Préhistorique de France organized a national survey of defensive earthworks which in twenty years recorded more than 3000 sites. In a similar way British and German archaeologists identified the existence of many native fortifications, distinct from those of the Roman *Limes*. Among the most outstanding European studies was that of the English General Pitt Rivers, who perfected the earliest techniques of settlement excavation by stripping large areas of South Lodge Camp, on the borders of Dorset and Wiltshire. The three Royal Commissions on Ancient and Historical Monuments began their work in 1908, whilst the Ordnance Survey had been recording archaeological monuments on its maps for many years. The name of A. von Cohausen is associated with German research on *Ringwälle* and he created the first corpus of these monuments in 1898. A number of late La Tène *oppida* were identified at the beginning of the twentieth century, but an overall picture had to await publication of the work of P. Reinecke in 1930. The discovery of a coin hoard at Stradonice, near Prague, in 1877 led to the plundering of a very rich site typical of the late La Tène. The publication of the report on the site by Píč in 1903 excited Déchelette because of its great resemblance to Mont Beuvray. In his *Manuel*, published in 1914, he demonstrated the remarkable uniformity of these late La Tène *oppida* all over Europe. At this time large fortified settlements appeared, from Hungary to England, with stone, timber or earthen ramparts, built on high ground and protecting what are in effect towns, with residential areas and artisans mass-producing artefacts that hardly vary from Brittany to Bohemia, and cult centres.

The notion that protohistoric settlement was distinctive and already considerably differentiated was thus well established by the beginning of the twentieth century, but the houses themselves and the structures associated with them remained largely unknown. In his *Manuel* Déchelette himself recorded the complete absence of archaeological data on houses of the first Iron Age period. His definition of La Tène 1 and 2 houses was very vague: 'Houses were not yet built in stone. Simple huts made of wood and branches with clay rendering and roofs of straw; they were no different from the primitive Neolithic thatched circular huts, half sunk into the ground. These "sunken hut floors" [*fonds de cabane*] can be found here and there. The remains are uniform in appearance: they consist of more or less circular depressions, filled with black soil mixed with organic residues, cooking refuse, and bones of domesticated and wild animals.' The vague concept of a 'sunken hut' which appears here was very widely used to designate structures revealed during excavation, the function of which excavators could not identify. Until very recently, most archaeologists have lumped under this convenient name simple patches of soil and traces of post structures as well as more or less regular pits, including even deep and narrow grain-storage pits in which it is difficult to imagine the presence of a human being. Ingenious theories, sometimes even supported by reconstruction drawings, have been put forward in vain attempts to resolve this problem and now form part of the corpus of major archaeological mistakes. The idea of the protohistoric dwelling which prevailed at that time among specialists and is still today to be found widely in French school textbooks was essentially based on Greek and Roman literary or iconographic sources, such as the works of Diodorus Siculus, Strabo and Tacitus and the reliefs on the Column of Marcus Aurelius or the house-shaped cinerary urns of eastern Germany. The excavations of the period were too small in area and the techniques used were too summary for a proper archaeological perspective to be obtained. The discovery of entire villages buried in peat-bogs was gradually to compel archaeologists to refine their techniques and to change their excavation methods in order to reveal building structures, even when they were poorly preserved.

The lake villages

In the mid nineteenth century a period of exceptionally low rainfall resulted in the discovery of the first lake villages on the shores of the Swiss lakes: a considerable amount of cultural material was collected from among the forests of piles set into the lake bottoms (Fig. 9). The founder of the Société des Antiquaires de Zürich, Ferdinand Keller, having been told by the village schoolteacher at Obermeilen, on Lake Neuchâtel, of the presence of these abundant remains, arranged for them to be excavated under the direction of this teacher and published a preliminary report in 1854, the year which thus marked the beginning of research on wetland sites in Europe.

The number of excavations in the Swiss lakes rapidly multiplied, spreading to the Lac du Bourget, Lake Constance, and the Alpine lakes in Italy. Many amateur archaeologists were involved in the work, to the benefit of their personal collections as much as the museums'. The earliest underwater excavation was carried out in the same year, 1854, at Morges on Lake Geneva, by F. Troyon, F. Forel, and A. von Morlot. When work began to control the rivers of the Jura in the 1870s new discoveries were made. The discovery of 'pile villages' did not affect the scientific world alone: all Switzerland was affected by lake fever. Lacustrine plays and novels, such as Friedrich Theodor Vischers's satire *Der Besuch* (The Visit) were published. Picturesque reconstructions of lake villages flooded almanacs and school pictures, whilst lacustrine displays formed part of historical costume processions.

The Swiss discoveries drew the attention of archaeologists to all the Alpine lakes. In France work began in 1863 and was to continue for twenty years under the direction of F. Perrin, L. Rabut, and Count Costa de Beauregard, all three members of the Académie de Savoie at Chambéry.

Interest in protohistory waned at the end of the century in favour of more remote periods. The work of V. Commont in the Somme valley diverted attention to the beginnings of man. Protohistoric villages were forgotten, in France at any rate. There developed, however, a substantial literature on them in Switzerland and Germany which was not challenged until the 1950s. Fom 1854 onwards F. Keller published the material found in the lakes along with plans of several areas of piles, and had no hesitation in reconstructing an entire village raised on piles, using comparative material from Swiss fishermen's cabins or lake settlements from Oceania. The numerous reconstructions of villages which swamped scientific publications and textbooks over the following hundred years were based not on a critical assessment of the excavated material but on simplistic theories constructed by analogy with ethnological data. It was not until after World War I that scholars began to question the true positions of these villages in relation to the water level on the lakes at the time they were occupied: were the houses and platforms built over the water, on dry land, or in an intermediate swampy zone? It was only

9
An array of piles at Cortaillod, Lake Neuchâtel. During work to control the waters of the Jura thousands of piles became visible, only the lower, submerged parts of which had survived. (Neuchâtel, archives of the Musée Cantonal d'Archéologie.)

recently that an answer could be given to this question, when it became possible to analyse the stratigraphy of the lacustrine sediments systematically. In the same way, analysis of house plans did not begin until the piles had been surveyed systematically, the timber species identified and precise dates obtained by dendrochronology.

The birth of modern excavation methods

The discovery of the lake villages popularized the image of protohistoric settlement, but the superficial interpretation that they were given did little to stimulate research. In contrast those villages where floors and wall footings were preserved in bogs and marshes contributed very valuable data for the development of knowledge. At Glastonbury (Somerset) Bulleid and Gray began in 1891 to excavate a village consisting of some sixty round-houses whose floors, hearths and wall bases were perfectly preserved. After World War I, A. van Giffen explored the *terpen* on the coast of the northern Netherlands. These artifical mounds contained superimposed settlements which ranged in time from the second Iron Age or La Tène period to the beginning of the High Middle Ages. The floor levels of the houses and storehouses, which contained much organic material, were preserved in the build-up of clay and were easy to interpret. The results of these excavations, which were carried out using impeccable techniques in both cases, encouraged scholars to study villages on dry land with more care, even though they were less well preserved.

The exploration of settlements built in wood, which left nothing in the ground but post-holes, pits and ditches, required large areas to be cleared with care and discipline, followed by observation and recording of the slightest remains. This technique, which was perfected on Roman forts on the German *Limes*, was applied by A. Kiekebusch on the Bronze Age village of Buch, near Berlin, and by G. Bersu on his many excavations. Systematic recording of post-holes and foundation trenches allowed house plans to be reconstructed, whilst analysis of the form, distribution and contents of pits helped in ascertaining their original functions and the processes and durations of filling them. Bersu occupies a premier place among the excavators who developed this technique. He first excavated the fortified settlements of the Goldberg in southern Germany and the Wittnauer Horn in Switzerland, two sites which are still fundamental references for settlement archaeology. He was appointed Director of the Römisch-Germanische Kommission in 1931 but two years later was forced to flee by the Nazis and took refuge in Britain. He explored a number of houses on the Isle of Man and the farm at Little Woodbury (Wiltshire). The latter, dating to the end of the Second Iron Age or Late La Tène period, consisted of a house and a large number of pits set within an enclosure. By means of the meticulous analysis of the structures that he found and the use of comparative material from the ethnological record, Bersu distinguished between grain storage pits, quarry pits and half-sunken workshops. The technique of excavation and the main lines of interpretation were established at this time, even for relatively poorly preserved settlements. It took more than twenty years for this approach to become fully accepted, especially in France, where confusion persisted into the 1960s.

Thanks to the information brought together in the inter-war years on larger area excavations, specialists in vernacular timber structures were able to propose possible reconstructions and to study the origin and development of building methods. The history of traditional settlements had in fact provoked some passionate controversy since the beginning of the century. The French idea of environmental control was opposed by the German tradition of a common prototype from which all the later variations derived. The discussion soon came to a halt owing to blind adhesion to Nazi theories on the part of some scholars, such as H. Reinerth. After the war A. Zippelius initiated a systematic survey of Iron Age settlements in southern Germany. Unfortunately his thesis has not yet been published, but most reconstructions of protohistoric houses in Germany have been his or are inspired by his theories. B. Trier, who in 1969 published a brilliant synthesis of non-Roman settlements in northern Germany, went along with his conclusions, in respect of both construction techniques and in the theory of the development of this form of architecture. It is always possible that archaeology may, at some unexpected time or place, reveal the existence of a building technique previously thought to have been a later innovation. However, from the beginning of the Iron Age man had at his disposal a number of highly developed techniques which allowed him to select a specific type of construction as a function of varied criteria, which would supply his needs and fit in with his culture as well as with the prevailing climatic conditions and the building materials to hand. So far as those architectural elements are concerned, which make it possible to distinguish at a glance regional styles or the characteristics of a particular human group, archaeology alone cannot decide on the basis of the meagre remains that have come down to us.

Recent research has tried to put settlements back into the landscape which surrounded them and to solve the problems of scale posed by the exploitation of sites of this kind, in a quest for the maximum yield of information. Under the influence of French prehistorians in particular, the meticulous analysis of the distribution of objects on undisturbed floors is attempting to reveal the traces of everyday life in houses and workshops. At the other extreme, large-area excavations and field survey techniques are seeking to place the narrow windows opened by traditional excavation in a wider framework where their true significance can be appreciated. Soil scientists and palaeobotanists are increasingly being encouraged to define the surrounding environment and to locate human intervention in the landscape. The scale of destruction of archaeological sites all over Europe since the end of the Second World War, and in particular the extraction of sand and gravels from river valleys, has contributed to the highlighting of the problem of the preservation and exploration of protohistoric landscapes.

Methods of research

3

When history can be revealed by archaeology alone

The basic characteristics of Europe stem from the two thousand years that span the Bronze and Iron Ages. The natural environment stabilized into a temperate climate and society diversified itself at the same time as the main political divisions were put in place. For this crucial time in our history we have only a small number of short texts from its final period, which have to be used cautiously, since they were written by authors from outside this 'barbarian' world. It is therefore archaeology that has to be interrogated about the way in which the peoples of Europe were created, how society, agriculture, and trade evolved, and when the various elements of this heritage – the organization of the land, the formation of provinces, and the major feasts on our latter-day calendar, which have survived in spite of many centuries of classical culture and Christianity – first appeared. Replying to these questions on the basis of material remains alone is something of a gamble: it is as though a race-course were to be reconstructed on the basis of a betting slip, but there is no alternative. Archaeologists find themselves confronted by a double paradox: they must first draw up general laws on the basis of individual pieces of evidence, and then they have to isolate, if not in fact identify, the specific historical events which alone are capable of explaining spatial differences or discontinuities in chronological evolution.

Scholars for a long time sought refuge behind historical evidence, and it is still difficult to make the general public understand that there was a gulf between primitive societies and the Gauls that Caesar encountered. Nowadays archaeologists are seeking to widen their field of action and to diversify their techniques so as to obtain an overall view of development at that time. The data that they can identify now should make it possible for the first time to reconstruct the characteristics and the economic evolution of the Bronze and Iron Ages; the nature and relative proportions of different types of production, the appearance of food surpluses, changes in exchange mechanisms and the development of new technologies are gradually being reconstructed using thousands of humble fragments of bone and pottery collected during excavations. The general trend of this development is characterized by a continuous striving for better productivity, but notable exceptions here and there accentuate original societies.

The essential nature of every society can only be understood from large and relatively well-preserved sites – villages, cemeteries or fossil landscapes, the layouts and organization of which reflect the principal characteristics of the human groups that planned them and lived in them. Although surviving sites of this kind are relatively numerous, those that can be excavated to acceptable standards are rare, since to explore them is costly.

Excavations have for the most part been carried out on small areas – a house, a pit, a handful of burials – which have enabled us to reconstruct certain aspects of daily life or to add another point on a distribution map, but make no contribution to better historical understanding. It is, of course, difficult for an archaeologist either not to react to a chance discovery or to abandon a threatened site to the bulldozers. Whilst it is unavoidable that rescue activities, in which the sites to be examined are the chance result of engineering works, will continue to be useful, such archaeological investigations should be matched by wide-ranging, systematic research projects which set out to tackle particular historical problems that have been defined in advance.

Excavation is in effect a sampling process, a window opening on a greater whole which we seek to understand in its totality. We shall proceed, therefore, to examine the different methods of approach and the tools that are currently available to us in interpreting the recovered data.

Settlements hidden in the landscape

Benefit can be reaped from most of the elements that figure in maps in studying the remains of the Bronze and Iron Ages (Fig. 10). On the one hand, the occupation of the landscape was conditioned by the same natural environment at that period as it is in the present day, whilst on the other the modifications introduced by man since then, such as buildings, roads, woodland clearances and place-names, derive more or less directly from the organization of the landscape in the pre-Roman period. But in order to

define this horizon accurately, the eye must be trained to detect inconspicuous forms which lie, as it were, between the natural features and the complex alterations due to human intervention in historic times: such forms include fortifications which follow the lie of the land, settlements which fade into natural terraces, and the identification of potsherds which are the same colour as the soil. The study of protohistoric structures thus assumes a considerable measure of experience on the part of fieldworkers, at whatever scale they are working and with whatever methods, along with a practised eye capable of detecting the details of patterns in the landscape, patterns that lack straight lines or right-angles.

Simply examining large-scale maps can provide valuable information: fortifications where the ramparts or ditches survive are represented either by the same conventions as breaks in slopes or quarries, or by appropriate symbols which show up earthworks

10

The contribution of cartography. Ordnance Survey One-Inch Sheet 158: the large-scale maps of the British Isles feature many protohistoric earthworks. (Ordnance Survey, 1967.)

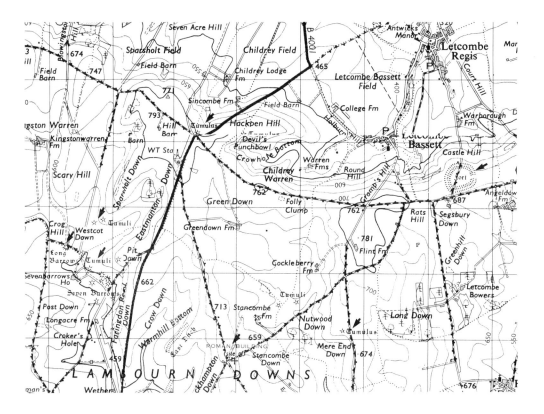

11
The contribution of aerial reconnaissance. Native farmstead at Tailly l'Arbre, Mouches (Somme) revealed by humidity and the dark colour of the ditches cut into the chalk. (R. Agache, SDA.)

created by man. A characteristic place-name, such as Caesar's Camp, La Châtre or the Heuneburg, will often catch the eye or confirm theories that the topography has already suggested. The main vestiges of ancient land divisions are shown on the maps of certain regions such as southern England. The interpretation of micro-relief may sometimes hint at the possibility of protohistoric settlement: the lines denoting fossil riverbanks shown by ridges no more than a few centimetres high in the Marsch region of Lower Saxony or in the north of the Netherlands indicate favoured sites for settlement research. This was where protohistoric villages were generally sited to provide protection against flooding by the North Sea.

The study of the vertical aerial photographs used for map-making provides much additional information. Stereoscopic viewing allows the micro-relief, earthwork ramparts and ancient field boundaries to be studied. If these photographs are taken at a time when the soil is not covered with crops, networks of lines of all kinds appear in the fields (soil-marks). The simultaneous examination of photographs taken with different types of film (panchromatic, infra-red, false colours) in association with field-name data and soil and vegetation maps make it possible gradually to reconstruct the main outlines of land-allotment systems.

Prospection using light aircraft has revealed a category of settlement that was completely overlooked before this technique began to be applied (Fig. 11). It consists of those which have been levelled and which can be detected from unequal ripening of cereal crops (crop-marks). They can also be detected during ploughing as soil-marks, when the ploughed soil contrasts vividly with the subsoil, such as gravel or chalk, or even in grassland during exceptionally dry periods (parch-marks). Hundreds of structures have been recorded in this way over the past fifty years: ditches forming simple or complex enclosures, usually curvilinear and broken by 'horned' (see Fig. 134) or 'corridor' entrances and packed with hundreds of pits of varying shapes and sizes. Our knowledge of isolated settlements, farms, stock enclosures and field systems has advanced considerably thanks to this technique, notably in the Paris basin and in southern Britain. The gradual reconstruction of the Danebury area in Hampshire by B.W. Cunliffe admirably illustrates the potential of this technique.

Aerial thermographic prospecting picks up the same type of structure, but under different conditions. Recording differences in temperature is optimal when the fields are bare and when the contrasts between night and day are very marked. The two techniques are thus complementary, and are suitable for use over equivalent areas.

More detailed research can start from this general framework. Geophysical prospection enables buried structures, pits, ditches, stone walls and concentrations of baked earth or metal to be detected. Various types of apparatus are available which can measure variations in electrical currents, magnetic fields or radio waves penetrating the soil when they strike a heterogeneous obstacle, which in most cases is the handiwork of man.

In certain conditions it is also possible to detect human occupation by measuring the amount of phosphates in the soil: the humus generally contains 0.3 per cent of phosphorus pentoxide (P_2O_5), but this level rises in habitation sites, livestock enclosures, cemeteries and shrines where the remains of sacrifices have been gathered.

Finally, the systematic collection of material from the surface of the ground has been developed considerably in recent years, under the influence of British archaeologists in particular. This involves methodically walking over the surfaces of fields, preferably after ploughing, in order to record all concentrations of artefacts and surface anomalies,

such as burnt soil or imported materials. Sampling procedures have been developed, with all the necessary statistical precautions, in order to obtain a satisfactory picture of a large surface area without in fact covering more than 20–30 per cent of it. The results of these surveys, which are of necessity diachronic (multi-period), are of particular interest in relation to protohistoric settlements, the slight and piecemeal nature of which have meant that they had been missed by fieldwalkers for many years.

The development of regional work of this kind has been vital in advancing the study of the Bronze and Iron Ages. Until recently our knowledge was based on the one hand on large defended earthwork sites, which are to be found all over western Europe, and on the other on founders' hoards, rich burials or coin hoards, which provide a spectacular but restricted snapshot of protohistoric society. The study of settlements in this period, which requires precise observations owing to their fugitive nature and at the same time the analysis of large surface areas in order to take samples that are representative of the whole, has today become possible owing to the judicious combination of all these prospecting methods. An overall analysis of a number of regions will give us a picture that corresponds most closely with the nature and the development of these societies.

Extensive or intensive excavation?

The same problems that we have described when dealing with prospection occur also when working out an excavation strategy: excavation has to be meticulous because the structures are delicate, but large surface areas must be examined, both in order to have the best statistical chance of finding significant remains and to understand the social differentiation or the overall organization of a village.

One of the first archaeologists to carry out an extensive excavation, A. Kiekebusch, justified his strategy at the Lausitz village of Buch, near Berlin (Fig. 12), by showing that he could only reconstruct its houses by accumulating information derived from a hundred buildings. His contemporaries reproached him for extending his excavations unnecessarily to remains that were unspectacular and repetitive. In fact, each set of foundations provided him with an

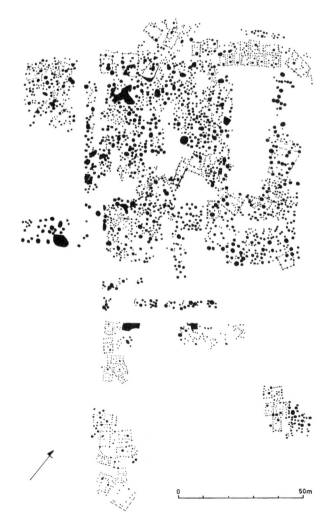

12
The earliest extensive excavations of dryland villages. Plan of the village of Buch, near Berlin. (A. Kiekebusch in J. Hoops, Reallexikon, *1981.)*

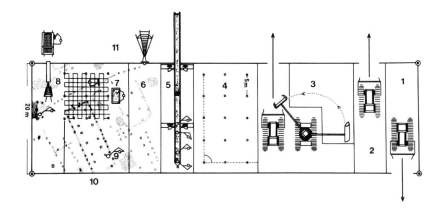

13

Method of excavating an undefended settlement in Lower Saxony. An example of excavation by artificial spits. (Right to left) The area is first stripped by machine (1–3), then divided into squares in order to collect finds (4); the excavators remove spits of constant 5–15cm (2–6in) thickness (according to the level), collecting sherds and other finds; spoil is removed by conveyor belt (5); photographs (6) and drawings (7) are made before opening up another strip. (W. Haarnagel, 1979.)

element of the puzzle: by adding them together he was able to reconstruct an acceptable model of the houses. The complete absence of extensive excavations in France until the 1960s led to the interpretation of ancillary pits, which Kiekebusch had identified as early as 1910 as workshops or grain-storage pits backfilled with refuse, as dwellings or 'sunken huts', corroborating prior judgements inherited from mistakenly interpreted historical sources. It should, however, be noted that, despite the modernity of Kiekebusch's principles, latter-day German archaeologists believe that his interpretations do not follow the field data closely enough. The plan of Buch is not accurate enough to be reliable, although the contribution of this excavation to methodology is still an important one.

Large-scale excavations are preferred nowadays, and sometimes extend to the nearest cultivated parcels of land outside the village proper, even though they ignore certain detailed data. This is often the case in the Netherlands and Denmark, where the foundations of houses, storehouses, and palisades are preserved in a clay-sand soil as coloured outlines. The building plans can be deciphered but the artefacts, which are scarce and show little variation, are of lesser interest except in so far as they can be used for dating. The archaeologists have therefore chosen to work in the

following way. Deposits are removed by machine down to a depth determined by the excavator, and a plan is then made of the visible structures, together with a record of any material on the layer that has been exposed. A second layer is then removed mechanically, its depth being decided by the archaeologist on the basis of his observations of the layer above. Once again structures and artefacts are recorded, and a further layer is removed, the process being repeated until the underlying natural soil is reached. Although some of the artefactual material is sacrificed, since the material removed mechanically is not examined, the speed of excavation means that several hectares can be stripped and in so doing a broad picture obtained, which is indispensable to an understanding of the site.

This technique of excavation, using 'horizontal spits' or 'artificial layers' (Fig. 13), was applied at the site of Feddersen Wierde (Lower Saxony), but here the layers were removed by hand and all the artefactual material was recovered. In this case the richness of the site, especially in wooden and bone objects, and its relatively small extent justified a more intensive and meticulous excavation.

On sites where the surface relief is more uneven and the occupation area more restricted, as at the Heuneburg (Baden-Württemberg), for example, excavation followed the occupation levels, which were successively removed. Unexcavated strips between the excavated surfaces, which gradually formed flat-topped baulks with straight sides, allowed the stratigraphy to be checked as excavation proceeded. However, for most excavations of protohistoric settlements a plan view is preferred. Large areas need to be opened up in order to be able to interpret the slight traces of structures: stratigraphical analysis is no more than a means of checking.

It should not be inferred from the examples given

above that the excavation of Iron Age settlements is always rapid. Under the influence of French palaeolithic archaeologists in particular, several excavation teams have attempted to carry out detailed analyses of the spatial distribution of objects, in the hope of discovering traces of the everyday life of the inhabitants, but the results have not always been very conclusive.

The study of settlement deposits

We studied a Middle and Late La Tène settlement at Levroux (Indre) in this way. It consisted of the remains of post-holes and pits dug into limestone and filled with a soil that had been completely churned up by ploughing. The density of objects in the pits was very

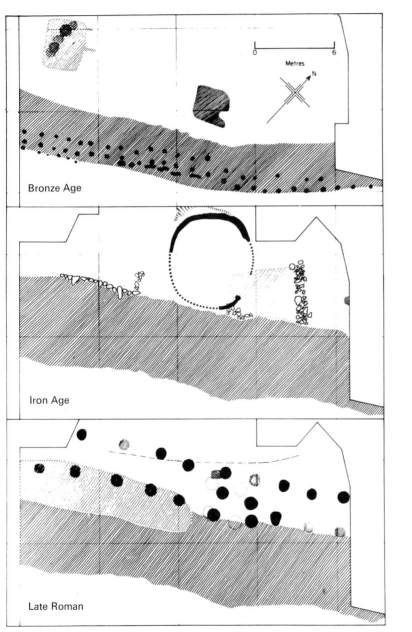

Bronze Age

Iron Age

Late Roman

14
Recent excavation of defences: the rampart at The Breiddin (Montgomeryshire). Excavation of a wide section of rampart enables the nature of the successive building layers to be better understood. (C. Musson in D.W. Harding, 1976.)

high, often more than 1000 fragments per cubic metre, and the fills were rarely stratified. In the hope of finding floors in place or deliberate deposits of artefacts in some of the pits, we attempted a detailed spatial analysis. Each object was recorded with its spatial coordinates and description and then entered into a computer which prepared plans, sections and projections as required. The different stages of filling could be reconstructed with the aid of graphics created automatically. However, none of the ten pits studied in this way contained any scrap of floor still in position. In most deposits of this kind, which have been disturbed by ploughing for generations, the chances of finding anything other than rubbish subsequently thrown into the pits are very slight. We therefore later adopted a more rapid method of excavating, which allowed us to extend the excavation over a larger surface area. Spatial analysis was then applied at the district or village scale, since the detailed study of life at the household scale was impractical.

At the Moel-y-Gaer (Rhosemor) hillfort, which had not been subject to ploughing, G. Guilbert obtained much more encouraging results by plotting not only potsherds but also every stone which appeared just beneath the turf, above an horizon into which the post-holes corresponding with the main occupation phase on the site had been dug. He was thus able to identify rectangular areas of cobbling which varied between 10 and 18 sq.m (108 and 194 sq.ft) in area; linear settings of stone which corresponded with palisade foundations, and spreads of potsherds and burnt stones up against lines of stones, which suggested open-air activity areas. The stone-packed areas were interpreted as supports for floors which had been swept regularly, since the houses produced no objects.

How to tackle hillforts of 20, 50 or 300 hectares

The methods used in excavating the immense hillforts that are the most outstanding monuments of the Bronze and Iron Ages in Europe also involve choices which have obvious consequences for the final interpretation. There is no question of stripping these settlements, which can easily cover 20ha (50 acres), in their entirety. It is usually the rampart which is excavated first; it is in fact easier to locate than houses, and the excavator knows that he will in all probability discover a succession of well-stratified construction phases and rebuilds which will provide him with a summary of the history of the site.

The traditional approach is to excavate a narrow trench which cuts through the rampart and ditch from top to bottom, a substantial expenditure of effort, and then to record the stratigraphic section, the various components of which are dated by material found in them during excavation. In the most fortunate cases it is possible for the archaeologist in this way to determine the main occupation phases on the site, but it is difficult for him, on the basis of such incomplete data, to reconstruct the structure of the fortification and hence the functions of successive constructions. Nevertheless, it is this evidence from a section of the defences which sums up our knowledge of hillforts in the majority of cases. Occasionally an attempt is made to extend the cutting into the interior of the hillfort, but without much success, since erosion has generally interrupted the stratigraphy. It is more effective to open up a large surface area which simultaneously uncovers part of the settlement and the rampart over a width of between 5m to 20m (16ft to 66ft) (Fig. 14). In this way the excavation strips the different levels of defences and the settlements which correspond with them in successive layers. This gives the archaeologist a plan view which alone allows him to identify the structure of the rampart and to establish a chronological relationship with the occupation phases inside the enclosure. All too often archaeologists are satisfied with slight indications, scarcely visible in the cutting, which lead them to visualize a type of fortification which fits in with a model borrowed from another site.

Graphic output as an indication of the progress of research

For a very long time protohistorians were constrained by the problems of presenting the results of their discoveries, and this discipline only developed when they became capable of illustrating their publications with accuracy. We are not referring here to the artistry of illustrations, since Napoléon III's atlas of *L'Histoire de Jules César* reached a very high level in this respect. However, accuracy in excavation recording, analysis of spatial relationships, the perfecting of effective and comprehensive cartography and the care taken in making three-dimensional reconstructions developed only very gradually.

Take, for example, Murcens (Lot), where (in the 1860s) E. Castagné was one of the first to compare his discovery of a rampart with internal timber reinforcement with Caesar's description of the defences of Bourges. It is impossible today to locate his trenches within an accuracy of greater than 100m (330ft). Although the rampart plans and sections have dimensions on them, they were completely reinterpreted by the draughtsman and the engraver, who erased all the surface irregularities so as to show a regular layout of timbers and stone revetments that fitted in with their interpretation of the find. Similarly, the plan of a perfectly circular house surrounded by 22 equally-spaced post-holes can in no way reflect the reality of what was found. Bulliot's plans for the *oppidum* of Mont Beuvray (Saône-et-Loire) or Bersu's for the Goldberg (Baden-Württemberg), which were cited by a number of writers up to the 1960s to justify talking of a hierarchical society or of a settlement in the process of urbanization, are more faithful to reality as observed during excavation; however, their lack of graphic precision is such that it is advisable not to use them. The preservation of records in archives and the frequent publication of unpolished documentation, interspersed with interpretive sketches, makes it possible nowadays to check and in due course to rework the excavators' interpretations.

Many archaeologists decline from the outset to interpret the constellations of post-holes which constitute the last trace of a settlement, on the pretext that there is nothing to be learnt from them. This attitude is justified when one is content to reason on the basis of a single small-scale plan. However, when an accurate record of every feature and of the distribution of their shapes and depths is available, more than half of the remains can usually be explained.

The best reconstructions are those which incorporate the largest number of the traces visible in the ground, have respect for the properties of the materials and techniques known at that time and succeed with the greatest economy of resources available in fulfilling the role allotted to them. Several possible solutions should always be explored, if only to demonstrate the limits of the certain, the probable and the possible to readers with little time to waste. Graphic reconstructions or models make it possible to locate the main three-dimensional spaces within structures. Full-size reconstructions, such as those at Butser Hill (England), Asparn (Austria), Lejre (Denmark) or Chassemy (France) make it possible not only to confirm the validity of theories, by observing how the buildings stand up to bad weather conditions, and to calculate the expenditure of labour and materials represented by a building, but also to correct the interpretation of certain remains revealed by excavation. P.J. Reynolds has in this way observed that runs dug by mice under the Butser Hill house-walls have left traces which are inevitably interpreted during excavation as foundation trenches.

At the larger scale of the village, the landscape and the region, protohistoric archaeology has for the past decade been following developments in cartography, graphic methods for the treatment of information, and spatial analysis. For example, the availability of specialist archaeological maps, notably the Ordnance Survey Map of the Iron Age in southern Britain, derived from information used for the general maps (such as the 'One-Inch' (see Fig. 10)), has enabled distributions which are entirely new and significant to be revealed: three synthetic studies and a number of colloquia published between 1973 and 1977 resulted directly from the appearance of this document.

We shall see later how it was possible to demonstrate, as a result of a controversy that lasted half a century, that a large number of the square enclosures measuring around 1ha (2.5 acres) which occur all over Europe north of the Alps correspond with Celtic shrines. The definitive publication on this subject was the *Atlas* of K. Schwarz (Schwarz, 1959), which contains nothing but maps, plans, and drawings: all the elements needed as verification were contained in these documents, which had no accompanying text.

A group of German scholars who met in Hamburg under the auspices of the journal *Archaeologia Geographica* between 1950 and 1960 developed systematic studies based on distribution maps, using graphical methods that had previously been set out in J. Bertin's *Sémiologie Graphique* (Bertin, 1967). The best way of defining and delimiting a culture must surely consist of drawing up distribution maps of objects, sites and place-names and making comparisons between them. Naturally certain biases have to be eliminated and these raw data must be weighted, taking account of inequalities in the research conditions between different regions, as a function of the preservation of sites and the state of advancement of excavations.

It is a great temptation to apply the models of spatial analysis that have been in use by geographers for several decades to the data available on protohistoric settlement. Action of this kind has the merit of making archaeologists look beyond their field data. A theoretical model of the landscape has to be drawn up on the basis of available data before returning to the field in order to check whether new discoveries can be fitted into the proposed scheme. The principal problems tackled by this type of analysis are settlement hierarchies, the delimitation of territories, the organization of exchange and distribution networks, and the process of urbanization. The main difficulties arise from the inadequacy of the models owing to the nature of the available data: models based on population distribution are applied using the surface areas of sites, which are assumed to correspond closely with the number of inhabitants. Reasoning is often based on a theoretical estimate of the needs of a primitive society, a vague concept which imperfectly conceals our ignorance. Finally, archaeologists can rarely affirm that the different sites in the survey were occupied simultaneously; if these models are to have any chance of approaching historical reality, therefore, it is essential to be able to date the occupation of these sites to within half a century.

Absolute dating methods

Because they had no contacts with the Mediterranean regions, which had already entered written history, there is no way of dating those protohistoric groups that were indigenous and independent. Their settlements, which only rarely contain valuable imported objects, most often lie outside those dating systems that are based on trade with the Near East and Greece. Recourse must therefore be made to dating techniques that measure elapsed time by means of physical phenomena. At the present time three such techniques are in use for protohistory: measurement of the carbon-14 isotope in archaeological remains with high carbon contents (especially charcoal and bone), measurement of thermoluminescence in heated stones and pottery, and measurement of remanent magnetism in pottery and furnaces.

The carbon-14 (radiocarbon) technique has, however, had some problems owing to variation in the carbon-14 content of the atmosphere over the millennnia. This had led to the establishment of a correction curve which has had the effect, so far as our period is concerned, of pushing back dates from 2000–1500 BC without having much effect on more recent ones. Uncorrected (uncalibrated) radiocarbon dates are written in lower case (bc, ad) and calibrated dates in capitals (BC, AD). Because of this margin of error it is not practicable to use single dates, but only series of dates. This means that the confidence limits can be narrowed, but it also implies that only complexes, such as villages, can be dated safely and not single features or burials.

The most valuable dating method for protohistorians is dendrochronology or tree-ring dating, which can be used when large pieces of wood are found in archaeological contexts. This is the first true absolute dating method since it provides dates in real calendar years (Fig. 15); it uses the annual concentric growth rings of trees, which can be studied on cut sections and

the thickness of which is related to climatic conditions. The succession of annual growth rings is similar for contemporaneous trees of the same species and these can be compared. They never repeat themselves over time. By studying increasingly old trees which overlap in time, a reference sequence of variable growths can be established, against which samples from excavations can be compared. It was American researchers who were the first to succeed in establishing a continuous dendrochronological curve between the present day and 5000 BC for the very long-lived Giant Sequoia. After a long period when they were struggling with a lack of data for the mid second and first millennia, laboratories in Switzerland and southern Germany have now succeeded in producing a tree-ring curve for the oak going back to the fifth millennium BC. Because of the often very slight nature of the variations and the number of parameters to be taken into account, the computer was soon applied to this technique. All species of trees are not of the same value for dendrochronology, and at present long sequences can only be produced for oaks and conifers. It is also necessary for the wood being studied, whether in the form of whole trunks or planks, to come from trees that are sufficiently well grown for their ring sequence to be compared with the reference sequence with a minimum of error.

Tree-ring dating does not only produce absolute dates. It permits relative dating to be obtained between one tree and another on a single site. In this way it is possible to check whether posts all belong to a single building and to detect repairs. Work carried out by Swiss archaeologists has enabled them to study how long a tree was seasoned after it was felled. Although like all physical methods it is subject to some uncertainties, tree-ring dating provides the most accurate dates and is an indispensible tool in settlement studies. By its use it becomes possible to study how a piece of land was occupied and the corresponding movement of settlement, year by year or even season by season.

Iron Age chronology still leans heavily on objects imported from the Mediterranean world which, when found in association with native material in a sealed group, allow a stage in typological evolution to be dated by reference to the historical record to within half a century. Some classic burial groups have been shown to be completely artificial creations, put together by antiquities dealers with little heed for historical problems. However, analysis of recent discoveries has demonstrated the reliability of the technique when the data is from a reliable context. The lapse of time between the arrival and deposition of

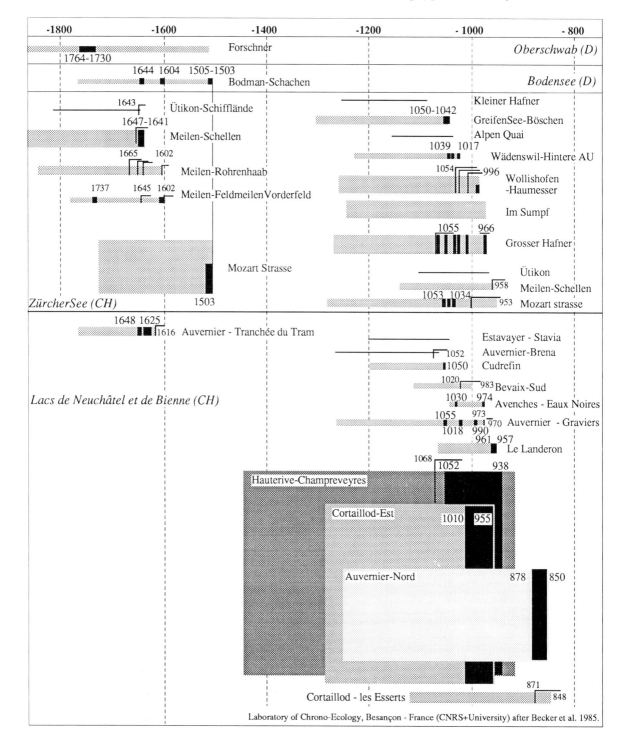

15
Dendrochronological dating of the Bronze Age German and Swiss lake-dwellings (after Becker 1985).

Laboratory of Chrono-Ecology, Besançon - France (CNRS+University) after Becker et al. 1985.

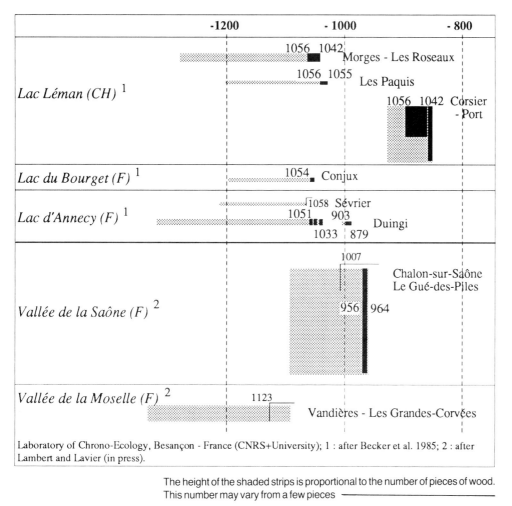

	-1200	- 1000	- 800

Laboratory of Chrono-Ecology, Besançon - France (CNRS+University); 1 : after Becker et al. 1985; 2 : after Lambert and Lavier (in press).

The height of the shaded strips is proportional to the number of pieces of wood. This number may vary from a few pieces ——————

to more than one hundred even to more than one thousand (Champreveyres, Cortaillod-Est)

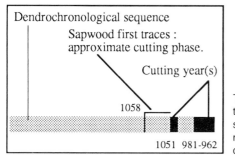

The analysis of a large number of pieces of wood increases the likelihood of correctly assessing the duration of a settlement. Though intrinsically accurate, the dendrochronological dates obtained from a few pieces may not be characteristic of the main occupation phase in a settlement.

an object in northern Europe, and even the manufacture of a copy there, is very short: luxury objects lasted as long as the fashion for them. Recent studies in this field have concentrated more on the reasons for these imports and on the effects of their being introduced on protohistoric society. From the Vix (Côte-d'Or) tomb to the thousands of amphorae found on Late La Tène settlements, the quality of imports became lower at the same time as they increased in quantity and the number of their customers grew. It is more difficult to date sites on the basis of these later objects, because they were sensitive to economic and commercial fluctuations of which we know little, even in the Mediterranean world; it therefore becomes necessary, as with local cultural material, to take quantitative aspects into account.

From 150 BC onwards the economy developed very rapidly and the quantity of imports increased exponentially. It began with the invasion of amphorae in the late second century BC, to be followed by building in stone, samian ware pottery, and the whole Gallo-Roman *instrumentum*. Within this rapidly-evolving framework it is necessary to date large series of objects, a relatively easy task, since settlement sites produce artefacts in their tens of thousands. It is the percentages of amphorae of different types, and the relative proportions of coarse and fine wares which allow one site to be dated in relation to others. During this period it is easy to follow the appearance of a certain type of object, its maximum development and its gradual replacement by another type since the wealth of examples available means that reliable statistical calculations can be made. Seriations proposed by archaeologists can be compared with other historical data, such as Gaulish coinage or Greek and Latin written sources.

Numismatists have at their disposal tried and tested methods for dating coins – direct analysis of motifs, studies of the weight and fineness of coins, reconstruction of series produced in the same workshop using characteroscopic methods. In this way they can obtain a picture of the economic development of a country which can then be keyed into the absolute chronology using documentary evidence. The documentary sources become more numerous and more precise during the second and first centuries BC. For the most part they refer to Gaul and Spain, but descriptions of Britain and Germany, although somewhat later, are of use in looking at the earlier period.

Thus we have at our disposal more varied sources for late protohistory than we have for the preceding centuries. However, this abundance of information only directs our curiosity into new fields, such as economics and politics. It is legitimate to question whether archaeologists' interpretations can be justified in so far as they always tend to extrapolate from the evidence upon which they are based.

Similar finds, similar interpretations?

In 1981 C.-A. Moberg brought together under the above title (Gothenburg University, Dept. of Archaeology. *Similar Finds, Similar Interpretations?*) nine essays on the interpretation of archaeological data, and in particular his own study of the Iron Age village of Glastonbury (Somerset), which we shall be examining later. This work posed a number of questions which are fundamental when studying non-literate cultures. To what extent do similar data justify similar interpretations? To what extent do preconceived hypotheses influence the understanding of data? Do similar models give rise to similar data? Do similar questions provoke similar interpretations?

Contrary to a widely prevalent view, archaeology is advanced less by new discoveries than by new theories. Chance discoveries may sometimes surprise scholars, but excavations are usually undertaken in order to confirm a hypothesis, and the excavator finds what he is looking for, or, more exactly, he only sees what he is looking for among the wealth of data that the soil yields up.

For decades scholars have shown little interest in settlements, on the pretext that they produce no useful data: in so far as the main preoccupation of the archaeologist is the establishment of chronology, this type of site is in fact of little help. Nowadays, however, the search is for information on food supply and daily life, ecology and agricultural practices; social organization and structures. The state of our knowledge of the Bronze and Iron Ages in reality permits the construction of very elaborate models, but the breadth of knowledge needed to take into account all the available data is already too great for a single individual. It is better to envisage several levels of approach and various themes, rather than an all-embracing view.

The scale of the work and the nature of the remains strongly condition the nature of the questions to be posed. We have seen that the study of domestic life becomes almost impossible where house floors have been destroyed and where refuse is swept up. In such cases it is necessary to move to another scale, analysing simultaneously a large number of pits and remains of foundations, in order to identify the repeated features that allow the definition of patterns in the data which may be significant pointers to the former organization of the settlement. Patterned elements, recognizable by the regularity, recurrence, orientation and density of archaeological objects and structures create an image of the village which may be somewhat vague but which is nonetheless sound. Social organization is enshrined in the plan of a community.

Let us pass now to a smaller scale: we should be aware that the number and size of the settlements that we know are so small that it is dangerous to extrapolate from them. We represent Hallstatt society in terms of the Heuneburg (Baden-Württemberg), but we know nothing of neighbouring enclosures such as the 'Grosse Heuneburg' and the Ipf, near Bopfingen, which seem to be more important, judging from their defences. In the same way, the farmstead at Little Woodbury (Wiltshire), which remained the model of the Iron Age farming unit in southern England for forty years, now seems from aerial photographs to have been no more than an annex to a much larger neighbouring enclosure, about which we know absolutely nothing (see Fig. 134).

Thus neither the nature of the remains nor the available resources can be overlooked when defining a research problem. Before interpreting data we must accept that we preserve only a few images of the past and at different levels. Each can only provide answers to a limited number of questions.

One Vix krater or 100,000 potsherds?

Archaeologists have often constructed theories on the basis of finds that are exceptional and unique: one house plan marking the transition from one type of architecture to another, a certain object that supplies the missing link in a typological sequence or on a hypothetical trade route.

The development of statistics has influenced archaeologists, whose tendency to extrapolate from a single piece of evidence has long been denounced. The presence of a piece of Chinese silk in a Hallstatt period grave is a curiosity, a record of a sort. In contrast, the appearance of thousands of Roman amphorae in Gaul fifty years before the conquest suggests intensive commercial penetration and a profound change in the habits of an entire society. Quantitative analyses based on sufficiently large samples make it possible to consider an appreciable number of fields of enquiry from the beginning of protohistory.

The relative lack of written sources should not blind us to the fact that we are dealing with societies that were already complex: it is no longer a matter of measuring the relative proportions of wild and domesticated animals, but rather of trying to find out how flocks and herds were managed, what their main role was – as working animals, for milk or for meat – and whether there was selective breeding. Settlements can reveal regional differences, complex social differentiations and rapid growth in production.

Models such as those of David Clarke and at times daring intuitions such as those of J.-J. Hatt have been very fruitful, even though they have not always been able to survive critical analysis of their basic premises. These are scenarios that are certainly closer to ancient reality than the deceptive rigour of typological and chronological categorization. In tackling the problems raised by C.-A. Moberg we incline to the view that the best interpretations are those which raise new questions: new interpretations – new discoveries, those which only a fresh approach can perceive.

The comparison of sources

The student of protohistory, and especially the last millennium BC, is fortunate in being able to compare various types of source – for example, archaeology, written texts and place names. Agreement or disagreement between these sources is constantly stimulating research: an archaeological hypothesis can clash with documentary data, or the latter may throw light upon the former. There is no question of looking in written sources for information that simply is not there, such as the locations of battles during the Gallic War, for example. Ancient texts often describe events that are unique and personalized, whereas archaeological data can only provide anonymous silhouettes. But words and objects can mutually illuminate one another; the background builds up around the actors.

This relative wealth of sources does not, however, allow us to look at these periods objectively. On the contrary, our present-day prejudices and preoccupations are always present when we reconstruct the past. Successive commentators on Caesar's histories, for example, faithfully reflect the political events which have rent Europe over the past two centuries. Works on the protohistoric landscape in the years between the two World Wars were profoundly affected by totalitarian ideologies. Nowadays stress is laid on the relationships between man and his environment and ecology and on the Celts, who are thought of as the first 'Europeans', rather than on the opposition between Gauls and Germans.

4
Raw materials
and building techniques

Iron Age settlement was essentially rural, and all the characteristics of its architecture were determined by the requirements and customs of a farming society. With a few rare exceptions, buildings were constructed using materials that were readily to hand and easy to work. The subtleties of construction came from long experience rather than from complex technology. The range of tools available was small and there was little specialization in them. Nevertheless, this lack of resources did not prevent the construction of a variety of buildings, perfectly adapted to climatic conditions, to the environment and to the functions assigned to them, but only an outline of which can be preserved by archaeology. When reconstructions are being made of protohistoric buildings, it should never be forgotten that the most likely solutions are those which make use of the simplest techniques, unless there are clear indications to the contrary.

Raw materials

Wood

Wood is the basic building material for the whole of temperate Europe. It occurs abundantly and is only replaced by stone in those regions where the latter is available for immediate use because it occurs in a naturally fragmented form, and on the Atlantic coasts where the relatively sparse vegetational cover is unsuitable for building purposes. Various species each have their own roles to play, by virtue of their hardness and resistance to compression, bending or fracture. Hardwoods are preferred for posts and framing. From the end of the fourth millennium BC, people dwelling on the shores of the Alpine lakes recognized the superiority of oak for major load-bearing elements in structures. Ash, alder and fir were also strongly represented. The use of conifers increased in the Bronze Age: some palisades, such as that at Auvernier-Nord on Lake Neuchâtel, were built entirely of fir stakes. At Fiave in the Trentino larch was used for piling. For other structural elements beech, willow, poplar, elm, lime and pine were all used. The presence of different species and the extent to which they were used depends on the local resources. In certain cases it is even possible to identify the type of woodland that adjoined the villages. Thus, it is considered that the Feddersee in southern Germany and the Wauwill and Thayngen marshes in Switzerland were bordered by alders, whilst oak woods dominated the shores of Lake Neuchâtel. Wood did not merely play an essential role in frames of houses, it was also used throughout buildings in the form of logs, planks, saplings and even branches and twigs. Small branches and twigs were often used mixed with stones and earth as foundation materials designed to raise floors up above water level. Wattling (flexible branches woven round stakes), which in most buildings supplied the framework for wattle-and-daub walls (see Fig. 24), was usually made of hazel. In order to obtain branches that were long, flexible and with few twigs, of the kind that have been discovered by excavation, it is necessary to select suckers from the stump of a tree that has been felled (coppicing). P.J. Reynolds stresses the fact that this implies long and careful forest management. The species available can determine the building technique chosen. The log cabin technique (German *Blockbau*) consists of forming walls of trunks piled horizontally and crossing at the corners: it is to be found principally in those regions where conifers predominate. The long, thin, light trunks of these trees are ideally suited to this type of architecture. Alongside the differential use of tree species there was selection of different parts of trees for applications related to their shapes and properties. Trunks were often cut above the first branching so as to preserve a natural fork which would be used as a load-bearing post in the frame. Domestic equipment similarly reveals an intimate knowledge of the physical properties of wood.

Flexible woods, hazel branches, osiers and reeds were used to make the wattling for walls and wickerwork as early as the Neolithic period, but the art of basketry had hardly developed before the end of that period. Very fine containers of wicker basketry, often 4–5 strands woven each way, have been found in Late Bronze Age lake villages. The use of bark is much older and more diversified. It was used for facing or in the form of woven strips as insulating material at ground level; it was sewn together to make cylindrical receptacles with flat bottoms; rolls of bark soaked in resin served as torches. Advantage was taken of certain specific properties: P. Pétrequin mentions cords made from lime or retted-oak-bast. Finally, the use of betulin, a gum produced by distillation from birch bark, is well known from all the lake villages.

Earth

Earth plays a not unimportant role in building. Sand, gravel, straw, grass and sometimes animal hair were used in the daub with which walls are rendered. This mixture is applied to the plaited wooden wattling of the walls. When it dries, the cracking caused by shrinkage of the earth is made good and a coating, usually finer and lighter than the main body of the walls, is applied to the surface. Recent reconstructions and comparisons with traditional buildings attest the solidity, economy and excellent insulating properties of this material. It would appear that cob and pisé

walls existed in the Bronze Age. They were constructed by gradually building up clods in the case of cob and by filling temporary wooden shuttering in the case of pisé; in the latter case, the wall was raised by successive compaction of layers of pisé. When complete, such walls would consist of earthen blocks in courses and generally with some form of staggered bond. This technique could only be used for walls at least 40cm (16ins) thick, often built on foundations made of unmortared stones or other materials.

When buildings of this kind fall into ruins, the earthen walls crumble, dissolve and become mixed with the subsoil, from which they become almost indistinguishable. As a result, nothing readily visible remains of such architecture. However, wall building required soil with particular characteristics of plasticity and coherence, even if some binder, such as sand, vegetable fibre or animal hair, was added to reduce the effects of shrinkage during drying. These characteristics are limited to clays with a restricted range of grain sizes. It was by studying the grain-size composition of sediment from the Bavois-en-Raillon (Vaud) site that J.-L. Brochier observed that the unusually thick clay fill of a small gully came from earthen buildings. Having been shown the type of remains to look for, archaeologists were then able to find elements of the foundations of these buildings. Turf layers with grass growing on them are also used in block form, especially in wetter regions (Fig. 16). The most famous example of a turf-covered roof is that from a house on the Isle of Man excavated by G. Bersu during the Second World War. A very even layer containing large pieces of burnt wood and Neolithic flints completely covered the floor of this Iron Age building. Bersu deduced that this was a roof of branches covered

16

Reconstruction of a house with peat walls and roof, Denmark. (H. Zangenberg, 1930.)

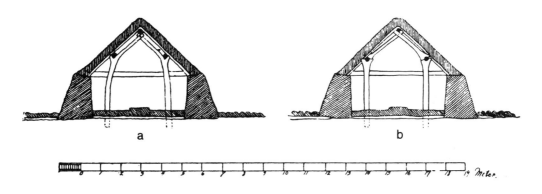

17
External facing of the rampart at Třísov, Czechoslovakia. (Excavation: J. Břeň. Photograph: O. Büchsenschütz.)

with turf taken from a Neolithic site. Not only roofs but also walls of turf are known from other regions, as, for example, Jutland. The cohesion of this material is ensured by the roots, since heat emanating from the hearth in the building combines with external humidity to keep them growing. At the fortified settlement at Nages, M. Py has uncovered a roof consisting of a frame of large branches covered by a thick layer of twigs and then another made of clay mixed with straw some 10cm (4ins) thick. These roofs, probably subhorizontal, were supported by the walls and edged with stone slabs.

The use of unfired mud brick or adobe is only known from the Hallstatt rampart of the Heuneburg (Baden-Württemberg) or from sites on the southern fringes of the continent. At the Heuneburg this is evidence of Mediterranean influences, confirmed by the imported materials on the site; it remains an example of technology transfer without a future by reason of its unsuitability for the climate of temperate Europe. Recently excavations on the Hallstatt site at Choisy-au-Bac (Oise) have shown that potsherds were reused, along with animal bone waste, as house foundations. They were in very wide use as insulating bases for ovens and hearths from the Neolithic onwards.

In the same way the use of clay as a floor covering is widely attested. In the west Swiss lake villages and in bog settlements it was used in large quantities for insulating layers over damp deposits. Some of these sealing layers, which had sunk under their own weight, had been renewed repeatedly. They were often placed over a layer of branches. Clay was also used as a sealing material, without wattle or cob, on log walls – at Clairvaux (Jura), Buchau (Baden-Württemberg) and Auvernier (Neuchâtel), for example. In domestic architecture it was always a local resource, although it could be transported several kilometres for certain funerary monuments of the period.

Stone

Over most of the continent, stone was used as a secondary building material until the end of the Iron Age. Even attempts at monumental construction, as at Třísov, (Fig. 17) are rather hesitant: here, two courses of large stones, set on edge in the external wall-face of the fortification appear to copy the Roman building style termed 'grand appareil'. Whether it was used for fortifications or even for dwellings, in those regions where stone was plentifully available it was always employed in a simple fashion. Walls without mortar (drystone) or with clay jointing were made from blocks that had been broken naturally or with hammers, and often carefully selected so as to reduce voids in construction. Walls with masonry facing and rubble-filled cores (Fig. 18) were known early, from the fifth millennium BC in the case of the great megalithic monuments, and from the third millennium BC for houses in sparsely wooded regions, such as the *garrigue* of southern France or the islands to the north of Scotland. In the former case, the facing was of limestone rubble or small slabs, and in the latter of carefully laid sandstone slabs. The filling was made of rubble of any kind. This technique developed later into the *murus duplex*, a wall construction with multiple internal facings within the wall-core. The slabs used at entrances were usually much larger since they had to support the thrust of the walls. In this area civil engineering lagged behind mortuary architecture, since in the Armorican barrows of the Early Bronze Age the slabs placed at the ends of the long sides of the funerary chambers had vertical grooves so that the slabs beneath could fit into them (perhaps imitating wooden structures).

Drystone revetted terraces and house foundations in stone appeared in the second millennium BC (at Savognin (Grisons), for example). This technique spread during the first millennium BC, and it is to be found in the Paris basin during the Late Bronze Age, at Catenoy and at Choisy-au-Bac (Oise). Stone began to be used for sills and floors; stone floors rarely covered the whole building but only those areas that were lived in. They often consisted of carefully-laid slabs. Corbelled false vaults, stone lintels and walls that were double-faced and reinforced with headers came into general use in those regions where flat stone was plentiful. The most accomplished form of this architecture developed throughout the Iron Age and into the first millennium AD on the north-west coast of Scotland and in the Northern Isles. Brochs were circular towers which could reach 14m (46ft) in height; their walls were very thick at the base and were double so as to allow space for an internal gallery and stone staircases (Fig. 19). These arrangements increased their solidity and made them easier to build. In the Orkneys not only the walls but also the internal fittings were made of sandstone slabs. As a general rule, stone was only used in combination with wood in order to improve living conditions within the structures or to compensate for a slope, to support posts or to protect wall bases against damp, to face a wall or to protect a timber-laced rampart against the effects of fire. In the form of roofing-slabs, it was also used to anchor roofs made of branches.

Techniques

Tools

The development of metallurgy in Europe, first of copper and then of iron, during the second and first millennia BC brought about profound changes in building tools. It was during these twenty centuries

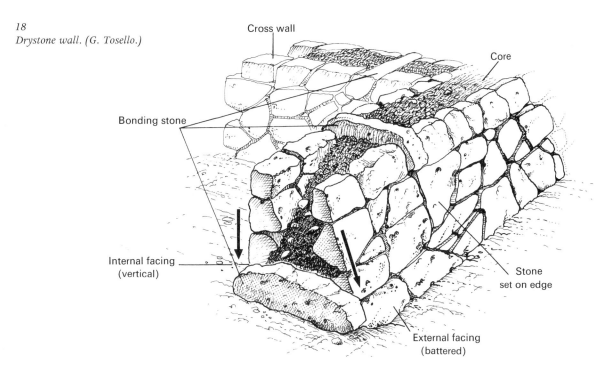

18
Drystone wall. (G. Tosello.)

Cross wall

Core

Bonding stone

Internal facing
(vertical)

Stone
set on edge

External facing
(battered)

Broch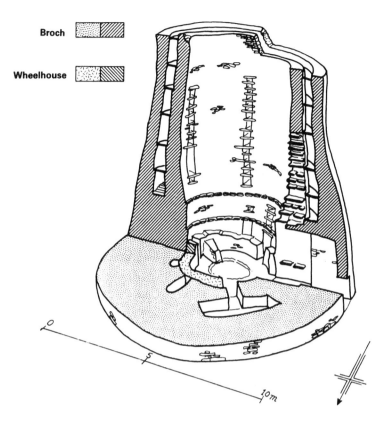

Wheelhouse

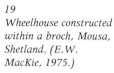

19
Wheelhouse constructed within a broch, Mousa, Shetland. (E.W. MacKie, 1975.)

that shaping and cutting tools evolved to achieve their modern forms. Although they later underwent considerable diversification in the Middle Ages, this was no more than variations on the basic forms in response to the increasing range of specialist tasks to be undertaken. The main tools of the carpenter and joiner stabilized their forms in this period: axes, adzes, gouges, chisels and gravers, along with wooden and bronze wedges. The last-named were flanged axes with butts flattened by repeated hammering, showing that they had never been hafted and that they acted not by being swung but by means of indirect percussion. Moreover they had broader blades than the more usual axes. Saws and augers for working wood did not appear until the Late Iron Age; saws are known from the Late Bronze Age but their small size shows that they were used by goldsmiths.

The changes that occurred in the Late Iron Age seem to have had less to do with the introduction of new technologies than with the selection of faster and more efficient tools. The fact that iron ore occurs in the whole of Europe ensured that iron was utilized everywhere. The cutting edges of iron implements are both more effective and more durable than their bronze counterparts. Complicated iron-working techniques can be observed, which made it possible by the Late Iron Age for a hard steel cutting edge to be obtained on a ductile blade. There was some diversification of tools linked with craft specialization and the rise of a professional artisan class (Fig. 20). The broad axe or hatchet, used for finishing, can be distinguished from the felling axe by its blade as well as its shorter handle. Alongside chisels and wedges, draw knives were in common use for smoothing. The bow saw only spread widely at the end of the La Tène period. For piercing wood bow-operated drills or spoon augers, of the type found in the Manching (Bavaria) *oppidum*, were used. The entire tool-kit perfected by the Celtic craftsmen of the second century BC survived with little change right up to the eighteenth century. The parallel progress achieved at this time both in tools and in building techniques suggests that craftsmen carpenters were working by the Late La Tène period.

Felling and cutting timber

There was a remarkable development in the techniques of building in wood between the Middle

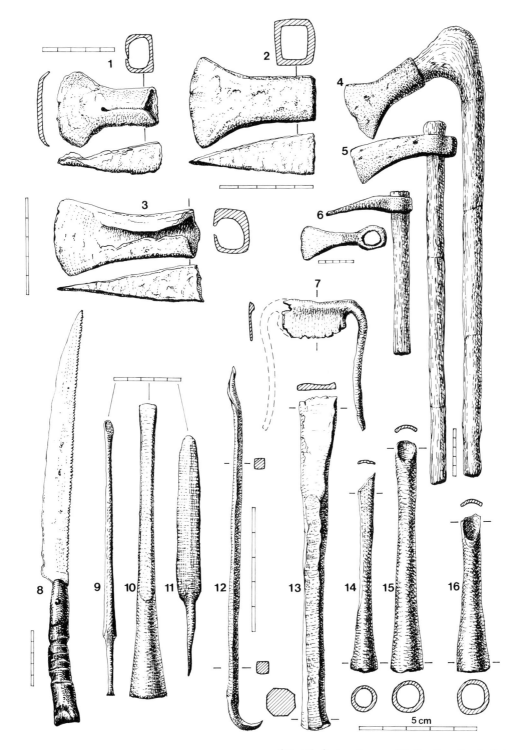

20
Iron tools. Axes (1–5); adze (6); draw-knife (7); saw (8); gravers (9–10); file (11); borer (12); chisel (13); and gouges (14–16), first century BC. (G. Tosello, after A. Rybová and K. Motyaková, 1983; B. Cunliffe, 1976; W. Drack, 1974; G. Chapotat, 1970.)

5 cm

Neolithic and the Iron Age, but this had no obvious relationship with improvements in the tools available. It was, however, a field where changes stem directly from enhanced tool performances. In the Neolithic felling and cutting was restricted to medium-size trees, the trunks being used either whole or split in two and only rarely split again into three or four. With the advent of metal, larger trees were tackled and they were often split several times. The lake villages can be studied to provide very precise evidence in this respect.

During the Middle Neolithic period the trees selected were between 10 and 20cm (4 and 8in) in diameter. At Auvernier B. Arnold has shown that the maximum diameter of felled trees increased considerably over two thousand years, attaining first 40cm (16in) and then 60cm (24in). These trunks were split several times in order to obtain a larger number of piles or planks. As a result there was a much greater exploitation of woodland, without this leading to the manufacture of beams or larger uprights. In the Late Bronze Age at Cortaillod-Est on Lake Neuchâtel the split piles were on average scarcely thicker than those from whole trunks. The sapwood removed during debarking was in general greater on split piles. Thus, it was an increase in solidity that was being sought rather than simply larger piles, since the sapwood, the living outer casing of the tree, is more prone to rotting.

As with felling, cutting up was carried out using axes and wedges. In the absence of saws, woodsmen made use of the splitting properties of wood up until the Iron Age. Trunks were split along the lines of least resistance, radial in the case of oak and ash, and concentric in fir. Piles and posts that were roughly circular, polygonal or rectangular were produced from oak and planks from fir. A characteristic phenomenon is the fact that oaks with diameters less than 15cm (6in) were used whole whilst larger ones, 15–30cm (6–12in) in diameter, were split into two, three or four; those of greater diameter (up to 60cm (24in)) being split into six or eight sections. Over 60cm (24in) the resultant posts were too large and further division would end up producing planks rather than posts or piles. For the most part these very large trees were not used. In the same way two separate groups of fir trees were exploited: the smaller, of 7–17cm (3–7in) diameter, were used whole as posts, whilst the larger, between 40 and 100cm (16 and 39in) in diameter, were made into planks. The concentric arrangement of these planks in relation to the trunk gave them a bowed section. They were therefore trimmed with axes and straightened by removing longitudinal shavings on either side. On this site the length of the planks was normally equivalent to four times the width.

The upright piles in houses were commonly 5–7m (16–23ft) in length, and sometimes longer, more than half of this length being driven into the ground. They were sharpened over a length of about 1m (3ft) (Fig. 21) and rarely debarked when they consisted of a whole trunk. To reduce the work involved, and also to prevent the sap rising up the length of the trunk, the posts were set head down. They often show evidence of wear on the pointed end, which B. Arnold attributes to their having been moved by dragging. Wear of this kind on the edge of a split trunk is proof that large trees were cut up where they were felled, or at least at a location some distance from the construction sites.

Beams and planks are much more rarely preserved. In the Early Bronze Age village found under the Mozartstrasse in Zürich, the alder cross-beams found in the earliest occupation layer measured 6–8m (20–26ft), rising to 6–10m (20–33ft) in the layer immediately above. The earlier ones had sections that varied from semi-circular to very flattened ovals, and still had their bark on. They had a rectangular hole at each end and in the centre. The later ones were rectangular in section and had two holes in the centre as well as the holes at each end. The tie beams were also found: they averaged 4m (13ft) in length and their flattened ends were oar-shaped in the case of the earlier examples. At Auvernier-Nord planks 5–7m (16–23ft) long were found, and a few as long as 10m (33ft). As at the Zürich site, these units of length appear to correspond with the dimensions of the houses. When house superstructures burn down, planks are the first things to be destroyed and so they are largely known from fragments. At Buchau H. Reinerth discovered oak planks 30cm (12in) wide by 2–3cm (1–1¼in) thick; Auvernier produced planks measuring 2–3m (6½–10ft) long, 30–40cm (12–16in) wide, and 4–5cm (1¾–2in) thick.

Jointing techniques

The Bronze Age witnessed few changes in jointing techniques in wood, and the Iron Age practically none. The main innovations appeared from the Middle Neolithic period, in the fourth millennium BC. It is not impossible that these may be even older, but earlier evidence, contemporary with the linear pottery culture long houses with five rows of posts, is missing. There has long been a desire to see the introduction of metal as the decisive factor in the progress in wood construction. It is now clear, however, that it was nothing of the sort, and that the earliest constructions

21
Piles from the village of Cortaillod, Lake Neuchâtel. The three pointed and debarked piles also show traces of previous use for other purposes: one has a circular groove, the second a dovetail mortice and the third an oblique notch. (B. Arnold, 1986.)

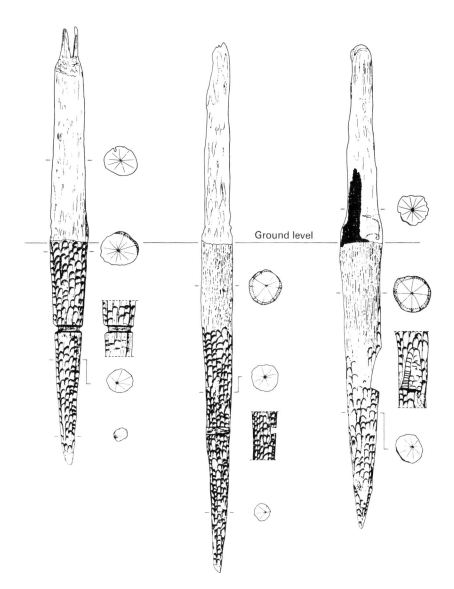

Ground level

were made using polished stone chisels and axes. However, the use of metal tools became widespread and in a way made techniques that had previously been reserved for making furniture or particularly well finished objects, such as fountains or carts, available for more commonplace applications.

Thus, the first dovetail mortices known are from a Middle Neolithic door or article of furniture found at Elgozwill, Late Neolithic cart-wheels from the Zürich Pressehaus (see Fig. 4.1), and a Middle Bronze Age fountain at Saint-Moritz, all in Switzerland.

Although a clear trend can be perceived in building construction, whereby the various elements of the walls and the structural timberwork associated with the roof are increasingly integrated with each other, there is no justification for asserting that there was regular progression of techniques from the simplest to the most complex. In the rural world of today well designed buildings exist which are surrounded by 'do-it-yourself' sheds built by the farmers themselves which are in no way superior to the earliest types of construction. From the beginning of the Bronze Age a builder could choose from a whole range of techniques those which were effective, solid and rapid in varying degrees, according to the intended use of the building and the likely length of time that it would be in use.

The work of Zippelius on these techniques is our best source of information at the European level. The many recent observations on lake villages have confirmed and complemented his hypotheses and they have been tested by experimental reconstructions. In so far as our data are for the most part fragmentary, we shall start with the simplest techniques and work towards the most complex, on the basis of data from excavations. The most elementary method used to join the timbers of a house frame is the plaited cord, dozens of which are to be encountered in lake villages. Using this method, structural elements can be joined which stay in place under their own weight. P.J. Reynolds has shown in his round-house reconstructions how the posts that support the roof can be joined together at the top by a simple tie, without any central post: the weight of the roof ensures general cohesion and distribution of loads. This type of assembly is easy to use and has the advantage of giving the structure great flexibility. In the continental four-sided buildings, the frame is of necessity more rigid, but cord lashing remains the favoured method of joining the various elements of the wooden superstructure.

Other techniques make use of the natural shapes of branches. The joining of upright posts to ridge-poles or wall-plates can be accomplished using a simple natural fork on which the horizontal beam rests (Fig. 22). This method, which is of great antiquity, can be found in all periods, from the Neolithic to the present day. Two slightly inclined posts joined together at their upper ends can also provide support. This 'scissors' construction has been identified at Aichbühl (southern Germany) from the Middle Neolithic, at Petit-Chasseur (Valais) on a small Early Bronze Age building, and at Zug in the Hallstatt period.

Like natural forks, of which they are a fabricated version, upright posts can be shaped in the form of a fork (checked) to accommodate the ridge-pole or thinned (half-checked) down at the top of the vertical element to consolidate the frame. Fiave (Trentino) has produced examples of piles shaped in this way to support planks, and also of similar types of structure, complete with mortice-holes. R. Perini is of the opinion that, in certain cases, these relate to the method of fixing extension pieces that supported the walls.

Mortice-and-tenon construction (Fig. 23) is also known from the Middle Neolithic; it may have

22

Posts with evidence of jointing, found in lake and wetland building settlements. 1: post with natural fork; 2: post with end tenons; 3: post with slot mortice; 4: post with halved joint; 5: post with mortice. (G. Tosello, after P. Pétrequin, 1983.)

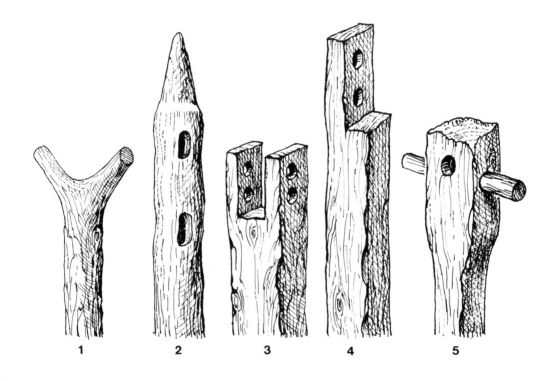

1   **2**   **3**   **4**   **5**

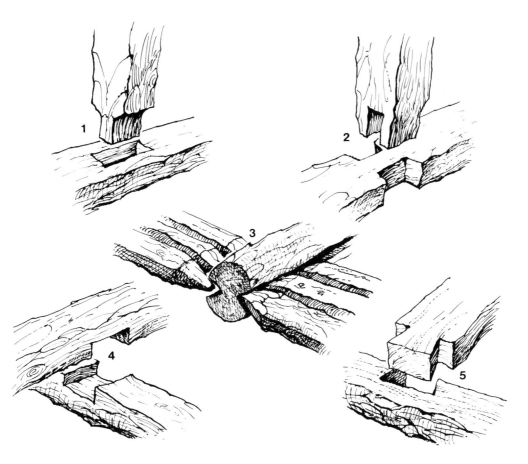

23

Principal timber joints used in the Bronze and Iron Ages. 1: mortice-and-tenon joint; 2: slot mortice; 3: rebated joint; 4: halved joint; 5: dovetail. (G. Tosello.)

appeared as a method of fixing handles to tools earlier, but there is no evidence available to support this. During the Bronze and Iron Ages it was used to fix upright posts into wall plates or sill beams. It was widely used to ensure rigidity in the joints between uprights and base-plates. From the Late Bronze Age it is sometimes to be found with pegs to anchor the tenons in the mortices. Halving joints were used for securing beams where they crossed, either at right-angles or obliquely. Older examples were not squared up and had roughly cut notches. In the Bronze Age, improved techniques led to only the lower element being notched in walls made of horizontal beams, so as to increase water-resistance. Later, notches were cut on the upper and lower sides of logs with depths equal to one-quarter of the section, in order to improve the

solidity and rigidity of the whole structure. This technique may have been in use in the Late Neolithic period in the construction of box ramparts (Ger. *Kastenbau*) with frameworks of the horizontal timbers only. It became very widespread with the growth of 'log-cabin' (*Blockbau*) building in the Middle Bronze Age.

The most highly developed technique, and that which seems to have been most difficult to master, was dovetail jointing, which was only represented by a handful of examples until recently. However, certain reused piles in the Late Bronze Age village of Auvernier have recently been seen to have notches in them characteristic of dovetailing. Even though it is not possible to establish a direct relationship between the number of archaeological examples of a technique and the frequency of its overall use, one may nevertheless consider that the use of dovetailing must have been limited, on account of both its difficulty and partly as long as craftsmen did not have iron tools available to them.

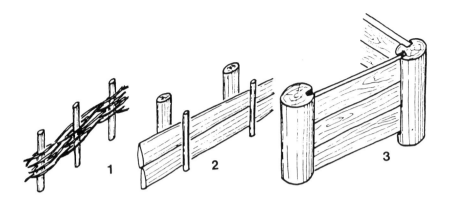

24
Walls. 1: wattles on stakes; 2: superimposed horizontal planks or false Blockbau*; 3: tongued-and-grooved horizontal planks with grooved posts. (After P. Pétrequin, 1983.)*

The problems of making planks during the Bronze and Iron Ages has already been described. Nevertheless, craftsmen were employing them in walls using a tongue-in-groove technique (Fig. 24). According to A. Zippelius, the earliest example is that found in the wooden mortuary chamber of the Leubingen (Saxony) burial mound, dated to the Early Bronze Age. A recent

25
Rebated jointing at the corner of a house from Biskupin, Poland. (National Archaeological Museum, Warsaw.)

discovery at the Middle Bronze Age settlement at Padnal-Savognin has shown planks joined together in this way, their ends being slotted into grooves in uprights at the ends and in the centres of the walls. A little later, in the Late Bronze Age, at Jemgum (Lower Saxony), the grooves in the upright were disposed radially and went through to the heartwood. At Biskupin (Poland), a narrow groove received the tapered ends of the logs (Fig. 25). Finally, the gate of the Altburg bei Bundenbach (Pfalz), as reconstructed by R. Schindler, used the same technique in the Iron Age. Lake sites have also produced posts and beams

with various types of slot – cut horizontally round the timber, oblique, etc – the use of which is not yet understood.

The Bronze and Iron Ages therefore represent a key period for wood working, with significant advances in tools and jointing techniques. To see equally important innovations in the art of carpentry it is necessary to wait until the full medieval period, between the twelfth and fourteenth centuries, as shown by J. Chapelot, with the general use of dovetail and mortice-and-tenon joints, wind-bracing in roof structures and the adoption of timber-framed walls. In the intervening period, the Roman occupation gave priority to stone for the most important buildings. Once this Mediterranean interlude was over, it is arguable whether the scarcity of iron tools in the countryside was a significant factor in the lack of development of wooden architecture for several centuries, or whether this should be attributed to demographic and economic stagnation.

5 House architecture

The birth of architecture

Bronze and Iron Age buildings present a wide variety of forms and dimensions, according to period and region. We do not have at our disposal enough data to allow us to follow this development in detail, either in space or over time. However, a general trend quickly becomes apparent: the constituent elements of the roof slowly became more robust and more solidly assembled so as to constitute a true frame. The walls underwent a similar evolution, so that the house became a coherent three-dimensional space which tended to detach itself from the ground: timber-frame construction (*Fachwerkbau*), many examples of which have come down to us from the Middle Ages, seems in fact to have been known from the Late La Tène period. The jointing techniques – halving, mortice-and-tenon, tongue-in-groove, dovetailing – are the same as those of the Neolithic period; however, the efficiency of metal tools allowed the increasing variety in the constituent elements of the timber framework (for details see Fig. 26).

Indications that allow us to reconstruct the different types of structure from this period are scanty and incomplete. We are compelled to argue on the basis of models borrowed from the ethnographic record: if we find a diagnostic frame element, this logically implies that a particular form of construction was being used. The problem is precisely that protohistoric men had at their disposal virtually the same tools as French farmers up to the eighteenth century, but we have no way of knowing whether they used them for the same purposes. However, in so far as the architecture in wood of the Roman period or the Middle Ages did not arise out of nothing, we have the right to propose a theoretical evolutionary model which fits between

Neolithic houses and those of the historical period.

It has to be said that in this enquiry the ancient authors are of little help: Strabo talks in his *Geography* of 'large houses that are round in shape' [*tholoeidis*] made of planks and wattling. This word is usually translated as 'round' but most European houses are rectangular. Only in the British Isles were houses generally round in plan. Caesar, who was sparing in his architectural descriptions, wrote that the houses in Britain were 'almost the same as those of the Gauls' (*De Bello Gallico*, 5,12). In fact, these men of the Mediterranean world were so struck by the materials used in these buildings, such as thatch, daub and wood, which tend to soften the lines of walls and roofs, that they paid little attention to their plans.

In this chapter we shall first examine the evolutionary model proposed by A. Zippelius for buildings based on earthfast posts, which are the most important group (Fig. 27). We shall then endeavour to interpret those house plans that are available in the literature in the light of this model. Finally, we shall analyse houses with load-bearing walls, the relative importance of which is difficult to estimate since they generally leave no traces in the soil.

Sets of post-holes

A. Zippelius looked at the problem of covering a rectangular space starting from two basic plans, indicated in the subsoil by two or three parallel rows of post-holes. The term 'single-aisled' is used when only two rows of post-holes are found and 'two-aisled' in the case of three rows. With the latter layout, the axial line of posts supports a ridge-beam on which the main weight of the roof is carried. The rafters bearing

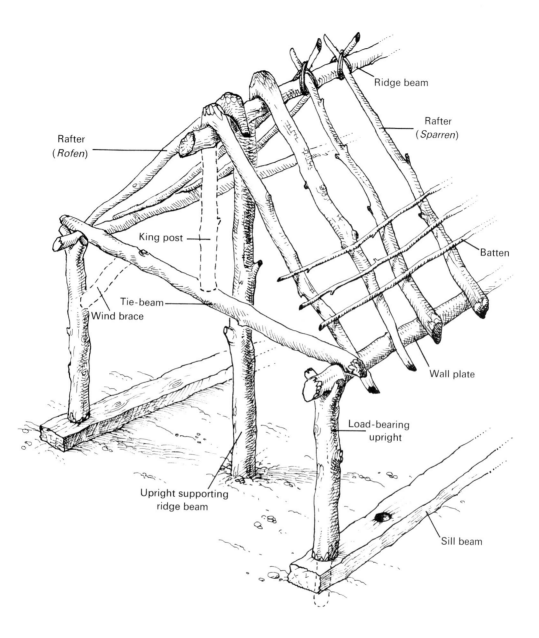

26

*Constituent elements of house frames during the Bronze and
Iron Ages. (Drawing: G. Tosello.)*

the roof itself are tied to this beam, whilst their farther
ends are carried on wall-plates, these being supported
by the two side rows of posts. A tie-beam may be used
to link the wall-plates at the ends of the building and
to fasten them to the axial post, but this does not play
an essential role in the balance of the structure (for

details see Fig. 27.1).

German archaeologists do not refer to rafters
(*Sparren*) but to *Rofen* when these timbers are set head-
down: the thicker section of the trunk is uppermost
and the disposition of the branches permits excellent
attachment to the roof-beam. In the present state of
knowledge in Europe, this *Rofendach* system, characterized by the attachment of these timbers to a ridge-
beam supported on an axial line of posts, is considered
to be the oldest and by far the most widespread

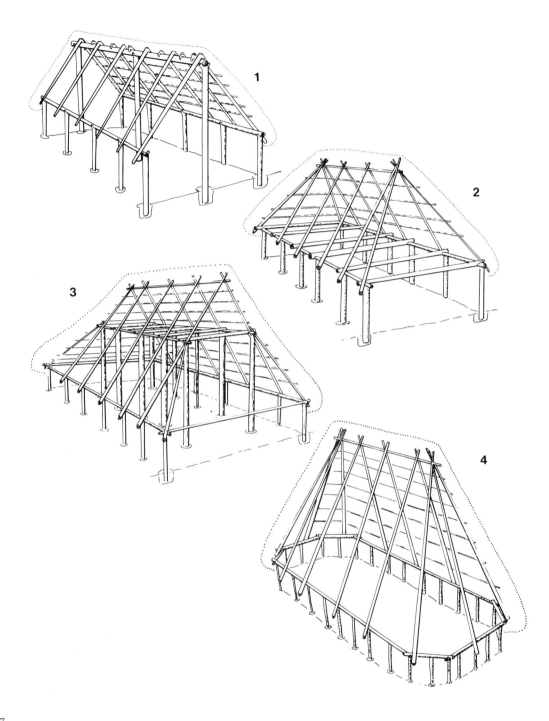

27

The four main types of construction on earthfast posts. 1: Two-aisled house, with ridge beam supported on an axial row of load-bearing uprights (Rofendach). 2: Single-aisled house, hipped roof with two faces, Sparren rafters joined in pairs: the stability of the structure is ensured by the tie-beams linking the load-bearing uprights; 3: Three-aisled house, with internal load-bearing posts connected by tie-beams; 4: House in which the roof is carried on the uprights set into the outer walls; these houses may also have some internal uprights, as at Verberie (Oise). (O. Büchsenschütz.)

technique up to the Late Bronze Age. Contrastingly, once the layout with one aisle, or even three aisles, reaches a certain size, it demands a completely different superstructure. Whereas in the system just described all the roof loading operates vertically downwards on a structure made up of elements placed on top of one another, single- and three-aisled layouts pose problems of lateral stresses which must be taken account of in planning the framework of the superstructure.

In single-aisled buildings the posts in each row are set carefully opposite one another: each is in fact joined at its top end by a tie-beam to a post set symmetrically opposite it in the other row. A wall-plate joins each post to the other uprights in the same row on the long axis of the rectangle. In this case the rafters are set on this wall-plate and joined in pairs to the ridge-beam. Thus in this case the ridge-beam has no load-bearing function, it merely brings together the pairs of rafters in order to avoid lateral slumping (Fig. 27.2).

This arrangement has a number of advantages: the covered space is not encumbered with axial posts; economies are made in the use of very long timbers; and it is no longer necessary to lift a heavy ridge-beam to the top of the roof before the rafters are set in place. The pairing of upright supports and rafters strongly encourages building in bays, which foreshadows the farms that were to follow later. In such buildings, the rafters are positioned with their heavier, thicker ends pointing downwards, since they no longer have to be fixed so firmly to the ridge-pole. In the German terminology, such rafters are *Sparren* and not *Rofen*. The summit of the roof frame is much lighter, and the weight of the roof is transferred down onto the tops of the long sides of the building.

A gable-end can be postulated at each end of a single-aisled house when there is evidence of an axial post in the middle of the short sides. Where this post is missing, there is a problem related to the weight-distribution of the framework of the roof. The difficulty to be overcome in the absence of axial posts in the end walls is the risk that the thrust of the roof, lacking any counterbalance, will cause it to tilt along its long axis towards one of the end walls. The solution is the use of a hipped roof, the two triangular faces of which are supported on rafters which start from the corners of the rectangle and join the first pair of rafters at the ridge. The back-thrust on the corner posts means that axial posts in the end walls can be dispensed with.

The layout without axial posts is only known from the Late Bronze Age, except for some small buildings with light roofs. Zippelius identified one of the first large buildings of this type at Künzing (Bavaria) on the basis of the rigorously symmetrical and closely set disposition of its two rows of posts (Fig. 28).

The third type of rectangular-plan building has three aisles, that is to say, four rows of posts. It is very difficult to say whether this resulted from the contraction, the evolution or the scaling-up of a simpler layout. By using a diagram which was more effective than descriptions, B. Trier has shown the main possible relationships, which are manifold (see Fig. 27.3).

In north-western Europe, and especially in Drenthe, more than a hundred such houses have been uncovered. They have two internal rows of strictly symmetrical posts; according to the size of the building, there may be between 5 and 23 pairs of such posts, equivalent to overall lengths of 17–40m (56–132ft) (an average of 25m (82ft)). These structures vary in overall breadth between 5 and 6m (16 and 20ft), the central aisle occupying approximately half of this. The surviving remains of the outside walls vary greatly: they are usually in the form of low walls of wattle (or sometimes of stone), which may be strengthened externally by posts. These outer walls in the majority of cases surround the double rows of internal posts on both the long and short sides of the building.

The reconstruction of these very large buildings has given rise to many discussions, among the most notable of which are those by van Giffen, Schepers, Haarnagel, Zippelius and Harsema (who rebuilt one of these houses). The following points should be borne in mind:

The posts in the two inner rows are linked by tie-beams and aisle-plates, which ensure a solid framework on which the rafters may rest; these elements also distribute lateral thrusts well above ground level.

In view of the relatively modest breadth of these buildings, each rafter is made of a single timber. These are *Sparren* since, in so far as the breadth of the central aisle is more than half the total breadth of the building, the point where they bear on the wall-plate is in the middle, or below the midpoint of, their length. It is therefore necessary to set them with their thicker sections down.

The exterior walls, or the outside posts which strengthen them, have an important load-bearing and stabilizing function: they support the bottoms of the rafters and therefore a substantial proportion of the weight of the roof. Archaeo-

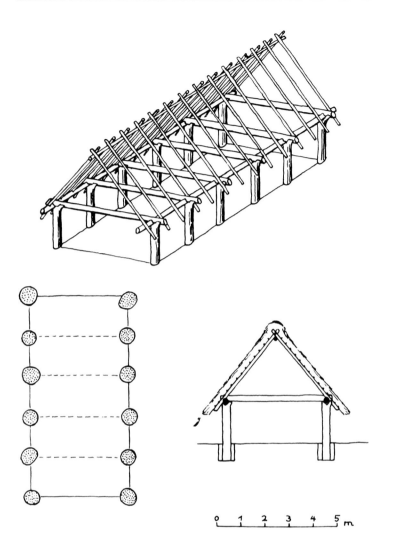

28
Building 3 at Künzing (Bavaria). The symmetry and large diameter of the uprights suggest that the ridge beam did not play a load-bearing role, since the rafters on the two sides are linked in pairs: the stability of the walls is ensured by means of the tie-beams. (A. Zippelius, 1975.)

0 1 2 3 4 5 m

logists have long thought, following the work of van Giffen and the Ezinge excavations, that these outside posts were inclined and that they buttressed the weak tops of the wattle walls. Harsema has shown that the measurements made at Ezinge were not convincing and that these external posts were in reality vertical. In his reconstruction of the Hijken house he put a wall-plate on them on which the rafters rested.

The roofs of these houses were in the form of canopies, their rounded ends giving an almost oval plan in some cases. Only the Late Bronze Age houses at Deventer had upright gables.

This characteristic differentiates these three-aisled houses from those in central Europe. In the latter, at least so far as ground plans are concerned, we are dealing with rectangular buildings constructed with stout posts at the corners and along the walls. From the Neolithic buildings at Charavines through to the Late Hallstatt buildings at the Goldberg, these were laid out with four lines of posts, almost identical in section and more or less regularly disposed relative to two axes of symmetry of the buildings (Fig. 29). It should be noted that the central aisle is not wider than the side aisles and, in consequence, it is always less than half the total breadth of the building. Several factors therefore distinguish this group from the north-west European group:

The roof is double-pitched and the gable-ends are vertical.

The rafters can be of either *Sparren* or *Rofen* type, owing to the narrowness of the central aisle.

The entire frame is carried on posts which concentrate the thrusts and sub-divide the structure along two orthogonal axes. The walls were not weight-bearing and were thus little more than light cladding, which has usually left no trace.

A. Zippelius drew attention to the large Hallstatt (First Iron Age) building from Befort (Luxembourg) which has an additional peculiarity. The posts that edged the central aisle are in fact not earthfast but simply packed lightly with stones. He proposes the reconstruction of

this building therefore with braces in order to stabilize the central aisle. We believe that they are not essential in this case: the side aisles are sufficiently anchored in the ground by their external posts to support the roof structure. The Befort house is at the crossroads of several traditions. However, we agree with Zippelius's statement that it represents a step in the gradual liberation of rectangular wooden buildings from reliance on earth-fast timbers.

The demise of earthfast timbers

Houses with earthfast posts are characteristic of the whole protohistoric period. This technique makes it

29
Reconstruction of a house from Cortaillod-Est from analysis of the types of pile remains and dendrochronological dating. All the piles are circular with the exception of two, which are split. The house was built in 934 BC, but a number of the piles had been kept in store for several years. It was rebuilt several times with the addition of reinforcing timbers, particularly in 907/903 and 902/898 BC before being abandoned around 891 BC. (P. Gassmann, 1984.)

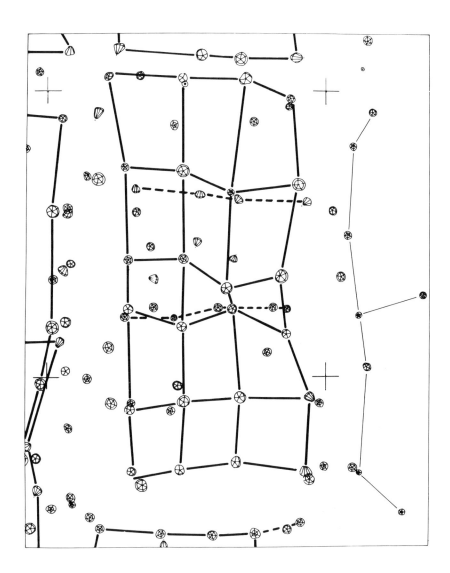

possible to counteract the lateral thrusts, which are of especial importance in rectangular buildings. It facilitates the building process in that the different frame elements can successively be attached to the main supports, which stay upright owing to the fact that they are set in the ground. It does, however, have one major drawback: neither the walls nor, in particular, the supports are insulated against ground water. Rotting of the uprights condemns the entire building in due course.

In order to avoid this it is necessary to use the technique of wind-bracing, with which we are familiar today in all wooden or metallic structures. Joints between two constructional elements – post and wall-plate or post and tie-beam – are kept rigidly at right-angles by means of a tie set obliquely and usually fastened by means of mortice-and-tenon joints, which forms the hypotenuse of a right-angled triangle. It thus becomes no longer necessary for uprights to be earthfast. They can even be insulated from ground water by setting them, as in contemporary sheds, on blocks of stone, or post-pads. The structure can also be reinforced by the addition of a sill beam which joins the bases of the posts.

A. Zippelius has proposed four stages in the theoretical evolution of the house, between reliance on earthfast posts and complete detachment from the ground:

1   The wall material does not rest directly on the ground but is supported on a sill beam fixed on the earthfast uprights;

2   The posts are simply set on the ground or on a stone pad; bracing is then performed by the angled timbers linking the uprights with the wall-plates or tie-beams;

3   A horizontal frame links all the uprights at their bases and tops; all the edges of the enclosed space which constitutes the house are defined by timbers that are morticed together;

4   The entire timber frame described in 3 is raised on a stone foundation.

All the elements and the knowledge needed for this evolution to take place were already available during the Iron Age. We have no tangible proof, however, of their having been used before the Roman period. Right up to the conquest, and in places beyond, building using earthfast posts remained the most common technique.

Is it possible to reconstruct post-built structures?

Having examined the theoretical evolution of earth-fast post structures, let us return to the evidence from excavations. How can the hundreds of post-holes found on settlements be disentangled?

It is first necessary to collect together all the available documentation and to consider not only the distribution of these post-holes but also their sizes, shapes and depths. Then, rather than looking for alignments, efforts should be made to isolate simple modules, attested in examples on the site being studied or observed on other comparable sites: squares, rectangles or trapezia composed of an identical number of posts. In fact, a module has a greater chance of corresponding to a functional building the more often it is found to be repeated on several sites. The more complex it is, the more specific it will be. It is worth concentrating on defining modules on levels where the preservation of wood removes doubts or on those that were only occupied for a short period and which thus offer distinct groups of posts.

We have collected several hundred plans of buildings from the Bronze and Iron Ages in northern Europe. Before presenting our interpretation of their construction and function, we shall summarize the steps which led us, along with other workers who have studied this problem, to favour certain forms and to isolate them from the mass of data available. The simplest form is the square defined by four posts placed one at each corner (Fig. 30, 1–4). Large numbers of these can be recognized on every site. They are generally small, 4–16 sq.m (43–172 sq.ft), which immediately excludes a large number of possible functions, such as use as dwellings. The very simplicity of this form multiplies the chances of error, because a layout of this kind can result by chance or from the confusion of two unconnected structures.

Among the plans available to us it is possible to observe considerable differences in section between the post-holes, which are not proportional to their distances from one another. It may be assumed that the

30a
Reconstructions and building plans of granaries. Four-post structures: Altburg-bei-Bundenbach (1,2), Manching (3), Dittenheim (4). Six-post structures: Altburg-bei-Bundenbach (5,6,7). Single-aisled: Levroux (8); Künzing (9); Altburg-bei-Bundenbach (10); Nový Bydžov (11). Nine-post structures: Owslebury (12); Altburg-bei-Bundenbach (13, 14).

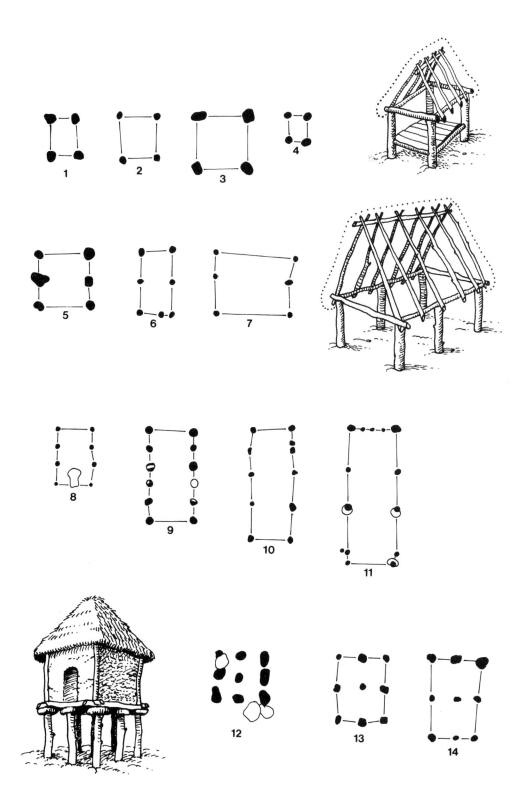

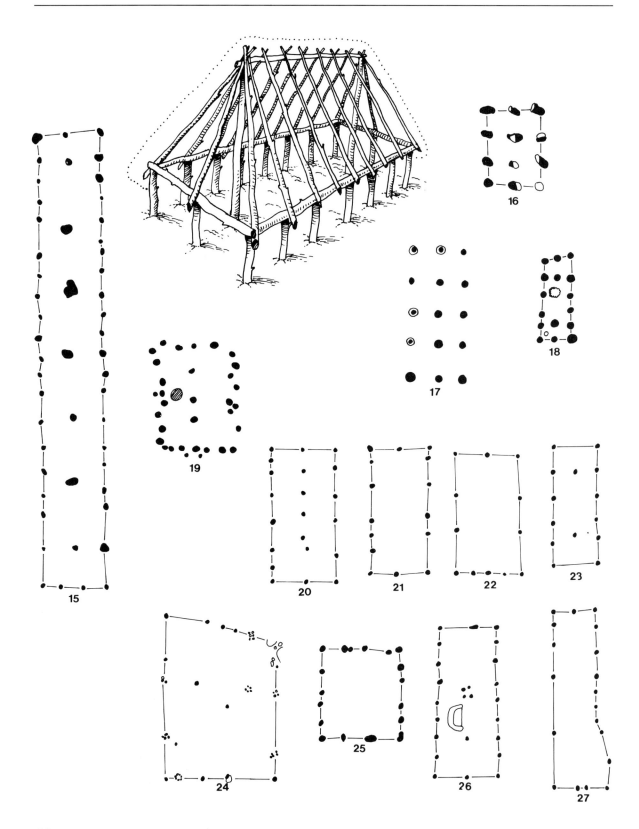

15

16

17

18

19

20

21

22

23

24

25

26

27

30b

Two-aisled structures: Manching (15); Künzing (16); Aiterhofen (17); Appelshofen (18); Holzkirchen (19); Goldberg (20, 27). Single-aisled with axial posts: Manching (21); Heuneburg (22,23). Structures with posts set into the walls: Befort (24); Altburg-bei-Bundenbach (25); Heuneburg (26); Goldberg (27). (G. Tosello, after A. Zippelius and F.-R. Herrmann, 1975; R. Schindler, 1969, 1977; W. Kimmig and E. Gersbach, 1971, 1976, 1983; J.R. Collis, 1970; O. Büchsenschütz, 1978; A. Rybová, 1964.)

forms with the smallest and widest spaced posts correspond to slight roofs and light loadings, whereas heavier ones, such as 5 and 12 in Fig. 30, were intended to support a floor or even an upper storey – a small granary, for example, or a tower.

There is frequently evidence of a pair of posts having been added. Thus, the figure shows a rectangle formed of three posts on each of its long sides. The same differences in post section and spacing can be identified as in the previous case. In addition, the length/width ratios distinguish squat (30.5) from elongated (30.27) forms. When the three posts are located on the short sides, it may be imagined that the axial posts supported a ridge-beam and so the structure comes into the two-aisled category. The relatively meagre nature of these buildings suggests various functions, such as storage, shelters for small livestock, or sheds.

If this rectangular form is extended by more pairs of posts, the dimensions can be substantially increased and the area enclosed can reach a critical size of 20–30 sq.m (215–323 sq.ft), making it possible to begin to talk of a 'house'. This was a single-aisled layout, well illustrated by Fig.30.9, the structure from Künzing (Bavaria) which Zippelius recognized as a prototype. It is reasonable to assume, at least for examples that are more than 5–6m (16–20ft) wide, that a tie-beam would have linked each of the pairs of opposed posts. Although this is a simple form, it required in practice a developed form of superstructure to cover so large a space.

Let us now go back to the square form in a more complex variant, which is often encountered. This is the nine-post structure, with three on each side and one in the centre, generally reserved for small structures (9–16 sq.m (97–172 sq.ft)). In many cases the posts were substantial in section and closely-spaced, as if they had to carry a heavy load. In most cases these would have been raised granaries, as shown by excavations on waterlogged sites and ethnographic parallels. An exception is the Besançon hut, which has the same layout but with slender posts.

Elongation of this form produces a two-aisled layout, the load-bearing elements being linked in threes. The Künzing (30.16) and Aiterhofen (30.17) sites in Bavaria have provided characteristic examples of this form. On the Heuneburg (Baden-Württemberg) the three rows of posts are more independent of one another (30.23).

The building from Holzkirchen (Baden-Württemberg) has five axial posts which clearly delineate a ridge-beam, whilst the supports of the lateral walls are disposed very irregularly (30.19). The number of internal supports for the ridge-beam is often reduced, no doubt with the intention of unencumbering the useful space inside the building. In the layout from Appelshofen (Bavaria) the symmetry of these supports also gives an indication of where the posts that have been eliminated would have stood (30.18). Here, as at Bundenbach in the Trier region, two internal supports have been preserved, with two more continuing this axis placed in the end walls. As long as there are posts on the axial line in the end walls, and even though there are no supports within the building, it is possible to reconstruct a gabled roof, as at the Heuneburg (30.22) and at Manching (30.21). However, if there are two internal supports close to the ends of the building and no central post on the line of the short sides, it is more logical to envisage the use of a hipped roof, as for example at the Heuneburg (30.23) and Manching (30.15). The examples that we have selected are relatively unambiguous, but there are many others where the profusion of supports makes it impossible to decide which layout the builder had chosen.

The three- or even four-aisled layouts in most cases pose no problems of identification: their plans stand out from stray post-holes in their vicinity from the moment of their discovery. However, before proposing an interpretation of their functions it is necessary to give careful attention to their size and to the distribution of load-bearing elements. The latter may be of the same section and delineate bays and aisles that are equal in width. The central aisle may be broader than the side ones and the external walls can be made of simple stakes or of a low stone wall. These variations imply different types of roof and different building traditions, and may relate to a variety of uses – large barns, elaborate houses, or multifunctional byre-houses.

Typological analysis reveals a whole group of structures which have not until now figured among the classic layouts: these are buildings with roofs that are wholly or mainly supported by posts situated on the exterior walls. The smaller ones, with seven to nine posts, are very similar to granaries in the arrangement of their supports, but with fewer, less substantial posts these were clearly not intended to support heavy loads. In larger buildings of this series, there are more posts on the sides. The Altburg-bei-Bundenbach (Pfalz) has a characteristic example of this group (30.25): 18 posts distributed along the four wall lines define an almost square area of 60 sq.m. (646 sq.ft). The longest buildings in layer 4 at the Heuneburg (Baden-Württemberg) and the subsidiary structures within the small fortification at Befort in Luxemburg: (30.24) also belong to this category. On these two sites it is interesting to compare the construction of other buildings which are nearby and very well defined, and have regular two- or three-aisled plans. These are clear cases of two architectural

schemes which are different, even though they are contemporaneous. At Befort, where there were only five buildings, the large five-aisled house contrasts with the other structures, which are smaller in area and of which most of the supporting posts are set in the walls. The small buildings associated with the large house at Neuhäusel (Westerwald) and the isolated buildings in the countryside around Ries (Bavaria) seem to indicate that layouts with posts set uniquely along the outer wall-lines, which are rudimentary but very flexible, were well suited for modest-sized houses or for certain utilitarian purposes.

A very similar principle was applied in two buildings, exceptional in their dimensions, that were

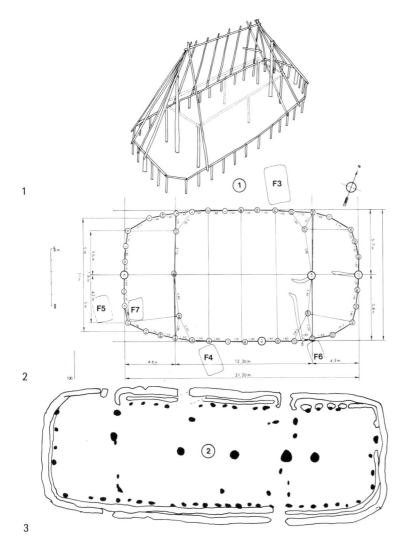

1

2

3

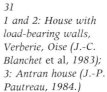

31
1 and 2: House with load-bearing walls, Verberie, Oise (J.-C. Blanchet et al, 1983); 3: Antran house (J.-P. Pautreau, 1984.)

found in France in recent years: Antran in Vienne and Verberie in Oise (Figs. 27.3 and 31). Like timber round-houses and houses with load-bearing walls, their superstructures were based on strong, closely spaced uprights placed around the circumference and their ground plans are more squat than those of the more conventional series of post-built structures. It is not possible to speak of a structural type or group, since we know only these two buildings, along with a few buildings that are more or less related to them. Nevertheless, their design is so accomplished and their size so impressive that it is difficult to believe that these are isolated examples. If new discoveries show that they do in fact constitute a western European group, this will form the natural transition between the rectangular structures on earthfast posts of central Europe and the round-houses of the British Isles.

Structures with load-bearing walls: the origin of the Alpine chalet

The pair of large oval houses just considered also represents the transition to structures in which the walls support the bulk of, or indeed the entire weight of the frame. The walls are made of superimposed logs or planks, generally laid horizontally, and there is either a complete absence of upright posts or they play no more than a secondary role. One difficulty immediately arises: these buildings leave almost no

traces in the ground and it is only in very special circumstances that their former positions can be discerned by archaeologists. It is therefore difficult to judge their relative importance *vis-à-vis* the other methods of construction.

Several types of jointing can be distinguished. The walls form a block of four solid walls made up of horizontal logs which cross at the corners: this is the true log cabin or *Blockbau* (Fig. 32). The logs are set directly on the ground or on low sills beams which form a plinth. When all the wood has disappeared, excavation may reveal stone blocks used for levelling up or wedging, low walls or sill-beam slots.

Ständerbau structures sit on the same type of foundations. This is a form of half-timbered construction in which the walls have either a framework of stakes, or posts that are generally joined by mortices and tenons to the cross-beams or sill-beams. They leave the same traces in the soil (beam slots or levelling stones *in situ*), and it is very difficult to avoid confusing these two series of structures. They can only be distinguished if traces of internal posts survive. Sill-beams appear very early in mountainous regions. They allow slopes to be compensated for by the use of footings of different heights. This technique is very common, for example in the Late Bronze Age settlement at Bavois (Vaud). It is the presence of posts in the centre of the building which allows this technique to be distinguished from that of the *Blockbau*. Structures of the *Ständerbau* type are also usually larger than their *Blockbau* counterparts.

The *Blockbau* technique was first identified in lake

32
Blockbau *construction. Reconstruction of a* Blockbau *building by F. Schäffer at the Open Air Museum, Asparn-an-der-Zaya, Austria. (O. Büchsenschütz.)*

or fen sites, where wood was preserved. The earliest-known example of this form of construction is not a house but a votive fountain of the Middle Bronze Age. This was an unroofed structure, more carefully constructed than ordinary buildings of similar date. The spring water was collected by means of two wells, each equipped with two wooden casings, one within the other. In one of these the outer casing was made of logs 15–20cm (6–8in) in diameter and 3.5m (11ft) long, with halving joints at the corners and their ends jutting out. The notches were in the upper part of the logs, although later these were to be on the underside as the first method resulted in water accumulating and speeding up the rotting of the wood. The inner casing was of planks 30–50cm (12–20in) wide and 10–15cm (4–6in) thick, stacked one on top of another and jointed with dovetails; the planks on the long sides jutted out and housed the worked ends of the planks from the short sides in slots. This is also the earliest known use of dovetailing in building.

The lake village at Zug-Sumpf has produced the earliest *Blockbau* houses (Fig. 33). The first two courses of the walls of two square buildings, of 3.1 and 2.6m (10 and 8ft) long respectively, were preserved, along with their corner joints. In view of their small size, they were probably granaries or lower floors designed to support a larger upper storey, of the type shown in houses in rock carvings from Val Camonica (Bergamese Alps).

Dendrochronology has dated the occupation layers at Zug-Sumpf to between 1282 and 1014 BC, and these structures occurred in the latest level. They are contemporary with the *Blockbau* houses from Greifensee-Böschen (Zürich) and also with those from the early phase at the Wasserburg, Buchau (Baden-Württemberg). The rectangular houses at the latter site were larger: 4–5m (13–16ft) long by 3 to 4m (10 to 13ft) wide. Those in the later village at Buchau, dated to the ninth to the eighth centuries BC, were even larger and were three-sided structures set round an open yard that is unique in Europe. Each of the three wings was about 10m (33ft) long and each house was made up of three to five rooms. These are without doubt the largest *Blockbau* structures known from the Bronze Age.

The only traces left by *Blockbau* structures are the stone or wooden footings they rested on. The Buchau houses were reconstructed from their floors and

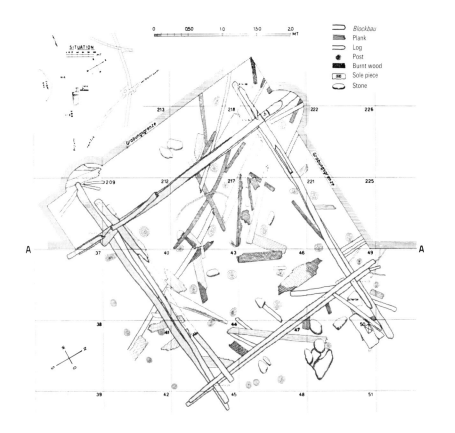

33

Plan of a Blockbau *structure from Zug-Sumpf in which the first two courses survive. (J. Speck, 1981.)*

scanty elements that survived from the jointing of their superstructures. Floors and morticed cross-beams allowed the same building style to be proposed for a Middle Bronze Age village far removed from the Alpine region: Várdomb, near Békés in the Hungarian plain, on the banks of the river Körös. The centre of the village was occupied by small rectangular structures, surviving as wooden floors surrounded in some cases by pegged beams. No post-holes were found associated with them. The small sizes of these buildings (3×2 m ($10 \times 6\frac{1}{2}$ft)) contrasted with those of the rectangular or trapezoidal post-hole structures that were also found on the site.

One hesitates between *Blockbau* and *Ständerbau* construction in the case of a high-altitude settlement in Switzerland: Padnal at Savognin (Oberhalbstein, Grisons) originated in the Middle Bronze Age with rectangular buildings whose drystone foundation walls were preserved. There was no evidence of post-holes within the structures, which contained hearths. At 14m and 20m (46 and 66ft) by 6m (20ft), these buildings were larger than those examined here so far. It cannot be affirmed that the cross-beams placed at the base of the wooden superstructure were components of a rectangular framework: it may be that this constructional technique was only employed on the two long sides, as at Bavois-en-Raillon (Fig. 34) from the Late Bronze Age or at Taubried and Thayngen in the Late Neolithic period. However, if it was indeed in *Blockbau* construction, Padnal is one of the earliest known examples. *Blockbau* was used in Poland in the Late Bronze Age. At Konin, for example, the outlines of the footings on wooden cross-beams and the clay floors of square or rectangular structures were preserved in a sand dune.

Some thirty Iron Age sites have produced the foundations of buildings on horizontal beams. They tend to be grouped around the Alps, especially in Switzerland and Austria in those regions where conifers predominate. At Hallein (Oberösterreich) the plans of three rectangular buildings were revealed by the low stone walls set at right-angles to a slope on which the sill-beams and cross-beams of the footings were set. At Salzburg-Hellbrunn it was the combination of an absence of post-holes around a well preserved floor and the imprints of logs on fragments of daub that suggested the presence of a *Blockbau* structure. In the Middle and Late Hallstatt level at Besançon-Saint-Paul traces were found of a two-roomed rectangular building measuring 8m by 5m (26 by 16ft) in the form of trenches with dark fill which preserved the outlines of horizontal beams; their ends jutted out at the corners and where the outer walls joined the partition walls, showing that these walls were certainly built with crossed horizontal beams. However, it is not possible to decide whether this was

34
Schematic reconstruction of buildings from Bavois-en-Raillon. (J. Vital and J.-L. Voruz, 1984.)

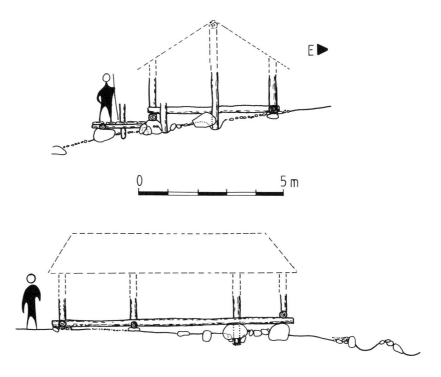

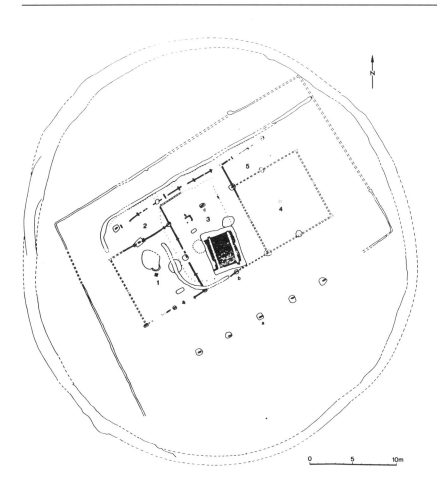

35
Structure built on a grid of horizontal beams and mixed constructions. House underneath Mound 4 at the Heuneburg-Talhau. (S. Schiek, 1985.)

Blockbau or *Ständerbau* because the remains of uprights morticed into the basal horizontal beams to act as a frame could not be identified.

In the famous fortified settlement of the Heuneburg (Baden-Württemberg) several levels of buildings were preserved in the form of 'grids' of beams measuring 2–3m (6½–10ft) square. The ends of the beams jutted out at the corners and so it is certain that the lowest course was joined by halving, but it is not known whether the walls were built in *Blockbau* style or whether the uprights were set into this grid, in which case they would only represent the base of the house and the support for the floor.

Some relatively well preserved houses have come to light under burial mounds near the Heuneburg. Mound 4 in particular had been erected over the remains of two buildings. The later of these had four rooms and covered 250 sq.m (2691 sq.ft) (Fig. 35). The load-bearing uprights, placed at the corners and in the centres of the sides, were set 1m (3¼ft) into the ground. Horizontal beams were set at the bases of the walls,

resting on regularly spaced wooden panels. Since the load-bearing uprights were squared from the beam level, with a regular 35 × 12cm (14 × 5in) section, it may be assumed that they were set into these beams. Crossed planks in the centre of each room supported an upright post which was preserved to a height of 10cm (4in), thanks to the protection provided by the mound.

Round-houses: a distinctive characteristic of the British Isles

The round-houses traditionally associated with the Gaulish hut are only found in the British Isles (Fig. 36). They are characterized by a continuous circular wall which supports a conical roof, the lateral thrusts from which are balanced radially. Various types may be distinguished by the solutions adopted to balance these engineering forces: either the rafters supporting the roof rest on a central forked post and on relieving posts set in a ring, or they are only supported by the external ring of posts and meet at the apex of the roof. Diametrically-opposed pairs of rafters are tied together at their lower ends so that they cannot slip outwards. These ties may have been composed of no more than intertwined withies which, under tension, are very strong. Reconstructions have shown that there is a third possible solution which is the most effective: the load-bearing posts are linked at their tops by timbers forming a wall-plate in a ring, or even better by a circular arrangement of interlaced branches, which act as a continuous girdle that is flexible and strong at the same time. An identical arrangement, but smaller in diameter, located about 1m (3¼ft) from the top of the roof is used when there is no central post. Since structural equilibrium is achieved by means of the unbroken wall-plate ring, wherever it is located the entrance is the weak point in the structure. For this reason it is often strengthened and developed in the form of a porch (Fig. 37). In the largest houses the roof rafters are supported on a double row of uprights. The combination of a ring of internal posts with a circular stone or turf wall which supports the roof is also known.

In excavations it is easy to recognize houses with central posts, but the only distinctive characteristic of houses with diametral ties is the absence of a central support and the strictly regular layout of the peripheral posts. This can only be discerned if older or later buildings have not confused the picture. Structures based on a circular lintel, moreover, also require rigorous symmetry in the post settings, and thus identical ground-plans can give rise to different reconstructions.

The outer ring of double ring round-houses is incorporated in the exterior wall, which often plays a secondary load-bearing role. There is thus no need for its posts to be deeply interred. It can be made of small-diameter stakes which act as the framework for the wattle-and-daub and leave almost no traces in the ground. It has only been recently that the use of more delicate excavating methods has allowed the archaeological traces that correspond to these slight outer rings to be revealed. By so doing it has been possible to show that the space occupied by these houses was greater than the area defined by the internal ring of

36

Hypothetical reconstructions of round-houses. 1: Central post; the axial post serves mainly to centre the top of the roof properly. 2: Tie-beams; tie-beams link diametrically opposed rafters in order to relieve the wall tops, which have a tendency to move outwards under the pressure of the roof. 3: Massive walls; the load-bearing role of the external wall is emphasized in buildings with stone walls. 4: Circumferential linkage: careful placing of posts and rafters allows the thrusts to be distributed over a less substantial wall. The top is kept stable by means of a continuous, flexible linkage. (After C. Musson, 1970.)

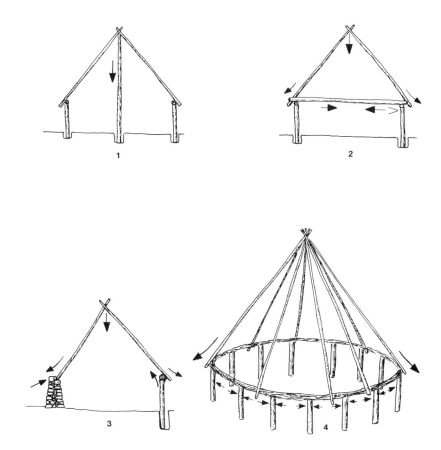

37

Experimental reconstruction of a round-house in timber and wattle-and-daub. The large Pimperne house. (P.J. Reynolds.)

posts, which had previously been interpreted as the remains of the outer wall. Circular house plans go back to the Late Neolithic in Britain, to Beaker contexts. Earlier they were rectangular or oval, their outlines being ill-defined, and they may well have been light structures. Exceptions include the three-aisled Lough Gur house from Knockadoon (Ireland), which measured 13m × 8m (42 × 26ft) and had stone footings, and that from Balbridie (Scotland), even larger with its 24m (79ft) long aisles.

Among the first round-houses were those at Gwithian (Cornwall), where a building in which the uprights formed a 4.5m (15ft) ring around a central post was replaced in less than fifty years by a larger structure. This was 7.6m (25ft) in diameter and had a much more elaborate plan: a double ring of stakes was strengthened outside by curving trenches and a porch, and there was no central post.

From this time onwards various layouts existed alongside one another, often on the same site, covering areas ranging from 28 to 88 sq.m (301 to 947 sq.ft) and with diameters between 4 and 10m (13 and 33ft). The layout, which consisted of a single ring of posts with a central one and an outer wall which should be reconstructed as lying outside the ring, was current throughout the Bronze Age. This is especially clear on hillside sites, where the houses were built on platforms that were partly scooped and partly terraced: the roof therefore rested on the edge of this platform. These sites, which are typical of the Bronze Age, became very common in the Highland Zone around 1200–1000 BC – for example, Green Knowe (Peeblesshire). Some of the houses of the Deverel-Rimbury Culture in southern England, from the second half of the second millennium to the mid-first millennium BC, also belong in this category, such as Itford Hill and Black patch (Sussex). The double-ring or ring plus ring-groove layout is known from the Early Bronze Age and developed during the second and first millennia BC (Fig. 38): examples are to be found around 1100 BC at Mam Tor (Derbyshire) and at Down Farm.

A variant of this type consists of a double outer ring of small-diameter stakes which had little or no load-bearing function. Depending on the gap between the two rings of stakes, the intermediate space may be assumed to have been filled by wattling covered with

38
1: Reconstruction of the Shearplace Hill house (M. Avery and J. Close-Brooks, 1969). Double-ring houses: 2: Moel-y-Gaer, house 14; 3: Pimperne (see Fig. 37); 4: West Plean, house 12; 5: Bodrifty, house E; 6: Little Woodbury, house 1. (G. Guilbert, 1981.)

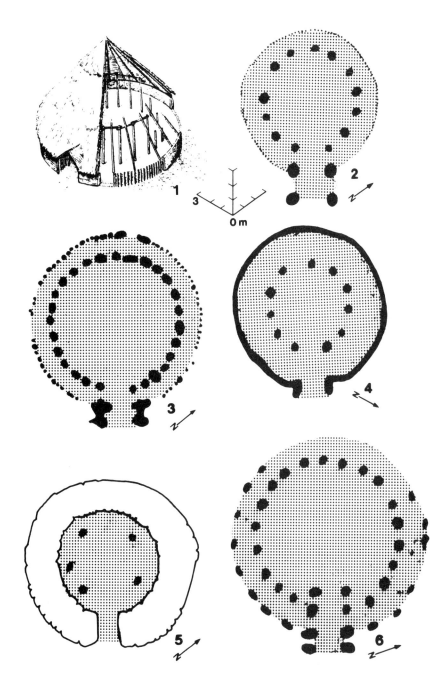

daub, by cob or by turf. This type of wall is known to archaeologists as a double-stake cavity wall. It existed in the Early Bronze Age (Downpatrick, Limerick), but it was most common in the second half of the second millennium BC, as at Shearplace Hill (Dorset) or Trevisker (Cornwall). In another variant of this type the posts or stakes forming the outer wall were very close together, but this is only known indirectly since it is deduced from the use of slots instead of post-holes, as at Downpatrick (Co. Down) or Rathgall (Co. Wicklow).

The use of a foundation trench round the whole

circumference of the ring of posts led to a type of house known in the Early Bronze Age, but which developed mainly in the Iron Age: the ring-groove timber house, in which the closely set posts were capable of supporting an enormous roof and enclosing an area of over 100 sq.m (1076 sq.ft). One of the earliest houses of this type was recognized at Houseledge (Northumberland). It was 8m (26ft) in diameter and was covered by a house edged with a circular bank in the mid second millennium BC. This type of structure spread to some extent from the Knighton Heath period (1400–1200 BC) when settlement became denser in hilly regions, such as Holme Moor, Dartmoor.

From the mid second millennium BC houses are found, often on top of constructions of rings of posts, in which the circular outer wall is built of drystone sometimes faced on both sides. The original thickness of these walls, which can be as much as 1–1.5m ($3\frac{1}{4}$–5ft), is often strengthened on reconstruction so as to attain 2–2.5m ($6\frac{1}{2}$–8ft). A ring of posts inside the building supports the roof. It appears in certain cases that this would have been destroyed when the building was reused, since stone slabs cover the post-holes. There is no central post.

These stone-walled buildings, which were often rebuilt several times, are well known from the hills of Dartmoor, where they have been preserved by the expansion of peat cover. This type of construction began in northern Britain in the second millennium BC and spread over the whole of the British Isles in the first millennium, no doubt associated with woodland clearance, which made building in wood less common.

From the Neolithic period buildings were erected in the Orkneys and Shetland Islands that were oval, circular or trefoil-shaped, whose plan was conditioned by the use of very thick (2–3m ($6\frac{1}{2}$–10ft)) drystone walls faced on both sides. Some internal posts laid out in an irregular ring supported a roof which rested for the most part on the walls. The scarcity of wood in these islands, which contrasts with the abundance of stone slabs, may explain this choice of construction. This seems to be confirmed by the recent discovery of a post-built structure beneath one of the stone buildings.

Slabs were widely used to strengthen entrances, in Dartmoor as well as in the northern isles, and to equip the interiors with partitions and tanks set in the floor. These houses can attain internal dimensions of 30–50 sq.m (323–538 sq.ft). Ness of Gruting, Benie Hoose and Yoxie (Shetland) date from the second millennium BC, whilst the first phases of the complex structural sequence at Jarlshof developed before the middle of the first millennium BC (Fig. 39).

The general lines of chronological development are known: the central post was gradually eliminated in favour of the internal ring of posts, which tended increasingly to be located close to the outer wall-line. The area covered tended to grow and diameters of 15–16m (49–52ft) are not uncommon by the middle of the first millennium BC. The entrances were developed in the most carefully built houses, emphasized by the use of stronger posts, by duplication of supports or by the addition of a porch. This was created by using thicker posts, sometimes jutting outside and sometimes forming a kind of passageway within the house.

The differences between the houses of the British Isles and the north European continent were not restricted to the general shape of the buildings, in the one case more rounded and in the other more angular. It was a matter of two conceptions that were completely different – certainly in form but also in the type of roof, the distribution of forces and the internal layout. Round-houses and rectangular houses on load-bearing posts are radically different in conception, and if there are some exceptions to this very clear-cut geographical distribution, these are in the main restricted to the field of religion. Several isolated rectangular buildings are known, and others standing alone among a group of round-houses, which have always been interpreted (rightly in our view) as temples – Heathrow (Middlesex), South Cadbury (Somerset) and Danebury (Hampshire).

We also know of some round structures on the continent that stand isolated among rectangular buildings, as, for example, at Manching (Bavaria) or the Altburg-bei-Bundenbach (Pfalz), the function of which is difficult to determine. Several Bronze and Iron Age settlements in Brittany have recently produced circular structures, such as Saint-Jacut-de-la-Mer (Côtes-du-Nord) and Le Talhouet at Pluvigner (Morbihan), which can be interpreted as domestic buildings. These discoveries confirm the fact that Brittany belongs to the Atlantic world. The rest of western France can be characterized by layouts that are intermediate between the central European and Atlantic traditions: oval forms, pitched hipped roofs and reinforced walls which support most of the weight of the roof, etc. The number of examples available is not yet adequate, however, to substantiate this hypothesis.

Footings, floors, walls and roofs

Most Bronze and Iron Age settlements leave only slight traces in the ground: post-holes and pits filled

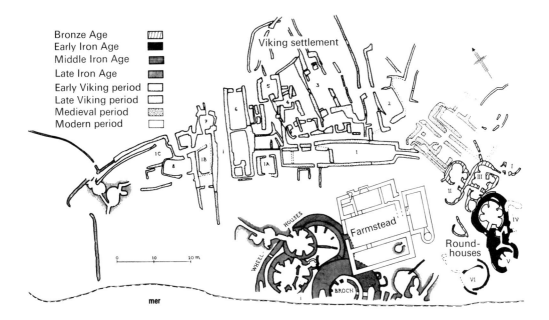

Bronze Age
Early Iron Age
Middle Iron Age
Late Iron Age
Early Viking period
Late Viking period
Medieval period
Modern period

Viking settlement

Farmstead

Round-houses

39
Jarlshof (Shetland). This unique group contains drystone houses of various types (round-houses with apses, wheelhouses) and a broch from the Bronze and Iron Ages, a Viking village and a medieval building. (E.W. MacKie, 1975.)

with rubbish. In order to reconstruct the architecture of houses in all its detail it is necessary to gather together information from all over Europe, and in particular from the lake villages, where organic remains have been preserved. The picture that we put together in this way is a little like Harlequin's costume. Regional characteristics, which may have been as numerous as in traditional settlements of the nineteenth century, are irretrievably lost.

The art of setting a post

In the types of house which were most frequently built in temperate Europe, the principal support for the superstructure, including the roof, was provided by upright posts. The post-holes and slots to accommodate these form the only foundations necessary for such buildings. In unstable soils and especially those subject to the phenomenon of thixotropy, such as the lake chalk which becomes liquid when it is subjected to compression, it is necessary to perfect special techniques which allow posts to resist continuing downward pressure as well as lateral forces. M. Magny has identified several solutions. Reinforced piles were driven into the lake chalk until they rested on the underlying moraine, a much stronger sediment. Since this does not always occur at the same depth, the builders cut their posts to different lengths so that their tops would always be at the same height. This implies that the inhabitants of the lake villages were aware of the differences in depth of the lake chalks, probably as a result of probing.

The technique of 'floating piles' was used when the the chalk layer was too deep or too thick to be penetrated completely. The stability of the posts was assured by the length and section of the part driven into the soil: the greater the diameter of the pile, the greater its resistance to compression and friction. The above two techniques were used in the Neolithic period and continued in the Bronze Age. At the Neolithic settlements at Clairvaux (Jura) and Thayngen Weier (Schaffhausen), the points of the piles went down more than 2m (6½ft) into the marl and they reached 3m (10ft) in the Late Bronze Age village of Auvernier (Neuchâtel).

Another response to this problem appeared in the Early Bronze Age, one which was more economical in the use of wood since the point of the pile fitted into a perforated wooden base or sole-plate. It was no longer necessary to drive the pile more than 1–2m (3¼–6½ft) deep, since this length was sufficient to counteract lateral pressures. Vertical stability was ensured by the sole-plates. These were cut from flattened cross-cuts or directly into trunks that still had their bark on, as at Grosser Hafner (Zürich). The recurrence of this technique, first noted in the Early Bronze Age at Baldegg, Arbon Bleiche and Meilen (eastern Switzerland) around the eighteenth century BC and then in the Late Bronze Age around 1100 BC at Zug-Sumpf and in the neighbourhood of Zürich, has led some authors to see indications of an oral tradition which survived during the half-millennium when the Swiss lake shores were abandoned. P. Pétrequin has opposed this interpretation: he has observed a sharp change in cultural, material and religious traditions around 1300–1200. The settling of the village in the local landscape was different, and, even though there were certain similarities in building methods and village layouts, they are as much the result of fortuitous convergence as of continuity of populations. The sole-plate technique first appeared at Hornstaadt on the shores of Lake Constance around 3250 BC.

The villages of eastern Switzerland and southern Germany showed evidence of the rapid assimilation of this technological innovation whereas those of western Switzerland (Lakes Neuchâtel, Bienne and Geneva), retained the reinforced pile technique throughout the Late Bronze Age. In northern Italy where, unlike the sites north of the Alps, the main occupation dates from the Early and Middle Bronze Age, other solutions were adopted which had more to do with reinforcing the wall-footings than with the construction of foundations in the true sense.

Settlement on the shore or on the water?

The adaptation of techniques for the construction of foundations in lake-margin environments was intended to ensure solid structures. But the problems posed by the footings of such buildings are connected as much with dampness as with stabilization in unstable soils. This question is linked with the water level in relation to the village, which also poses delicate problems of interpretation for archaeological sites that are today completely submerged or on dry land and covered with peat. It is in fact difficult to determine from archaeological layers alone whether the ground was under water throughout the year, during certain seasons of high water level or merely on occasions when the water level of the lake rose exceptionally high. A number of criteria have enabled

P. Pétrequin to distinguish settlements built on the water from those on dry land, notably the state of conservation of the faunal remains and of pottery, which is better in the former case. Evolution over time generally resulted in the village moving from the shore towards open water, as at Clairvaux (Jura), with resulting changes in building techniques.

From the Neolithic period the necessity of avoiding damp floors led to houses being raised by means of increasingly complex footings, in wood (Switzerland) or earth (Italy). At Thayngen (Schaffhausen), a marshy Middle Neolithic site, the floors of some of the houses were set on logs placed horizontally on the foundation piles. There are even double systems of this kind, the floor being set on the upper level, thereby creating a sort of underfloor gap.

One new solution which gave greater stability appeared at Fiave (Trentino). The extension of the Middle Bronze Age village towards the lake was carried out on piles with a timber raft on top, composed of longitudinal tie-beams bearing transverse poles. The load-bearing posts, which had rectangular mortices at the level of submerged natural deposits, were kept in place by a small square-section hardwood peg which was set into the mortice and rested on the transverse poles.

Three types of footings existed side-by-side in the village. In the middle of the island the houses were built directly on the ground; in the area covered by water they were built on the raft described above; between the two, in the first extension zone, they were built on an 8m (26ft) wide bed of stones, which in turn rested on a bed of branches and tops of pine trees, held in place by pine and larch logs. All the load-bearing posts were reinforced with horizontal pieces of wood which either surrounded or pierced them.

The coming of sill-beams

Another technique which appeared in the Middle Neolithic period consisted of passing the load-bearing upright through one or two horizontal stabilizing elements known as sole-plates or shoes (Fig. 40). When the stabilizing component ran the full length of the footings it was already in effect a sill-beam since the walls were built on it. This technique was used at La Motte aux Magnins at Clairvaux (Jura) in the Early Bronze Age. Subsequently it was regularly used as footings for *Blockbau* and *Ständerbau* buildings. Structures built on floating piles are more common in western Switzerland whereas piles on sole-plates predominated in eastern Switzerland.

40
Chronology of the technical development of sill beams and sole-plates for piles from the Middle Neolithic period to the Late Bronze Age. (P. Pétrequin, 1983.)

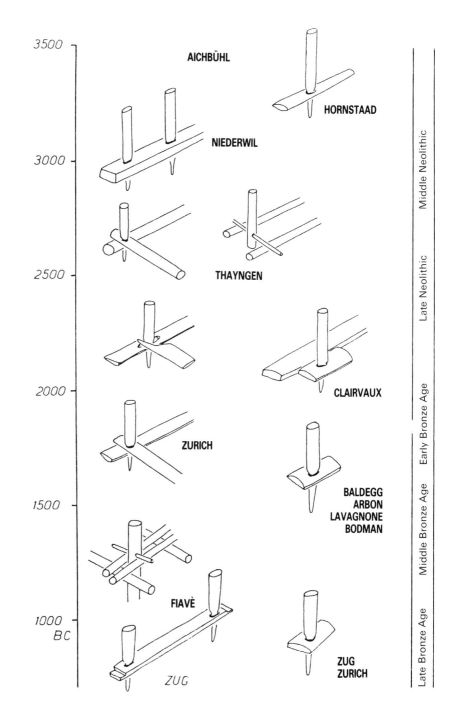

In a house at Risle, Seegen (Aargau), the sill-beams rested on a dozen stone blocks. Imperceptibly we thus pass to true stone footings. These were known as early as the Early Bronze Age in the Jura and the Swiss Alps, in particular at Padnal-Cresta (Grisons), and at Mot-tata, near Ramosch (Grisons) in the Late Bronze Age. In rare instances, as at the Late Bronze Age site at Hohlandsberg (Haut-Rhin), stone footings directly supported uprights. In the north and west of Britain low stone walls supported walls of turf.

Mounds and terraces

Settlements on embanked ground are not uncommon. In many fortified sites on high ground it was necessary to modify the slopes so as to be able to build on them. The shelf or terrace could be continuous or separate for each house, as at Heidetränk, near Frankfurt-am-Main, in the Late La Tène, or in many of the British hillforts. At Kestenberg (Aargau) three successive terraces have been identified. The 5–6m (16–20ft) wide terraces at Wittnauer Horn are delimited by a low stone wall reinforced with heavy timber beams.

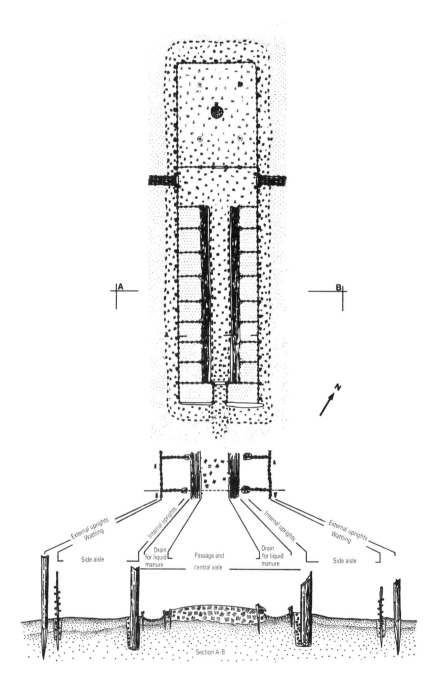

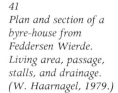

41
Plan and section of a
byre-house from
Feddersen Wierde.
Living area, passage,
stalls, and drainage.
(W. Haarnagel, 1979.)

On several marshy sites the houses are raised up. At Toszég (Hungary) in the valley of the Tisza, which is liable to flooding, earthen banks seem to have been revetted with rows of stakes or wattle walls, traces of which can be seen outside the houses, parallel with their walls.

In the village of Feddersen Wierde, on the low-lying North Sea coast, and constantly threatened by the sea like so many settlements in the Marschen region, are found what are known as *Wurten* or *terpen*, which are identical in purpose. These are mounds formed of rubbish and the remains of earlier settlements upon which the new houses were built, as a precaution against the sea and its dangers. In the historic period the *Wurten* of all the houses were joined together and the village was thus established on an artificial hill.

Floors

The surface on which the people who lived in a house moved about is rarely preserved. Beaten earth floors were probably the general rule, as they were in much of rural Europe until the modern period. Archaeologists have on a number of occasions analysed the composition of floors, which might include gravel, sand and clay, depending on local resources and climate. It is necessary to read what P.J. Hélias has written on the restoration of such a floor to understand the amount and quality of the work needed to tamp down a mixture of this kind properly (*Le cheval d'orgueil*, 1975, p. 437). It should not be thought that food debris piled up on the floor when the building was occupied. It was on the contrary a carefully tended surface that was regularly swept. Sometimes excavation reveals a layer that has been hardened and reddened by fire. It is always difficult to determine whether this burning happened during building or accidentally at the moment of destruction.

In one of the houses at the Heuneburg (Baden-Württemberg) there is a *Lehmziegel* floor, probably made from squares of baked clay. This discovery is still, however, an exceptional one. Some of the Late Bronze Age houses in the Shetland Islands, at Jarlshof and Clickhimin, have floors covered with sand. As usual, however, the lake and bog settlements have provided the best data. In the Late Bronze Age settlement at Auvernier-Nord, a bed of hazel twigs is covered with a series of clay surfaces. Wear from foot-traffic and gradual sinking of the floor required frequent resurfacing, to the extent that at the La Tène site at Glastonbury (Somerset) ten successive floors can be counted, gradually building up into a kind of mound. The Early Bronze Age sites at Clairvaux (Jura) preserve floors made of a mixture of clay and chalk. The byre-houses of northern Germany have different floors, depending on the use of each room: living-space, workshop, store, byre or passage (see p. 107). They are separated from one another by planks or timbers fixed in place with small stakes (Fig. 41).

Wooden floors are attested from the Middle Neolithic period in Switzerland and Germany. The most spectacular find is that from the Mozartstrasse in Zürich, which dates from the Early Bronze Age (Fig. 42). It is probably the surface of an open space, since it measures 20m × 10m (66 × 33ft). It is made up of

42
Wooden floor, Zürich-Mozartstrasse, Early Bronze Age. (M. Mörreisen, 1982.)

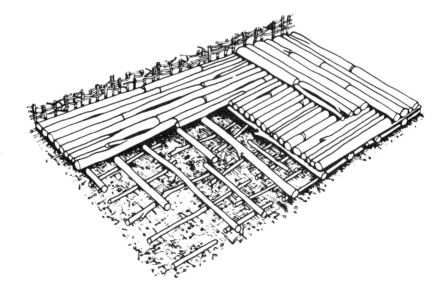

several layers of timbers at right-angles to one another: from bottom to top it is composed first of twigs, then of long logs laid out parallel to one another and spaced regularly; then of other logs laid perpendicularly to the lower layer and interspersed with heavier beams. Two layers of logs, again at right-angles to one another, cover the whole ensemble. Along the eastern edge there is a low wattle wall and the sole-plate posts associated with it may correspond to buildings.

At Buchau (Baden-Württemberg) in the Late Bronze Age the wooden floors were made of closely set round logs set on a grid of pine trunks and covered with a 10cm (4in) layer consisting of a mixture of sand and clay. Substantial timbers were mixed with bundles of alder and birch branches at the Lausitz site of Biskupin (Poland). Differences in the texture of floor deposits sometimes allow the identification of internal partitions, zones where special activities were carried out, and passageways. In the late Bronze Age houses at Dampierre-sur-le-Doubs, the wooden floors only covered half the internal space within each building.

Entrances and porches

In the rectangular post-built houses of continental Europe the roof rested on the wall-plates; these only exerted downward pressure on load-bearing posts, which did not need to be spaced equally. The entrance was therefore marked only by a wider spacing between two posts on the long or short side, and there were often several entrances. This can easily be seen on the plans of the Toszég, Perleberg, Emmerhout or Verberie houses. In well preserved houses they may be marked by a wooden sill – at Salzburg-Liefering (Austria), for example. On the other hand, they cannot be distinguished on *Blockbau* buildings, where nothing more than the first courses are known, and these are continuous. It must simply be assumed that entrances were narrow, since they weakened such structures.

Some doors are known, made of planks or a panel fixed on to a wooden frame, as at Wetzikon (Berne). They were made of oak and mounted on pivots at Altburg-Niedenstein (Hesse) and Glastonbury (Somerset). Sockets in the stone sill, in which the door pivot turned, permit the identification of doors in many buildings in which they have disappeared.

The presence of keys or rather latch-lifters is attested from the end of the Bronze Age. The way in which locks worked, already complex, can be reconstructed, even though they may have been made completely of wood. They consisted of a bolt which slid between two brackets. Lake village specialists believe that they have identified keys: these were bronze shanks, 40–60cm (16–24in) long, the upper third being bent at a right-angle. They ended in a ring, often decorated with other rings or bird heads, set in the same plane as the curved section. The key had to be inserted through a hole in the door, so that its point was placed on the bolt. Rotation of the angled upper part made its point displace laterally, thereby drawing the bolt. Although one may be somewhat sceptical of such an arrangement and question whether these bent shafts were in fact keys, there is no doubt that bolts have been found in these settlements. It was above all in undefended settlements and *oppida* at the end of the Middle La Tène period that the custom of locking certain buildings became common.

Variegated and decorative walls

In describing the houses of the Germans, Tacitus wrote that 'they did not use even stone or tiles, they used untrimmed tree trunks for every purpose, without any heed for beauty or pleasure' and in so doing expressed the contempt in which the Latin culture held buildings that were not in stone. But he contradicted himself in almost the next sentence, when he wrote: 'Certain parts are coated with earth that is so pure and so brilliant that it imitates paint and strokes of colour' (*Germania*, 16).

It should not be overlooked that walls play a very important role in rural architecture, since it is they that carry the main part of the decoration of a house. It is almost exclusively on this surface, restricted yet free of technological constraints, that cultural, regional and social differences can be expressed.

The style of the builders or successive repairs sometimes result in various techniques being used for different walls of a house. We know an example at Besançon (Doubs), of a building in which two walls are made of planks nailed on load-bearing posts whilst the other two are preserved in the form of a sole-plate made of clay and amphora sherds.

With protohistoric houses it is necessary to distinguish between those in which the roof is carried on posts, and those in which the walls take the weight of the roof. In the latter case the wall is massive in construction, thick and relatively unbroken, whereas in the former it is a simple cladding, independent of the general structure of the house. Almost all the materials used at the period lent themselves to one or the other technique. They were used sometimes as filling elements and at others as supports. Walls in mud-brick, pisé or brick were only used for short periods, and on the Mediterranean fringe of Europe. Stone was only used on its own when there was a complete lack of timber, especially in some of the islands off the Atlantic coast.

Let us now look at structures with load-bearing timber walls. In the *Blockbau* technique, the horizontal beams acted both as walls and as supports for the roof. The difficulty lay in piercing holes in them

without compromising the overall balance. No evidence of windows has survived, in excavations or in documentary sources, but we are able to reconstruct doors thanks to kindred types of structure. At Jemgum (Lower Saxony), in a Late Bronze Age house (Fig. 43.2) where the walls are made of superimposed beams kept in place by pairs of stakes placed inside and outside, the door frame consists of earthfast upright posts with grooves, into which the ends of the beams fitted.

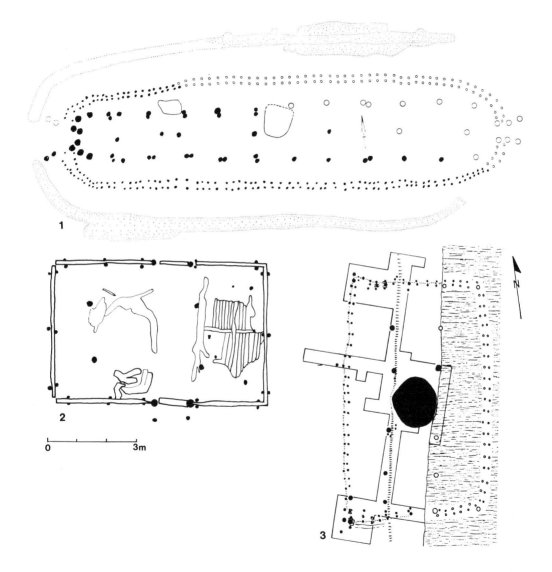

43
1: *Zijderveld, Netherlands (Middle Bronze Age): four-aisled house. The wall is made from two rows of stakes. (The open circles show areas where the evidence did not survive and the reconstruction is suggested.) (R. Hulst, 1973.)*
2: *House from Jemgum, Lower Saxony. The walls are*

horizontal beams, held in place by pairs of stakes. (W. Haarnagel, 1957.)
3: *House from Chassemy (Aisne). The right-hand area (shown shaded) was destroyed before excavation. (M. Boureux, R.M. and E.S.-J. Rowlett, 1969.)*

This type of joint is extended at Biskupin (Poland) to the whole structure: the roof rests on posts set in the ground which all have vertical slots into which the horizontal beams that formed the walls fitted. Walls are also known which consisted of vertical beams or planks slotted into a sill-beam or fixed to the load-bearing posts.

We know much more about structures which combine load-bearing posts with a cladding, which is generally made of wattle-and-daub. Excavation produces many fragments of daub that still retain the imprint of branches.

The wall stakes are usually on the same alignment as the load-bearing posts, but in north-western Europe and Britain the walls can be displaced outwards. At Toszég (Hungary) in the Middle Bronze Age the load-bearing posts were, by contrast, placed outside the wall, which here was constructed over reed wattling.

There are also walls made of strengthened wattling: the stakes which support the flexible branches are systematically paired (Fig. 43.1). Examples are a Late Bronze Age house at Andijk (Netherlands) and the La Tène house at Chassemy (Aisne) (Fig. 43.3).

The gap between the two rows of stakes can vary between 30 and 60cm (12–24in). Several hypothetical reconstructions of these walls have been proposed. They may have been made of daub, or even of horizontal logs, in the continental rectangular houses. Turf blocks are suggested for the round-houses of Britain or in the lands of north-western Europe. This type of material disappears without leaving any trace. Excavations in Scandinavia have made it possible to reconstruct houses in which the walls are formed of peat at the base and daub above (see Fig. 16). The excavators of Padnal-Savognin (Grisons) have raised the possibility of the use of pisé in the Middle Bronze Age, and the same theory has been put forward in the case of Bavois (Vaud) because burnt daub has been found there without wattle imprints. It is only in the Mediterranean regions that this technique is attested from the third century BC, at Marignane, Éguilles (Bouches-du-Rhône), and La Lagaste (Aude).

Sometimes minute examination of fragments buried in the remains of houses can give an idea of the sealing-up of cracks and the finishing of walls. At Buchau and Toszég imprints of moss, bracken and animal hair have been found which were intended to fill the gaps between the timbers. Clay fragments can preserve the shape of the logs which made up the walls of *Blockbau* houses, as at Padnal. Pieces of daub with rounded cut-outs found on Otománi sites in Rumania and at Fort-Harrouard (Eure-et-Loir) may be window edging. Traces of paint have been found at Spišský Štvrtok (Czechoslovakia) and in several sites in eastern Germany: some fragments had red and white coatings on them. At Levroux (Indre) in the undefended village on the site of the later Roman arena built at the end of the Middle La Tène period the yellow daub was covered with a grey layer, which was itself coated with some kind of whitewash.

Upper storeys

Archaeological structures rarely have any surviving height. In the best-preserved cases no more than a few wall courses survive. Roofs and lofts are thus only known through indirect observations. By analogy with more recent buildings and because one may attribute a certain logic to prehistoric builders, it is reasonable to assume the former existence of an upper storey beneath the roof when the internal weight-bearing structural posts are either particularly substantial or found in pairs, in excess of the likely requirements to support the framework of the building At Lovčičky (Moravia) at the beginning of the Late Bronze Age, house E, the largest in size, 20m × 7m (66 × 23ft), consisted of two aisles with a row of central posts and two partitions dividing the building into three equal parts. The central posts of the western third were associated with six posts to form a rectangle measuring 5 × 3m (16 × 10ft). Since the post-holes of the wall-lines were larger and slightly more numerous in this part of the building, whilst there was also a foundation trench extending several metres, this reinforcement can only be interpreted as providing support for a loft beneath the hipped roof.

The discovery of timbers whose dimensions do not coincide either with the spacings between the supports or the frame members sometimes constitutes solid evidence for a suspended floor. This was the case at Auvernier, where the floor consisted of a coating of clay and where the timbers in question could only have come from a loft. At the Goldberg (Bavaria), the posts of the 'acropolis' buildings were all very large without being spread out one from another, also an indication of an upper storey (see Fig. 123). Archaeological proof is rare, but experimental reconstructions and calculations of the likely strength of structures show that upper storeys must have been common.

Roofs

Excavation for obvious reasons provides almost no information about how buildings were roofed; the

44
1: House-urns. (top)
Obliwitz (Pomerania,
Poland); (bottom left)
Willsleben (Germany);
(bottom right)
Königsaue (Germany)
(O. Büchsenschütz.)
2: Val Camonica, rock
at Bedolina. Rock
carvings from the
Bronze and Iron Ages
showing a field system
linked by tracks, houses
with upper storeys,
people and animals.
The houses were carved
later than the field
system. (Centro
Comune di Studi
Preistorici.)

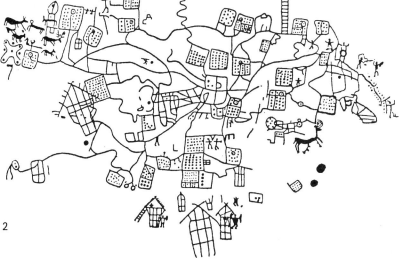

1

2

conditions must be exceptional for any evidence to be preserved. Most roofs must have been of thatch. At Buchau the houses were roofed with reeds. Aquatic plants were probably used in all those regions where they were available. Wooden tiles or shingles were found at the eponymous Hallstatt site. Stone slabs were also used, as, for example, at Castaneda (Grisons). Earth, or more precisely blocks of turf, was used in northern Europe, in Scandinavia and in the British Isles, for example on the Isle of Man.

In southern Gaul also earthen roofs were used, but they were quite different. M. Py described a roof at Nages (Languedoc) preserved by a fire: 'This roof was made of a layer of large branches, which provided a framework; then came a thick layer of twigs, which were found, like the beams, in the form of charcoal; finally, the twigs were covered with about 10cm (4in) of pisé, that is to say, clay mixed with straw' (Py, 1978, p. 157). Flat stones set on the tops of the walls attempted to consolidate the whole arrangement, but these roofs were still fragile, given the high winds and rainfall in these Mediterranean regions.

In the north there was more to fear from rain and snow than from wind. Roofs were steeply pitched, in most cases more than 45–50°. At Biskupin (Poland) and Feddersen Wierde (Niedersachsen) rafters and wall-plates have been found, along with the slots into which they were fixed, from which it was possible to calculate this pitch approximately. The experiments of P.J. Reynolds at Butser Hill have clearly shown that roofs with inadequate pitches collapse under the weight of snow or very heavy rain.

The house-urn from Königsaue, which shows a high double-pitched roof of which the short sides are triangular, gives a good idea of the proportions of protohistoric house frames. Renaissance Flemish paintings and the large barns (*granges-chapiteaux*) that still survive in the Limousin also give this image of an ancient Europe of steep roofs. House-urns (Fig. 44.1) in which cremated ashes were collected, were used in Poland, in central Germany and in Latium during the Hallstatt period. Although these usually represent granaries rather than houses, they provide unique evidence of the general appearance of protohistoric buildings.

The rock engravings of the Val Camonica in northern Italy and Andorra are another source of information about the superstructures of Bronze and Iron Age houses. They show houses set on platforms, like Alpine chalets, and equipped with lofts and double-pitched roofs. Certain ones, such as that of Bedolina, give a very complete view of protohistoric settlement since they also include representations in plan of landholdings, with fields and tracks (Fig. 44.2).

6 Fortifications

Thousands of enclosures

The fortifications erected during the Bronze and Iron Ages constitute the most impressive group of monuments that have come down to us from protohistory. Several thousand sites spread over the whole of Europe were laid out on a grand scale with the construction of banks and ditches, in order to provide defence for a human group or simply to affirm their power. They are often hidden by vegetation, except in Britain where they are set in pastureland, and they are beginning to become known by the public as a result of the environmental movement. This awakening of conscience has happily come at the very moment when the existence of these monuments is threatened by the advent of modern earth-moving equipment.

These ramparts in earth, stone and timber often run for several kilometres; they can exceed 10m (33ft) in height and the volume of earth and timber required to build them is enormous. Works of this kind imply well defined planning on the part of an organized and stable human group, capable of setting up complex civil engineering projects and of ensuring long and costly maintenance. Fortifications of the type we are discussing here have nothing in common with animal enclosures or with emergency refuges thrown up hurriedly by an army in the field or by people under pressure from an invader. Their immense size, the complex structure of the ramparts and the traces of permanent settlement found inside most of them all show that these enclosures had a high place in the minds of their builders.

There have been those who have tried to explain their development in terms of an endemic climate of insecurity, and invasion theories have seized upon remains of this kind. Historians have linked the more recent of them with Celtic invasions, the raids of the Cimbri and Teutones, and the Roman conquest. The more the investigation of these sites advances, the weaker these elegant theories become: ramparts appear, disappear and change shape without relation to the development of weapons or siege methods. On a single site settlement may precede fortification or follow it. In no region does the spatial distribution of fortified enclosures in a region provide a clear guideline which might imply the defence of a frontier or a strategic network, for example.

Layout and construction of enclosures

The earthen hillforts of southern England are so well preserved that it is possible to reconstruct the stages in their construction from what is still visible on the surface. At Ladle Hill (Fig. 45) the remains of the quarries which supplied the building-materials are visible behind the rampart or in irregularities in the course of the ditch. Slight variations in the bank show that the builders often worked in teams, each being responsible for a limited length of the bank and ditch which were later joined together. After the course of the work had been traced by a small ditch, the teams were allocated to sections of it. They began by removing the upper layers of the ditch, which were dumped in the interior, behind the rampart. It was only when they reached the chalk layer that they stacked up chalk blocks to form the bank. The work was interrupted, however, even before the different sections had been joined together.

The roughly circular area enclosed by the *vallum* (i.e. the bank and ditch) was 3.3ha (8 acres); it was

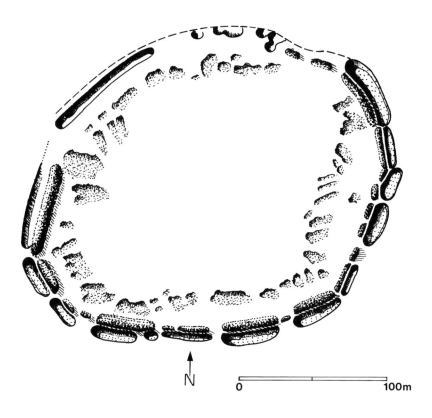

45
Unfinished hillfort at Ladle Hill (Hampshire). (After S. Piggott, 1931.)

about 700m (2296ft) long and, according to S. Piggott, the work was shared out among a dozen teams. Experimental archaeology has shown that a man working with an antler pick and an osier basket could extract and move 1–1.3 cubic metres (35–46 cubic feet) a day.

Using the data from Ladle Hill, A.H.A. Hogg estimated that 12,500–17,000 working days would have been needed to dig the ditch, build a bank 4m (13ft) high, tapering from 7m (23ft) broad at the base to 1m ($3\frac{1}{4}$ft) at the top, and crown it with a palisade, for which a thousand stakes would have had to be made. A human group of 200 people, equivalent to the work of 150 adult males, could have completed this work in about a hundred days.

The organization of work

Hogg quotes the example of Camps Tops at Morebattle (Roxburghshire), where the eight buildings grouped in an area of 0.2ha ($\frac{1}{2}$ acre) could have housed forty people. The double rampart could have been completed in two months. This seems a reasonable length of time to us today, in relation to the service that these

defences could have rendered. There are, however, small enclosures surrounded by much larger fortifications. In this case there must either have been a greater occupation density or an external group assisted in the work: the enclosure could have been a refuge or a strongpoint for the surrounding undefended settlements.

It is easy to understand how larger enclosures were built because they require proportionally less work in relation to their potential population capacity. If a 4ha (10 acre) fortification housed sixty people per hectare (2.5 acres), it would only need 2–4 months of work.

In any case we believe it is important to stress that works of this kind required collective organization, with one man or a group of men in authority, and, no doubt at an early stage, the involvement of specialists, especially when bank structures and entrance designs became more complicated. Above all, however, the construction of such an enclosure implies planning,

46 (Right)
Siting of enclosures in relation to topography. 1: promontory fort; 2: contour fort; 3: ridge fort; 4: fort backed on to a cliff edge. (G. Tosello, after J.L. Forde-Johnston, 1976.)

decision-making, and an implementation stage, followed by permanent maintenance. In the absence of anything else, these structures are still today the most obvious sign of the development of political organization during the Bronze and Iron Ages.

Fortifications in the landscape

Protohistoric defensive works were systematically constructed on natural features favourable to defence. The course of the rampart follows the crest of a slope, cuts off a promontory or backs onto a cliff or a watercourse (Fig. 46). The builders knew how to take advantage of different locations, and the relief or the natural drainage network would be no more than one of the many factors which determined the selection of a site. In some extreme cases the choice made seems to us to defy logic: the triple ramparts of the small Chesters hillfort in East Lothian (Scotland) are laid out beneath a hill which overlooks it by some 15m (49ft), from which attackers could bombard the defenders with projectiles. The defences of several Late La Tène *oppida*, such as Závist (Czechoslovakia: see Fig. 140), Heidetränk-Talenge (Germany: see Fig. 47), or Mont Beuvray (France: see Fig. 141) ran down across the contours of the valleys around the hills on which they were positioned. Huge fortresses, but ones which seem militarily to make little sense, were thus created.

Defensive works could be concentrated on a single weak point and be constructed to a uniform standard over the whole length of the ramparts, or constitute a strong refuge within a much larger enclosure, principally as a function of the terrain but also according to the prevailing customs of each period and culture. Internal divisions are usually attributable to successive enlargements or conversely to a reduction in the original plan. The scarcity of excavations and the number of special cases will only permit us to advance the hypothesis that Neolithic and Bronze Age peoples often used promontories, which they cut off from the main plateau with an earthwork, whereas the Celts of the Late La Tène period preferred contour defences around the summits of one or more hills.

It should be made clear that the use of the term 'hillfort' in the region that is the subject of this book relates to relatively low-relief features: these enclosures take advantage of a landscape irregularity, a river meander, a *cuesta* or outlier, the low hills of central Europe, or the plateaux or downs that edge depressions. The zone in which they occur stops short at the foothills of the Alps, and at the outlying hills which border the great north European plain. The selection of a site seems to have resulted from a compromise between natural defensive potential and the disadvantages that might arise from the choice of a site far removed from the centre of a territory. At the local scale, the topographic setting of hillforts seems often to have been simply copied: how else can the development of a chain of enclosures on the edge of the plateau along the entire length of the lower Somme, on the cliffs that overlook the Seine near Rouen, or on the north bank of the Loire near Tours be explained? The typology of defensive enclosures is connected more closely with the nature of the local relief than with cultural choices. Topography also often dictates the size of the area to be fortified: this should not be overlooked when attempting to estimate the population of a region on the basis of settlement size. On the other hand, certain sites, such as the Dünsberg (Hesse), the area of which varied from one period to another, clearly show a deliberate intention to establish a certain size for the settlement by fortifying first the summit of the hill, then halfway down its slopes, and finally the entire feature.

Fortifications were generally restricted to points without natural defences: a cross-rampart some tens of metres long could be adequate for the defence of a promontory. This economical solution prevailed for most of the Bronze and Iron Ages, but the Late La Tène period saw the appearance of continuous ramparts enclosing the entire settlement, even in those places where artificial defences seemed not to be required. In such cases the wish to delimit the urban area with a monumental construction clearly went beyond the requirements of protection.

Rampart technology

In the majority of cases the rampart consisted of a bank and ditch. A counterscarp bank sometimes lay outside the ditch, which could, like the bank, be double or triple. All those defences which, by reason of their size and construction, can be distinguished from a simple palisade, fall into two distinct categories: banks which present a sloping surface to the exterior and walls with vertical external faces. It is impossible to estimate the relative importance of the two types because their present-day aspect is in all cases the same as the first series. However, several dozen sections through these banks have very often shown structures of the second type. Superimposition of one type upon the other is frequent. It is difficult to appreciate the reasons for the choice of one method or the other, but it is clear that each had its advantages and disadvantages.

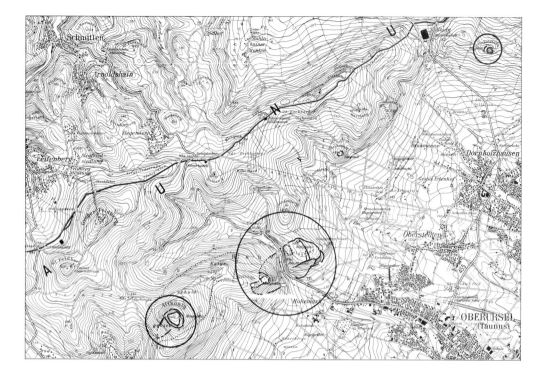

47

Enclosures in the Taunus, north of Frankfurt-am-Main. The location of the Taunus fortified sites is typical: the protohistoric enclosures occupy the lower hills of the massif, alongside the Wetterau plain, whereas the Roman limes runs along the line of the crests. The earliest enclosures (the Altkönig to the south-east or the Altenhöfe in the centre) are on hilltops and were built in the Early La Tène period. The large oppidum of Heidetränk-Talenge surrounded two previously fortified hilltops, by means of an immense rampart pierced with six gateways, which runs down the slopes of a valley. It is typical of the large earthworks of the Late La Tène period. (F. Maier 1985.)

Massive banks and vertical walls

A bank of earth or stone can be built quickly with relatively unskilled labour. It can resist fire, battering rams and natural erosion so long as the slope has been properly calculated and the material carefully chosen. It has the disadvantages of covering a large ground surface as its height increases and of being rather vulnerable when it is not high enough. If attackers are confronted by a vertical wall 4–8m (13–26ft) high, this obstacle can only be surmounted by the use of scaling ladders or materials capable of filling up the ditch. Other ways of attack are using a battering ram to make stone walls collapse or setting fire to timber fortifications.

Ladle Hill is a classic example of how massive banks could be built in chalk regions using material taken directly from the ditches. On a steep hillside, by contrast, earth can be tipped down the slope to create a bank while at the same time constructing a terrace in the interior of the enclosure. The chalk of southern England, which is relatively easy to dig out and then compact down in order to form a bank, is very resistant to the relatively warm and wet climate, with the result that the ramparts of Maiden Castle (Fig. 48), Hod Hill or Danebury still preserve their original profiles. In regions with less stable soils, a covering of turf or stone capping is needed to prevent slippage. Wide flat-bottomed ditches tended to replace V-section ditches towards the end of our period, because they are easier to dig than deep ditches and are more resistant to collapse. Mortimer Wheeler defined the Fécamp type, which combines a wide flat ditch, sometimes with a counterscarp bank in front, with a massive triangular-section bank which can vary from 6 to 9m (20 to 29ft) in height.

It should be noted that this category is spread over the whole of Gallia Belgica, whereas preference was

48
Aerial view of the triple earthen ramparts and monumental entrances of the major hillfort of Maiden Castle. (Cambridge University Collection of Air Photographs.)

given in Brittany and Normandy to timber-laced ramparts to protect the settlements. The development of these wide ditches can no doubt be explained as being due to a concern to distance the ramparts from both siege engines and projectile launchers. Owing to the lack of excavations, however, we know little about how the banks were built: were they new constructions or were they the result of late refurbishment of vertical-walled ramparts? Recent sections through the defences at Amboise (Indre-et-Loire), Châteaumeillant (Cher) and Saint-Thomas (Aisne) have revealed that these banks covered timber-laced ramparts.

A group of enclosures defended by banks over 8m (26ft) high needs to be distinguished. Above a certain height, the effectiveness of earth ramparts can be as great as that of vertical walls. At Otzenhausen (Pfalz), Murs (Indre) and Ipf, near Bopfingen (Baden-Württemberg) it is obvious that it is the sheer size of the earthworks that dissuaded attackers.

By joining the external slope of the bank and the internal face of the ditch in the same plane, the Late La Tène military architects in south-eastern England

obtained differences in height of 16–25m (52–82ft). B. Cunliffe calls these 'plain style' defences, and they developed at the same time as multiple defences in the especially favourable conditions of that region.

Timber-laced ramparts

In continental Europe, where the climate is more extreme, and in all those regions where the subsoil is less homogeneous, efforts were made throughout protohistory to build vertical walls reinforced by an internal wooden framework. Two groups can be distinguished, on the basis of the position of the timber uprights in relation to the outer cladding: frameworks with horizontal timbers and those made up of vertical posts (Figs. 49–50).

Ramparts of horizontal timbers

In these ramparts the horizontal timbers were simply laid on the ground; intersecting timbers ensured that

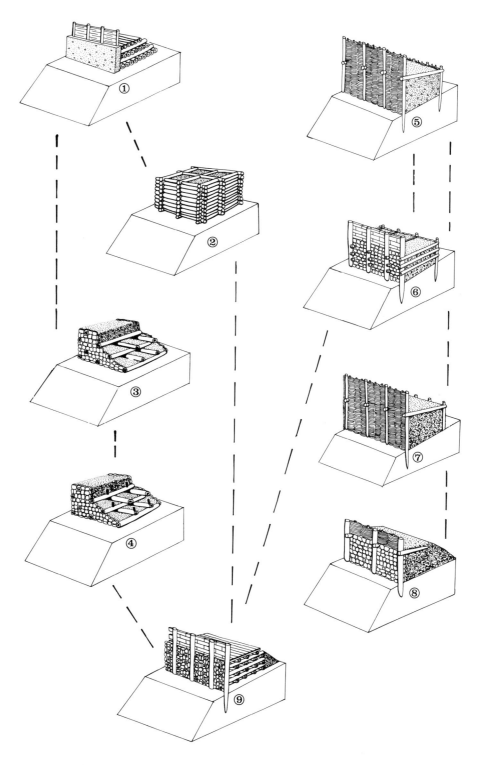

49

The main types of rampart: 1: Rostbau *type, all-wood construction; 2:* Kastenbau *type of box walls; 3: Ehrang type, very similar to* murus gallicus, *but lacks the iron spikes; 4:* Avaricum *or* murus gallicus *(often with an internal ramp), with iron spikes at the intersections of timbers; 5: Box ramparts. Whilst the spacing of the vertical elements can be variable, the distinctive trait is two parallel rows of earthfast timbers; 6: Altkönig-Preist type. A variant on no.5, these are notable for the segments of stone wall-facing and the heavy use of internal transverse timberwork; 7: Hod Hill type. In this variant of no.5 the vertical timbers of the internal wall-face are no longer earthfast; 8: Kelheim type. This represents further simplification, in which the verticals of the front face are tied back into the core of the wall; 9: Mixed series. The wall at Basle-Münsterberg combines traits of the* murus gallicus *(including nails), the Kelheim series and the long-established* Kastenbau *walls. (O. Büchsenschütz.)*

91

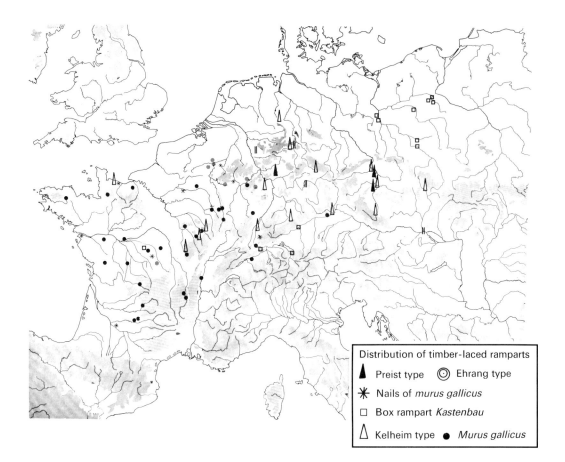

Distribution of timber-laced ramparts

▲ Preist type   ◎ Ehrang type

✳ Nails of *murus gallicus*

□ Box rampart *Kastenbau*

△ Kelheim type   ● *Murus gallicus*

the rampart was stable and the external face was vertical. Three main types based on this basic layout have been observed.

Firstly *Rostbau* or grid construction consists of alternate courses of longitudinal and transverse beams laid directly upon one another. Halving joints and a covering of earth prevented any lateral slipping of the edging elements. Secondly, in the *Kastenbau* technique, the horizontal timbers were piled up upon one another so as to form true timber walls which divided the interior of the rampart into boxes. The only rampart of this type known in France, at Moulins-sur-Céphons (Indre), consists of two rows of rectangular boxes with an overall breadth of 7m (23ft). This seems to have been a prototype, since its construction has been radiocarbon-dated to the Chalcolithic period.

Murus gallicus

The third type of construction with horizontal timbers is the famous *murus gallicus*, described by Caesar in his *Gallic War* in connection with the siege of Bourges:

50

Distribution map of the main types of rampart in continental Europe (O. Büchsenschütz.)

'Gallic walls are always built more or less on the following plan. Baulks of timber are laid on the ground at regular intervals of 2ft along the whole line on which the wall is to be built, at right-angles to it. These are made fast to one another by long beams running across them at their centre points, and are covered with a quantity of rubble; and the 2ft intervals between them are faced with large stones fitted tightly in. When this first course has been placed in position and fastened together, another course is laid on top. The same interval of 2ft is kept between the baulks of the second course, but they are not in contact with those of the first course, being separated from them by a course of stones 2ft high; thus every baulk is separated from each of its neighbours by one large stone, and so held firmly in position. By the addition of further courses the fabric is raised to the required height. This style of building presents a diversified appearance that is not unsightly, with its alternation of baulks and stones each preserving their own straight lines. It is also very serviceable and well adapted for defending a town: the masonry protects it from fire, the timber from destruction by the battering-ram, which cannot either pierce or knock to pieces a structure braced internally by beams running generally to a length of 40ft in one piece. (*De Bello Gallico*, 7,23: translation E.V. Rieu).

The broad outlines and some specific details of this description have been confirmed by modern excavations. For example, the use of the word *effarciuntur* to designate the stacking of stone blocks roughly jammed in between the timbers to form the outer face corresponds very accurately with observations made during the excavation of the *murus gallicus* at Levroux, which is geographically the closest example excavated to modern standards to Bourges. Ramparts of this type built in regions where the limestone splits easily, as at Murcens (Lot) or the late example at Vertault (Côte-d'Or), have a more even external face, and still today have a remarkable appearance.

It is surprising that Caesar makes no mention of an entirely new element in the history of timber ramparts, which has been observed in most excavations of structures of this type. This is the iron nails, 20–30cm (8–12in) long, that were intended to join the timbers together. Dozens of these have been collected along the entire lengths of ramparts, in such quantities that on several sites local peasants gathered them up for making small tools. The effectiveness of this method of joining is dubious: the ramp built up against the rear of most examples of the *murus gallicus* gives better protection against battering rams than the use of nails.

The *murus gallicus* appeared late in the western part of the Celtic world on the continent, probably not until the second century BC, and continued up to the Gallo-Roman period. It was preceded chronologically by the so-called Ehrang type, in which the unnailed timber framework was laid out in the same way but which had stone facings on the interior as well as the exterior. The basic framework continued in the series of *muri gallici* but the use of stone facing and, above all, of iron nails were new and distinctive elements.

Ramparts with vertical timbers

The second group that can be distinguished among timber-laced ramparts is defined by the use of vertical posts set in the ground, which ensured the stability of the external face. This method of construction developed from the simple palisade. An earthen bank piled against the internal face of the timber revetment gives protection against battering rams, but the pressure that the mound exerts introduces a risk of forcing the uprights to collapse outwards. To counteract this disadvantage, horizontal timbers firmly attached to the uprights are required to anchor the wall into the bank. They could even be attached to an internal wall built of upright posts, which increased the solidity of

51
Rampart at Nitriansky Hrádok (Slovakia). This structure of the Mad'arovce culture, dating to the Early and Middle Bronze Age, is one of the earliest timber-laced fortifications in Europe. (A. Točik, 1981.)

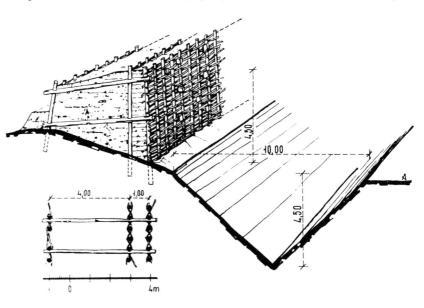

the whole structure and limited the surface area covered by the rampart. All the variations of ramparts with facings of upright timbers are determined in relation to this structural problem (Fig. 51).

In the Iron Age the external wall no longer had the appearance of a palisade: the upright timbers were located 1–3m (3¼–10ft) apart and the intervening spaces were filled with walls of stone, planks or interwoven branches. Excavators often find no more in the ground than traces of the vertical timbers and the lower courses of the walls, when these were made of stone. The horizontal bracing timbers are rarely preserved, whilst traces of the perimeter walkway or a possible parapet have almost always disappeared. English usage normally terms such walls which incorporate both vertical and, often inferentially, horizontal timbers 'box ramparts' (and British archaeologists have defined several series of these); but they differ substantially from the *Kastenbau* (lit. 'box built' technique identified by continental scholars.

The simplest form consists of two rows of upright earthfast timbers which constitute the internal and external walls and which must have been linked together by horizontal timbers at the top of the rampart. An internal bank reinforces the internal wall-face at Hollingbury (Sussex). At Hod Hill (Dorset), the uprights of the interior face are not set into the ground, but simply act as a means of anchoring the horizontal timbers, which are buried in the mass of the rampart. According to Cunliffe, the development of this type led to a structure in which the exterior facing of upright timbers was fixed into the bank by means of a single row of horizontal timbers. They were held inside the mass of the bank by the weight of earth alone, or by means of a light bracing system which has completely disappeared. This type of structure only leaves vestiges of the external facing in the ground, and in rare cases traces of horizontal timbers in the earthen fill.

The development towards the end of the period of internal ramps, which offered better resistance to battering rams and allowed easier access to the perimeter walkway for both men and siege engines, explains the gradual disappearance of internal facing walls. The same general development can be observed in ramparts with horizontal timbers in the period when *oppida* flourished.

The considerable progress in the quality of excavation over the last fifty years explains the rapid evolution of classifications and the appearance of sub-categories or mixed examples. Such variants are normal when several structural solutions existed side-by-side within the same culture. Builders could choose between a limited number of variables: horizontal or upright timbers, vertical interior facings or ramps, simple jointing techniques or the use of nails. None of these elements was obviously superior to any other and the different solutions were equally valid and corresponded with cultural traditions rather than with technological requirements.

It is clear from certain structures, moreover, that concern over appearance was more important than solidity: the most striking example is that of the rampart in level 4 at the Heuneburg (Baden-Württemberg). This was a faithful copy of a Greek mud-brick rampart set on stone footings and flanked with rectangular bastions. This monument, which imitates a model well known from Magna Graecia, is one of the imports from the Mediterranean world found in the settlements and princely tombs of the Late Hallstatt period. This technique, wholly inappropriate for the Württemberg climate, was soon abandoned in favour of a timber box rampart, a technique that had already been used on the same site. The appearance of nails in the *murus gallicus* should be interpreted as a cultural phenomenon, unrelated to any technological necessity. The explanation of this extravagant method of construction should be sought in the development of craftsmen specializing in metalworking or the birth of the idea of the 'town,' where the defences could represent a symbolic or juridical boundary.

Stone ramparts

We have already seen that some massive defensive banks were built entirely of rough stone blocks piled up unsystematically. There are also much more sophisticated structures with vertical walls built of natural slabs or roughly dressed stones.

The simplest drystone constructions consisted of inner and outer vertical faces, filled with rubble. In order to strengthen them the external face could be battered, by reducing its thickness from bottom to top, or the two faces could be linked by cross-timbers. Another technique was to encase one or more supplementary wall faces within the rubble core of the fortification. This variant is known as a *murus duplex*, using Caesar's terminology (*De Bello Gallico* 2, 29), although he does not provide a description of this term. In several instances the interior face of the fortification resembles the steps of a staircase, strengthening the main wall and giving access to the top of the wall for defensive purposes.

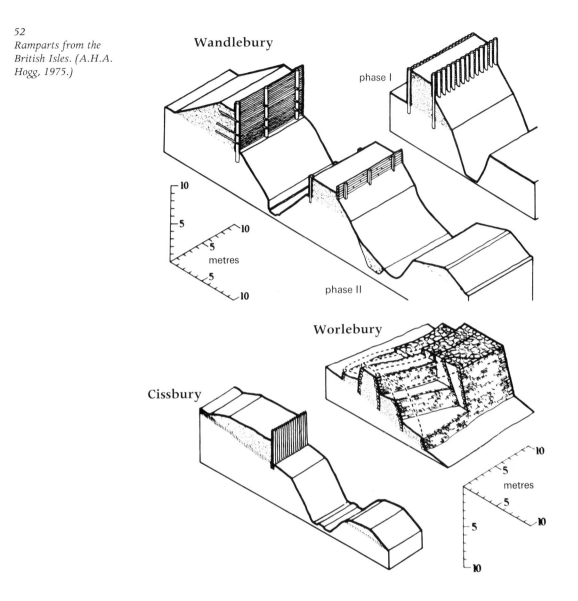

52
Ramparts from the British Isles. (A.H.A. Hogg, 1975.)

The same variants are to be found in widely distant regions at different times: it was the availability of material which guided the builders. Examples are the Steinsburg (Saxony), with its triple ramparts in basalt, and the many hillforts in the British Isles (Fig. 52).

In Burgundy many fortified settlements were built from the Neolithic period onwards on the limestone uplands of the Auxois and the hinterlands of Beaune and Dijon. The existence on these plateaux of a stone that splits naturally into slabs favoured the development of a form of drystone construction that was used for houses and burial cairns as well as for defensive works. J.-P. Nicolardot has demonstrated the scale

and the variety of these defences, which often preserve traces of several superimposed walls from the Neolithic period through to the Iron Age. The promontory fort at Myard in the commune of Vitteaux was defended in the eighth century BC by a drystone rampart built on the ruins of the Neolithic defences. Three solid square towers were built into the exterior wall. A fourth, larger tower was probably added later, since it was only built up against the wall. At Châtelet d'Etaules (Fig. 53), the superimposition of successive walls resulted in a rampart 7m (23ft) high and 26m (85ft) wide at its base. The Bronze and Iron Age ramparts built on the Neolithic core resulted in several

*53
Superimposed ramparts at Étaules (Côte-d'Or). This 6m (20ft) high bank is made up of several fortifications built one on top of the other in the eight-third centuries BC. (Reconstruction: J.-P. Nicolardot, 1983.)*

level platforms, at least on the interior face. The latest rebuild, at the summit, was some 2m (6½ft) wide, and was strengthened at its top (as were several of the lower stages) with upright timbers set parallel to one another and wedged with stone slabs set on edge.

On the Mediterranean littoral defensive works were built almost exclusively using the drystone technique from the Neolithic period onwards. As early as the Fontbouisse culture round-houses set within drystone enclosures evoke some form of fortress by virtue of their form. It was in the Iron Age above all, however, that true forts were built, protected with *muri duplici*. Solid rectangular towers appeared in the fifth century BC, to be replaced in the third century by semicircular towers. Their monumental function is confirmed at Mauressip, where one of the towers is faced with stonework in the Classical 'grand appareil' manner.

The foothills of the Vosges, which dominate the plain of Alsace, are also crowned with drystone structures, neither the function nor the dating of which have yet been firmly established. They have produced finds which range from the Bronze Age to the medieval period. Some seem to be true defensive works whilst others are more like cult centres. The Purpurkopf at Grendelbuch and the Petit Ringelsberg at Oberhaslach are largely buried beneath immense heaps of stones. The most famous site is the Mont Sainte-Odile, where the large stones are joined together by wooden tenons, inserted into the stones with dovetails. This enclosure has not been excavated systematically and so the dating of this altogether

exceptional structure remains uncertain. H. Zumstein has shown that the rampart was restored in the late Roman period, but he believes the original construction to have been earlier.

'Vitrified forts'

Place-names, popular legend and even today some archaeological literature give a large place to 'vitrified' or calcined forts. Stone blocks that have been melted and fused together by heat or cores of heat-altered lime have been found within the mass of collapsed stonework derived from the fortifications at some 150 sites. Most of these are to be found in Scotland and the Massif Central. They have excited the curiosity of scholars and many different theories have been put forward to explain this phenomenon.

In the early nineteenth century their origins were attributed to fires lit by lookouts to communicate information. Writers of this period were preoccupied with relations between hillforts, and every site description was accompanied by comments on the surveillance of the surrounding land. A bolder theory attributed the vitrification to lightning, which would thus seem to have a predilection for protohistoric defences. Finally, there were certain writers who believed the cause to relate to a technique developed in order to increase the compactness and cohesion of the rampart materials. Even though carrying out such a project in regions of crystalline rock would assume that an enormous amount of wood was available, it is easy to see how valuable a process would be that produced a rampart that was stronger than one made of reinforced concrete. The heat-altered cores of lime, however, which writers such as Drioton believe they identified in the hearts of walls in calcareous areas, would seem to be of more limited interest.

In 1930 Gordon Childe succeeded in melting stone blocks in an experiment carried out on a reconstructed rampart, but the choice of inappropriate materials has been criticized. Youngblood showed in 1978 that combustion of the framework of a timber-laced rampart would not produce vitrification unless a fire had been deliberately kindled and manipulated for that purpose. I. Ralston repeated the experiment in 1981 with a rampart 9m (29ft) long, 4m (13ft) wide, and 2.40m (8ft) high. He built it with timbers interlaced internally, the ends of which projected from the face. Several lorry-loads of wood were tipped in front of the rampart and set alight. The temperature in the core of the rampart rose only gradually. It fell every time the wind scattered the flames in different directions instead of directing them on to the rampart. Several vitrified fragments were found in the remains of the rampart, which had partially collapsed because of the heat. It is thus obvious that an intense fire, carefully managed in favourable meteorological conditions, is needed to produce vitrification.

In his excavations in Burgundy J.-P. Nicolardot has revealed some new factors relating to the 'cores of heated lime' beloved of early twentieth century writers. At Myard the remains were those of a house built up against the walls, the carbonized timber frame of which had produced charcoal. The coloration and texture of the limestone were the result of changes occurring naturally. At Châtelet d'Étaules what had been considered to be calcined rock was in fact a tufa taken from a stream that ran at the base of the defences.

In every case that has been studied up to now, the action of fire has never left any regular or systematic traces which alone could be considered as proof of the use of vitrification as a constructional technique. These have always been localized observations or irregular traces and never a wall that had been truly fused by fire. Ralston, moreover, has shown that the map of vitrified or calcined enclosures corresponds fairly closely with the distribution of timber-laced enclosures, dating between protohistory and the Middle Ages.

Are these the traces of attacks on fortified settlements? The siege technique most widely used until the Romans arrived consisted in fact of battering the tops of ramparts with missiles in order to dislodge the defenders and then to set fire to the gates before bursting into the interior. It is unlikely that in the heat of the action the attackers would have sufficient time to build a fire that was intense enough to produce vitrification which, as experiments have shown, needs a great deal of combustible material and a favourable wind. Certain Scottish forts are, moreover, vitrified over their entire perimeters. It is easier to imagine that vitrification was the product of systematic destruction by an enemy after the settlement had been taken and often pillaged, in order to mark the irreversible nature of the defeat.

Gates

The position of a gate is determined as a function of the topography. Thus in promontory forts or those on the edge of a plateau the gate is often to be found between the end of the rampart and the cliff. When attackers began to be armed with swords and shields, the builders of defensive works strove to produce a compulsory route to reach the gate which forced the attackers to leave their right sides unprotected. The aim was to compel attackers to advance parallel to the rampart with their unprotected right arms exposed to the defenders for as long as possible.

On level ground, a long entrance passage crossed the thickness of the rampart in such a way that the defenders dominated the attackers. The break in the bank was reinforced with upright timbers on both sides in order to define a form of corridor. This was lengthened either by inserting an angle into the passage or by extending the ramparts on either side of the entrance towards the site interior, thereby producing an inturned entrance.

The oldest examples of complex gateways have been found in eastern Germany and Poland (Fig. 54). Two rows of vertical posts edge a narrow extended passageway, the floor of which is made of horizontal timbers laid side by side. At Senftenberg the entrance corridor turns to the right, runs through the core of the rampart, and only emerges 15m (49ft) further on after a fresh turn to the left.

On the continent monumental gateways developed in the La Tène period. These consist of three parallel rows of substantial post-holes, one row set on the axial line of the entrance passage, and the other two aligned close to the edge of the fortification on either side. These were designed to carry a wooden superstructure – a footbridge or a tower – which ensured both continuity of movement around the rampart and protection of the entrance. In the Late La Tène period

54
Biskupin (Poland), (O.
Büchsenschütz.)

55
Dinorben (Wales). (A.H.A. Hogg, 1975.)

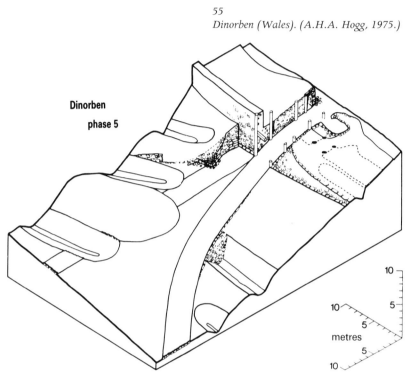

Dinorben

phase 5

54–55
Reconstructions of
fortified entrances. No
more than a simple
break in the ramparts
in earlier periods,
gateways assumed an
increasingly
monumental character.
The presence of guard
chambers or a covered
passage-way implies
control of people and
goods.

the bank was enlarged so as to form a corridor directed towards the interior of the enclosure by means of a return on the rampart on either side of the gateway. These inturned entrances are so common in *oppida*, from Brittany to Hungary, that their presence on an unexcavated site is a strong presumption that it belongs to the Late La Tène (Fig. 55).

Double gateways developed in Britain at the beginning of the Iron Age; they were flanked by 'guard chambers' in wood or stone in parts of southern Britain. Their presence suggests that there were permanent guards on the entrances to settlements: were these soldiers watching over those who came in or agents for collecting tolls? Inturned entrances with walls jutting into the interiors of enclosures spread in the second century BC. With the development of multivallate defences double entrances evolved which compelled attackers to move round a large central mound masking the entrance and protecting the interior of the hillfort. Danebury (Hampshire) and

Maiden Castle (Dorset) are the best preserved examples of this type.

Outer defences

The immediate environs of hillforts could be protected in various ways. Sometimes a counterscarp bank precedes the bank, which can be double or triple. It has been established, especially in Britain, where there are numerous examples datable to the later stages of the pre-Roman Iron Age, that multiple defences were built in order to distance slingers from the interior of the enclosure. *Chevaux de frise*, which are preserved only if they are made of stone, are much rarer. Traces of wooden *chevaux de frise* dating from the Late Bronze Age have, however, been identified at South Barrule (Isle of Man). They formed a thick barrier of stakes, the first being set vertically at the very foot of the rampart and the others inclined towards the exterior. Several examples are known from France and Germany. Stone *chevaux de frise* are generally dated to the Iron Age. They are known from the Iberian peninsula, Wales, Scotland, Ireland (e.g. Dun Aengus), and some Hallstatt C sites in central Europe.

Spatial analysis of fortifications

There are two different approaches to the study of protohistoric fortifications. One is to excavate a judiciously selected site carefully, in order to determine its chronology, its development and, if possible, its function. The other is to compile an inventory of the largest possible number of enclosures, from which

56
Distribution of fortified sites in England and Wales, classified by size. (J.L. Forde-Johnston, 1976.)

to draw up a typology and general ideas about the occupation of the land. It is postulated that the surface characteristics of the defensive works – size, location in the landscape, layout and nature of the banks and ditches – are adequate to assign a period or date to it and to determine its function. In reality it is only by combining the two methods that it becomes possible to break free from both narrow particularities and superficial generalities.

The British Isles

Analysis of the size, typology and distribution of fortified enclosures in the British Isles is especially meaningful; the conditions for field survey are in fact excellent. The hillforts are located on high ground covered with pasture or moorland, where not only the defences but also the foundations of houses are preserved in the form of micro-relief. Several studies based on the Ordnance Survey map (1967), which

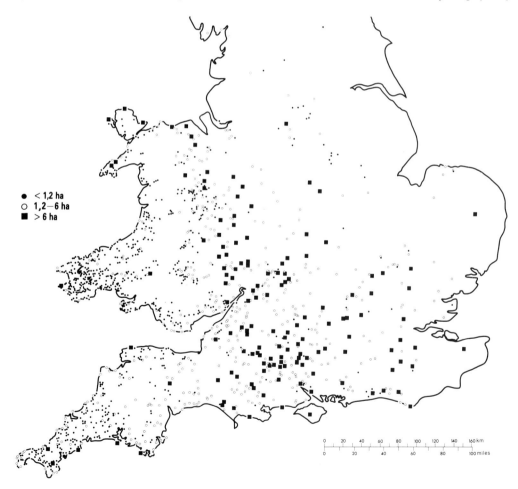

● < 1,2 ha
○ 1,2–6 ha
■ > 6 ha

records 1310 enclosures in southern Britain, were made between 1967 and 1976.

The results of these typological studies have been particularly interesting. The distribution of sites is very uneven (Fig. 56): they are very numerous in the west (Wales, Cornwall), and their density diminishes progressively towards the centre and the east of the country, where they are totally absent. This contrast is still further accentuated by the differences in surface area. Cornwall and Wales contain the majority of enclosures smaller than 1.2ha (3 acres) in area.

Medium-sized enclosures (1.2–6ha (3–15 acres)) are to be found essentially in a central triangle bounded by Liverpool, Plymouth and the Thames estuary. The largest enclosures have a similar distribution, with a special concentration around Salisbury and in the Severn valley. Forde-Johnston (1976) identified two traditions on the basis of size: that of Wessex, with enclosures of over 2ha (5 acres), and that of the west, with much smaller surface areas (Fig. 57). This is a meaningful division in that each of the latter series corresponds to the settlement of a very small human

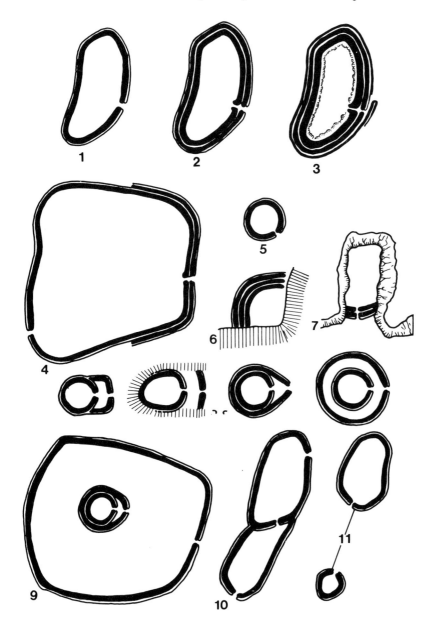

57
Typology of enclosures in Southern Britain. Types 1–4, 10 and 11 belong to the Wessex tradition, the remainder to the western tradition. (J.L. Forde-Johnston, 1976.)

group somewhere within their territories. The locations of the Wessex enclosures, by contrast, relate closely to the relief, and their size leads to the conclusion that they were occupied by larger communities. Forde-Johnston went on to distinguish several sub-groups on the basis of size (2–12ha (5–30 acres), 12–20ha (30–50 acres), over 20 ha (50 acres)), type of rampart (simple, reinforced, multiple), and situation in the landscape (edge of plateau, promontory).

All the authors who have studied this corpus stress the differences in social organization that such a diversity of forms presupposes. The need for defence produced a constellation of tiny enclosures in the west of the country; the larger sites of the Marches and Wessex indicate that this requirement was met collectively. In the east of England, contrastingly, this pressure generally did not give rise to defensive structures that are easily recognizable in the landscape. It should not be forgotten, however, that most hillforts are not dated and that this analysis takes no account of the evolution that took place over the thousand-or-so years when they were in use. It is evident, however, that with time the size of enclosures increased and their defences became increasingly complicated. Multivallation and complex entrances developed relatively late, principally in the south.

North-eastern Europe

Antoniewicz's map (1966) records nearly 2300 'pre- and protohistoric' defended sites in Poland. This survey well illustrates the uneven density of enclosures betwen one region and another: it varies from 1.3 to 21 per 1000 sq.km (386 sq. miles). Even taking account of the potential effects of successive rebuilding on a single site, there are certain regions where defended sites remain rare. On the other hand they are a typical element of the protohistoric cultures of Masuria, and above all in the south-west of the country: during the closing phases of the Lausitz culture they increased in number as their surface areas decreased.

The work of Herrmann and Coblenz in the former DDR has demonstrated a quite distinctive pattern through time (Fig. 58). In the northern plain enclosures are rarely more than 2ha (5 acres) in area. They often occupy an islet in a lake or marsh, and their ramparts are regular in plan, either oval or circular. In the south promontory forts of 9–35ha (22–86 acres) can be distinguished from a series of smaller sites, with surface areas of 0.7–18ha (2–44 acres) and consisting of a citadel and a residential zone. A sharp reduction in surface area can be observed between Hallstatt A-B

(the Late Bronze Age) and Hallstatt C-D (the First Iron Age). *Oppida*, frequently newly-established sites, do not occur at the end of the Second Iron Age in what was East Germany. At this time, however Hallstatt or Early La Tène fortifications were reoccupied and sometimes enlarged.

Central Europe

Western Germany provides a distribution pattern of hillforts that shows strong internal contrasts. None is known from anywhere in the entire northern plain. Those in central Germany are modest in size. By contrast, the largest fortified sites anywhere in Europe have been discovered on the Danube and the Rhine, covering several hundred hectares. The largest is that at Grabenstetten (Baden-Württemberg), which occupies a plateau that covers 1500ha (3706 acres). Most of the enclosures in this group are late: the construction of defences, if not occupation, is no earlier than the end of the Middle La Tène period. Those in central Germany and Bohemia had longer histories of use, which are sometimes perceptible even in the layout of the defences.

Recent studies of the Late La Tène enclosures in the whole of central Europe have highlighted this general movement towards the creation of huge fortified settlements on high ground which characterizes the *oppidum* civilization. The development of smaller enclosures, which were occupied throughout the Iron Age, is more difficult to follow. Despite their small size, they were often protected by timber-laced ramparts which could attain impressive dimensions. In the absence of excavations, they are still little known; the exploration of these sites, which has begun in the Ardennes, the Pfalz and Westphalia, will bring new ideas on the subject in the years ahead.

France

In France protohistoric enclosures are medium-sized, lying between those in Britain and those in central Europe. They cover 3–25ha (7½–62 acres), only a score exceeding that size. As in the rest of Europe the larger ones are late; nevertheless, there is an appreciable number which possess the typical attributes of *oppida* (*murus gallicus*, imported objects) but the area of which is no more than a few hectares.

The distribution map of dated enclosures has many gaps in it, but already it reveals a very uneven distribution in terms of enclosed areas, according to region and period. In Burgundy, for example, there is a large number of very small enclosures west of Dijon which seem to have been occupied alternately with undefended settlements from the Neolithic period up to the beginning of the Iron Age. In the Late La Tène period, by contrast, only a handful of large enclosures, such as Mont Beuvray, Alésia and Mont Lassois (Vix), preserve traces of occupation, as though all defended settlement was concentrated in the capitals of provinces.

The immense *oppidum* of Villejoubert in the Limousin contrasts with the other enclosures of the region, which are small. In Brittany Wheeler postulated a hierarchical organization between provincial capitals, secondary enclosures and small coastal promontory forts, which he termed 'cliff castles'. The validity of this model depends upon the contemporaneity of these settlements, which remains to be confirmed.

The national surveys in the early twentieth century in the Var and the Alpes-Maritimes recorded several hundred small enclosures perched on the summits of the limestone massifs which dominate the coast and its hinterland. Here both ramparts and houses are built in the drystone technique. A systematic survey is in progress to determine their function, their main characteristics and their dating.

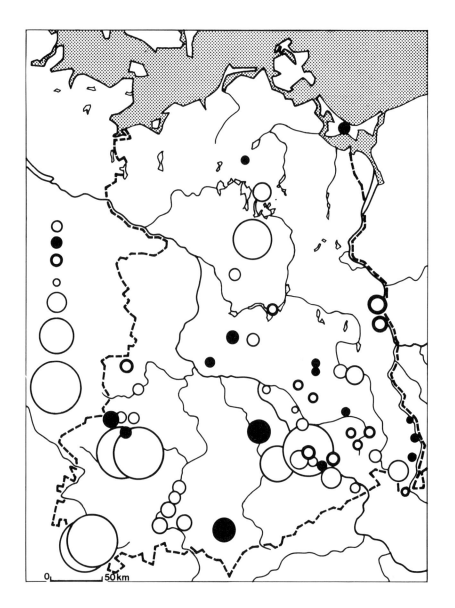

58
Map of Late Bronze Age and Hallstatt enclosures in eastern Germany. The surface area of enclosures diminishes progressively from the Late Bronze Age to the Hallstatt period. Circles denote (from top to bottom, as shown at left of map): Bronze Age; Iron Age; Bronze and Iron Ages; less than 0.5ha (1 acre); 0.5–2ha (1–5 acres); 2–6ha (5–15 acres); 6–70ha (15–173 acres). (T. Postic, after J. Herrmann, 1969.)

102

Chronological summary

The earliest defended sites appeared in the Late Neolithic period. The latest settlements of the *Linearbandkeramik* culture – at Köln-Lindenthal in the Rhine valley or at Darion in Hainault – were surrounded with ditches and palisades in the fifth millennium BC. The Middle Neolithic period (fourth and third millennia BC) is characterized by large enclosures with interrupted ditches and the first upland defended sites. The second half of the third millennium BC saw an increase in defended sites with multiple ditches and banks, as in western France, or with drystone ramparts flanked by solid masonry towers, as in southern France. Middle Neolithic ramparts, made of earth and cobbles and surmounted with a palisade, were often reoccupied or increased in height in subsequent periods: at Catenoy, in Oise, a vertical-faced rampart of Late Bronze Age date replaced the palisaded Chassean bank.

Some protohistorians believed that they could identify phases of fortification over the whole of Europe which corresponded with periods of disturbance. In fact no such generalized phenomena exist, but rather regional developments. In the Early Bronze Age settlement was too dispersed in north-western Europe to result in the creation of true defended settlements. The ditches surrounding certain roundhouses in Britain only served to delimit non-defensive enclosures. Upland settlements such as Savognin in the Grisons (Switzerland) were not fortified.

In southern France, the Camp de Laure at Rove (Bouches-du-Rhône) continued the tradition of the Chalcolithic enclosures, with its large drystone wall reinforced with massive towers every 8m (26ft). The way certain populations lived behind palisades in the Swiss lake villages or on the margins of some lakes in northern Italy, however, indicates a localized concern to live in a protected settlement.

Many sites of the Hatvan and Otománi cultures in Slovakia, Hungary and eastern Romania are surrounded by earth ramparts and wide ditches. A circular or rounded plan is common and sometimes there are two concentric ditches, each enclosing part of the settlement, as at Varsand in western Romania. Further to the north it was during the transition from Early to Middle Bronze Age, in the Véteřov culture and then the Mad'arovce culture, that defended sites began to increase in number, perhaps in response to the expansion of the Otománi culture from the south-east.

With the emergence of the Lausitz culture in the thirteenth and twelfth centuries BC the settlements in southern Poland were surrounded by simple fortifications with the appearance of the characteristic cultural traits of the Mad'arovce and Véteřov cultures at Nowa Cerekwia or the Otománi and Piliny cultures at Maskovice, coming from the Carpathian region. The influence of the Otománi peoples seems to have operated at greater and greater distances from their homeland.

From the Late Bronze Age onwards fortifications played an essential role in settlement history. They were reoccupied or modified periodically, at dates and in ways that varied from region to region. Everywhere, however, and in every period they remained in the background as refuges, even when they could not house a large part of the population.

Some Late Hallstatt settlements in the regions lying to the north and north-west of the Alps demonstrated ostentatious wealth in the structure of their ramparts and the presence of imported luxury goods. The most striking example is the rampart in level 4 at the Heuneburg (Baden-Württemberg). The relatively small size of these enclosures suggests that only a section of the people lived in them permanently. From the fifth to the second century BC they were eclipsed in many regions by the development of lowland settlements. It is difficult to demonstrate occupation levels for the Early and Middle La Tène periods on these upland settlements, even though the ramparts may here and there have been reconstructed or repaired. In fact the rich levels of the Late La Tène period have masked or destroyed them. Nevertheless these defended sites were occupied continuously in regions such as the Ardennes. In Britain B. Cunliffe has even been able to put forward an evolutionary model for the construction of gates and ramparts, which evolved without a break over the entire first millennium.

The development of *oppida* in the Late La Tène period was a general phenomenon. All over Celtic Europe vast enclosures were built, surrounded by a continuous monumental rampart. The areas enclosed were much larger than hitherto. These sites have certain urban characteristics, but at the same time the choice of upland locations and a return to timber-lacing shows how attached the Celts were to their traditions. We shall examine this point further in the context of the civilization of the *oppida*.

Enclosures, occupation, peoples

How should these enclosures be interpreted in relation to social and historical evolution? J. Neustupný has drawn attention to the intermittent nature of their periods of occupation and abandonment and the complementary nature of their relationship with lowland settlements. J.R. Collis has sought to show that they had different functions according to region and period. However, he has warned archaeologists against an over-hasty interpretation of distribution maps. An example serves to show that the spatial distribution of badly dated enclosures leads to mixing up several different chronological groups.

The risk of chronological confusion also limits the use of methods of spatial analysis. I. Ralston has tested several techniques on those regions where Late La Tène fortifications are relatively well known: Limousin, Berry and Picardy. Methods borrowed from geography assist in the better exploitation of data, in that they offer a different view from that of the crude map. Care should be taken, however, not to draw direct historical conclusions from this. Most of the methods assume that all of the sites are known and that they were all occupied at the same time. Moreover, their size is measured in terms of population, whereas here it is considered as a function of surface area.

Scholars have for too long considered that protohistoric fortifications reflect only the existence of armed conflict. In reality they played a complex role in protohistoric societies, which built and maintained them at considerable cost. They were constituent parts of systems of land holding and they symbolized the possession of territory in a monumental way. They could shelter animals or harvests, a garrison or craftsmen, a sanctuary, a market, or a princely residence. They are characteristic elements of European cultures during the first millennium BC and mark all the stages in political and economic development. It is difficult to know which social group controlled them and what precise role they played in the defence or conquest of a territory. Caesar describes for us a complex situation at the end of the period, a sharing of power between the inhabitants of the *oppida* and the nobles living in the lowlands. Although it was burdened with archaic characteristics, this long tradition facilitated the rapid urbanization of temperate Europe from the early days of the Roman conquest.

7 Houses and daily life

the organization of settlements

Protohistoric settlement, which was essentially rural in nature, was organized so as to provide shelter for men and animals while providing the opportunity for food production and craft activities to be carried out. Apart from the large fortified sites, it was an essentially agricultural economy, orientated towards meeting the requirements of family and village units.

The proliferation and differentiation of buildings throughout protohistory reflected intensification of agricultural and craft activities, and first diversification and then specialization in tasks. Buildings also illustrate changes in family and village structures. The Danubian long-house with several hearths was lived in by an extended family and could provide a shelter for crops and animals. In temperate Europe it was gradually superseded by individual houses occupied by nuclear families consisting of no more than parents and children. Ancillary structures were built to house crops and animals, and in due course craft activities as well.

Methodological problems

It is no easy task to determine the functions of buildings on the basis of their architecture alone, especially when all that is left is a ground-plan and a few elements of the superstructure. Nevertheless, typological analysis can reveal the existence of certain types of structure that are characteristic enough to be associated with a specific activity – granaries by virtue of their closely spaced heavy posts and grain storage pits, which can be distinguished from other types of pit by their greater depth and narrow openings. Other structures, particularly those used for housing men or animals, are less clearly distinguishable: some are dug into the ground, others set into or above ground level, whilst their plans are equally variable. It is none the less possible to establish some subdivisions in the series of buildings on the basis of a number of indications: for example, the design of the building itself, differences between neighbouring buildings, the location of the hearth, or the internal arrangements, and the contrasts that these reveal. Those buildings which can be identified as houses cover a large area, rarely less than 20 sq.m (215 sq.ft), and they testify to a certain concern for comfort.

In situ Bronze and Iron Age floors are rare. It is only sudden destruction, combined with exceptional conditions of preservation, that can give us an idea of what a protohistoric 'interior' was like; there are no surviving contemporary illustrations to help us to reconstruct internal arrangements. The repeated association of a particular range of artefact types with a specific building category allows the use of the structure to be identified. Other sources that can help in this process are a few rare texts or plastic representations from antiquity, together with ethnographic comparisons.

Pit-dwellings?

So long as the areas covered by excavations were small, archaeologists failed to identify post-built structures and concentrated on the pits and holes of many shapes and sizes that are to be found scattered all over protohistoric settlements. The vague concept of a 'sunken floor' was applied to all these structures indiscriminately, and bell-shaped grain-storage pits, ditches, multi-lobed quarries and workshops were all collected under this convenient but meaningless label.

In *Germania* 16, Tacitus provides evidence of the existence side-by-side of post-built structures and pits within the same settlement:

> It is a well-known fact that the peoples of Germania never live in cities, and will not even have their houses set close together. They live apart, dotted here and there, where spring, plain or grove has taken their fancy. Their villages are not laid out in Roman style, with buildings adjacent or interlocked. Every man leaves an open space round his house [*domum*], perhaps as a precaution against the risk of fire, perhaps because they are such inexpert builders ... They have also the habit of hollowing out caves underground [*suffugium hiemi*] and heaping masses of refuse on the top. In these they can escape the winter's cold and store their produce. In such shelters they take the edge off the bitter frosts; and, should an invader come, he ravages the open countryside, but the secret and buried stores may pass altogether unnoticed or escape detection, simply because they have to be looked for. (Translation H. Mattingly.)

Some writers have deduced from this that post-built structures were used as summer homes whilst the pits housed people during the winter months. This interpretation distorts the meaning of the text, in which the word *domus* is used solely with the meaning of a building at ground level. The expression *suffugium hiemi* is much vaguer: should it be interpreted as a refuge for humans or for perishable foodstuffs? In fact, Tacitus was conflating two types of pits with different functions: pits covered with dung reserved for working with wool, and grain-storage pits, which were different in shape and were not roofed in this way. The terms that he uses only permit the idea that the Germans temporarily left their houses to protect themselves against exceptionally cold conditions in below-ground structures that were ordinarily used for other purposes. The houses themselves are described much further on in Tacitus's text, where he is contrasting the Veneti, who like the Germans were a sedentary people, with their nomadic neighbours, the Fenni: 'They [the Veneti] are to be classed as Germans, for they have settled houses, carry shields ...' (*Germania*, 46: translation H. Mattingly). Does he mean merely that their houses were fixed, or is he alluding to the technique of load-bearing earthfast post construction? We cannot answer this, but it is none the less clear that the houses of the Germans had nothing to do with underground structures.

Current archaeological evidence offers a qualified solution to this problem. There were in fact below-ground dwellings in the Iron Age, but they can be distinguished from other pits by their size and shallow depth. It is more correct to describe these as semi-sunken dwellings, since they are never deeper than 0.50–1m (1½–3¼ft) below ground level. They are not common in western Europe during the Bronze and Iron Ages since, as A. Zippelius has shown, the tendency here was to specialize in post-built structures and pits, the latter being ancillary to the former. Both large- and small-scale excavations in central and eastern Europe have revealed the existence of semi-sunken structures that were used as dwellings: they are well known from Bronze Age Poland but only rarely in association with post-built or *Blockbau* structures. They can be distinguished from true pits by their shallowness and by the existence of a floor and, on occasion, a hearth.

Casual reading of ancient texts and inappropriate excavation methods have created a picture of crude and undifferentiated protohistoric settlements. Recent observations, in contrast, have suggested that the real picture is one of change through time and space. Domestic activities took place inside or outside dwellings, and sometimes on flagged surfaces. Houses could shelter both men and beasts, and all types of work were carried out within them. There was a perceptible development over the two millennia concerned. This resulted in a multi-purpose settlement with diversified structures where agricultural and craft activities were removed from dwellings and installed in specialized ancillary buildings, and where the interior and the enclosure gradually encroached upon the exterior. Whilst houses continued to shelter men and animals and some work was still carried out inside them, they were divided up by partitions, separating the living area from the rest. Ancillary buildings served as granaries, barns, byres or workshops. By the later Iron Age in the southern part of the area considered here, kitchens had become recognizable and increasingly became separate rooms. Family groups and village communities penned their animals up in enclosures and marked their possession of land with ditches around fields or banks of earth or stone at the boundaries of their holdings. Although we cannot yet demonstrate it, we would argue the case, on the evidence of settlement organization described later, for a social organization that was different from that which prevailed in the Roman world. Family life and activities did not centre on a courtyard that was not visible from outside but were distributed between an interior and an exterior space with less clearly demarcated limits.

Interior arrangements

Internal divisions

Although internal partitions that form part of the basic construction of buildings may be rare, they occur throughout protohistory. It is often a matter of a local tradition which applies to most or all of the houses in one village, yet is completely unknown in a neighbouring community. Divisions of this kind are almost always present in buildings over 20m (66ft) in length.

Internal divisions manifest themselves in architecture in three ways. The first, characterized by the byre-houses of northern Europe, is shown in the building itself by a change in the spacing between the central posts in one half and the other, and by their being doubled up in some instances at the junction. This change is emphasized by the presence of a hearth in the residential section and by entrances in the outer wall-line close to the position of internal division. In some cases this may be represented by a partition wall: the partition wall in the Bronze Age house from Zijderveld (Netherlands) consists of five posts instead of three, and in the Iron Age house found on the same site twelve small posts duplicate the two load-bearing posts. Division into two sections is most common, but there are examples from all periods of buildings divided into three. These may have only one hearth or, less frequently, two, as at Trappendal (Fig. 59) and Ristoft (Jutland) or Emmerhout (Drenthe) from the Late Bronze Age.

The second tradition belongs mainly to continental Europe and includes bays, which may be built in the same way as the external walls, in the *Blockbau* houses

of Buchau (see Fig. 62), for example, or in lighter materials. The third tradition is confined to the stone houses of Scotland, Shetland (see Fig. 61) and Orkney. The rooms are set into the thick masonry of the external wall and form more or less open apses.

The term *megaron* is often found in the archaeological literature when referring to two-roomed houses. It is applied to houses from all over Europe, but it is an abuse of the term. In Greek architecture the *megaron* is the main rectangular room entered from a vestibule without a facade and open to the exterior, with one or two timber supports forming a portico (B. Holtzmann). Although it is possible to conceive of Greek influence making itself felt as far as Hungary, where the Neolithic has certain aspects in common with the Balkan cultures, it is in no way plausible in respect of regions lying further to the north or west. Only at Tószeg (Hungary) do the anterooms in certain cases lack an end wall in the true megaron style. On most other sites it is a matter of two-roomed houses, the layout of which is so obviously dictated by architectural considerations that any resemblance is due to convergence rather than to influences coming from the Mediterranean. The location of the hearth in the inner room, the larger of the two, also highlights the logic of the domestic organization. At Toszég the anteroom is usually separated from the main room by a reed screen, but it can be closed off with a true wall of load-bearing posts and contain a second hearth (Fig. 60). The post alignment inside the Early Bronze Age long house at Březno (Czechoslovakia) defines interior walls one-third of the way along and at the end.

There are sometimes dividing walls inside the British round-houses which are represented partly by

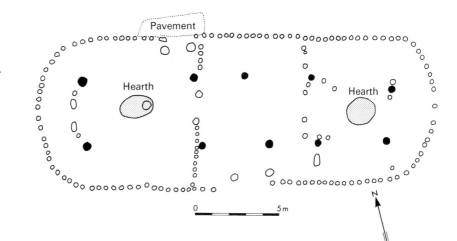

59

Three-aisled house at Trappendal, Jutland (Late Bronze Age, Montelius Period III). It is divided by partition walls into three rooms, two of which have hearths. (C.J. Becker, 1982.)

Pavement

Hearth

Hearth

0   5 m

N

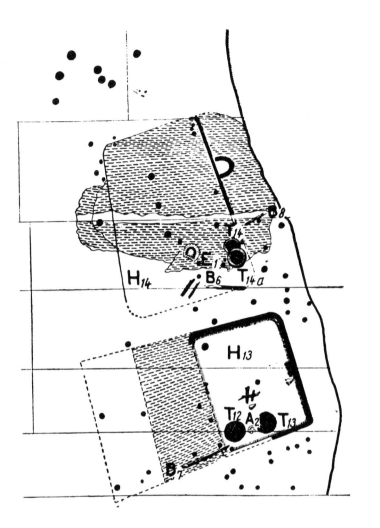

60
*Houses from Tószeg
with three rows of
posts (Late Bronze
Age). House 13 consists
of two rooms and a
covered patio; part of
the beaten earth floor
has survived. The
hearth (T) is set up
against a wall in both
houses (H13 and H14).
Remains of planks and
logs (B) were still in
place in the walls. (J.
Banner, I. Bóna, and L.
Márton, 1959.)*

stake-holes. In those regions where the houses are built in stone, rooms take the form of apses, arranged round the central room (Fig. 61). These apsidal chambers are separated from one another by the masonry of the exterior wall in the Bronze Age and by partition walls in the Iron Age. In the large Middle La Tène farm at Verberie (Oise) an area of 25 sq.m (269 sq.ft), defined by a light wall, the foundation trench of which has survived, may have been devoted to specialized activity or the dwelling proper inside a multi-purpose building (see Fig. 31).

The plan of the early first millennium BC houses at Buchau (Baden-Württemberg), with two wings projecting from the ends of the central range, is so far unique in Europe (Fig. 62). Built using the *Blockbau* technique, they comprise three to five rooms, two or three of which have hearths. Since these nine houses

replace the 38 houses of the preceding century and the total available space enclosed remains the same, it is reasonable to wonder whether this may not be due to regrouping of families. This would be a rare but not unique phenomenon, comparable with the way in which buildings of 25–50 sq.m (269–538 sq.ft) at Bavois (Vaud) were replaced by others covering up to 100 sq.m (1076 sq.ft) at the end of the second millennium BC. Buildings of over 100 sq.m begin to occur in the Hallstatt period at the Heuneburg (Baden-Württemberg) or the Goldberg (Bavaria), but they existed alongside smaller buildings and began to reflect social differentiation.

Very often, however, there are no internal partitions; it is only the type of use which governs the organization of space, and this can only be understood if the floor and furnishings have been preserved.

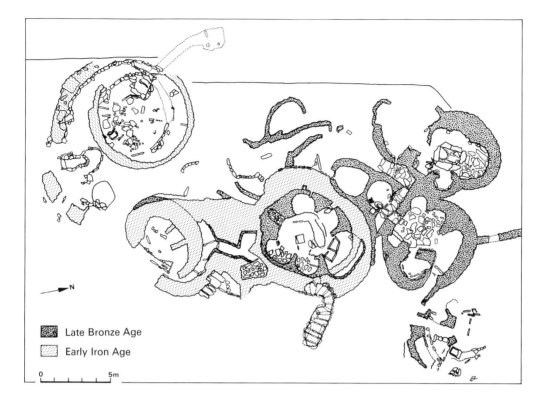

61

Late Bronze Age houses from Jarlshof (Shetland). Houses with drystone walls that had been reconstructed several times. Each contained a hearth of slabs on edge, stone tanks, one or more paved areas and an angled underground entrance. (T. Postic, after J.R.C. Hamilton, 1956.)

62

Wasserburg at Buchau. The large two-winged farm, granary, and ?byre of the upper level lie on top of three small houses in the lower level (Baden-Württemberg, Late Bronze Age). Open squares: hearths of the later period; shaded squares: hearths of the earlier period. (H. Reinerth, 1976.)

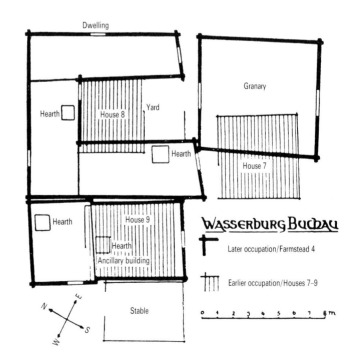

Ovens and hearths

A hearth is often the only element surviving inside a house, but the presence of a hearth is not always an adequate criterion for identifying the function of a structure. In many cases it occupies a central or axial position: in round-houses it is often in the centre, whilst in three-aisled houses it is found in the centre of the third bay, i.e. in the middle of the section occupied by humans. In other cases, such as Buchau or Biskupin, it is closer to the wall. Sometimes it is put outside the building, in the immediate vicinity.

The accessories found associated with them show that hearths would have been used for boiling, braising and roasting. The increase in coarse, durable pottery in the late Neolithic period can be related directly to the general adoption of direct cooking on the fire, which partially replaced indirect heating methods such as boiling with the aid of heated stones. Frequent finds of caramelized remains of boiled cereals in the bottoms of pots provide direct proof of this. Bronze and later iron spits replaced thin branches of green wood for roasting, whilst the pot-hangers that spread widely in the Iron Age are connected with the cauldrons used for cooking soups or stews.

Domestic hearths do not, however, reflect the progress made by craftsmen in the mastery of fire. When used for cooking or heating of houses they are very similar to those of the preceding millennia and are evidence of skills acquired much earlier. A more economical use of fuel seems to have been sought, as shown by the Chalcolithic hearths from Charavines (Isère): A. Bocquet describes these as small hearths containing embers replenished with branches and twigs of beech, a wood whose heating qualities are well known. In fenland and lake-margin sites more complex hearths were constructed, with a foundation of branches or logs, sometimes covered with fir boughs or birch bark, often topped with a coating of clay, on top of which the hearth was built, to protect it from moisture.

The construction of domestic hearths was essentially aimed at confining them within fixed limits, so as to protect the building against the risk of fire. The various arrangments that are known are connected with local methods of construction and resources — stone or clay, according to their availability. Bowl hearths are less common than in earlier periods, being replaced by flat hearths, usually circular, more rarely square, and by cooking pits. They vary in size from 0.70 to 2m (2 to 6½ft). Over most of temperate Europe they consist of a clay base with pebbles on top. These bases often rest on foundations of stones or potsherds

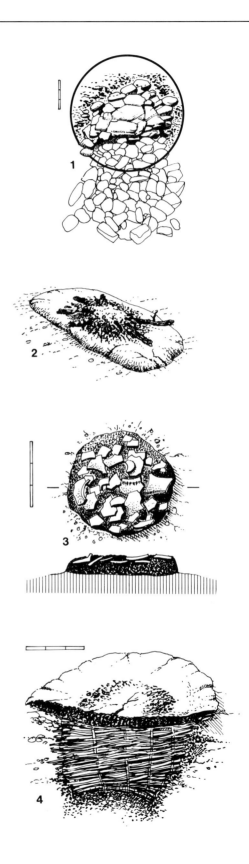

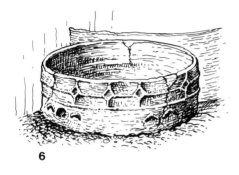

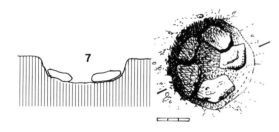

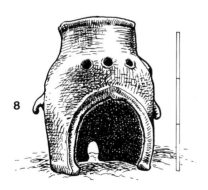

63
Protohistoric hearths and heating structures.
1: Hearth paved with small stones and with a platform of large slabs in front (Padnal, Savognin, Grisons). (After J. Rageth, 1977.)
2: La Tène clay cooking plate. (After Musée de Martigues catalogue, 1984.)
3: Hearth on a plinth of sherds and clay. (After J. Banner and I. Bóna, 1974.)
4: Hearth on frame of hazel wattling (Auvernier). (After B. Arnold, 1981.)
5: Hearth of sandstone slabs (Skara Brae, Orkney). (After C. Renfrew, 1983.)
6: Hearth with edging of decorated clay (Tószeg, Hungary). (After J. Banner et al, 1959.)
7: Cooking pit (Coulon, Vendée). (After J.-P. Pautreau, 1978.)
8: Portable oven designed to receive a cooking vessel (Füzesabony, Hungary). (After T. Kovács, 1977; Drawings: G. Tosello.)

mixed with clay, and may be finished off with an edging (Fig. 63.3). At Tószeg several hearths were positioned so as to straddle two rooms and were divided in two by a low wall on the line of the partition wall. A type of hearth common in the La Tène period was made of a circular slab of baked clay, as, for example, at Les Baux-de-Provence in the second century BC (Fig. 63.2). 'Hearth plates' similar in shape and size to Roman flanged tiles have been reported from the Gaulish sites at Aulnat and Levroux, but their function has not yet been properly elucidated.

In areas of building in stone, hearths are often square or rectangular and are marked by stones or slabs. Platforms of this kind are found in Alpine villages such as Cresta, Mont-Vallac, or Padnal-Savognin in the Grisons (Fig. 63.1). The hearths from Padnal-Savognin are flat or dished and edged with small stones or carefully lined. In some cases the hearth was closely linked with a more substantial pit filled with charcoal remains and heated stones. Another variant consists of a deeper pit associated with a bowl hearth, both filled with stones and charcoal. In every case these pits are connected with ovens, the superstructures of which were broken down at the end of each cooking period.

In the stone houses of Shetland and Orkney, the flagged edges of the hearths form boxes with clay bases, as at Skara Brae (Fig. 63.5), Rinyo, or Jarlshof. At Late Bronze Age Hohlandsberg (Alsace), hearths with clay or pebble bases were often built between one or two partition walls and the back wall of the house. In some cases, such as the house of the potter or house 3 at Linsenbrunnen (Alsace), there was also, alongside the main hearth, a second one set into a kind of outhouse edged with low walls, which M. Jehl and C. Bonnet have interpreted as a kitchen. Two hearths also built into walls in the northern sector of Linsenbrunnen but at some distance from the dwelling houses are argued to have served communal functions: one is described as a 'baker's oven' because of its similarity to the nearby pottery kiln, which it resembles in form but without the associated debris of potsherds. The other may have been used for spit-roasting because of the many burnt deer bones found close by.

In southern Europe, where clay played an important role, hearths give an impression of how house interiors may have been decorated. They are built on a plinth of clay and potsherds and often coated with the same material as the floor; in plan they are round, oval, or, more rarely, rectangular, and measure between 0.60 and 1.60m (2 and 5ft). At Tószeg they are flat and at floor level, isolated from the rest of the room by means of a channel a few centimetres wide or by a base set into earlier occupation layers. These were followed by shallow dished hearths, called bowl hearths by L. Márton, and hearths edged with a low wall. In the later levels the edges are higher and horseshoe-shaped. In some cases they are ornamented with relief decoration consisting of simple geometric motifs – horizontal cordons, triangles, lozenges and spirals. Some of them have two or four ventilation holes arranged diametrically and internal brackets on which cooking pots would have been set (Fig. 63.6). Many pot supports have also been found, in the form of truncated cones or crucibles. Similar hearths equipped with holes for rabbling or poking the fire are known from sites such as Apátdomb (Hungary) and Donja Dolina (Yugoslavia) dating to the Iron Age. Other hearths, at Toszég and Tiszaluc, are covered with a clay grid (probably strengthened with wooden rods).

The first portable ovens have also been found in Hungary (Fig. 63.8). They take the form of inverted vessels with an opening at the top where the pots to be cooked were placed and one or two openings at the base for adding fuel and for draught.

Hearths are often accompanied by accessories. In the Rhine-Switzerland-eastern France region crescent-shaped firedogs are found in the Bronze Age. They are so small that there is a question about what they were used for. Ceramic or iron firedogs became widely used in the Iron Age, often with animal-head terminals, along with cauldrons and pot-hooks. The large double firedogs or andirons of the Late Iron Age were used on open hearths. Found in association with cauldrons (Fig. 64) and drinking vessels, they are a reminder of the importance of ceremonial meals and feasts for the Gauls. We must conjure up a picture of one of these bronze cauldrons, known both from archaeology and the many Irish legends in which they play an important part, hung above the hearth.

The problem of smoke removal, which has led several authors to formulate various theories about types of chimney or openings in roofs, causes no

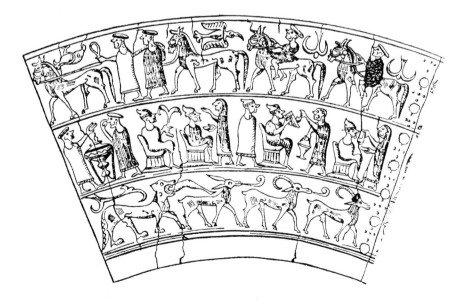

64
Sixth-century bronze situla from Vače (Slovakia). The complete decoration consists of a procession on horseback and in chariots and a festive scene similar to the Greco-Roman symposium – men seated on chairs are served with drinks previously mixed in a cauldron set on a tripod. These articles of furniture and ceremonial vessels are sometimes found in Hallstatt princely graves. (After J. Déchelette, 1914.)

65
Ovens and hearths in an Iron Age house at Maiden Castle (Dorset). (R.E.M. Wheeler, 1943.)

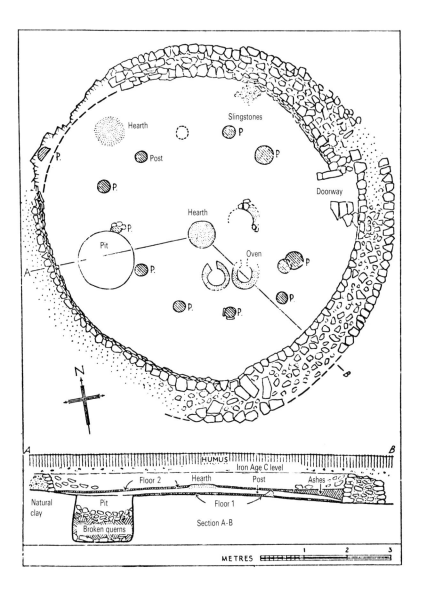

problems in thatched houses, where the roof covering allows air to pass through easily. Indeed, P.J. Reynolds has shown that an opening at the top of a conical roof sucks up sparks and puts easily inflammable roofing materials at risk. One of the earliest conduits for evacuating smoke belongs to an oven in a First Iron Age (Hallstatt) house at Entringen (Germany): the pit oven was connected with the exterior by means of an inclined duct.

Ovens first appeared in the Neolithic. At Early Bronze Age Tószeg (Hungary) the oven was alongside the hearth. It was built on a base of stones or potsherds, its cob walls being built on a framework of flexible sticks and topped with a rounded roof. The walls were usually horseshoe-shaped and surrounded the base in all those sites where clay structures are well preserved such as Bronze Age Tószeg and Várdomb (Hungary), and in the Iron Age at Maiden Castle (Dorset) (Fig. 65) and many of the *oppida*, such as Saint-Blaise (Provence). They can be reconstructed as domed ovens, with a single combustion and heating chamber. This has an opening at its base into which first fuel is introduced and then, when the oven has heated up, the food to be cooked. These hemispherical or ovoid ovens are identical with the cooking ovens still to be found in the eastern Mediterranean. Whether they were sited within or outside dwellings seems to depend on local rather than regional traditions, since the location varies from site to site. The oven with a ventilation duct at Entringen referred to above was located alongside a hearth. Houses at Hallstatt Biskupin (Poland) all had hearths but no ovens. Ovens are rarer than hearths in houses before the La Tène period and do not occur in small houses. At the Hohlandsberg the only structure that might have served as an oven was set between two low walls and the retaining wall of the village. This was perhaps one of the earliest covered ovens. At Hallstatt Choisy-au-Bac (Oise) the two domestic oven bases were found in 3m- (10ft-) long outhouses, one of which was built up against a house.

Craft furnaces have also been found in the ancillary buildings of settlements. These reflect technological progress earlier than domestic ovens, which did not incorporate such improvements until several centuries later. Thus the fifth-century BC ovens found at Martigues are the distant descendants of craft prototypes from the Bronze Age (see Fig. 85.2). They consist of four superimposed independent elements. The nearly cylindrical base, set on the ground, acted as a hearth. At the top it had a central opening through which heat and smoke rose. Above this was the cylindro-conical cooking chamber, which was surmounted by a perforated plate with a cylindrical rim on which a lid with a central opening rested. Thus hot air circulated from the hearth up to the top of the oven. The hearth could be fed during the cooking process. However, the upper components had to be dismantled in order to put food in or take it out. J. Chausserie-Laprée postulates several functions, including slow cooking on the embers, conservation of food by smoking and drying of cereals. It is likely that while in use the component parts of the oven were sealed hermetically with one another with clay or dung, in the same way that this is still done in the Mediterranean.

Domestic ovens must have been used principally for baking unleavened bread of cereal flour, but they would certainly have had other uses. It is known that part of the cereal crop was roasted or parched, but the ovens used for this purpose have not yet been identified.

Furnishings

If we are to believe Strabo, 'the Gauls slept on the ground and took their meals seated on straw couches' (*Geography*, 4;4,3). At first sight this statement seems to be confirmed by the archaeological discoveries.

Furnishings are rare or non-existent in protohistoric houses. However, the same is true for furniture as for the upper parts of houses: most of the information has disappeared and very special conditions of deposition are necessary if any indications are to come down to us. H. Reinerth mentions beds and wooden chests at Buchau (Bavaria), but there is no graphical evidence to support his statements. However, benches made of wattle and daub are known from Hungary. Some Bronze Age round-houses from Stannon Down (Cornwall) have series of stakes running for some 40cm (16in) along the walls. They may have served as the supports of benches or shelving. Benches were built into the walls of some semi-sunken rooms in central Europe. At Biskupin (Poland), all the houses had a wide bunk to the left of the entrance (see Fig. 71).

There was also a bench in hut 1 of Les Tremaïe at Les Baux-de-Provence, but in a context of domestic activities rather than sleeping (see Fig. 72). Clay benches were in fact a Mediterranean fitting which became common in southern France between the fourth and second centuries BC but which seem not to have spread to the north. On the other hand, the presence of traces of wood and large nails makes it possible to argue for the existence from the La Tène period onwards of wooden chests in houses, as at Etival (Vosges). The stone furniture in the Orkney houses (Fig. 67) is completely exceptional.

It is also necessary to take into account vegetable materials of all kinds, which must have played a very large role in houses. Lake villages such as Clairvaux (Neolithic to Early Bronze Age) in the Jura, which have been the object of intensive botanical studies, give some idea of this importance. Tons of plant material were brought into the village by dug-out canoe, both for everyday requirements and for constructional purposes. Vanished beds have to be reintroduced into the bare interiors that excavation has demonstrated. They may have been made of leaves, twigs, moss, grass, seaweed, hay or straw.

A number of seats are known, but these have all been found in funerary contexts and seem not to have been used in everyday life. In the Bronze Age there were the folding wooden stools from northern Germany or Denmark, such as that from Guldhøj (Jutland), or the stools with legs of the kind found at the bottom of a funerary shaft of the second century BC at Pomas (Aude).

These modest remains give a rough picture of the interiors of houses. However, the scenes depicted on some Hallstatt situlae from Italy and central Europe give a glimpse of a much more refined world which used chairs with curved backs, stools and beds with

66
Klinè *from Hochdorf (Baden-Württemberg), second half of sixth century* BC. *A bronze couch on which the dead man was lying in the burial chamber of the Hallstatt grave-mound. (J. Biel.)*

legs. The archaeological remains of these ceremonial beds are not to be found in houses but in certain 'princely' tombs containing Mediterranean imports. The discoverers of the princely grave mound at Hochdorf, near Stuttgart, estimated that the bronze couch with curved back or *klinè* (Fig. 66), on which the dead man lay was not made locally but came, like the great bronze cauldron, from south of the Alps.

Inside the protohistoric houses one must add to the pottery, sherds of which are found, and the wooden or basketry containers which proliferated from the Bronze Age onwards. They must have combined to give dwellings a much more cluttered appearance than that which emerges from excavation. In the Neolithic period pots were suspended in nets. It may be assumed that a number of objects would have been hung from the walls or the beams. Utensils, tools, hunting weapons and fishing equipment would have been stored in the houses. At Biskupin (Poland) these were left in the outer room, and as a result it was possible to identify a fishermen's quarter in the heart of the village on the basis of the fishing gear in those houses.

Outside the regions of lake dwellings, pits are often found inside houses, especially in Czechoslovakia, Poland (e.g. the Lausitz site at Konin) and England. Some of these pits contain utilitarian objects, such as storage jars, but some also contain other materials, such as potter's equipment in the cave of Planches

(Doubs) in the Late Bronze Age and stocks of slingshots at Iron Age Hod Hill (Dorset). They sometimes served as hiding places for precious objects: at Early Bronze Age Spišský Štvrtok (Slovakia) 'chests' dug into the floors of houses contained gold and bronze objects. Discoveries of hoards of this kind often occur in unfavourable circumstances, so that we do not know whether the amber beads and bronze pendants found inside a wooden box in the upper levels at the slightly later site at Barca (Slovakia) came from within a house or not. At Buchau, however, it is clear that a chain of rings and pendants was buried directly in the ground behind house 1, just like the hoard of bronze weapons and tools. The same applied to the wooden box found a few years later which was swallowed by a cow along with the water in which it was being conserved and disappeared before its contents had been investigated!

Discoveries from the Swiss lakes have shown that these boxes made out of wood or bark often contained precious objects. That from Grosser Hafner in Zürich was a jewel box and contained a necklace. Although their construction and dimensions do not differentiate between houses, discoveries of this kind show that some of their inhabitants were very affluent.

Organization of domestic space

Certain favoured sites give an impression of the organization of domestic space: special conditions of burial and preservation have meant that the floors have survived, together with traces of furniture and fittings. Their layout makes it possible to get an idea of

67
Interior of house 1, Skara Brae. The use of local stone for both the furnishings and the structure itself ensured its preservation. In the centre can be seen the hearth, and on the right there is a cupboard with two shelves and tanks. (Drawing: P.-Y. Pavec.)

interior arrangements and the lifestyle within them.

In north-western Europe at the beginning of the second millennium a settlement of peasant fishermen in a dry environment where trees were rare resulted in the local resources being used in an exceptional way. The houses at Skara Brae (Orkney) were buried under sand and domestic rubbish, which ensured that the walls were almost completely preserved. They were of drystone construction and provide a very rare example of stone furniture (Fig. 67). The small square houses with rounded corners consisted of a single room measuring 20–35 sq.m (215–377 sq.ft). The walls were up to 2.40m (8ft) high and 2–3m (6½–10ft) thick. At the tops of the surviving walls the beginning of corbelling could be discerned. There was a square central hearth edged with stone slabs. Built up against the walls were items of furniture made out of slabs of the local sandstone and set on carefully-built low drystone walls. There were two box beds which would have been filled with heather, one of which (the man's?) was larger than the other, a 'dresser' with two shelves 0.80–1.30m (2½–4ft) high, fitted niches and a recess that was paved or provided with a drain. The floor also had boxes or troughs lined with slabs, often sealed with a clay coating. The limpet and cockle shells found inside them suggest that they may have been used as tanks for holding or even raising fish. Several slabs piled on top of one another may have formed a bench near the hearth in house 1. In another house a stone slab used as a working surface sited near the

doorway, had on it a whalebone bowl, a mortar and two pots. These island sites from northern Scotland are characterized by the use of whalebone and sandstone for making vessels and tools. The later houses at Jarlshof and Gruting produced less information, but the stone furnishings still included a hearth, troughs, a quern, a drain and flagged floors in some of the rooms, the entrances and the corridors.

The houses at Fragtrup in northern Jutland are, to the best of our knowledge, the only Late Bronze Age houses in Scandinavia that still have floors surviving. House I, 18 by 7m (59 by 23ft) was divided into two by a partition and a slight difference in level (Fig. 68). The constructional details and the furnishings suggest a tripartite division: a corner for eating and cooking in the section with a lined floor near the hearth; domestic activities and storage in the centre of the house; and craft activities in the second room. The sleeping areas may have been along the walls near the hearth. A 1.20m- (4ft-) deep well and a small storage building completed this part-domestic, part-craft settlement which produced much high-quality pottery.

At Dean Moor (Devon) at the end of the second millennium BC the stone-built round-houses were divided in two sections, occasionally by means of a partition wall. The lower section near the entrance was the working area where cooking and craft activities were carried out round the hearth and the cooking pits, as shown by the potsherds, flint chips and loomweights found there (Fig. 69). The upper

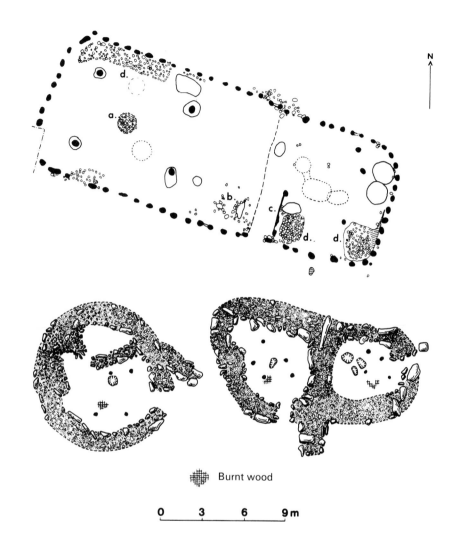

68

Plan of the Bronze Age house from Fragtrup (Denmark). The interior is divided into two rooms by a partition wall and a difference in floor level. On the left is the living area with hearth (a), two benches on stone supports (d), and pits; in the centre there is a storage area filled with coarse pottery jars and a corner reserved for flint working, and on the right there is a room for craft activities, with two stone-floored areas (d). (B. Draiby, 1984.)

69

Bronze Age houses at Dean Moor, Dartmoor (Devon). Interior layout of round-houses: alcoves or partition walls form the interior divisions. (J.V.S. Megaw and D.D.A. Simpson, 1983.)

⊞ Burnt wood

0   3   6   9 m

part, slightly set into the slope of the hill and less well lit, was kept more or less empty and was used for sleeping. A few centuries earlier, at Black Patch (Sussex), the same division is to be found, with a storage area further into the house. However, several round-houses, some of which must have been used for animals, already show indications of complementary functions being located in neighbouring groups of structures and this developed considerably from then on. At Glastonbury (Somerset), for example, round-houses could be used as dwellings or as kitchens, workshops or byres from the fifth century BC on.

At Biskupin (Poland) in the seventh century BC some hundred houses carefully aligned along parallel streets (Fig. 70) were identical in their internal organization. They measured 9 by 7m (29 by 23ft) and

were divided into two rooms (Fig. 71). Small lofts under the rafters were probably used for storage. The hearth was situated in front of the house at Néry (Oise) in the mid first millennium BC and cooking took place outside, using coarseware vessels. Finer wares were used for eating and drinking inside the house.

There are several La Tène period houses in southern France which give an idea of domestic organization. At Martigues in the fourth century BC the houses seem to be cluttered with cob-lined grain silos, large jars known as *dolia* and other storage vessels, which lined three of the walls. The fourth side was reserved for cooking, with the oven, the clay hearth plate, the quern and some flat stones. A space of 2 by 3m (6½ by 10ft) was kept free in the centre. Storage seems to have dominated other functions in a smaller hut. At Les

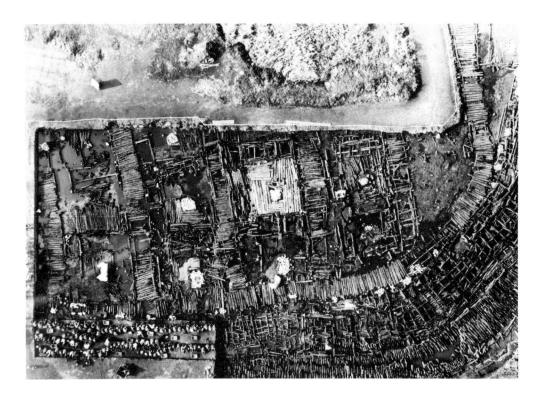

70
*Aerial view of the seventh-century BC village of Biskupin
(Poland). The rectangular* Blockbau *houses form continuous
parallel rows and are separated by corduroy streets of
horizontal logs. (National Archaeological Museum,
Warsaw.)*

Baux-de-Provence in the late second century BC the
interior space was divided into three sections in house
1 at Les Tremaïe (Fig. 72). One was for storage in *dolia*
and clay storage vessels, the second was for food
preparation, with a mortar, a whetstone, a wine flagon
and small drinking vessels, and the third was for
cooking, with a cooking plate and vessels for putting
on the fire. A bench running along the wall and two
clay shelves completed the furnishings. A few square
metres were left free in the centre of the room and
adjacent to part of the bench. It would be a mistake to
consider this congestion as in any way exceptional.
The large number of potsherds in occupation layers
confirms this. At Auvernier-Nord B. Arnold has
calculated that each of the houses in the village
contained between 50 and 200 pots, and generally
more than 100. Even if they did not all belong to the
same phase of occupation, the number of pots in use at
the same time in a given house must have been
substantial.

The above examples come from all over Europe and
relate to very different cultures, but they reveal
general trends common to all ancient rural settlements. The main room was used for all domestic
activities, even when there were other rooms. The
hearth played a central role. Life was lived at ground
level, and most activities were certainly carried out in
a squatting position.

Although the relationships between the layouts of
spaces and their functions are becoming clear, we have
virtually no idea about the connections that the
patterns may have with social structures. Ethnographic studies have shown us how important these
links are in the organization of life and in the
distribution of activities between the sexes, between
age-groups and between families, as well as the place
of each individual in the household. Research is not
yet far enough advanced to provide answers.

External domestic arrangements

Cobbled areas

Flagged or cobbled areas or pavements are often to be
found outside houses. The archaeological remains

71
Village houses at Biskupin. Each has a main room with a central hearth and a raised area to one side for sleeping. In front there is a vestibule running the length of the house for working tools and implements. (National Archaeological Museum, Warsaw.)

found show that the same activities were carried out on them as in the interiors of the houses, as at Shaugh Moor (Devon) in the mid first millennium BC (Fig. 73). Flint working was common. At All Cannings Cross (Wiltshire) the archaeological discoveries corresponding with domestic or craft activities – querns, flint tools and waste, and potsherds were recovered from various areas. At the beginning of the first millennium at Berlin-Lichterfelde (Germany) the paved area, which measured more than 300 sq.m (3230 sq.ft), was located some distance from the house. It was surrounded by rubbish pits (with pottery wasters, loomweights, spindle whorls and stone waste). Paved surfaces of this kind are known from all those regions where stone is abundant and were used for a variety of purposes throughout the protohistoric period.

Corn-grinding areas

Very few traces of grinding activities have survived in proportion to the amount of time they must have taken up, at least until the invention of the rotary quern. Using a primitive saddle-quern around an hour and a half would be needed to produce 1kg (2¼lb) of coarse flour. This means that several hours had to be devoted each day to this monotonous task. Up to the second century BC a large flat stone with dressed edges and surface was used for corn grinding; this was the surface on which the grain was crushed using a hand-held smaller stone, the rubber, in a back-and-forth movement. The lower stone could often weigh as much as around 30kg (66lb). P. Ribaud has shown that at Late Bronze Age Auvernier the weight of these pads varied between 20 and 45kg (44 and 99lb), the rubbers being 30–50cm (12–20in) long and weighing 5–20kg (11–44lb). Elsewhere grinders seem to have been smaller.

The plano-convex form is that most frequently encountered but in certain regions it was replaced by other forms in a local tradition – concave saddle querns in Britain, trough querns in Scotland and Scandinavia. A flattened tetrahedron form known as

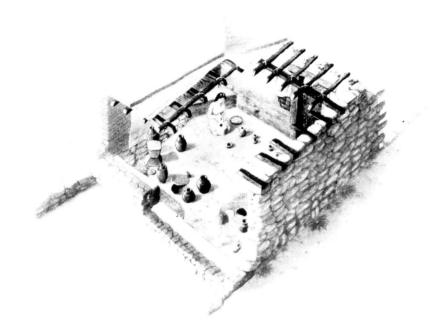

72
Reconstruction and plan of a La Tène house from Les Trémaïe, Les Baux-de-Provence. The contents of the single living room include a cooking corner with hearth (a), a storage area filled with containers (1–4), and a sleeping corner with a clay bench (b). (G. Tosello; plan: P. Arcelin.)

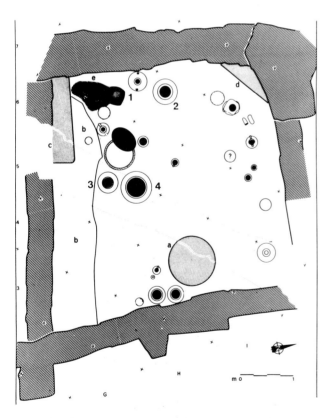

'Napoleon's hat', the point forming the base, predominated in Iron Age Germany. A large number of querns had a convex base which was intended not for setting them up but rather so that they could be chocked up to give a slight inclination to the working surface.

The places where querns were used are rarely discovered; they most often come from rubbish pits or are identified reused in drystone walls. Ethnographic examples suggest an explanation for this fact. Although they were very simple objects, saddle-querns were only of use so long as the (grinding) surface was satisfactory. When this became too deeply hollowed or irregular they had to be reworked, by trimming their sides followed by levelling of the surface, until eventually they were thrown away or used for grinding other materials because they had become too small. V. Roux has shown that in Mauretania the women turn them over after use so as to preserve the working surface; once they become worn they are used for crushing other plants. Querns have been found face downwards in the barley deposit in house I at Ness of Gruting (Fig. 74) and house IV at Jarlshof (see Fig. 61).

In the few cases where they have been found *in situ* they occupied various locations in the houses: near the hearth and along the walls in the two Chalcolithic houses at Conquette (Hérault), or scattered around the interiors and present in almost every house at Late Bronze Age Auvernier, near Neuchâtel. A plano-

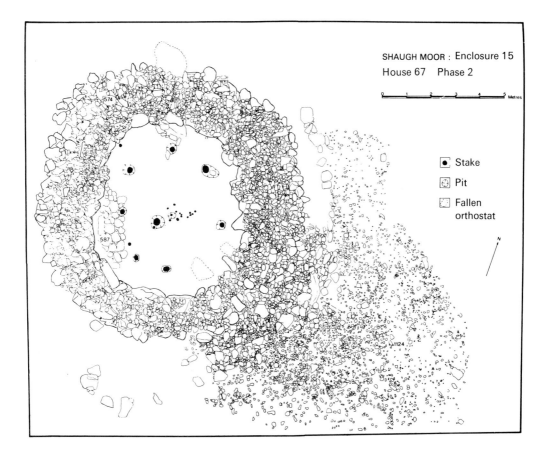

73

*Bronze Age house 67 from enclosure 15 on Shaugh Moor
(Dartmoor). The house with its sunken, angled entrance has
a cobbled working area outside. The internal layout includes
a flagged area and a drain that passes beneath the wall.
(G.J. Wainwright and K. Smith, 1980.)*

convex quern was wedged in the ground with a row of
small stones at Late Bronze Age Berlin-Lichterfelde, so
as to keep it at an angle. This arrangement, which was
certainly intended to be permanent, was installed
along the wall outside one of the houses. No rubber
was found nearby, only in the rubbish pits. The
querns from House II at Jarlshof (Shetland) or Weston
Wood (Surrey) were also fixed in place with stones. It
seems therefore that whenever a quern is found in its
original location it is set in position using subsidiary
elements which includes at least a stone packing.

To judge from the contents, the four Middle Bronze
Age round-houses at Black Patch (Sussex) had different functions, and the only quern found on the site
came from the hut which contained pottery vessels
but no craft elements. This is one of the earliest
indications, along with the Weston Wood hut, of a
covered space being given over to corn grinding.

During the Iron Age querns are to be found in all
houses on sites such as Hrazany (southern Bohemia).
At Partenheim (Rhein-Hesse) the quern was adjacent
to a stone seat in a 40cm- (16in-) deep pit inside a
roofed workshop-cellar. Those which seem to be *in
situ* are located in ground-level buildings that also
contain an oven or in small outhouses with floors
slightly below ground level, as, for example, at
Radovesice (Bohemia). At fourth-century BC Martigues (Provence) the two components of the quern
were up against the wall, alongside the oven, in that
part of the hut reserved for domestic activities. It is
thus very likely that cooking and storage of foodstuffs
were progressively found in specialized sections of
dwelling houses or were located in a separate building,
and that the querns and grinding activities gradually
occupied a fixed place in those areas.

The rotary quern appeared in the second century
BC, first in southerly regions, under Greek and Italian

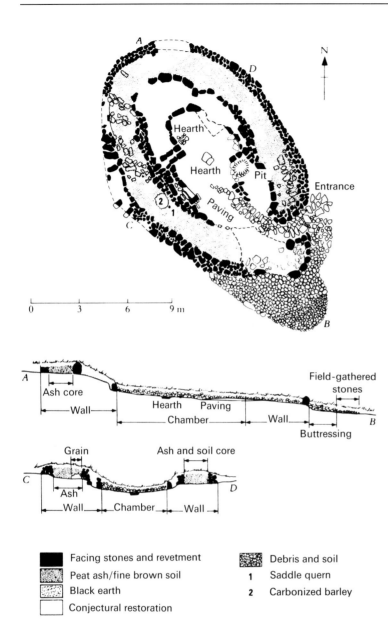

Plan and section of
Bronze Age house 1 at
Ness of Gruting
(Shetland). The double-
faced stone wall with a
core of soil and ash
contains a pit filled
with grain (2) and
covered by an inverted
quern (1) in its south-
west corner. The
internal layout includes
two hearths, a pit, and
paving in the angled
entrance corridor. (P.J.
Fowler, 1983.)

influence. It slowly spread over the whole of Europe, but without replacing the saddle quern completely. It is relatively standardized in form: the fixed part (*catillus*) and the moving part (*meta*) formed a cylinder of around 30–40cm (12–16in) diameter and height. The *catillus* had a central hole to receive the central pivot. The *meta* was perforated right through to receive the handle used to turn it. M. Dembinska, who has studied the development of these devices in Poland, estimates that the yield was three times better (1kg (2.2lb) of flour in half-an-hour) with a semi-rotary quern and nine times better (1kg (2.2lb) in 10 minutes) with a rotary quern.

Some rotary querns were not used with complete rotation but with a reciprocal motion, like those from Gellérthegy, Budapest, in the La Tène period (Fig. 75), where they were located up against the wall and so could not be used with a full circular motion. In this semi-rotary mode two handles were fitted to the *meta* with the aid of a leather strip or something similar.

The intensive and probably daily use of these querns made it necessary for them to be replaced periodically. There was a gradual shift from domestic production using local materials in the Bronze Age to quasi-industrial production involving trade over 100km (60 miles) from the manufacturing site.

Cooking pits

Heating structures outside houses provide evidence for various methods of cooking as well as craft activities. Cooking pits include round, oval, and rectangular holes of varying depths. Their fillings consist of charcoal, ashes and burnt stones. The walls show signs of heating. At some sites in Germany and Denmark they are found in dozens or even hundreds, as at Late Bronze Age Zedau in the Altmark or Raga Hörstad in Skåne. They are less common in the rest of Europe. At Coulon (Poitou), for example, fifteen cylindrical pits 1m (3¼ft) in diameter and 5–40cm (2–16in) deep had been dug into the limestone. Large stones set at the bases of some of these pits seem to have acted as supports. In the absence of products cooked in them, it is difficult, if not impossible, to identify the exact function of these pits.

Other pits exhibit recurrent characteristics that are definite enough for modern comparisons to be found for them. These are shallower, rectangular and filled with a layer of charcoal and ashes covered with a layer of burnt stones. They are generally called 'Polynesian ovens', although their distribution is worldwide, and

are used to cook vegetables and meat wrapped up in leaves by sweating or steaming. An intense fire is kindled in the bottom of the pit and stones are put into it and brought up to red heat. Then, the larger embers having been removed, the food is added, in between layers of leaves, and the whole is covered with earth. Cooking takes about two hours. D. Ramseyer has identified structures of this kind at Jeuss in Fribourg Canton and had dated them to the Hallstatt period. At Late Bronze Age Berlin-Lichterfelde two pits 70cm (28in) in diameter and 50cm (20in) deep must have been used for the same purpose. Their walls were lined with blocks of feldspar mortared with clay and covered with a clay coating which showed evidence of having been fired to high temperatures.

The British Isles have produced examples of groups of more complex cooking pits which combined cooking with boiling water, roasting and steaming. The survival of this type of cooking area until the medieval period and references to them in the Irish epics facilitate their archaeological interpretation. Three types of structure are associated at sites located in marshy areas or close to water: a rectangular reservoir of planks or stone slabs is set into a pit and kept filled with water, supplied either by the water-table or a nearby source of water. Near one of its ends is a hearth on which stones are heated to be thrown into the water to bring it to boiling point. Heated stones are also put into another pit used for braising or

75

Plan and reconstruction of the elevation of the La Tène house from Budapest-Gellérthegy (Hungary). The internal layout includes an oven, a pit used for craft activities, and two querns placed up against the wall. (L. Vargha, in E. Petres, 1976.)

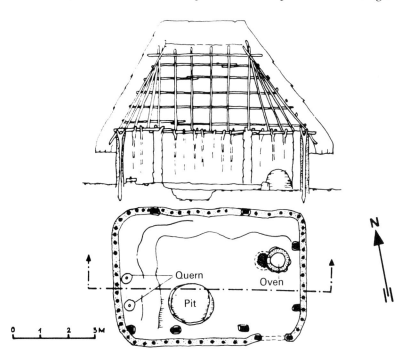

Quern

Oven

Pit

0 1 2 3M

N

steaming. These heated stones are thrown on heaps near the pits which can be as large as several cubic metres. Several dozen sites of this kind are known from Ireland, western England and the northern isles of Scotland. They can easily be recognized by their heaps of burnt stones.

The Irish *Fullacht Fiadh* are seasonal (summer or autumn) camps, the name of which is associated linguistically with deer hunters. A late text, the *Forus Feasa as Eirinn*, describes how the hunters sent their assistants halfway through the day to dig two pits, one for roasting and the other for boiling the game killed during the day. They built intense fires in which stones were heated up before being put in the two pits. The selected site was usually a hill where there was plenty of wood and a nearby marsh. The pits discovered at Ballyvourney or Kilnee correspond exactly with these descriptions. At Ballyvourney I a pit lined with stakes and filled with water was flanked by two hearths in a semi-circle (Fig. 76). There was also a stone-lined pit for steaming and an oval hut in which the stakes in the interior probably corresponded with

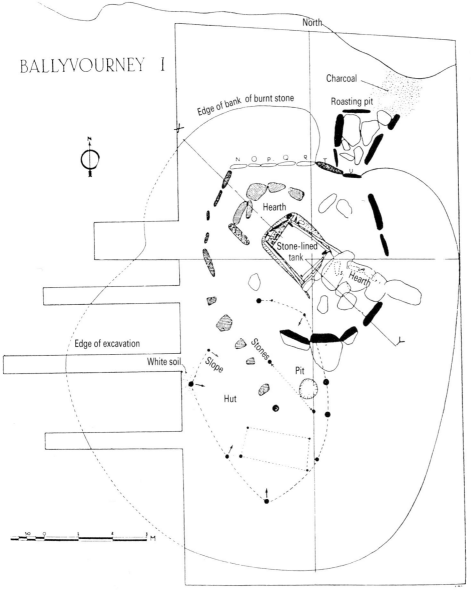

76
Fullacht Fiadh, Ballyvourney, Co. Cork (Bronze Age). In this temporary site two hearths served the central sunken pit and the roasting pit to the north. Burnt stones were thrown on the surrounding heap. To the south stakes indicate the site of a hut. (M.J. O'Kelly, 1954.)

racks on which the deer carcasses would have been suspended. The whole site is surrounded by a pile of burnt stones measuring 27 cubic m (953 cubic ft). In northern Scotland these cooking areas are often associated with more permanent structures and the amount of burnt stones can be as much as several tons, as at Liddle Farm I (Orkney).

This tradition began in the second millennium BC and lasted throughout the following two thousand years. These sites hark back to culinary practices which not only recall the origins of Irish stew but also a special type of social organization in which groups of hunters roamed over the Irish countryside living on the results of hunting and gathering over a season.

Culinary activities

Information about cooking in protohistory remains very fragmentary, gleaned from chance discoveries. It has always been believed that ground cereal was used solely for making flat unleavened bread and porridge. A recent discovery, however, has shown that leavened bread existed as early as the Late Neolithic. At Douanne on Lake Bienne a carbonized loaf has been discovered made of fine wheat flour, along with a fragment of a barley loaf. A caramelized deposit at the bottom of a vessel from the Planches cave may have come from the fermentation of beer which was abandoned when fire destroyed the house. Stocks of acorns in Scandinavian and English houses or that in the granary at Pègue (Drôme) do not all seem to have been connected with animal feed. Roasting followed by careful grinding is necessary to make the resulting flour edible.

Cooking pits and ovens show that boiled and roast meat was also eaten, wild animals being gradually replaced by domesticated animals. In certain places dog also found a place on the menu, as at Bronze Age Bovenkarspel (Netherlands) or La Tène Villeneuve-Saint-Germain (Aisne), where the skin was also tanned. The ages at which domestic animals were slaughtered can be used as evidence for the increased importance of milk as a foodstuff during the Bronze and Iron Ages. Fish formed an important dietary complement, and occasionally frogs. The study of plant macro-remains provides information about the plants, berries and fruits that were eaten – cereals, peas, vetches, apples, blackberries, raspberries, strawberries and nuts in particular. There were also plants that are nowadays not considered to be edible such as fat hen. Aromatic herbs were also being used.

The only method of preserving that has been proved archaeologically to have been in use was drying, since dried half-apples have been recovered from lake villages. However, smoking was also used, whilst salting, reported as being used by the Gauls, must have spread from the Hallstatt period onwards, or even the Late Bronze Age, when there is evidence for salt pans and mines being developed.

Caves as alternative settlements

The existence of Bronze and Iron Age occupation levels in caves has never ceased to intrigue archaeologists. Why live in this damp, dark environment when there were opportunities to live in the open air? The work of P. Pétrequin and his colleagues in Franche-Comté has now supplied some answers to this question. Caves often served as refuges for short-term occupation during troubled times. In so far as they can be subjected to detailed analysis, these archaeological deposits, sometimes over 1m (3¼ft) thick, can be broken down into a succession of short occupations. Thus, the Grotte des Planches at Arbois (Jura) served as a refuge settlement at least seven times in a century in the Late Bronze Age. Groups of six to fifty people sheltered there for some weeks or months and tried to recreate their domestic space in a temporary fashion. The most important occupation (corresponding with layer D2) comprised seven hearths divided into two groups, each having a granary and an area for storing cereals in baskets or storage vessels and sharing a common stock enclosure (see Fig. 97). Small storage pits contained what may be considered to be the basic domestic equipment for each hearth (in both the figurative and the literal senses) – spindle whorls, potters' burnishers, small personal ornaments, shells or pyrites blocks. Other caves have produced evidence of temporary occupation protected by walls or palisades, such as that at La Baume de Gonvillars, or the shelter at the Source du Dard at Baume-les-Messieurs. P. Pétrequin has recently shown that caves were used in periods of instability when villages were changing their locations. In eastern France, and probably elsewhere, this type of settlement represented a means of finding a replacement for undefended settlements comparable with lake villages or hillforts. This phenomenon is attested in Britain, Belgium and Italy. In France many caves have levels stretching back from the Middle Ages to the Iron Age or the Bronze Age, as at the Grotte de Saint-Roman (Côte-d'Or). They are especially numerous in southern France, and a number are located deep underground, as in the Grotte de Labeil at Lauroux (Hérault) or the Grotte du Hasard at Tharaux (Gard).

8 Activity areas and social spaces

Storage pits and buildings

Harvesting of regular seasonal resources led the peasants to organize the means of storage so as to be able to spread the use of the crops over a longer period, whether these were wild or domesticated plants. Thus there are numerous storage places in settlements, varying in shape and size according to the method of conservation and the intended use of these reserves – above-ground, ventilated storage or restricted, below-ground storage for cereals and leguminous plants; smaller short-term storage for family use or enormous long-term storage for the whole community. Many arrangements were in use, reflecting both technological constraints and social organization. They range from large buildings to multiple vessels in pottery, basketry, wood or even fabric.

Buildings and below-ground structures for food storage are among the earliest ancillary constructions to appear within rural settlement. Pits are first found in the Upper Palaeolithic; they increased in number during the Neolithic and are to be found in their hundreds on protohistoric sites. Some sparse references by classical authors mention buildings used specially for storage. Diodorus (5, 21.5), for example, writes of buildings to contain harvests. Strabo (4; 5,5) reports what Pytheas has to say, in a rare example of confidence in the latter, about the mysterious island of Thule situated to the north of Britain: 'They thresh corn in large buildings, after having brought the ears there, because the sky is never without clouds and the lack of sun and the rain make it impossible to use outdoor spaces.'

Internal arrangements

Barns and granaries can be distinguished from houses by differences in layout, such as the absence of floors and hearths in the former or strengthening of the posts in the latter in order to support the weight of the grain. The best proof is still provided, however, by cases where a building has been destroyed by fire, carbonizing the grain *in situ*.

In the Jura at Clairvaux, in the Early Bronze Age as well as the preceding period, space in this village built on piles is limited and so food was stored inside each house using pots and baskets. In Early Bronze Age Toszég (Hungary) grain was stored in large pots or in horseshoe-shaped structures inside the houses, but there may have been a communal store in the handful of structures without hearths or clay-sealed floors.

A little later, at the end of the second millennium BC, the two *Blockbau* houses at Zug-Sumpf (eastern Switzerland) are considered by P. Pétrequin to have been granaries because they measure no more than 2 by 2.5m (6½ by 8ft) (see Fig. 33). His interpretation is based on the presence of many carbonized grains and fruits in the occupation layer. He linked the introduction of specialized storage buildings with developments in agriculture and the long life of the village. One or two centuries later, however, the village of Auvernier seems not to have included barns; nevertheless, the existence of timbers that did not belong to the roofs has led B. Arnold to assume the existence of grain lofts in all the buildings.

In a few rare cases a granary can be identified from the presence of storage jars. At the Hallstatt settlement at Pègue (Drôme), for example, a 4 by 8m (13 by 26ft) structure post-built on stone foundations contained a very large number of receptacles constructed of cob; these were set on stone flags or raised areas (Fig. 77). They contained acorns, stocked separately, a little barley and wheat (compact wheat and emmer wheat plus a little einkorn).

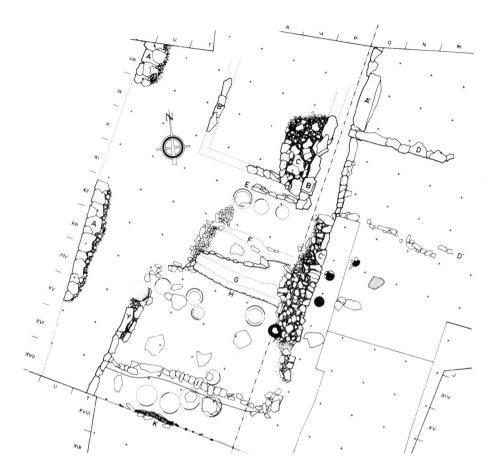

77

*Granary from the
Hallstatt (late sixth
century BC) level of the
oppidum of Saint-
Marcel-du Pègue
(Drôme). The walls, set
on stakes or set on
stone foundations,
enclosed three stepped
levels where jars and
cob receptacles which
contained grain and
acorns were stored.
Excavated by J.-J.
Hatt, C. Lagrand, and
A. Perraud. (C.
Lagrand and J.-P.
Thalmann, 1973.)*

Raised granaries

Raised granaries can easily be recognized in a village from the square or rectangular layout of their four, six or nine posts. The close-set, substantial posts are seen as having supported a raised floor capable of bearing heavy loads.

Among the house-urns found in tombs in eastern Germany and Poland, those from Obliwitz and Woedkte are examples of structures with clearly defined floors, raised on four posts in the case of the former and six in the latter. This type of structure is still to be seen in Spain and Scandinavia, where it is used for storing crops. There are clearly marked circular mouldings on the supports of the Obliwitz urn: these correspond exactly with the disks, flat stones or sometimes old millstones set on top of the posts of Spanish granaries to prevent the access of rodents (see Fig. 44).

The simplest form is the four-post structure, with side lengths of 2–3m ($6\frac{1}{2}$–10ft) in most cases, although this may reach 5m (16ft), as at Manching (Bavaria) or in Britain (see Fig. 30). The most typical form consists of nine posts arranged in three rows in order to distribute the weight evenly; they vary in size between 2 and 6m ($6\frac{1}{2}$ and 20ft) square. There are intermediate forms with six or eight posts, and also larger granaries built on twelve or sixteen posts. The largest structure of this type is that from Ézinge, which consists of 34 posts and covers 120 sq.m (1292 sq.ft): it is not out of the question that these supported a single platform.

The village of Feddersen Wierde (Lower Saxony) produced an exceptionally well preserved granary: this was a nine-post structure surrounded by a wicker fence with a gate facing that of the byre-house enclosure. This layout suggests frequent comings and goings between the two buildings. In the *Wurten* (terp settlements) of northern Germany each granary is paired with a house. At single-unit farms in Britain, such as Tollard Royal (Wiltshire), the enclosure contains one or two granaries alongside the house itself. An entire area located away from the houses is reserved on larger settlements such as Moel-y-Gaer or Danebury for groups of small square structures: this layout emphasizes the different functions of these two types of building (Fig. 78).

Granaries with different plans can exist side by side on the same site. They are relatively few in number on Bronze Age sites, but they became characteristic features of Iron Age settlements. The considerable technological constraints, related to the weight of grain involved and the need to preserve it in a well ventilated place, resulted in raised granaries being remarkably stable in form over the centuries. This type of structure is a recurrent element in settlements over the second and first millennia BC.

Barns

Barns, which are structures that are larger than granaries and are used for more than one purpose, can sometimes be distinguished by virtue of their architectural characteristics. In Scandinavia a distinctive series of rectangular structures appears some distance from farms or villages. The central row of posts is aligned slightly obliquely to the side rows and there is no floor or hearth inside. The filling of the post-holes is sandy and less rich in organic materials than that of the contemporaneous houses, as if they had been erected on virgin soil unaffected by man or beast. Becker suggests the function of these structures may be related to those built for storing crops in the historical period during deforestation. At Grøntoft (Jutland) they may slightly antedate the Early Iron Age farms.

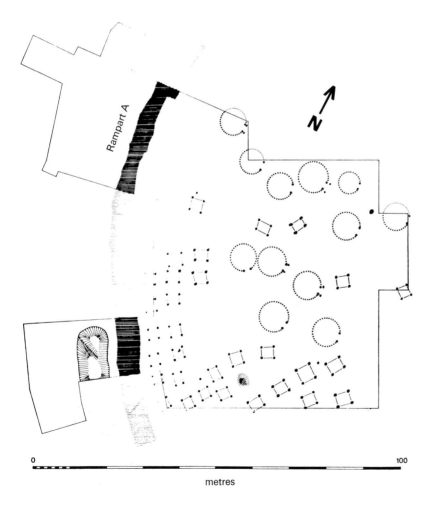

78
Late-seventh-century BC hillfort of Moel-y-Gaer, Clwyd (Wales). The excavated part revealed an area of round-houses and an adjoining area of square granaries. (G. Guilbert, 1975.)

0   100

metres

A. Zippelius interprets three three-aisled structures from the village of Goldberg (Bavaria) as barns. They are some distance from the group of houses and may have served the entire community. We shall come back to this problem when considering village plans.

Storage pits

Storage pits can be distinguished from the innumerable pits found all over protohistoric settlements by their characteristic shape (Fig. 79). They are usually circular in plan and generally small, being only rarely more than 3m (10ft) in diameter. The depth is usually equal to or greater than the maximum diameter. The opening was originally smaller in diameter than the maximum diameter of the pit. These characteristics stem from the need to have as large a storage capacity as possible with the smallest possible opening, which usually seems to have been worked out so as to allow a man to get inside. A. Villes has observed that in Champagne in the La Tène period the average diameter of the aperture was 60–70cm (24–28in).

The principle of how these storage pits functioned has been confirmed experimentally by P.J. Reynolds, as well as by many ethnographic parallels: the threshed grain is tamped down and the pit is filled up to the top, the opening being sealed with a plug made of clay and straw. The oxygen in the pit affects the

79

Forms of storage pit. The most common are bell-shaped, cylindrical and truncated cones; after their mouths collapse erosion gives them a more open and wider profile. (O. Büchsenschütz.)

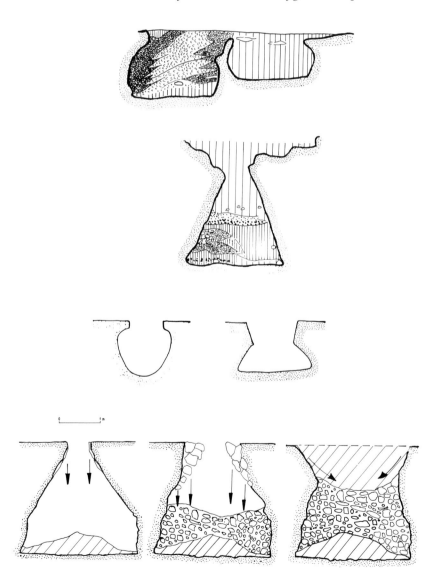

grain near the walls, but it is quickly used up and the atmosphere inside stabilizes. Grain can be preserved in this way for several years.

These pits are also distinguishable from quarry pits, which are shallower in limestone areas and generally appear as a series of contiguous scoops, the remains of working with picks. They have also been interpreted as rubbish pits: in many cases this is what they were used for after they ceased to be used for their original purpose. But why would anyone dig a pit right in the middle of a settlement, sometimes into hard rock, in order to put rubbish in it, when it would be easier to spread it around some distance from the village? It should also not be forgotten that the increase in the amount of rubbish is a very recent urban phenomenon: in the countryside until a short time ago practically all rubbish was used for feeding animals or for fertilizer, whilst broken objects were mended or converted to other uses where possible.

The discovery of carbonized grain at the bottom of these pits in some exceptional cases has provided direct evidence of their original function. Mention may be made of the pit from the valley of the Moulins at Cannes-Écluse (Yonne) or the undated examples from Saint-Christophe-en-Bazelles (Indre). At Little Woodbury (Hampshire) G. Bersu identified three types of pit which may have been used for storing grain: cylindrical pits, bell-shaped pits and globular pits. All the pits at Danebury (Hampshire) were cylindrical, probably because of the nature of the rock there, an especially hard chalk. Pits in the form of truncated cones, carboys or barrels have been reported from Champagne. More than one type may be found on the same site, as at Suippes (Marne).

The archaeological record has provided no evidence about the plugs used to seal these pits or the covers that may have been placed over them in certain instances. These no doubt consisted of a light roof supported on stakes, the traces of which have been lost through subsequent ploughing. Ethnographic studies have shown that the choice of a pit for storing grain may correspond with a desire to conceal harvests. In such cases there will be no superstructure visible at ground level. Algeria in the nineteenth century provides a good example of this practice: when Bugeaud's columns realized that by finding their grain stores they could have villages at their mercy, the plugs using for sealing pits were made thicker so that a French bayonet could not penetrate them.

Settlement plans show that storage pits only rarely occurred inside houses. In the village of Radesovice (Bohemia) they were separated from one another, as if each house had its own. They were all grouped together, almost in the centre of the enclosure, at Little Woodbury (Hampshire): G. Bersu was able to show that the inhabitants had about six in use at a time. Excavations extending to 3ha (7½ acres) of the fortified settlement of Danebury in the same region have produced 860 pits: extrapolation gives a figure of 5000 for the whole site. They are grouped together, some distance from the houses.

Like other structures for storage, pits are not typical of a single period or region. They are a frequent, but not universal, feature of settlement sites in those areas where the subsoil permits this type of storage and when the technique becomes known to the local inhabitants. They are not found in the marshy areas on the north coast of Europe. In the British Isles they are only found in the sedimentary regions of the south-east. V. Kruta has observed that in northern Bohemia they are common in the Late Bronze Age and Early Hallstatt period, numerous and large in size at the end of the Hallstatt period and in the Early La Tène period, and that they decrease in number in the centuries that follow. It is known, moreover, that storage pits existed in historic times in certain micro-regions or villages and were commented upon by neighbouring peoples or visitors as curiosities. In the nineteenth century engineers tried without success to make large storage pits based on the same principle of controlled atmosphere.

Open-air storage

In Armorica, where archaeologists have recorded many underground refuges or souterrains, it is not impossible that part of the harvest may have been placed in these artificial caves dug into the rock. They appear as small chambers linked together by passages and with several entrances. A good many of them are dated to the Iron Age.

This is a different form of storage, since the grain is taken out as and when it is needed. This is probably the same practice as that used in the deep open pits in Champagne that A. Villes calls 'cellars', the contents of which are protected by a covering that has generally left no traces. At the fortified settlement at Sainte-Geneviève at Essey-lès-Nancy, a pit with flat bottom and vertical walls proved on excavation to contain a layer of grain in which the shapes of the posts that supported the roof but which were not set into the subsoil were still discernible.

Feddersen Wierde (Lower Saxony) produced structures that were 1m (3¼ft) wide by 1.50m (5ft) long and 60cm (24in) deep with sloping walls kept in place with interlaced sticks. One of these contained hazelnuts that had been deposited in sacks. The fortified settlement of the Pierre d'Appel at Saint-Dié (Vosges), where wood is relatively well preserved, produced other types of receptacle: rectangular pits, dug into the sand and first edged with stones and then lined with fir planks nailed together, contained grain, querns and nutshells. These spectacular examples remind us that evidence from excavations is always only partial, since almost all structures in organic materials will have disappeared.

Basket containers have been found on sites in wet environments and in burnt layers. Baskets abound on the sites at Zürich, Neuchâtel and Clairvaux. The Grotte des Planches in the Jura has yielded new information thanks to the exceptional state of preservation of the structures and to very careful excavation. Layer D1, dated by P. Pétrequin to the late second millennium BC, contained two series of carbonized timbers and small posts arranged around postholes aligned over lengths of 4 and 5m (13 and 16ft) respectively. The excavators reconstructed two granaries with narrow bases and on sloping sides supported by piles. The grain was no doubt stored there in pots and baskets. Large storage jars were found all around. The floor was littered with carbonized grain which had been scattered around during flooding. It should be noted that, in general, excavations produce no more than a few hundred grammes of grain after very long sieving operations.

Dolia, large globular jars made of clay or cob, or wooden chests were also used for storage. At Ensérune (Hérault), *dolia* replaced storage pits inside individual houses in the fourth century BC, although pits continued to be used on a terrace at the eastern edge of the village. J. Waldhauser has shown the correlation between the distributions of *dolia* fragments and small pits covered with light roofs in a village in northern Bohemia. However, although pits co-existed with structures of this kind, the nature of the foodstuffs that they contained remains difficult to establish.

Enclosures, byres, and stock pens

Enclosures

Animal husbandry brought with it very early on the need to control the movements of the animals to ensure that they were fed, that they could be selected for slaughter, that the females could be milked and, above all, that they were prevented from straying on to the cultivated lands. Enclosures thus appear as early as the Danubian Neolithic period and increased over the whole of Europe in the succeeding centuries. These were formed by means of fencing, ditches or stone walls, according to the region or the resources available. Fenced enclosures were directly associated with settlements. They were built next to individual houses or surround the entire settlement. In the latter case they were intended as much for keeping livestock in as for defending the village.

The same applied in the case of ditched enclosures. The bank and ditch at Biskupin, dating from the Early Bronze Age, is considered to have been an animal enclosure which would have held up to 500 beasts. In

80

Fengate, Peterborough (Bronze Age). Fields and meadows are delineated by double ditches broken by narrow gateways. They are reached by sunken tracks which separate two rows of fields. a: Overall plan of the modern field system and that in protohistory (thicker lines); b: protohistoric fields. (F.M.M. Pryor, 1976.)

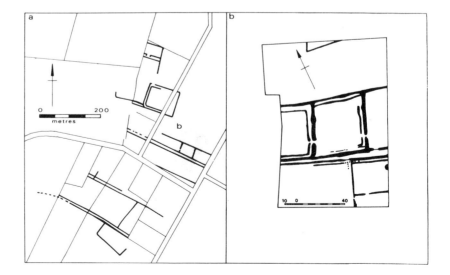

certain favourable circumstances it is possible distinguish pasture from arable: at Fengate in eastern England a field system originating in the late Neolithic period spread over an area of a 100ha (250 acres) during the second millennium BC (Fig. 80).

In south-western England and northern Scotland houses were often set in plots delineated by drystone walls. It is assumed that some of these enclosures alongside houses were used sometimes as gardens and sometimes as stock pens. On Dartmoor the field systems were sited on the lower slopes of hills and ran together so as to enclose the hilltops, which were used as communal pasture for each settlement.

Some exceptional finds have revealed structures which leave such faint traces that they generally escape notice. At the Grotte des Planches in the Jura the communal stock enclosure in layer D2 was made using two rows of stakes, 8m (26ft) wide and some 10m (33ft) long (see Fig. 97). These stakes supported fencing panels made of perishable material which were sufficiently solid to prevent the rubbish that was strewn all around from getting inside the enclosure. The soil is blacker and richer within this enclosure than elsewhere and seems to have been trampled down. This enclosure must have been used for medium-sized animals (pigs or sheep) rather than cattle, in view of the difficult access to the cave.

Byres

The great innovation of the protohistoric period was the development of the penning of animals and the creation, over the whole of northern Europe, of a new type of structure which joined the byre to the house proper. Elsewhere byres remained separate buildings. The presence of thick layers of dung near the houses at Tószeg (Hungary) shows that there must have been byres there, but the traces of their light construction were not found by the archaeologists.

Cattle seem not to have been kept in the lake villages. P. Pétrequin has shown that at Clairvaux during the Neolithic and Early Bronze Age the presence of some excrement, in very small quantities, suggests that small animals (goats, pigs and sheep) were present on the site periodically but not cattle. The absence of hearths in some of the houses in the first village at Buchau (Bavaria) and the existence of separate buildings, distinct from the U-plan houses of the second village, argue in favour of the existence of byres (see Fig. 62).

Having at one time considered all the round-houses in the British Isles to be dwellings, British archaeologists are now modifying their views and are seeking to identify ancillary buildings through differences in the diameters and contents of these buildings and in the organization of the immediate surroundings. At Black Patch (Sussex), dated to the mid second millennium BC, P.L. Drewett has suggested that the fifth hut in a hamlet of houses aligned in a row may have been used for housing young animals, since it contained virtually no furnishings and was surrounded by a fence which separated it from its neighbours. Deverel-Rimbury settlements of the second millennium BC in the Cranborne Chase area of southern England, for example, often contain round-houses in pairs, the smaller of which must have been an ancillary building. Recent excavations are beginning to produce remains of light rectangular structures that are distinct from dwellings, as at Shaugh Moor (Devon), where they were no more than 3m (10ft) wide. The British Isles are different from other parts of Europe by virtue of the large number of enclosures there, which testify to the preference for keeping animals outside.

It is, however, possible to recognize byres inside certain houses. Some of the rooms in the stone houses of Shetland and Orkney are considered to be byres because of the highly organic black soils that they contain. They are sometimes flagged, with a drain. The ring made from a whale vertebra fixed into the wall of house II at Jarlshof may have been used for the tying up of an animal.

Byre-houses

The most important innovation in the Bronze Age was the introduction of a new type of building: the byre-house, which contained a dwelling and a byre under the same roof. It appeared at the beginning of the second millennium BC in the Low Countries, and then shortly afterwards in northern Germany and the whole of southern Scandinavia. It continued in use throughout protohistory and survived until the nineteenth century in Friesland.

H.T. Waterbolk, who has devoted many studies to byre-houses, considers that the following traits are indications which directly or indirectly demonstrate their existence, when the features noted appear in one part of a building only: the presence of plank or wattle cross-partitions which form a line of single or double boxes, additional uprights set along the rows of internal load-bearing posts; a channel or gutter on the longitudinal axis of the building; a flagged or timber floor; supplementary posts spaced regularly along the side walls; longitudinal partitions starting from one of the shorter walls or from an internal cross-wall; closer

81
Three-aisled byre-houses in the Netherlands (1–5), and Scandinavia (6). 1 and 2: Emmerhout, Drenthe (Bronze Age); 3: Elp, Drenthe (Bronze Age); 4: Hijken, Drenthe (Hallstatt period); 5: Ezinge, Drenthe (La Tène period); 6: Hovergård, Jutland. (H.T. Waterbolk, 1975; C.J. Becker, 1982.)

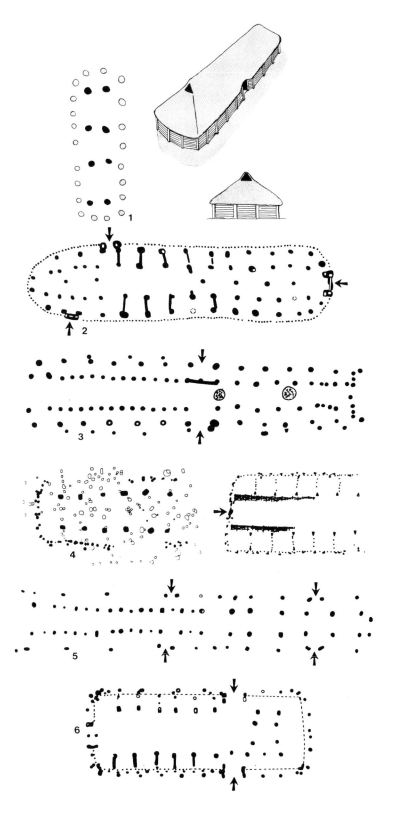

and more regular spacing of the load-bearing posts; or finally a door on one of the short sides (Fig. 81). These arrangements are intended to provide stabling for cattle in stalls, removal and recovery of liquid manure, and separation between man and beasts. It should also be noted that there are no hearths or small finds of domestic character of any kind in the byre section and that the floor, when it survives, is rich in dung. In the Low Countries the byre is located in the eastern section of the building.

Although partitions to form stalls are rare in the Bronze Age, the division of the structure into two or three sections and changes in the spacing between load-bearing posts is already clearly discernible. The stalls were more distinctly marked in the Iron Age and entrances opposite one another in the centre of the two long sides became very common. The characteristics described above did not appear in Scandinavia before the Iron Age, with one exception, Hovergård (Jutland). There was a general trend towards shortening these buildings and at the same time making them wider. The 40, 60, and even 80m (130, 195 and 260ft) long byre-houses disappeared at the end of the Bronze Age and were replaced by buildings 10–20m (33–66ft) long.

The byre-houses in Holland were built to accommodate a large number of animals – 20–30 in the largest building at Emmerhout and those at Elp, and even 30–40 head in the largest, which was 40m (130ft) long. The numbers were always smaller in Scandinavia, where the longest buildings would have housed 10–20 cattle and the smaller 4–10.

The size of stalls varied over time, and became smaller. This gradual change accords with the observations of zoologists, who have noted a substantial decrease in the size of cattle during the Bronze and Iron Ages. It is not yet known whether this decrease in size, which has been observed all over Europe, was due to the stock rearing conditions, to deterioration in pastures or to a more general evolutionary phenomenon, since wild animals were also affected. The rearing of smaller animals, such as pigs, goats and sheep, has not left such visible traces in the archaeological record, but the bones found in occupation layers show how important they were – 15–27 per cent at Bovenkarspel, for example. They may have been housed in some buildings which have single or double internal partitions but no stalls.

Byre-houses afford the best proof available to us at the present time of continuity in rural life between the protohistoric period and the present day. Although the medieval Saxon farms to which they are related seem to derive in fact from monastic barns, they testify equally to the persistence of a certain style of rural settlement from the Bronze Age to the present. This type of building did not become established in the rest of Europe, the Hallstatt house at Befort (Luxembourg) being at present its most southerly manifestation. Byre-houses testify to the establishment of an arable-pastoral economy in which the penning of stock played an important role, whether on a seasonal basis or otherwise. It necessitated the storage of large amounts of animal fodder and consequently increased granary space.

Craft installations/workshops

The range of activities conducted in villages was considerably extended during the Bronze and Iron Ages. Before the Bronze Age, the economy was essentially agriculturally-based and locally-focused. By the end of the Iron Age the situation had become much more complex. An increase in trade, greater division of work and social stratification are all apparent. Greek and Latin writers mention the presence among the Celts of craftsmen whose workshops and highly-specialized products are found in the *oppida*. Certain activities, such as weaving and pottery, which had hitherto been domestic, became autonomous and special installations were provided for them. These annexes to settlements were organized according to the demands of technology and are often characterized by structures that are smaller and less carefully built than domestic units.

Outside the wetter regions, sunken-floored ancillary structures become more common. There may have been a diffusion of this type of structure from east to west, since they are known from the Neolithic in eastern Europe. They provide good heat insulation in the continental climate against winter temperatures, whilst in the Atlantic climate they ensure an appropriate level of humidity for activities such as weaving. A. Zippelius relates their eventual disappearance to the appearance of stoves in the medieval period.

They are common in Germany, particularly in the south-west in the vicinity of the Rhine. They are never more than 5m (16ft) long. Sometimes the supports for the roof are indicated by two post-holes in the main axis of the rectangular plan or by a combination of four or six post-holes. B. Stjernquist has recognized the same type of structure in Scandinavia, always close to post-built houses. They increase in number with the transition from the Iron Age to the Roman period.

In France it is relatively easy to distinguish shallow

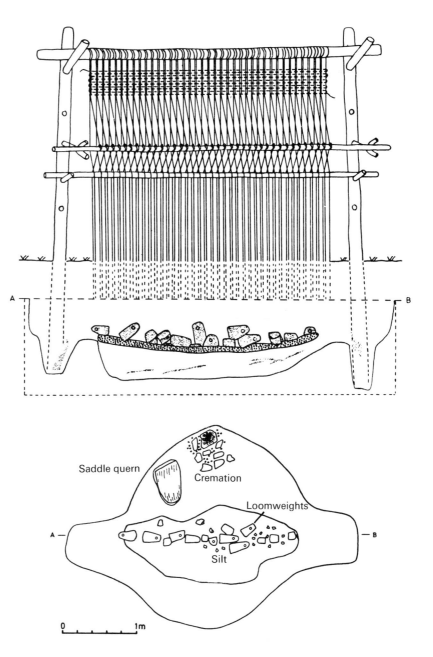

82
Late Bronze Age weaving hollow at Wallwitz, Kr. Burg (Lower Saxony). The loomweights found lying in a line in a pit between two post-holes permit the reconstruction of a vertical loom set into the pit. The cremation and the quern are more recent. (H. Stalhofen, 1978.)

Saddle quern

Cremation

Loomweights

Silt

A — B

0 _____ 1m

rectangular pits from those deeper pits which Alain Villes calls cellars and which relate to storage. On some dozen sites these are associated with post-built structures. Their surface area is never more than 10 sq.m (108 sq.ft). Only rarely were their roofs supported on posts. They became common during the second Iron Age (the La Tène period).

During the La Tène period in Czechoslovakia, southern Poland, and Hungary the most common type of structure was rectangular, measuring 4–5m (13–16ft) long by 2.5–3.3m (8–11ft) wide. The depth in relation to present ground level varies between 40 and 90cm (16 and 36in). Two posts, sometimes more, were located on the main axis, near to or actually set into, the shorter walls. They probably supported a double-pitched roof. Structures of the same type found in France for the most part do not have post-holes sunk into the sub-soil. At Villeneuve-Saint-Germain (Aisne)

135

traces of the supports for the roof are visible in the filling of a La Tène structure.

Weaving workshops

The archaeological evidence for weaving activities is usually no more than the presence of spindle whorls. These are cylindrical or biconvex rings of baked clay with a central hole which acted as inertia flywheels for the spindles. Stone or baked clay loomweights, and occasionally weaving-combs, are also found. Their presence in most reports of excavations of protohistoric settlements illustrates the important role of weaving in everyday life.

83
1: Iron Age rock engraving from Val Camonica (Adige). It represents a vertical weaving loom with three shed-rods and loomweights. (O. Büchsenschütz after E. Anati.)
2: Decoration of the situla from Sopron (Hungary). On the left a woman wearing a dress is working at a vertical loom set up in a pit. (S. Gallus, 1934.)

1

The traces left by looms are similar all over Europe. Bronze Age settlements produce series of grouped loomweights, sometimes ranged along the walls of houses, as at Black Patch (Sussex) or Dean Moor (Devon). In some better preserved sites these are associated with a pair of post-holes less than 1m (3¼ft) apart, in which the uprights of the loom were set. This was the case at Trevisker (Cornwall), where the pairs of post-holes were 60–90cm (24–35in) apart. The loom was sometimes set in a pit: at Cock Hill (Sussex), ten loomweights were found in a row at the bottom of a pit inside a building of the second half of the second millennium BC. At Late Bronze Age Wallwitz (Saxony) the loom was installed in an external pit flanked by two post-holes, between which 27 loomweights were aligned (Fig. 82).

The use of hollows for weaving became increasingly common in the Iron Age. This custom survived into the Roman period and the Middle Ages owing to the humidity in these pits, which made the textiles easier to work. An Iron Age settlement at Dalem at the mouth of the Elbe contained a ditch measuring 3 by 4m by 50cm (10 by 13ft by 20in) deep which must have been covered by a double-pitched roof. Two parallel rows of loomweights some distance apart suggest that the loom may have been inclined.

The vertical loom of the type corresponding to these installations is now well known. It appears on rock carvings in Val Camonica, consisting of two wooden uprights joined by a horizontal beam at the top, from which the warp threads were suspended (Fig. 83.1). Three shed-rods are shown, along with a row of

2

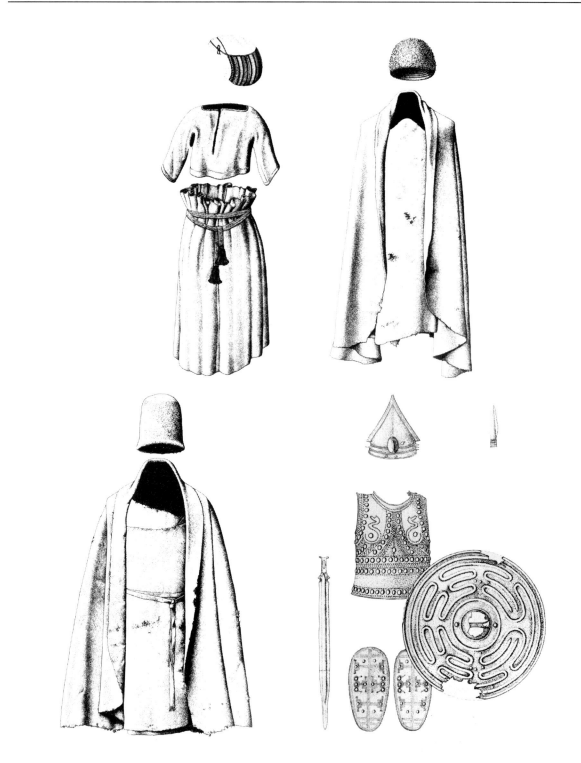

84
Costume. Clothing, which is rarely preserved, is characterized by the amount and quality of the stitching involved to adjust the material to fit the body. Armour was reserved for a few warriors. (H. Müller-Karpe, 1980; P. Schauer, 1975.)

loomweights. From a slightly later period, the loom depicted on the Hallstatt situla from Sopron (Hungary) was set up over a pit; it had several shed-rods (Fig. 83.2). Looms of this type are often set up in pits so as to increase the length of the cloth produced, since this is determined by the height of the loom. They were in use over the whole of protohistoric Europe and remained in use for a long time in northern Europe and Iceland. Their use made it possible to produce high-quality cloth in plain weave. From the Iron Age onwards the use of four shed-rods made it possible to produce twill weave and its variants. The use of tablet-weaving for borders led to the production of garments that were very durable and allowed many decorative effects to be created. Tacitus talks of the luxurious ceremonial cloaks with striped borders the Germans had which were the envy of the Romans. Pliny also mentions that German women wove in cellars and that linen twills were among the most favoured cloths in Gaul. Scottish tartan designs may owe their distant origins to the fabrics of the Iron Age, since woollen cloth decorated with squares in several colours of a similar pattern have been found in Jutland.

Exceptional conditions have preserved clothing in certain Danish burials (Fig. 84). The men wore capes and tunics, the women sleeved, seamless blouses and long skirts. A short cord skirt and hairnets have also been found. The first trousers appeared later, along with long dresses worn like a *peplos*. However, since these were found in rich graves, often under burial mounds, it is possible that they were reserved to a small, privileged part of the population.

Although luxury fabrics spread among the elite classes, raw materials that took a long time to produce were not squandered. The tunic from Bernuthsfeld (eastern Frisia) was made up of no less than forty pieces. Vegetable and animal remains found on archaeological sites reveal the diversity of fibres used, for vegetable as well as animal fibres were employed. In addition, materials that seem somewhat inappropriate to modern eyes were used. Hair from deer or cows' tails was added to wool, and nettles or bark tow were mixed with flax or hemp when these were not available or in short supply.

Pottery kilns and production

Pottery occupied a dominant place in daily life from the time that it was invented in the Neolithic. The majority of the vessels used were pots of baked clay and they had to be replaced periodically. For this reason many settlements have produced remains related to pottery production. In the Bronze Age this was performed in a reducing atmosphere, as shown by the colour of the resulting pots, varying generally from brown to black, and it was carried out in kilns. Most of these kilns have disappeared since they had to be dismantled, at least partially, in order to remove the pots once fired.

The simplest kilns consisted of a single chamber in which the combustible material and the pots were placed simultaneously. The protohistoric kiln found at Le Cèdre (Andorra) was a portable one: unfortunately it has not been dated. It was in the form of a truncated cone, tapering from 90cm (35in) in diameter at the base to 85cm (33in) at the top; there was a 45cm (18in) opening at the top and another, reduced by a 20cm- (8in-) wide flange on the base. When in use it must have been set directly on the ground.

Kilns consisting of two chambers, one on top of the other and separated by a perforated floor, are usually only known from their hearths, set in pits, more rarely from the walls of the lower chamber, and almost never from the firing chamber itself, which was demolished when the kiln was unloaded, as was the case with the Late Bronze Age examples from Cronenbourg and Achenheim (Alsace).

The earliest kiln made up of detachable elements appeared in the Late Bronze Age. The Sévrier kiln owes its preservation to the fact that it was found 4m (13ft) below the surface of Lake Annecy on the site of the lakeside village of Crêt-de-Châtillon (Haute-Savoie). It comprised a heating chamber in two parts with an internal volume of 120 litres (32 gallons) and a lower element consisting of a floor plate with numerous perforations and edged with a cylindrical wall on which a cover in the form of a truncated cone with a central chimney could be located (Fig. 85.1). When it was operating, this furnace must have been placed over a pit in which the hearth was slightly set forward so as to ensure the best possible circulation of hot air. Four rings and a number of rolls, all in highly burnt clay, which would have been used as saggers for wedging the pots in the kiln, were found nearby. Fragments of perforated floor plates suggest that similar kilns were used on the sites edging the shore of the Lac du Bourget (Savoie). Similar fragments have recently been found in the Yonne and Provence (see Fig. 85.2).

A certain number of kilns from the Hallstatt period are known in which the pit is divided into a hearth section and an empty heating chamber, in which the hot air would circulate before passing into the kiln chamber proper through the perforated floor plate. This was the case, for example, at Besançon-Saint-Paul (Doubs).

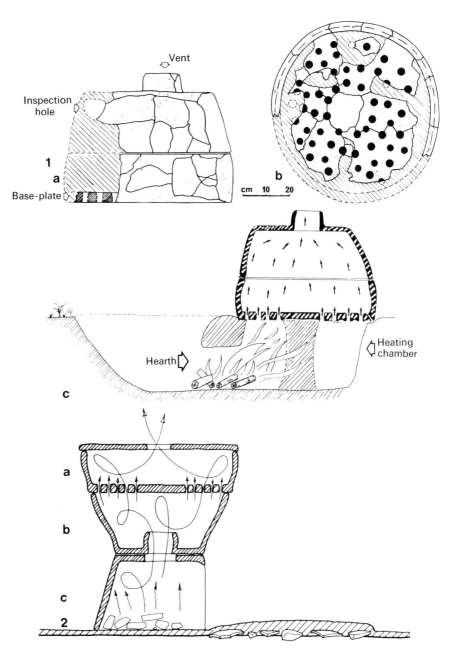

85

1: Late Bronze Age kiln from Sévrier (Haute-Savoie). The dismountable firing chamber (a), the base of which was perforated, was used on top of a pit which served both as a hearth and as a heating chamber (c).

2: Late fifth- early fourth-century kiln Martigues (Bouches-du-Rhône). The firing chamber (a) was set on a dismountable heating chamber (b) which in its turn rested on a portable hearth (c). (A. Bocquet and J.-P. Couren, 1975; catalogue of the Musée de Martigues, 1984.)

The kiln from the Hohlandsberg (Alsace) is much larger and belongs to another group, the horizontal-draught kiln. It was built of stone bonded with clay and set up against a small building. It consisted of a hearth 3m (10ft) long by 1.5m (5ft) wide ending in an apse and a perpendicular firing chamber 2m (6½ft) long. Clay support-rings and wasters were strewn all around the kiln. The kiln found in the middle of one of the hamlets of the Hohlandsberg (Linsenbrunnen II) belonged to the same horizontal-draught group, but it was made of clay on a wooden framework and was much smaller (2m (6½ft) long).

There are certain indications that production was still largely on a domestic scale in the Late Bronze Age. At Auvernier on Lake Neuchâtel pottery wasters were present in large quantities on the sites of four houses,

139

which shows that pots were being made within the village itself. At the Grotte des Planches pottery burnishers formed part of the domestic equipment and were hidden, along with spindle whorls, in the pit or the container associated with each of the seven hearths which contained domestic objects. The patterning of the finds here may indicate that the hearths are attributable to two family groupings: those set more deeply in the cave are characterized by a much more conservative taste in pottery styles than those located nearer its mouth, which can easily be explained in terms of family traditions.

The kiln from the Hohlandsberg of the same period testifies by contrast to collective production. More than 30,000 sherds representing at least 450 different vessels were found close to the kiln and in the associated lean-to shed. This was obviously a level of output that went beyond manufacture for simple domestic needs, or even perhaps for the village itself. In this respect the Bronze Age may be considered to mark the beginning of the process that led from domestic to craft production. In the Iron Age domestic and craft production continued side by side, but the latter began to predominate, particularly from the second century BC, when cheap mass-produced wheel-made pottery production spread.

Metal-producing installations

The production of metal artefacts in villages required both know-how and raw materials: ores or smelted metals and wood. The bronze smith in a village was involved at the same time in casting and forging metal, as shown by casting refuse and slags. There is, however, a very marked contrast between the thousands of manufactured objects found all over Europe and the modesty of remains of metalworking installations. All that were needed in fact, were a hearth, a crucible, an anvil and some moulds. Only the first of these was fixed: crucibles and anvils could be recovered after they had been used and either thrown away or used for other purposes, to such an extent that the only archaeological traces of metalworking activities are most often a hearth or a heating pit, and casting refuse, to which can be added moulds, broken crucibles and fragments of nozzles. There should be no illusions about the quantities of artefacts made by the bronze smiths: the several hundreds or even a thousand bronze objects found in certain lake settlements represent occupations lasting from a score to a hundred years, which reduces the average annual output to a much lower level. The stock of the bronze smith at Auvernier in the Late Bronze Age, for example, comprised 185 objects. In such circumstances this activity must most often have been sporadic or seasonal rather than continuous.

In Britain, Scandinavia and temperate Europe the many Bronze Age foundries thus seem to have been somewhat makeshift – one or two pits surrounded by casting refuse or slag on the outskirts of settlements. Certain examples are more explicit: at Les Rives, Saint-Germain-du-Plain (Burgundy), L. Bonnamour found a furnace used for melting down scrap bronze items: the rectangular pit measuring 3m (10ft) by 80cm (31in) by 40cm (16in) deep had heavily-burnt steep sides and a base lined with limestone. It was connected with a

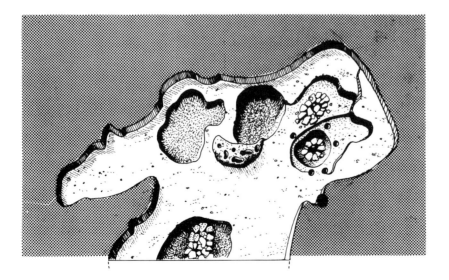

86
Middle Bronze Age metal workshop from Lovasberény, western Hungary. Here are visible hearths, a pit, possibly used for ore-roasting, and a bench with depressions that acted as crucibles. (T. Kovács, 1977.)

second, smaller pit used for ventilation. Several hundred fragments of melted bronze were recovered from the fill, along with two pieces of nozzle and lumps of clay from the superstructure of the furnace. The pit was surrounded by rows of stones set on edge, which might have formed the foundations of a chimney.

These installations were usually open to the sky. In such cases they were often located on the edges of settlements, as at Thwing (Yorkshire), a fortified Late Bronze Age site, where the open-hearth furnace pit was built up against the rampart. The metal furnaces were situated beyond the last house in the Hallstatt village of Choisy-au-Bac (Oise).

Roofed workshops were less common. The earliest known date from the Middle Bronze Age, the workshop at Lovasberény (Hungary), is the best preserved example (Fig. 86). It was situated in a rectangular shed with a sunken floor. It contained two hearths, hollows dug into the floor and lined with clay, and a clay bench set on a base of sherds with long, cylindrical, and hemispherical depressions in it used for bronze casting. Crucibles and a mould for belt fasteners were found on the floor. It was constructed in the craft area of the twin enclosures at Lovasberény. At the Late Bronze Age hillfort of Rathgall (Ireland) the workshop,

although built inside a large post-built structure and containing several hundred moulds, was situated just outside the rampart.

The most significant remains of metalworking activities in quantitative terms, however, occurred on certain fortified sites, such as Spišský Štvrtok (Slovakia) or Fort-Harrouard (Eure-et-Loir). Several specialized workshops were installed in small sunkenfloored buildings on the latter site.

For the Bronze Age the most impressive metalworking installations come from Scandinavia, where the site of Hallunda, south of Stockholm, must certainly have been a regional production centre in the late second millennium and the first third of the first millennium BC. This is the oldest known example of batteries of furnaces: six out of twelve were situated in a building 18m (59ft) long at some distance from the houses.

Despite the advent of iron metallurgy, production conditions remained on a modest scale in the Hallstatt period. However, although the fifth- or fourth-century BC smith's workshop at Kestor (Devon) consisted of just one water-tank, one furnace, one reheating hearth and an anvil, it was housed in the largest building on the site and bears witness to the increasingly important place that metalworkers held

87

The Iron Age smith's house at Round Pound, Kestor (Dartmoor). It is divided into living and working areas, with a forging hearth, a smelting furnace and a drain to take water outside. (A. Fox, 1973.)

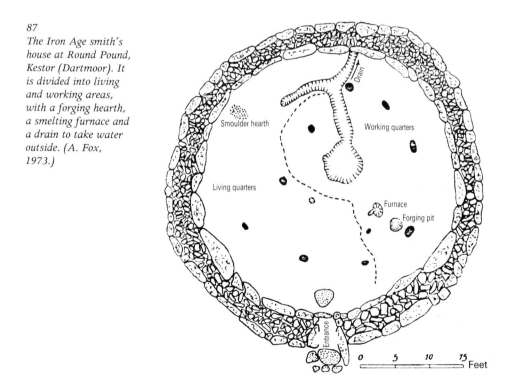

141

in this society (Fig. 87).

Gradually the production of bronze and iron increased over the whole of Europe. During the later centuries BC the large byre-houses of Scandinavia were often flanked by a small rectangular structure with or without internal posts in which large quantities of slag have been found (Hodde, Grønbjerg, Skole).

With the appearance of *oppida* in the second century BC metalworking installations developed considerably and began to constitute true craftsmen's quarters. The late-nineteenth-century excavations at Bibracte (Saône-et-Loire) revealed a group of workshops in the northern part of the enclosure, near one of the gates.

Throughout the whole protohistoric period metalworking activities were integrated into the everyday lives of both villages and larger communities. As F. Sigaut has observed, technological innovations in this field were not confined to precious objects or weapons for the privileged classes. Iron very rapidly came to be used as much for ploughshares, sickle blades, chisels, axes or hammers as for swords or spearheads. Its generalized use led to substantial increases in productivity in agriculture and crafts, which went on to have repercussions on the whole of socio-economic life.

The provision and management of water

Water was managed in two ways in settlements: it was stored in ponds, wells, springs and cisterns and it was removed by means of ditches, drains and soakaways. Wooden piles and earthen platforms raised buildings above the water level.

Water storage

From the Middle Bronze Age onwards a pond became a common element of settlements in the British Isles. Two of the five circular houses at Black Patch (Sussex) built on the same terrace were accompanied by a pond at the front of the courtyard. In the later centuries BC the raised village at Feddersen Wierde in northern Germany contained oval ponds which measured 2.50–10m (8–33ft) long.

Wells, which had been known since the Neolithic, multiplied during the Bronze and Iron Ages. When they were dug into the sedimentary rocks, like the well at Wilsford (Wiltshire), which was 30m (98ft) deep, or those at Levroux (Indre), dating from the La Tène period, they were unlined. Those which went

through less stable sediments needed wooden linings. These were generally tree trunks split in two, hollowed out, and then reassembled, so as to form a pipe. The Fontaines Salées Saint-Père-sous-Vézelay, which were highly regarded from the Iron Age onwards for the curative properties of their waters, belong to this group. Sometimes, as at Late Bronze Age Senftenberg in eastern Germany, this arrangement was strengthened with a casing of planks. In the Iron Age the casing of the well was made of wickerwork. Some of these wells were not very deep, sometimes less than 3m (10ft). They were fed as much by water filtering in from above and by ground-water as by the water table and quickly dried up in dry summers.

Although evidence of religious practices is very rare in protohistoric settlements, it is common around or within water sources. Wells and springs often contain ritual deposits. This was the case in one of two wells at Berlin-Lichterfelde (Fig. 88). From the La Tène period onwards installations are found which have a post in association with a water source, particularly in the *Viereckschanzen*, those rectangular enclosures, probably ritual in function, generally found located outside settlement zones.

The presence of human bones in wells should be linked with the existence of human sacrifice, which is attested in Celtic societies. The Wilsford and the Levroux shafts mentioned above contained them. Lossow in eastern Germany is a good example from the Hallstatt period, with over 50 wells on a defended site some 40m (130ft) above the Oder. Many of these produced mixed human and animal skeletal material, often with the limbs still articulated and so distinguishable from the animal bones found in nearby domestic rubbish dumps. One well contained a complete stag and another the complete body of a man which had been put into the well bound, head first and face down. This is a position very rarely found in cemeteries. These customs should also be connected with the deposits of human remains found in caves or rock fissures. Arrangements around the margins of settlements bear witness to complex relationships with the underworld. In the La Tène period some wells possessed or acquired a funerary function, such as that in the Lagaste cemetery at Pomas (Aude) dating from the first century BC.

More prosaically, the water supply to fortified sites always posed problems, and it is for this reason that some defended enclosures were built so as to include springs inside their enceintes: examples are Třísov (Bohemia) in the La Tène period, or Altburg Niedenstein, where water was stored in wooden cisterns. In La Tène *oppida* cisterns were often dug into the rock.

88

Late Bronze Age well from Berlin-Lichterfelde, Germany. The 3m- (10ft-) long lining, made of a hollowed-out tree-trunk, is filled for one-third of its height with material which casts doubts on its having been an ordinary well. About a hundred small pots were laid in several layers over a foundation of branches and enlaced twigs. These pots contained the remains of willow catkins, lime flowers, grain, orache and aromatic herbs and must therefore have been put there in the spring. It is not certain whether it would have been possible to draw water from the well afterwards. Pots continued to be put in the well, which was eventually sealed up with branches, reeds and stones. (A. von Müller, 1964.)

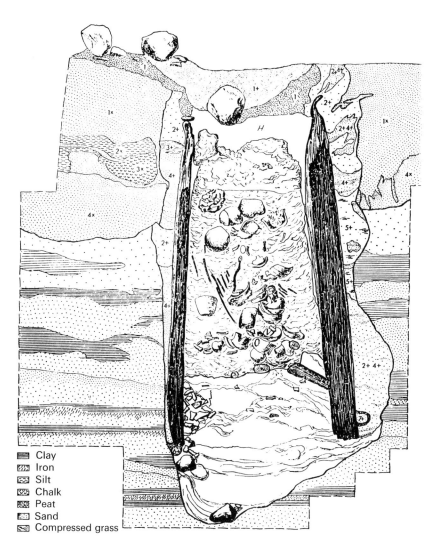

Clay
Iron
Silt
Chalk
Peat
Sand
Compressed grass

The cistern at Padnal (Grisons) is the oldest known and must certainly represent a technological achievement for the early part of the Middle Bronze Age (Fig. 89). It is 4.8m (16ft) long by 3m (10ft) wide and is set into a 10m (33ft) wide hollow. It was made out of planks rebated together and mounted in morticed upright beams so as to form a horizontal frame, which was itself set on cross-beams. The cistern served both to catch rainwater and melted snow and to collect groundwater, which drained into it by means of gullies. It is not certain whether it was used as a drinking-water supply since it was located below the hamlet and there were streams nearby. When the settlement was rebuilt towards the end of the period the hollow was filled with mixed materials and can

have been no more than a soakaway.

The care lavished upon the construction of springheads distinguishes them from wells and testifies to the importance accorded to them. They were built with wooden casings using meticulous craftsmanship. The two Middle Bronze Age springs at Saint-Moritz (Switzerland) are the earliest examples known of the use of *Blockbau* construction and of dovetail jointing in architecture. The Hallstatt springs at Ivanka pri Dunaji (Slovakia) had double casings, but the interior one was square and built of planks. The Feddersen Wierde spring in the La Tène period was constructed of planks fixed into a morticed wooden frame. Another consisted of a pit lined with a wall of turf blocks reinforced by interwoven and rammed

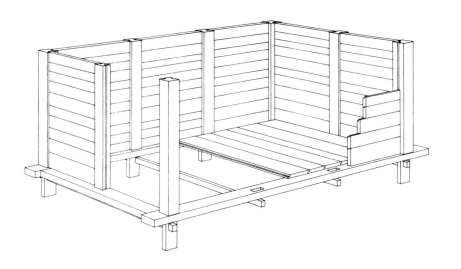

89
Reconstruction of the Early/Middle Bronze Age cistern at Padnal, Savognin, Grisons. The wooden container measuring 4.80m by 3m (16ft by 10ft) was made of tongued-and-grooved planks set into uprights that passed through the beams that made up the base. (J. Rageth, 1986.)

branches set in clay and with a floor also made of branches.

Like wells, springs contained offerings, pots, weapons and other bronze objects. Evidence of similar actions can be found at fords, when the amount of material left by protohistoric people is such as to make it impossible to explain its presence simply as accidental losses. These practices must also be related to the burial of men and women, often bound and sometimes strangled, in the bogs of Denmark, northern Germany and Britain. The peat environment that mummified them has provided us with incomparable information about clothing in both the Bronze and Iron Ages.

Drainage

Water management is not solely related to its collection. In many sites, and especially in north-western Europe, it was necessary to divert water away from settlements, so as to keep them dry. Drains, soakaways and ditches were among the methods in general use for this purpose.

British settlements included provisions of this kind as early as the second millennium BC. Houses with drystone outer walls often had radial drains running from a point on the ring of internal posts to outside the walls. These were usually channels 30cm (12in) wide and 50cm (20in) deep, covered with irregular stone flags. They passed beneath the wall through an aperture with a flagged lintel and in some cases terminated in a soakaway or a ditch, as was the case in some of the houses at Shaugh Moor (Devon) from around 1000 BC. In other regions, houses with wattle-and-daub walls were encircled by a circular drainage channel, distinct from the foundation trench for the wall stakes.

On the continent it is in the settlements on the slopes of the Jura and the Alps that drains and soakaways can best be discerned. At the Late Bronze Age settlement at Bavois-en-Raillon (Vaud) drainage ditches and soakaways were dug around or close by the houses until the whole of the bottom of the valley was filled with settlement refuse. On present evidence it would appear that drains played no part in structures with beaten earth floors in other regions.

By contrast, the digging of drainage ditches developed considerably in the low-lying lands of the Netherlands and northern Germany, which were liable to flooding. Houses from the Zuider Zee up to the mouth of the Ems were surrounded with ditches, ending in front of the entrance, from the late second millennium BC – as, for example, at Bovenkarspel. The ditches there were cleaned out and redug every time the houses were rebuilt. The settlement was crisscrossed in every direction by other ditches which served to delimit and drain the agricultural holdings or to encircle the round platforms where sheaves of corn or hay were stored. With an increase in humidity and a rise of the water-table in the first millennium BC it became necessary to reinforce the drainage of the houses by creating an earthen platform surrounded by a ditch, a new arrangement which appeared around 800 BC at Bovenkarspel. It spread to many other settlements in the course of the centuries that followed. These platforms were first made from the spoil from the ditches and later included the ruins and refuse of settlements that were being reconstructed

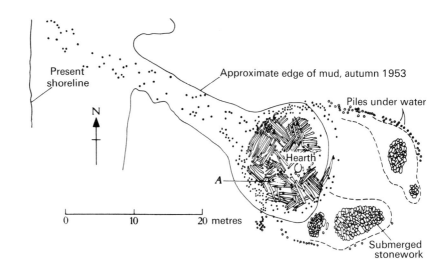

90
The La Tène period crannog in Milton Loch (south-western Scotland). This was an artificial island made of rubble and branches secured by piles on which a round-house was built, the floor of which, made of crossed logs, has survived. It was reached by means of a track of planks on piles. (C.M. Piggott, 1955.)

continuously. These are known as *terpen* in the Netherlands and *Wurten* and *Warften* in Germany. At first, each man-made mound supported a single house, but in the later centuries BC they began to accommodate several houses and finally the whole village, as at Ezinge (Netherlands) or Feddersen Wierde (northern Germany).

In a very different region of Europe the ditches of the *terremare* of Emilia in the second millennium were primarily for defence and were reinforced with earthen ramparts, as at Castione di Marchesi or Montata. However, they also protected these villages built on earthen platforms from flooding.

In Ireland the crannogs (artificial islands created from rubble confined within piles) were established in lakes and marshes for reasons of protection. They were anchored by means of wooden piles which retained the heterogenous filling materials – branches, earth and stones. A platform, which might or might not have a log base, usually supported a single house, sometimes with ancillary buildings (Fig. 90). They were first known in Ireland but have since been recognized in Scotland. As with the lake villages, water here was used for defence.

Social spaces

Roads and trackways

Very few traces of prehistoric roads remain anywhere in Europe. Later transformations of the landscape have destroyed or obscured them everywhere, apart from a few regions such as the plateaux and hills of the British Isles or the low country of the Netherlands, northern Germany or Denmark. The extensive excavations carried out on the uplands of Wiltshire and Devon or in the Somerset Levels have revealed roads that are linked with settlements and 'Celtic fields' (see p. 160). These are the sunken tracks created by the repeated passage of livestock or by the banks and lynchets that defined the fields. Sometimes they linked farms with one another and sometimes they linked farms with fields, as at Plumpton Plain A (Sussex) or Shearplace Hill (Dorset) in the late second millennium BC. At Fengate, on the edge of the East Anglian Fens, ditches ran alongside the rectangular fields, and edged a rectilinear network of trackways: the corresponding embankments must have disappeared. All these trackways were for local use and the longest stretches known do not exceed a few hundred metres in length. It is reasonable to assume, however, that the network of which they formed a part spread over the whole of the corresponding 'Celtic field' system, over distances of 1–3km ($\frac{1}{2}$–2 miles) on Dartmoor, for example, in the second millennium BC.

In the peat and marshy areas of Britain and the Low Countries a special system of land management was used which appears to have no parallels in central Europe. From the end of the third to the middle of the first millennium BC the villagers living on the edges of, or within, the waterlogged Somerset Levels built wooden trackways which crossed the marshes and linked up the higher ground. They range in length from a few hundred metres to more than 2km (1 mile) (2.5km ($1\frac{1}{2}$ miles) in the case of the Abbot's Way, built

145

at the very beginning of the second millennium BC). The simplest of these consisted of tree trunks set longitudinally and butting on to one another. Others had foundations or a network of branches pegged down with stakes, the solution adopted on the most recent, the Viper's Track, which dates from the mid first millennium BC. The most complex consisted of a base of branches on which longitudinal trunks were set, these in turn being surmounted by morticed cross-planks kept in place with wedges set vertically. The Sweet Track (1090–1070 BC) and the Meare Heath Track (1030–890 BC), where the trunks were set transversely and the planks longitudinally, belong to this category (Fig. 91). Similar trackways also existed in Ireland. They went out of use everywhere when the growth of peat or a rise in water level forced the inhabitants to leave a region that had become too inhospitable. The frequent presence in these settlements of nets and fishbones (especially of eels) makes it possible to establish a link between these trackways and exploitation of the resources of the marshes.

In Lower Saxony and the Netherlands many lengths of timber trackways are known, from some hundreds of metres to 3km (2 miles) in length. They did not cross marshlands but went from its edges to the centre, rather than linking settlements. Some were quite wide and were furnished with foundations that were solid enough to support a cart, like the Nieuwe Dordrecht, built around 1890 bc, on which a wooden wheel was found. Others are narrower and made of planks set end to end and linked by means of an arrangement of cross-members fixed into the ground with upright stakes (Emmercompascuum and Klazienaveen-Nord, from the late second millennium BC). Three such stretches of track from the Bronze Age and three from the Iron Age are known from the Emmen region. They may have been connected with the exploitation of bog iron ore, nodules of siderite (iron carbonate) formed by precipitation from ferruginous water, since they passed close by an area where these nodules were formed. Moreover, a fragment of iron rod was found on one of these tracks, whilst the nearby settlement at Emmen contained iron slags. The investment of considerable construction materials and working time in such projects is somewhat perplexing, given the fact that these tracks can only have served for a few years because of the continual rise in the level of the bog.

Without exception, no major communication links are known, even from the La Tène period. An origin in protohistory can, however, be attributed to some roads stretching over more than 100km (62 miles), such as the Jurassic Way, which links the Cotswolds and the Yorkshire Wolds, or the Harroway and the Pilgrim's Way, which link Salisbury and Folkestone, each more than 200km (124 miles) long. On the continent the *chaussées Brunehaut* of northern France often prove to have originated before the Roman period and their alignments are known over several dozen kilometres. Some of the Alpine passes were in use as early as the second millennium BC.

There are many indications of the use of carts with wooden wheels. Ancient authors refer to several examples: Diodorus Siculus, for instance, reports that Cornish tin reached the coast by cart on the Ictis highway, whereas in Gaul it was transported by packhorse. Distribution maps of objects show that waterways formed the basic means of communication. Material was generally transported in dug-out canoes, but the Scandinavian rock carvings and ancient texts provide evidence of larger vessels capable of crossing the Channel and of coastwise trade along the Atlantic and North Sea littorals. Hoards of continental Bronze Age objects found off Dover and Salcombe are evidence of ships coming from the continent being wrecked. The diffusion of Baltic fossil amber over the whole of Europe as far as Greece and the coasts of Syria and Phoenicia testifies to the effectiveness of these exchanges which were based on 'down the line' trade along the major continental rivers.

Streets and open spaces

Streets were slower to be introduced into protohistoric villages. Over much of Europe the 'agglomerated villages' of German-speaking archaeologists contained only unorganized open spaces between the houses, as did the linear villages of northern Europe. Streets began to appear in settlements established in more restricted areas – lake villages, upland settlements or fortified meanders – and houses were built in parallel rows. These were not always proper streets but rather regular open spaces, especially where the ground was only accessible in periods of low water. They were always covered with rubbish.

Proof of the deliberate planning of streets comes from the seventh century BC: at Moel-y-Gaer (Wales) the granaries were laid out in six concentric rows parallel to the rampart, whilst the houses were more or less regularly arranged in two lines a little way away (see Fig. 78). At Biskupin (Greater Poland) twelve parallel streets separated rows of houses sited side by side and joined up with a peripheral street which followed the line of the ramparts (see Fig. 70). *Oppida* such as Manching, Danebury or Hod Hill contained streets which crossed the entire defended area,

91
Late Bronze Age wooden trackway at Meare Heath (Somerset). It was made of planks set on cross-members held in place with small stakes and stabilized by means of a foundation of branches and logs (beneath the soil and not visible in this photograph). More than 2000m (6560ft) of its length is known. (J.M. Coles.)

without, however, constituting a true street network. In the first century BC streets ran across Mont Beuvray (Burgundy: see Fig. 140) and Manching (Bavaria: see Fig. 138) and joined specialist districts, such as those of craftsmen. Streets were not yet anything more than unbuilt spaces for circulation. At the end of the first century BC the houses at Villeneuve-Saint-Germain (Aisne) did not always open on to the streets but rather on to courtyards, despite the regular layout of the street system (see Fig. 141).

In similar fashion, the eccentric location of the earliest open spaces in lake villages or fortified settlements, such as Senftenberg (eastern Germany) in the early first millennium BC or Biskupin in the seventh century BC, gives the impression rather of an unoccupied space or one used for temporary penning of animals. There were, however, more or less central open spaces at Dampierre-sur-le-Doubs (Doubs), at Perleberg, near Berlin, and at Buchau (Baden-Württemberg) in the Late Bronze Age. The 200 sq.m (2153 sq.ft) wooden platform in the Mozartstrasse site at Zürich shows that concern to make a public open space had manifested itself as early as the Early Bronze Age (see Fig. 42). This public square did not, however, acquire its status as the monumental centre of the urban area, invested with political and religious functions, until the Roman conquest. The social meeting places of the Celtic world as such still in fact elude us, since they are not the objects of specific definition within the urban space. This perspective helps to explain the reflection by Tacitus quoted above (p. 106) about the open spaces which surrounded the houses of the Germans.

Funerary space: cemeteries

Organized funerary space did not in general form part of the urbanized area during the Bronze and Iron Ages. There was no place for the dead inside settlements. Unlike the Middle Ages, when graves were grouped round the church, protohistoric cemeteries were separated from villages. There are even periods, such as the early first millennium BC, for which only the cemeteries are known for parts of Germany and Hungary, and not the settlements. In Switzerland, on the other hand, it is the cemeteries corresponding with the lake villages that have not yet been discovered, apart from that of Boiron (Vaud).

Nevertheless, wherever there is good documentation cemeteries are found associated with villages but at distances from them varying from a few hundred metres to several kilometres. At Březno (Czechoslovakia) in the Early Bronze Age two cemeteries, each containing some forty graves, were found in association with two distinct groups of buildings (see Fig. 108). In the Lausitz Culture of Germany and Poland the cemetery could remain in one place even though the village itself moved several times (Woryty in Masuria and Bodzanowice in Silesia are examples from the Late Bronze Age). Many fragments of human bone are found in settlements, but it remains difficult to explain these since they do not conform with contemporary funerary rites. These include dismembered bodies in ditches or wells and unusual skeletal postures (tightly flexed or squatting, for example, in the ditch of the fortified site at Cezavy, near Blučina; dismembered children in the defensive ditch at Hradisko in Moravia in the Middle Bronze Age). In some cases there is evidence of dismemberment or even defleshing of bodies which suggests human sacrifice.

It has been seen earlier that some wells contained human remains. Those which in the La Tène period were clearly funerary in character form part of

cemeteries, such as the Lagaste cemetery at Pomas (Aude) in the first century BC or those of Vieil-Toulouse and Cavaillon. In many regions potholes, crevices and caves were also used as burial places. These are known from all the limestone massifs of Europe. In southern France, particularly in Languedoc, caves were the most common burial sites during the Bronze Age and sometimes remained in use over several periods – for instance, the Grotte du Hasard at Tharaux (Gard).

The dead were therefore consigned to the fringes of settlements, the boundaries of village territories. In Britain barrows often acted as markers of such territories. The stone walls which delineate individual holdings and were laid down in the late second millennium BC on Dartmoor include a number of earlier barrows in their alignments. The construction of many stone cairns, whether funerary or otherwise, on ridges marking watersheds in the Plym Valley or on the North Yorkshire Moors in the early second millennium BC shows that there was already a concern to give land distribution a material form, which was developed later in the form of reaves (linear dry-stone boundaries). Subsequently, in the Iron Age, the grouping of burials in cemeteries meant that monuments of the dead no longer served to delineate territorial boundaries. The settlements of the dead thus remained clearly separated from the settlements of the living, although they may have contributed to affirming the continuity of the rights of the living over their own lands.

Religious space

Our knowledge of religious practices in the Bronze and Iron Ages is very scanty and very disparate. It relates for the most part to the later period, when Roman cults had modified the visible aspect of religion. We know almost nothing of everyday cult practices. Nevertheless, one dominant trait emerges clearly from the data that have been collected together: cult sites were separated from settlements until late in the La Tène period. The few sanctuaries that are known were built deep in the countryside and cannot be linked with any specific settlements. In some cases they served a vast area over several centuries. One of the most striking examples is the great megalithic monument of Stonehenge, where the circles of dressed stones were successively added to over the third and second millennia BC.

In Drenthe in the Middle Bronze Age the small wooden building at Bargeroosterveld, set on four posts and surrounded by a circle of stones, is isolated in the middle of a bog. The slightly later site of Černčin (Moravia) consisted of a large hollow in the form of a cross in the middle of which there was a horse burial. These sacred sites are connected with natural elements – water, the earth, forest, the sky. Like Stonehenge two millennia earlier, Libenice was built with reference to the position of the sun at the solstices. This is one of the best-preserved sanctuaries of the Celtic world. It consists of an oval ditch measuring 80m by 20m (262 by 66ft), orientated north-west/south-east, which surrounds a sunken structure and the inhumation grave of a woman. Excavation showed that a stone pillar, a stone circle and posts defined the axes linked with the solstices. Remains of sacrifices were found in pits dug at the foot of the walls of the sunken building. This complex was in use for 25 years, around the beginning of the third century BC. No trace of any settlement has been found in the neighbourhood.

It appears that from the Hallstatt period some fortified settlements may have been established on sacred sites in central Europe. One of the earliest sanctuaries associated with a settlement was found at Závist (Bohemia). Firstly there was a cult enclosure in the Hallstatt period; then, in the Early La Tène period, substantial foundations in drystone construction some metres high were built on a terrace of the acropolis overlooking this 170ha (420 acre) enclosure, apparently to carry religious buildings of some kind.

Other sacred sites are known only from deposits of objects or bodies, or by light structures. At Ostaburg-Zedau in the Altmark of eastern Germany, 145 hearths ranged over a length of 310m (1017ft) have been dated to 750 BC. Caves were also used for depositing hoards. One of the most spectacular is that from Býči Skála, near Brno (Moravia), which produced, in addition to rich bronzes characteristic of the Hallstatt period, traces of sacrifices of various kinds: cereals and animal and human bones, arranged with great care but for a purpose that eludes us.

The importance of sacred springs persisted during the Roman period, with the famous wooden ex-voto from Chamalières (Puy-de-Dôme) and the Sources de la Seine (Côte-d'Or).

One group of sites that has recently been identified emphasizes the survival of certain religious sites from the Late Bronze Age through to the La Tène period. These are to be found from northern to west central France, and perhaps also occur in the lower Rhine valley. A good example is Acy-Romance in the Ardennes. Late Bronze Age ritual enclosures with ring-ditches crossed by timber footbridges and with post-built entrances were replaced in the Early Hallstatt period by long rectangular enclosures with ditches revetted with wattling and entrances strengthened with posts. One or two rectangular structures were built inside the enclosures. The ditches often contained the scattered fragments of a single pot or a hoard near the entrance. These enclosures did not have a funerary function since no graves were found inside them. Cremation or inhumation graves were found all round them, singly or grouped into small cemeteries, according to period. B. Lambot interprets these structures as the successive indications of a sanctuary of regional significance, connected with settlements some kilometres away. Sites such as Villeneuve-au-Châtelot (Aube), Antran or Valdivienne (both in Vienne) may also be interpreted in a similar way.

Woodland enclosures

Another category of structures, whose sacred function and dating have been well established, thanks in particular to the definitive work of K. Schwarz, are also removed from settlements. These are regular four-sided enclosures or *Viereckschanzen*, with sides measuring 60–150m (197–492ft) in length and most enclosing an area of 5000–15,000 sq.m (53,821–161,463 sq.ft). Each is surrounded by a bank, usually with an external ditch with no break at the entrance, both of modest size. A gateway, often defined by massive timbers, is located in the middle of one of the banks, orientated to the south, east or west. Unlike protohistoric fortified enclosures they were not sited so as to benefit from the natural protection of an escarpment or water: most of them are on flat or slightly sloping ground.

In all the regions of Europe where they have been recorded they are irregularly distributed, with areas of intense concentration and others where they are completely absent. They are often found on poor soils, which are today generally still covered with forest. In Bavaria K. Schwarz has located them at the edges of or beyond lands under cultivation.

All the artefactual material recovered from these sites comes from the ditches or near the gateways, but in no case has any occupation layer been found in their interiors. The dating evidence in them all comes from the Late La Tène period.

Excavation of the Holzhausen enclosure allowed K. Schwarz to demonstrate the cult function of *Viereckschanzen*. Like many of the others, this enclosure had a monumental gateway, an absence of occupation in the interior, a post-built structure, and wells. It is clear that the precise nature of the enclosure was of little

149

importance: palisades and banks served successively to define a space which did not change from one period to the next. The building was reconstructed several times in the same place and there is no equivalent of its special ground plan to be found in Celtic settlement architecture.

K. Schwarz has rightly interpreted these structures as component parts of a sanctuary. Thus the enclosure delineating the sacred ground, the wells in which sacrifices were carried out, and the temple, surrounded by a kind of peristyle or gallery, which was transformed into a stone building in the Gallo-Roman period.

Five *Viereckschanzen* with wells have been excavated so far in Europe, among them that at Tommerdingen (Bavaria), where the well contains a pile packed with stones, and three with post-built structures. The distribution of these enclosures covers almost the whole of temperate Europe.

Weapons and human sacrifices

From the La Tène period onwards sanctuaries were built in a number of late fortified sites. The recent exploration of the sanctuary of Gournay-sur-Aronde (Oise) has completely changed our understanding of Celtic religion in the Middle and Late La Tène periods. This is an enclosure with sides 40m (131ft) long built inside an *oppidum* on flat ground and covering 12ha (30 acres); it consists of several contiguous enclosures backing on to the river. The sanctuary proper is surrounded by a wide ditch broken by a gateway. A wooden building was erected inside in the late third century BC, rebuilt twice before the Roman conquest and a third time in the Augustan period; in the Early Empire it was replaced by a stone *fanum*. The Celtic origins of these small square Gallo-Roman temples is thus confirmed once again. It is, however, the meticulous analysis of the extraordinary deposits found in the ditch which has supplied new information. The excavators showed that the offerings were 'exposed' in this ditch, which was lined with timber and very carefully looked after. A wooden palisade outside the ditch, with returns lining the entrance, concealed the offerings from the view of people outside the sanctuary. These offerings consisted largely of hundreds of weapons. These artefacts, which had been 'sacrificed' by means of violent blows as well as the rust which slowly eroded them in the ditch, were associated with cattle, sheep and pigs. Finally, twelve humans had been deposited in the ditch after having been decapitated. All these objects were systematically destroyed, the animals and

humans being slaughtered. The skulls were removed in order to be exposed and the limbs rotted in pits before being exposed in their turn in the ditch. J.-L. Bruneaux stresses the fact that maintenance of a sanctuary of this kind required there to be a permanent staff who may have assisted the famous Druids referred to in written sources.

Some 50km (31 miles) to the north of Gournay the lower levels of the Gallo-Roman sanctuary at Ribemont-sur-Ancre (Somme) produced in 1982 another structure of a type hitherto unknown. A pile of human long bones belonging to some 200 individuals, mainly young men, was found in the corner of an enclosure slightly larger than that at Gournay, defined by means of a ditch and a *vallum*. The bones were laid out systematically on top of each other to form a structure around an empty space, the roof of which may have rested on a post located in the centre. Some weapons contemporary with those from Gournay were found at the base of the structure. Study of this extraordinary find has not yet reached a stage when a definitive interpretation can be advanced.

From sanctuary to temple

At Gournay we can observe in spectacular fashion how the square Gallo-Roman temple surrounded by a gallery emerged from the wooden prototypes of the Celtic period: ritual requirements imposed a new layout on the classical architecture imported from Italy. Similarly, in Britain the sanctuaries which appeared on the fortified settlements of the later centuries BC are clearly distinguished by their square plans from domestic structures. At South Cadbury (Somerset) a building in which the long sides projecting beyond the facade are reminiscent of a *pronaos*, was associated with two pits which contained in particular newborn calves and weapons. It was rectangular in plan and measured 3 by 4 m (10 by 13ft). Four square buildings occupied the centre of the fortified settlement at Danebury (Hampshire); the largest, 5m (16ft) square, is reminiscent of the Heathrow (Middlesex) temple, which also had a gallery, like the temples of Roman Gaul.

Now excavation methods have become more precise, fragile structures that in the past would have been overlooked are being studied minutely, and can even be interpreted long after the excavation has finished, by means of comparative studies or analysis. The corpus of Bronze and Iron Age sanctuaries is now developing rapidly. Many questions remain to be answered, in particular that of the exact function of the *Viereckschanzen*. However, we can already state that religious architecture developed greatly in this period. The relationships between settlements, land holdings and cult sites seem to have evolved substantially over the second and first millennia BC. Although the subject of pre-Celtic and Celtic religions remains little understood, certain changes can be clearly distinguished: sacred and cult sites developed first outside settlements, and in the Bronze Age there were no recognizable collective religious areas within villages. Firedogs and other objects that are described as 'ritual' testify to the existence of domestic cults of which we are almost completely ignorant. The first cult buildings erected inside settlements were in the Hallstatt period, but it was above all the La Tène period that saw them proliferating, at the same time as settlements themselves changed in character and location and the influence of the Mediterranean world manifested itself in many aspects of Celtic civilization. Alongside temples with peristyles or galleries built in settlements, the rural and forest cult centres continued to be important, as shown by the relatively late blossoming of the *Viereckschanzen*. Rural cults maintained their place in Gallo-Roman religion and gave it an identity of its own within the Roman Empire.

Although the Celts and their predecessors seem close to us in matters of technology, they become much further removed when one begins to explore their social organization and their values.

Conclusion

At the end of this chapter domestic life in protohistoric settlements seems to have become familiar to us. The main living space was organized around the hearth and life went on there: a mixture of sleeping, cooking and many other activities. The layout of these settlement units is comparable with that of farms in historical times. Certain activities gradually acquired a permanent place within a specialized building – barn, granary, byre, workshop. In this respect the Neolithic period and the Bronze and Iron Ages may be shown to form an integral part of the history of rural settlement in Europe.

This type of settlement seems closer to us when we study only its material aspects. We are always conscious of the consequences of the constraints imposed by the environment, by raw materials and by the techniques used. In these material aspects the similarities with more recent times are very strong. They might be less so if we knew the way in which family relationships fitted into this domestic space. What were the respective places of men and women, older and younger children, within a household?

By contrast, when we turn our attention to social spaces – village squares, cemeteries, cult areas – the Celts and their predecessors seem much more remote from us. None of the sites we have studied has a public open space that was organized in the same way as those whose development we can study in ancient Greek and Roman society. Even when they are associated with villages, cemeteries are separated from them in space. Cult sites are associated with the elements of nature – sky, water, forest – and until a late period were divorced from settlements. The protohistoric period seems to have been not only the time when the western rural world was formed but also a civilization greatly different from our own, whose distinctive characteristics we are only now beginning to understand.

9 Settlements in the landscape

The natural environment within which protohistoric man evolved is not fundamentally different from our own. Overall, the conditions in which these farmers worked are comparable with those of historic periods. When we are prompted by curiosity to examine a particular region or period, however, we become aware of significant differences in the climate, the flora and the nature of the plants being cultivated. In this Europe, characterized by the juxtaposition of small landholdings in which the balance and the products are very diverse, any change in natural conditions, however small, has repercussions on the whole rural economy.

From the dry Sub-Boreal to the wet Sub-Atlantic

The entire Bronze Age took place during the relatively dry Sub-Boreal climatic period. These conditions remained relatively stable until the fourteenth century BC. In central Europe at least, the wetter thirteenth and twelfth centuries were followed by three drier centuries. Transition to the Sub-Atlantic climate took place more or less abruptly, according to the region. The horizon recorded in certain peat-bogs, which seems to hint at sudden climatic degeneration, in reality covered the whole eighth century BC: average humidity grew rapidly but not in the catastrophic way that earlier scholars believed. The development between the seventh and second centuries BC was much slower. Rainfall increased again in the first century BC. This development can be observed best in marginal areas, such as coastal and mountainous regions. In certain areas they resulted in severe ecological disturbances, in some cases irreversible. In

this way the Dartmoor hills in south-western England and part of the Drenthe region in the Netherlands were covered with peat-bogs and rendered unsuitable for cultivation between the beginning of the first millennium BC and the fifth century.

Settlements had been evolving on lake shores since the middle Neolithic. Successive occupations and reoccupations were related primarily to economic and historical influences. The greatest rises in the water-level of the lakes, however, caused temporary or permanent abandonment. Thus in Switzerland during the Middle Bronze Age village sites drew back from the lake shores, whereas occupation continued on upland sites and also along the Italian lakes. The Late Bronze Age was a period of favourable conditions when not only lake-shore and hill-top settlements multiplied but the upper valleys were also colonized. This phenomenon did not survive the climatic degeneration of the eighth century: the lake shores were abandoned following the flooding which marked the end of the Bronze Age and permanent settlement receded from these areas finally at the beginning of the Iron Age. Climatic deterioration was not so much the main cause of change as the event which precipitated transformations that the new historical, social and cultural context had made inevitable.

On the flat coastal lands of Holland and Lower Saxony even small variations in sea-level either exposed huge areas fit for settlement or flooded some that had already been colonized. The marine transgression of the Atlantic period ended in 2500 BC, and throughout the Bronze Age the sea receded, revealing a vast expanse of clay and sand which linked the Friesian islands with the present-day coastline. The Sub-Atlantic transgression covered this surface again between 700 and 100 BC, sealing previous occupation levels beneath 50cm (20in) of clay. It receded again in the first century BC, freeing a smaller area which men settled and defended by means of earthworks when the sea returned in the second century AD.

New species, new plants

Removal and transformation of the woodland cover

The landscape changed partly under the influence of man, who encouraged the development of certain species at the expense of others. His activities, however, often only served to reinforce, and in some cases combat, the larger trends resulting from climatic changes. It is therefore possible to distinguish between the general evolutionary pattern – best considered in relation to those widespread tracts of woodland which remained in a natural or semi-natural state – and localized sequences attributable to human management. Depending on the nature and location of sampling for ancient plant remains, it is possible to obtain information about both phenomena.

Dutch and German archaeologists who have studied occupation levels on the southern coasts of the North Sea have been working with palaeobotanists since the 1920s. In these waterlogged contexts, where organic remains are remarkably well preserved, excavations have yielded as much information about the natural environment as about human activities. The spectacular results of this collaboration have encouraged scholars in other regions to develop their efforts in this direction, even where the conditions for preserving organic remains are less favourable.

The study of pollen produces the most reliable results when sampling conditions are good. The date and the process of formation of the level in which they were deposited must be known accurately. Factors such as whether the sample has been collected from a site which reveals human activity and the details of its topographic setting dictate the extent to which the results are representative. Palynologists separate pollen from sediments, identify and count the individual grains of each species, and compile statistical tables according to agreed standards. As the number of samples collected over Europe grows, so our view of the landscape becomes more accurate.

The studies of plant macro-remains – seeds, charcoal or even wood itself, recovered from waterlogged deposits – give information about the plants used by man, since they are generally collected from places where man was living and working. J.-C. Miskovsky

outlined a synthesis of such evidence for France in 1976. Mixed woodland of oak, elm and lime declined at the beginning of the Sub-Boreal. Beech came in from the east and expanded slowly towards Normandy, Brittany and even the Pyrenees. In the south-west, clearance was responsible for the expansion of hazel, whilst the warm, dry climate favoured the development of Mediterranean plants. Oak and Aleppo pine dominated in the south-east.

Human intervention became very significant from the beginning of the Sub-Atlantic, especially in northern France: deforestation is clearly marked, but regeneration of woodland still occurred. Beech and hornbeam continued their expansion, in places accompanied by alder. In the south-west, the flora of the present day became established, with maritime pines and heather and bracken moorland. In the Pyrenees, where beech and alder predominated, pine advanced at the expense of fir, whilst hazel was planted by man in the valleys. The south-east was covered with pine, box and Mediterranean plants. Fir was widespread in the Massif Central, and it was accompanied by beech in the northern Alps and the Jura, whilst higher up spruce predominated, which in turn was associated with larch in the Alps.

Diversification and expansion of cultivated plants

During the Bronze and Iron Ages agriculture assumed the fundamental role that it retained up to the Industrial Revolution. It was the main activity of the majority of the population, whose subsistence it ensured. Technological developments included the domestication and introduction of new species, better fitted to the natural conditions and the tastes of different groups. Cereal diversification also made it possible to sow at different times of the year (Fig. 92.1).

In the Neolithic cereal production was confined essentially to emmer and club wheat. Einkorn, naked barley and millet were already known. Regional specialization of species began with the Bronze Age. In northern and central Germany, the Netherlands and Britain barley expanded rapidly during the Bronze Age. Naked barleys were gradually replaced by hulled varieties. During the Gaulish period (Second Iron Age) this cereal was used for making beer. Spelt increased in importance in Switzerland and southern Germany during the Late Bronze Age. Rye, which had been cultivated in eastern Europe since the Neolithic period, progressed into southern and central Germany during the Iron Age, accompanied by oats and spelt. It did not reach its maximum expansion on the siliceous

153

	NEOLITHIC	BRONZE AGE	IRON AGE	HISTORICAL PERIOD
Einkorn				
Emmer wheat				
Spelt				
Compact wheat				
Naked barley				
Two-row barley				
Rye				
Oats				
Millet				
Panic grass				
Peas				
Lentils				
Beans				
Flax				
Hemp		?		
Poppy				
Hybrid lentils				
Hazelnuts				
Acorns				
Apples				
Pears				
Cherries	?			
Morello cherries				
Sloes	?			
Wild plums	?			
Plums				
Damsons				
Apricots				
Peaches				
Vines	?			
Dogwood berries				
Chestnuts	?			
Walnuts			?	

92
Schematic diagram showing the appearance of plants in northern Germany. 1: Cereals and leguminous plants; 2: Fruits. (U. Willerding, 1969; K. Behre, 1970.)

German plains until the end of the Iron Age, no doubt because of its excellent resistance to cold. Wheaten bread was a Gaulish speciality whose quality was lauded by classical authors (Pliny, *Natural History*, 18.68).

In Britain spelt and hulled barley were the cereals most cultivated throughout the first millennium BC. Winter-sown, they were used alongside the spring-sown cereals, emmer and naked barley. C. Burgess has pointed out that it was the fact that these cereals were harvested on different dates that led Diodorus Siculus to assert that there were two harvests a year in Britain.

At the present time it is difficult to give a more detailed picture or to comment on other regions of Europe without tackling the problem of the representativeness of the samples analysed. Samples are becoming more numerous in every country, but there are still strong inequalities, by virtue of the state of preservation of grain and the distribution of specialists available to carry out analyses. Moreover, we are still awaiting syntheses of the results obtained in recent years on the dating and identification of agricultural implements, ard-marks and other traces of cultivation and the reconstruction of working cycles. Within the next decade we shall doubtless have a detailed view of the development of agriculture during the Bronze and Iron Ages for a good many regions.

Development of leguminous plants and domestication of fruit trees

Observations carried out in Germany, Switzerland, Poland and Czechoslovakia have shown the increasing importance of leguminous plants, which are of only marginal importance in the present day when the potato has assumed a major role in food supplies. Peas and lentils are known from the Neolithic. Broad beans appear during the Bronze Age in the Polish Lausitz Culture, in central Germany and in Switzerland, where remains of cabbage and turnips were also identified. Vetches were eaten in the Iron Age. Acorns and beech-nuts were stored on some sites, as were hazelnuts, but we know nothing of their food role. The Tollund bog man from the early first century AD had been ritually strangled before burial; his stomach retained the remains of a cereal-based porridge.

So far as fruits are concerned (Fig. 92.2), it is not always easy to distinguish when gathering ceased and arboriculture began. Apple is frequently found on Neolithic settlements. Pears, sloes, cherries, strawberries, blackberries and raspberries are also found in the Late Bronze Age. Rare grape pips testify to the existence of wild vines, but wine remained a luxury import. Vines and apricot trees appeared in the lower Rhône valley at the end of our period and on a restricted scale, but the cultivation of these fruits, as well as the peach, only really became established after the Roman conquest. Oil-producing plants, such as poppy and rape, should not be overlooked, nor fibres such as flax (attested in the Neolithic) and hemp, the origins of which are obscure but which were known in the Iron Age.

A slow and difficult technological development

Like other human activities, agriculture benefited from the appearance of metals, but the profound changes in the very design of working tools were not closely linked with the basic material. Their development is everywhere complex and difficult to localize.

Ard and plough

The evolution of ploughing implements is characteristic of this phenomenon. There is considerable evidence for the existence of ards pulled by a pair of cattle all over Europe at the beginning of the Bronze Age: rock carvings in Sweden, on Mont Bego above Nice and in the Val Camonica in the Bergamese Alps provide especially helpful examples. Danish peat-bogs have preserved examples of wooden ard stocks, and yokes have been found at Swiss lake settlements. These ards cut through the soil without turning it over, and one of the Val Camonica rock carvings shows a man who appears to be breaking up the clods of earth with a hoe behind the ard (Fig. 93).

The first iron shares appear in Palestine between the twelfth and tenth centuries BC. However, the first metal components known in eastern Europe, and which typify that region, are coulters. The Thracians and Dacians combined this with a share on sole-ards in the second century. Shares of a special, almost triangular, design from Illyria turned the soil over on both sides. No metal mould-boards are known, but these devices may have been made of wood.

From the first century BC the Celts were using narrow iron shares. Although M. Beranová has gone as far as to suggest that the beginnings of iron working among the Germans led to very conservative attitudes technologically, the Celts seem on the contrary to have colonized new territories over the whole of central Europe thanks to their superior technology, but one which has not left any spectacular material remains.

93
Harnessing, harrowing, and ploughing as shown on rock carvings from Val Camonica (Bergamese Alps). (G. Tosello, after M. Beranová, 1980.)

Pliny writes of a ploughing implement equipped with two wheels used in the Grisons and the Tyrol in the first century AD, which has been identified a little hastily as a true plough. In fact the latter does not necessarily include a wheeled carriage, and is distinguished essentially from the ard by its mould-board and the equipment which allows the soil to be turned over to one side. M. Beranová claims to be able to distinguish from the asymmetry of some surviving specimens, evidence for experiments to this end from the second century BC. This remains a controversial question and would justify more intensive research.

In parallel, cultivation by hand remained important: this is attested by many iron tools – hoes, picks, spades and even different types of rake in the Balkans (Fig. 94).

Harvesting

The manufacture of bronze sickles developed widely from the middle of the second millennium BC. This was a relatively small implement, with a balanced shape, well adapted to hand use and fixed by means of a tang or a rivet into a wooden handle. The large iron sickles that appeared in the mid first millennium BC, similar in shape to modern examples, clearly imply a broader motion on the part of the harvester. Iron scythes are also widely distributed, from the Balkans to the site of La Tène itself, although they are not found in Roman Italy. Specialists debate whether they were used solely for cutting grass or whether they were also used in harvesting cereals.

Data on the height of the cut in harvesting and the techniques of threshing are still very fragmentary.

Recently these problems have been studied by experimental archaeology (the work of P.J. Reynolds), by analysis of plant macro-remains and by fruitful meetings among archaeologists, historians, ethnologists and agronomists. Bringing together all these complementary studies should make it possible in a few years' time to put together an accurate picture of this chain of processes. The question of yields, where P.J. Reynolds has obtained some spectacular results, is also of prime importance. From a technical point of view the Celts were capable of both intensive agriculture ('gardening') and also of extensive agriculture over large areas, as shown by the famous Gallo-Roman reaping machine used in the plains of northern France and Belgium.

We have already drawn attention to the question of returns, in terms of output, which manifests itself at the milling stage with the development of the rotary quern, from the second century AD over all central Europe. The opening up of large quarries, the products of which were distributed over distances of up to a hundred kilometres, demonstrates the success and importance of this innovation. Examples of such quarries are known from Mayenne, Switzerland, and Bohemia.

The unevenness of the surviving evidence that we have for the Bronze and Iron Ages does not mask the real technological progress that was achieved. Striving for good yields began in the middle of the La Tène period and the progress achieved was such that in this field the Romans had as much to learn from the lands that they colonized as they had to offer.

From pastoralists to specialized stock-breeders

Relationships between men and animals seem also to have developed during the Bronze and Iron Ages in a similar way. Livestock regimes were increasingly

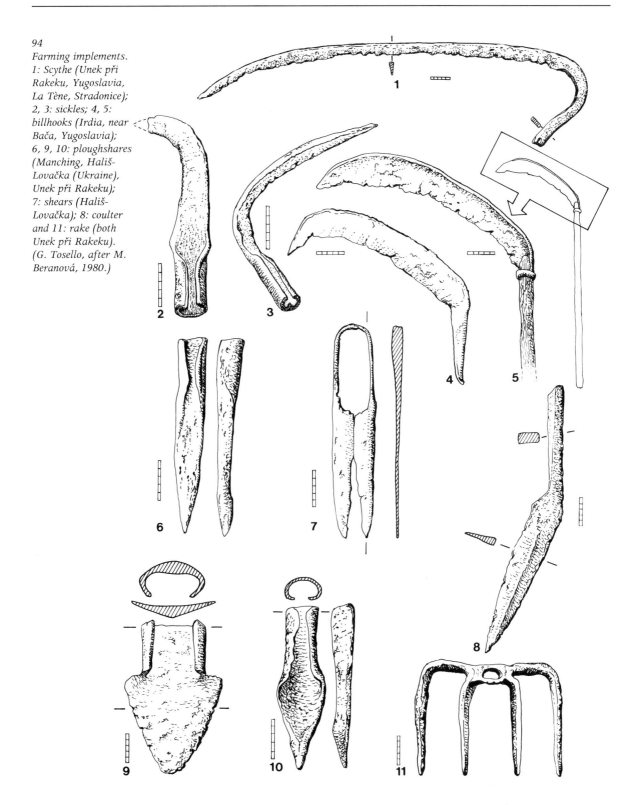

94
Farming implements.
1: Scythe (Unek při
Rakeku, Yugoslavia,
La Tène, Stradonice);
2, 3: sickles; 4, 5:
billhooks (Irdia, near
Bača, Yugoslavia);
6, 9, 10: ploughshares
(Manching, Hališ-
Lovačka (Ukraine),
Unek při Rakeku);
7: shears (Hališ-
Lovačka); 8: coulter
and 11: rake (both
Unek při Rakeku).
(G. Tosello, after M.
Beranová, 1980.)

controlled and oriented towards human needs – meat, dairy products and traction power. Methods of analysis and interest in these questions have made rapid progress over recent decades.

Large quantities of animal bones are needed if zoologists are not to restrict themselves just to the identification of the presence or absence of certain species but rather to try to establish their relative proportions. It is also useful to measure the size of animals in order to see their development and to estimate the amount of edible meat produced. The determination of sex, of castrates and of age at slaughter also make it possible to reconstruct the objectives of stock-rearing for each species.

Hunting products steadily decline in percentage terms in deposits that consist of food debris. In the Chalcolithic period they vary between 70 per cent and 30 per cent, but on Iron Age settlements hunted species often fall to less than 1 per cent of the bones recovered.

Cattle, sheep/goats (associated in statistical data because of the difficulty of distinguishing them anatomically from one another), pigs and dogs make up the overwhelming majority of bones from settlements. Horses, which, as we have seen, were not harnessed until the end of the Bronze Age and were only ridden from the beginning of the Iron Age, are very much in a minority, although they were eaten. Birds are difficult to identify: ducks and geese are present at an early stage, but chickens appear for the first time in the Hallstatt period in Bohemia and southern Germany.

From the Bronze Age onwards the percentages of different species vary from one country to another, and even from one region to another. It should be borne in mind that the figures quoted here are based on numbers of individuals, not on weight of meat. In Poland, pigs predominated over cattle, then came sheep and goats. In Czechoslovakia, cattle preceded pigs and sheep/goats, which were equally represented. The spread of the latter in northern Europe is sometimes related to deforestation. In France they are more numerous throughout the south and on the middle Loire. Cattle and pigs are the principal species represented in the east whilst the three groups are in equal proportions in the Paris basin. Throughout the Iron Age pigs increased proportionately, especially in the North, and sheep predominated in the South and Centre-West.

Although an increase in pig raising can be observed over the entire Celtic world, the Iron Age is characterized above all by the variety of its herds. Specialists are nowadays attempting to identify ranges of live-stock that are characteristic of certain types of site: from the beginning of the Iron Age settlements are known that are entirely given over to animal husbandry and others where a small herd is associated with polyculture, whilst there are significant regional variations. The samples available are still too few for solid results to be forthcoming.

The study of age at slaughter reveals the growing importance of dairy production and the use of animals for draught purposes. The number of cows grows in proportion to the number of males. Herds are better managed and controlled. This development has to be related to the extension of the practice of providing housing for animals at the end of the Bronze Age.

Recent research has shown that castration was already being practised at this period. However, general species development seems not to have been mastered. Although sheep grew heavier during the La Tène period (Second Iron Age), cattle and pigs seem to have decreased in size over the first millennium BC.

Thus, during the Bronze and Iron Ages agriculture and animal husbandry made remarkable progress in temperate Europe. From Caesar to Augustus the Roman army had no supply problems. Cereals and salted products early on played an important role in exports into Mediterranean markets. The origin of this surplus is to be found in intensive exploitation of the soil and of all the available resources.

The birth of administrative divisions

Scholars such as G. Roupnel and H. Hubert were aware as early as the 1930s of the fundamental role played by protohistoric developments in the shaping of the landscape and the agricultural economy of temperate Europe. Roupnel stressed the original character of these protohistoric cultures: 'The creation of the countryside is the characteristic product of our West. It is the nature and the spirit of its civilization. It is as typical of this civilization as the development of the *polis* is to the Mediterranean societies ... We are the oldest peasant peoples of history.' He located the chronological position of this people between history and prehistory: 'Whereas in the Mediterranean south it was the sea that attracted man and the rule of hunting clans persisted in the northern forests, in the centre, in that giant clearing of the ancient continent, the humanity of herds and fields developed.' The subdivision of landscapes and the vast increase in the number of small units of landscape in central Europe were major factors, according to Roupnel, in the settling process that turned early nomads into farmers. It was they who established territories which were able to provide all that was required for subsistence.

Although current research largely confirms some of the intuitive statements of Roupnel and Hubert, the arguments that they put forward to justify these are no longer acceptable. For Roupnel, France offered three 'rural economy systems'. The south, with its nucleated settlements, strongly influenced by the Mediterranean economy, was a world of its own. The west presented a landscape of enclosed fields and dispersed settlements. Like England, the Netherlands and western Germany, the centre, north, and east of France constituted in his eyes 'the true countryside'. Around nucleated villages the fields were divided into three blocks, related to the communal practices of triennial rotation and empty pasture. In each block the individual fields formed long parallel strips. For him, Neolithic peoples were responsible for setting up this communal system, which achieved full development during the Bronze Age. He considered the Celts a warlike people, a vanguard of the Germans who long remained at the stage of elementary agriculture. With his views visibly upset by Hubert's book, which appeared while he was putting the finishing touches to his own work, he admitted that the Celts had of necessity to adopt the system of their predecessors in the Rhine and Paris Basin regions. In the less populated west they imposed their own primitive and individualistic system.

Hubert did not contrast the Celts with earlier peoples. He believed that waves of immigrants followed one another and that the Celts were experienced farmers. The landholding systems in both east and west France were in his view attributable to the Celts, but they were at different levels of development. He stressed comparisons with medieval Ireland and Wales to interpret bocage (a landscape of small enclosed fields interspersed with woods) as a primitive stage in the Celtic economy and the eastern landscape as a more developed one.

In his book on the evolution of the French rural landscape, which appeared in 1934, R. Dion was much more cautious in explaining the origins of and reasons for the organization of the countryside. He began by rejecting the notions of environmental determinism: neither the river systems nor the underlying geology influenced the organization of agriculture and settlement, even though men did take advantage of the special possibilities within the regime that they selected. The oceanic climate of the west and the Mediterranean climate of the south had in his opinion a much more important role to play and modified the agricultural systems significantly. We know a great deal about the distribution of different field systems from the eighteenth century onwards. From this period we have at our disposal reliable descriptions of land allotment thanks to the work of Arthur Young, the maps of royal routes of Trudaine and the early maps of large estates.

Almost all the land lying to the north-east of a line running between Rouen and Lyons was cultivated communally on the open-field system, corresponding to the 'true countryside' of G. Roupnel. Triennial rotation, which presupposes division into three blocks in which each person's holdings were evenly distributed, involved alternation of winter wheat, spring cereals and fallow. In Dion's view, early farmers did not have access to spring-sown cereals, and so cereals did not take up as much as a third of the land: it was merely a matter of a few furrows taken from the stock-raising grassland, where different livestock were already being rotated.

Dion rightly relates several modern texts on operating this system to a few sentences that Caesar and, in particular, Tacitus devote to the organization of agriculture among the Germans: Caesar wrote (De Bello Gallico, 4,1) of the Suebi: 'No land, however, is the property of private individuals, and no one is allowed to cultivate the same plot for more than one year. They do not eat much cereal food, but live chiefly on milk and meat and spend much time in hunting' (translation E.V. Rieu).

He explains that, after a year of cultivation, half the men devote themselves to warfare, being replaced in the fields by those who were campaigning the previous year. But elsewhere (6,12), when speaking of the Germans, the reasons for this practice, astonishing to a man of the Mediterranean, seem less clear: 'The Germans are not agriculturists, and live principally on milk, cheese and meat. No one possesses any defined amounts of land as private property; the magistrates and tribal chiefs annually assign a holding to clans and groups of kinsmen or others living together, fixing its size and position at their discretion, and the following year make them move on somewhere else. They give many reasons for the custom: for example, that their men may not get accustomed to living in one place, lose their warlike enthusiasm, and take up agriculture instead; that they may not be anxious to acquire large estates, and the strong be tempted to dispossess the weak; to prevent their paying too much attention to building houses that will protect them from cold and heat, or becoming too fond of money − a frequent cause of division and strife; and to keep the common people contented and quiet by letting every man see that even the more powerful are not better off than himself' (translation E.V. Rieu).

Tacitus's description seems to be more objective: 'For agriculture, the villages take possession of a certain area of land in proportion to the numbers of workers; then this is divided up according to rank; the immensity of the land facilitates this division. Every year they take more fields and land is never lacking.' (*Germania*, 26).

Following Fustel de Coulanges, Dion interprets this text as the description of a system in which the planted areas, although much smaller, were already subject to a system of communal exploitation and regular movement around the defined territory, in which he saw the origins of the practices observed in north-eastern France, Belgium, and north-western Germany during the eighteenth century.

By contrast, the west and south of France were subject to the system of undivided private property of Roman law. Corn alternated with fallow or sometimes beans, and 'catch' crops such as turnips could be inserted between harvests and sowing. Animals were excluded from the cultivated part of the territory, the *ager*. They could use the permanent scrub of the *saltus* and in due course the *silva* which delineated the boundaries of the territory.

We will not dwell here on the many modifications that Dion himself made to this very schematic picture of eighteenth-century France, because his work is only of interest to us as an explanatory model for late protohistory. Before analysing the systems that have been proposed recently for this period, let us look at the data that has been collected in the field.

'Celtic fields'

It was O.G.S. Crawford in 1923 who introduced the term 'Celtic field' to denote those fossil land divisions characterized by the low-relief, lyncheted boundaries that separate them. However, as early as 1660 J. Picardt observed similar remains in Drenthe, long interpreted as the work of the Romans. In the Netherlands A. E. Van Giffen identified them as fields shortly before World War II: he succeeded in showing that the earthen banks overlay soils that had already been cultivated and that, in the region he was studying, they were earlier than the fifteenth century. The main areas of 'Celtic fields' are to be found in countries bordering the North Sea – Britain, the Netherlands, northern Germany, Sweden and Denmark.

For J.A. Brongers, who has recently taken up again the study of these remains in the Netherlands, they were constructed to control the humidity of the soil and improve its quality. All the fields he has recorded are located in zones of Pleistocene sand which usually cover an impermeable stratum. The earliest belong to byre-houses of the Middle and Late Bronze Age, at Bovenkarspel, for example. They become very common in the Iron Age. The Vaassen group, which has been intensively studied, was created around 600 BC and continued in use until AD 150 (Fig. 95.1). They were first delimited by tracks on which the earliest banks were constructed; then rectangular blocks were set up on two orientations, north-south and east-west; their higher banks make it possible to distinguish them from later sub-divisions. They respected burial mounds built in the preceding period. These large banks, which defined the long rectangular land parcels, were built during the phase when the fields were being cleared of their infertile contents in order to be enriched with humus, whilst the square sub-divisions corresponded with the use of the land for cultivation, since this shape was best suited to the techniques of the period. 'Celtic fields' generally disappeared from the Netherlands during the Early Roman Empire. A few examples have survived, however, either crowned by hedges or edged by little ditches.

In northern Germany this type of field system is also attested on the sandy moraine soils from the beginning of the Iron Age. The individual fields covered 1000–3600 sq.m (10,765–38,751 sq.ft) and the banks were 50cm (20in) high and 8–16m (26–52ft) wide. These groups are associated with isolated farmsteads or hamlets whose location moved quite frequently. The Flögeln group survived until the end of the first century AD.

In Schleswig-Holstein and Denmark they are found on the morainic sands, where they form groups of 200–1400ha (494–3459 acres) with individual plots of 2000–3000 sq.m (21,528–32,293 sq.ft). They were in use from the Hallstatt period until the beginning of the Roman period. Before World War II Hatt recorded 33 groups, and the figure has now risen to 480.

'Celtic fields' are also known from southern Sweden. Some 92 groups have been recorded on the island of Gotland: they range in date from the Iron Age to the end of the Roman period. The plots, smaller than those of continental Europe, cover 500–1000 sq.m (5382–10,765 sq.ft). It is estimated that a surface of 600 sq.m (6459 sq.ft) could have been ploughed in a single day and that a family could live on the produce of 2 ha (5 acres) in this case ploughing required some thirty days' work annually.

These fossil field systems are especially well preserved in Britain, in the form of low banks on the chalk uplands or low stone walls in western and northern

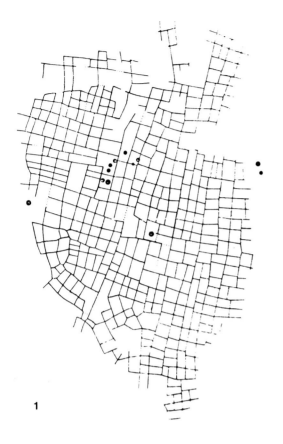

1

regions. Some groups in Ireland, the Orkneys and eastern England have been dated to the third millennium BC, and from the second millennium BC in the rest of England. They achieved their widest extension, however, during the Iron Age and the Roman period, thus lasting longer than those on the continent. Field size varies from 1000 to 5000 sq.m (10,765 to 53,821 sq.ft), and in shape they are usually nearly square, although some are clearly rectangular. It appears that the basic size corresponds with the area that could be ploughed in a single day using the implements and the techniques of the period, i.e. cross-ploughing. According to C. Burgess Bronze Age farms often lay adjacent to field systems of 6–8 ha (15–20 acres).

The Iron Age 'Celtic fields' on the chalk uplands of the south-west were integrated into landholdings that additionally included enclosed settlements and pastures. At Woolbury (Hants), for example, they butted up against a large ditch which led to a hillfort, on which the main boundaries of the landholding seemed to converge (Fig. 95.2). The pasture area can be identified from the ditches that delimit it and, indirectly, by the presence of burial mounds that have not been obliterated by ploughing. In this type of arrangement, which is also found at Danebury or Ladle Hill, both also in Hampshire, the hillfort certainly played an important role in the storage of grain and fodder as well as the penning of livestock.

95
1: 'Celtic fields' at
Vaassen, The
Netherlands. (The dots
are barrows) (A.
Brongers, 1976.)
2: Fossil field-system,
Woolbury
(Hampshire). (B.W.
Cunliffe, 1974.)

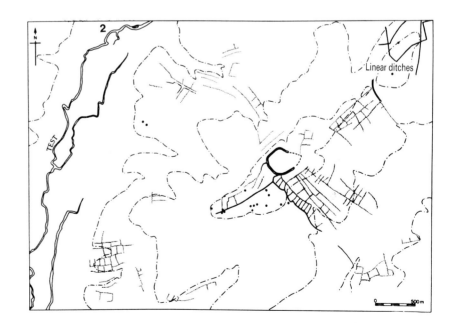

French archaeologists have been actively looking for landholding systems of this type but so far they have only been found in areas marginal to the main agricultural regions. Some forests in Lorraine and the western slopes of the Vosges have preserved in fossil form groups of fields defined by low walls resulting from clearance and including settlements. Their dating has not yet been determined accurately. The system of banks recorded by J.-M. Couderc at Cravant (Indre-et-Loire) is more closely related to the 'Celtic fields' of northern Europe. In the present state of knowledge, it seems to date back at least to the Roman period.

Contrary to what Roupnel and Hubert believed, the *bocage* of the west of France has nothing to do with any Celtic land-allotment system. It is in fact a very recent creation, dating to the seventeenth to nineteenth centuries according to P.-R. Giot. The Breton landscape was much more open in the Iron Age. Farms defined by an enclosure which contained both humans and animals were located on hilltops. Banks of the kind used to delimit plots are rarely preserved, but occur on the coast where they have been overwhelmed by sand dunes. Caesar's text gives very little precise information about the landscape. The Roman general does, however, evoke the laid hedges (i.e. made of shrubs with interlaced branches) of the Nervii which stopped any cavalry charges.

It is clear that the study of these surviving field systems should not lead us to imagine the whole protohistoric landscape as being divided into small enclosed fields. The role of woodland and natural grassland or unenclosed deforested land remains of considerable importance. For more than 90 per cent of the surface of Europe all traces have been irretrievably erased, since natural erosion or modern deep ploughing have destroyed the protohistoric horizon. We have no way of knowing whether the majority of these lands were enclosed or open.

Nevertheless, the 'Celtic fields' show that, from the Bronze Age in England, there was a wish to improve the lands on which human groups had settled permanently. Building banks indicated the desire to control soil humidity and to prevent erosion or incursions by animals. It suggests the import of more fertile soil or manuring. This raises the possibility that these techniques were practised equally in all the cultivated areas.

It is, however, difficult to date the introduction of these methods. British authors consider that the introduction of byres automatically led to manuring of fields, but this remains to be proved. How should we think of those innumerable regions where archaeology has produced no indisputable evidence of animal shelters? There is no tangible evidence that the practice of rotation had begun to spread. P. Wells believes that it already existed in the Hallstatt period, but he offers no proof of this.

The handful of agronomists who, like F. Sigaut, have seriously studied these historical problems stress the diversity of systems and conditions necessary in order that an agricultural implement or practice can be considered viable: scythes can only be used in harvesting if the field is cleared of stones and levelled, manuring is only worthwhile if it can be transported at the lowest possible cost, the *vallus* (the wheeled Gallo-Roman reaping machine whose teeth remove the ears) can only be used for harvesting certain types of cereal, etc. There are so many well formulated questions, to which archaeologists are still unable to provide answers.

The *saltus* and pastures

The presence of byres obviously implies that a significant part of the territory was devoted to pasture. It should be made clear that the woodland contributed to the feeding of animals, which browsed on leaves and, in the case of pigs, ate acorns. It is very difficult to find the precise location of pastures in territories. Many authors believe, in our opinion correctly, that a not inconsiderable portion of the 'Celtic fields' were reserved for animal husbandry. Enclosing the fields meant that flocks could be routed either along the paths or to these grazings without impinging upon ripening crops. We have already seen the example of Woolbury, analysed by B.W. Cunliffe, where a specified part of the territory was reserved for pasturage.

Long ditches are also evidence of the existence of flocks and herds, whose wanderings they would restrict: these are the 'ranch boundaries' which spread over many kilometres of southern England, designed to separate two territories. The enclosures round settlements in these regions, and also round some farms in Norway or northern France, with funnelled or winged entrances (see Fig. 134) were intended to direct animals towards their nocturnal or seasonal shelters. In most cases we are unable to say whether pastures and cultivated fields existed side-by-side on the same pieces of land or whether they formed separate groups, and we do not know their relative sizes.

Prehistorians and geographers propose functional models which A. Gallay has summarized and synthesized in a remarkable manual on settlement: the territory comprised the agro-system, a rural space resulting from woodland clearance and composed of fields (cultivated) and the *saltus* (waste land), and the natural environment (*silva*), in which man's only incursion was as a predator (Fig. 96.1). The following schema develops this perspective. The uses of the territory surrounding the settlement are defined in terms both of the labour input required and the distance to be covered in order to reach each zone.

In a study of the village of Glastonbury (Somerset), D.L. Clarke proposes a model for the exploitation of the resources of the territory which has the merit, in going beyond what can be proved by tangible data, of being closely adapted to the natural conditions of this valley and to what we know of the Celts in the second century BC (Fig. 96).

This schema is first of all conditioned by the marshland in which the site was established, which is more or less unusable between November and May. Clarke goes on to distinguish three zones in the territory: the *infield*, cultivated for barley in winter; the *outfield*, for spring wheat and peas alternating with fallow; and what may be called the *silva*, represented here by the marsh, which is exploited for its reeds and as pasture. It should be added that the author also suggested that there was active exchange with people living on the neighbouring high ground, which is crowned with hillforts, perhaps in the form of transhumance of animals. In these conditions, which are admittedly somewhat special, it is difficult to classify this territory with the collective system of the north-west European countryside or that of the west and south of France, as defined by R. Dion.

G. Lambrick, following up the work of D.W. Harding on the upper Thames valley, has shown to what point farming activities in different settlements can be narrowly specialized. His work was carried out on the small Middle Iron Age units in the floodplain and on the first terrace at Farmoor and Appleford, on an enclosed settlement on the floodplain at Hardwick, and a hamlet at Ashville. He has shown that there was

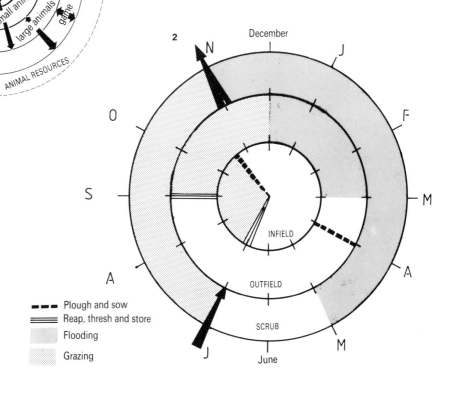

96
1: *Land-use model. (A. Gallay, 1982.)*
2: *Model of exploitation of land, Glastonbury. The author takes account both of the distance from the village (concentric circles) and of the different seasons of the year during which the land is used for various activities (segments within the circles). (D.L. Clarke, 1972.)*

seasonal settlement on the floodplain, utilized for a short period and devoted exclusively to cattle and horse raising. Farms were established on the terraces which produced evidence both of agricultural activity and animal bones suggesting the presence of flocks of sheep on the higher ground.

Opencast mining of lignite in recent years has provided Czech archaeologists in north-western Bohemia with immense areas that are rich in settlements and burials from the Hallstatt period to the Late La Tène to study. In an area of 80 sq.km (31 sq. miles) J. Waldhauser recorded 64 settlements, 59 cemeteries and two fortified sites for an occupation period of 700 years. The areas of human settlement are related to the hydrographic network, but both the smallest streams and the largest rivers were avoided.

Survey revealed the existence of empty sectors, which allowed the author to identify micro-regions of 5–10km (3–6 miles) in extent, each separated from the next by a distance of 1–5km ($\frac{1}{2}$–3 miles). Each of these consisted of several settlement areas of different types: the simplest was a single farm devoted to stock raising, agriculture, or both, with or without a group of tombs. Larger units were reminiscent of small villages, with a cemetery and surrounded by fields, in which craft activities were being carried on from La Tène B onwards.

Waldhauser notes the importance of buffer zones between inhabited zones, which according to him remained uncultivated *silva*. It is this not insignificant part of the territory that we shall examine next.

Woodland

Although archaeological progress has made it possible to obtain an idea of the different types of territory, the exploitation and extent of uncultivated areas is still imperfectly understood. Historians have long taken the name *Gallia comata* ('hairy Gaul') literally: for them the Celts inhabited simple clearings in the forest which at that time covered most of the land.

J. Harmand has shown in a famous article that even Caesar's text does not permit such an interpretation (Harmand 1969): the Roman general did not give a picture of Gaul as being particularly wooded, something which would have made an impression on a man from the Mediterranean south. He reported that the progress of his troops was only hindered by woodland between Besançon and the plain of Alsace (*De Bello Gallico*, 1,39).

The word *silva* and its derivatives are used 61 times in *The Gallic War*. It is used 12 times about Britain, 8 times about the lands beyond the Rhine, 32 times about the land between modern Belgium and the left bank of the Rhine, and only 10 times about lands lying further to the south or west. It is never used about the Breton countryside. In most cases it relates to woodland in an otherwise open landscape. Harmand notes that in the territories of the Menapians, who retired behind a continuous line of woodland and marshes (*De Bello Gallico*, 3.28; 6,5), Caesar was able to cut down a vast clearing very quickly in order to dislodge them.

In reality the only true forests, which Caesar describes in a few sentences, were the forest of the Ardennes, stretching from the Rhine to the lands of the Remi (around Reims); that which separated the Menapii from the Morini, the forest of Bacenis, between the Suevi and the Cherusci, on the right bank of the middle Rhine; and the Hercynian forest, which extends in Germany along the banks of the Danube.

M. Clavel, who does not believe in either 'Hairy Gaul' or the radical deforestation suggested by Harmand, insists on the very important role of woods in the battles of the Gallic War. Caesar often recalls a Gaulish tactic which consisted of falling suddenly on Roman columns and taking refuge as quickly as possible again in the cover out of which they had surged, as soon as the enemy recovered themselves (*De Bello Gallico*, 2,19). He wrote that 'The forest appeared from one end of the Gallic War to the other to be a decisive factor in the tactics, at one and the same time offensive and defensive, of the Celts. It was the end for them when they abandoned the protection of the woods for fortified towns.'

This rather provocative conclusion in fact poses the true problem of Gaul on the eve of the conquest. It is true that the Celts were finally defeated in a siege war, as the campaign of 52 BC well demonstrates. It is also true that the most heavily-wooded land, in which *oppida* were few or small and scattered, such as Belgium or central Germany, put up the longest resistance or escaped Roman pressure. In our opinion the Gaulish Celts had long before this pushed the forests back to the fringes of their territories and had for half a century been establishing these fortified towns, to which we shall return and which they could no longer abandon, even when Roman superiority in siege techniques was obvious. The contradictions in their war tactics culminated in the campaign of 52 BC in Berry, when Vercingetorix practised the traditional scorched earth technique but failed to burn Bourges (Avaricum), 'the most beautiful city in Gaul'. At the time of the conquest the forest was broken up into small woods and copses in the middle of a largely open landscape, at least in the Paris basin, the centre and the west of Gaul. In addition, the Celts had concentrated all their fighting forces in agglomerations that they were incapable of defending, lacking as they did adequate political structures and military knowledge.

Although we have stressed the extent of deforestation in the La Tène period, it should not be overlooked that woodland played an important role in the Iron Age civilizations. It provided wood, which was the favoured raw material of Gaulish craftsmen, not only for the frames of buildings but also for vessels, barrels and carts, which were considerably more developed there than in the rest of the ancient world. It was a natural reservoir for all types of game and no doubt also made a contribution to the pasturing of domestic animals.

The richness and diversity of protohistoric agriculture

The role played by protohistoric farming in the shaping of the European landscape can only be appreciated with the aid of historical data. The approach of Roupnel and Dion, however, leads to some extent up a blind alley, in that it considers protohistory to be a homogeneous whole and the evolution of the landscape as a linear phenomenon. It is only possible to take note of those aspects which are directly related to later development. Any cyclical effect or retrogression is excised. Moreover, this approach seems to take no account of the existence of successive technological levels in the course of protohistory, which bring with them very different ways of exploiting the land and to some extent condition the degree of sedentariness and permanence of settlement. These factors, however, play a fundamental role in the relationships linking settlements with their territories and to the resulting landscapes. It is true that the successive transformations have only been clearly understood in recent years and that precise data are only available for a few regions where palaeobotanical studies have been more developed than elsewhere. However, whether it be in Franche-Comté, in Switzerland, in England, in the Netherlands or in Scandinavia, the same phenomena can be observed: there is a clear relationship between the length of occupation of villages and the type of farming practised. When the land is exhausted, the village must move on to fertile soils or ensure that it is regenerated by means of improved techniques. Changes in the location of villages may be irregular or organized and cyclic. In the former case it often only comes about at the end of a crisis in the course of which internal or external demographic pressure on the village may play its part.

When the whole territory is occupied competition develops for fertile land. At the historical level this manifests itself in the form of raiding, war and the destruction of villages. In the landscape it is marked by the fortification of settlements and the establishment of territorial boundaries in order to affirm property rights more effectively. When the chronology is rigorously examined, it is seen that such upheavals only concern a restricted area at any given time. It can happen, however, that destabilization gradually looms larger, leading to general relocation of villages at the regional level, a reorganization of exchange mechanisms and to new methods of farming.

The work of P. Pétrequin and the palaeobotanists G.-N. Lambert, K. Lundstrom-Baudais, and H. Richard on Lake Clairvaux was the first to demonstrate this model, which is equally applicable to a number of Swiss lake villages. Their conclusions are based on the one hand on the length of occupation and abandonment of the different Neolithic and Early Bronze Age villages around the lake and on the other on the state of vegetal cover when they were reoccupied and rebuilt. The seven settlement sites were each occupied on up to eight successive occasions. Dendrochronological analysis made it possible to ascertain very accurately the dates when houses were built, in real years, and the length of time they were abandoned. In the Middle Neolithic (3400–2400 BC) it appears that there was only one village in existence at a time, which lasted for 16–40 years and was then abandoned for a period of 50–150 years. This lapse of time enabled the forest, which had been lightly cleared, to regenerate. In the Late Neolithic (2400–2000 BC) and again in the Early Bronze Age (2000–1700 BC), several hamlets were able to co-exist. The period of occupation of the villages lengthened and the periods of abandonment became shorter. The timber used for house building came from trees that had sprung from stumps: there was not sufficient time for the woodland to regenerate completely between two occupation phases. Pétrequin deduces from these data that a long fallow farming system in the forest based on irregular cycles was succeeded by a similar system with shorter fallow periods and more regular cycles. The fallow-scrub system gradually replaced the fallow-forest system, to use the Boserup terminology. The shores of Lake Clairvaux have not been settled since that time, but the Swiss Bronze Age lake villages testify to longer and longer periods of occupation, up to a hundred years at a stretch. The corresponding agriculture cannot have been other than fallow-scrub or short fallow farming with crop rotation.

Other indications, indirect in some cases, are also

available of this slow transformation of farming practices and the introduction of crop rotation. The increase in the range of cereals available brought with it species that were more resistant to cold or better adapted to certain areas, but most important of all was their ability to be sown at different seasons.

Protohistoric farming practices led, as we have seen already, to the complete relocation of villages for variable periods. This resulted in radical changes to the landscape, territory by territory, with a more or less incomplete return to woodland, scrub or pasture. Some of these relocations correspond with crises. They are now well known at Clairvaux, where the transition from Middle to Late Neolithic was represented by new farming methods, changes in village organization and length of occupation, and reorganization of the exchange system, which substituted a preferred southward axis for an east-west one. Transition from the Late Bronze Age to Hallstatt Iron Age is also shown by the distribution of settlements: in the Combe d'Ain valley, the Late Bronze Age IIIb settlements are less numerous than before, they are usually fortified and they are situated on the edges of the Jura; in contrast the Hallstatt sites are all situated higher up, on the limestone plateaux. Pétrequin believes that it is likely that the Hallstatt people arrived from the east at the end of the Late Bronze Age and gradually installed themselves on the sparsely populated higher ground before they became overlords of the whole territory. In fact the Hallstatt cemeteries of the region lasted from Late Bronze Age IIIb through to the Middle Hallstatt period and contain the graves of a warrior aristocracy at the rate of an average of one grave per generation, which may be that of the tribal chief.

It is, however, also possible to look at these crises in a wider perspective, especially when they affect very large regions. They are assuredly associated with the problems of demographic pressure and have an effect on the settlements themselves, which are fortified, and on the landscapes, which are gradually broken up by territorial boundaries. Britain is an especially favourable field for this study, due partly to its long tradition of field survey, but also because of the restrictions imposed by the islands and the relatively small areas involved. Pollen analyses show that woodland took over again and deforestation diminished for the first time in the mid third millennium BC, and then again in the first third of the second millennium BC. Woodland clearance continued at a regular rate throughout the rest of the second millennium and the first millennium, but at the expense of grassland. In establishing correlations between all the possible indicators for pastoral and agricultural activities, R. Bradley was able to discern a major increase in arable land around 1200 BC, both preceded and followed by an increase in herbaceous plants in pollen diagrams, i.e. an increase in pasture between the Early and Late Bronze Ages. Transition to the La Tène (Second Iron Age) is also characterized by a peak in the surface area of arable land. Substantial clearances, attested in Yorkshire and East Anglia between 400 and 300 BC, gave rise especially to the extension of pasture in the latter region.

Successive landscape changes do not always involve increases in areas available for farming or intensification of agriculture. On Dartmoor, for example, it was the territorial system established in the mid second millennium BC that was the most extensive and elaborate. Stone walls several kilometres long, known as *reaves*, separated the high land reserved for communal pasturage from the slopes and valleys, which were divided up into rectangular fields by means of low walls aligned with or at right-angles to the reaves. Round-houses were built in the valleys and among the fields, sometimes inside and sometimes outside enclosures. The work of Andrew Fleming has demonstrated the remarkable homogeneity of the whole system, which obviously derives from an overall design and effective collective organization. His excavations, like those at Shaugh Moor for example, show that most of this was carried out between 1600 and 1200 bc (1800–1400 BC in calibrated dates), and most probably in an even shorter time. The fields, delineated by walls or banks, must have served more often for enclosed pastures than for arable farming, since there are no lynchets, which result from ploughing, in evidence. Many of the enclosures near or around the houses have no gateways: they may have been gardens or cereal fields, with agriculture taking second place to animal husbandry. This land-allotment system divides Dartmoor up into ten territories of 150–3300ha (371–8154 acres), which include all the fields in the valleys, the lower ground and part of the higher ground. It replaced a much less formal system dating from the late third millennium when the region was still in the process of deforestation. The houses then rarely had enclosures and wood was used for walls and palisades, in due course to be replaced by the reaves. Small groups of fields were established near the houses and were accompanied by clearance cairns. Only funerary monuments, such as stone circles and cairns, are to be found on higher ground. Occupation density decreased during the Iron Age. Pollen analysis indicates a reduction in woodland clearance and some recolonization by trees and shrubs. The expansion of peat bogs on the higher ground reduced the land available for farming. The only complex of enclosure, houses and fields of the mid first millennium BC is at Kestor. The Dartmoor region was reoccupied in the Middle Ages, but even then it was on a modest scale and the fields round the farms covered smaller areas. Their contours follow the topography and hydrography of the region, unlike those of the second millennium BC

The Dartmoor case may be an exceptional one by virtue of its marginal situation. However, similar breaks in development are frequent: at Fengate, near Peterborough in eastern England, the system of rectangular fields or meadows surrounded by ditches dates from the end of the third millennium BC and was in use throughout the second millennium. It bears witness to a pastoral economy which made complementary use of the water resources of the Fens. It succeeded a Neolithic agriculture in woodland clearings and was replaced in the Iron Age by an agro-pastoral economy which no longer felt it necessary to make so clear an imprint of its ownership on the land.

In Wessex, the linear or cross dykes or ranch boundaries, which delimited more pastoral lands, were superimposed on the 'Celtic field' systems on Salisbury Plain, for example, and are evidence of an economic shift from agriculture to animal husbandry during the first millennium BC, or perhaps a little earlier. The same phenomenon occurred again in this region in the later Middle Ages, owing to the rising price of wool. Similar reorganizations of the landscape can thus take place, although not necessarily from the same causes. There are unfortunately very few dated dykes, but it is tempting to see in them a phenomenon complementary to that of the hillforts, which are typical of the first millennium BC. The foundations of the European landscape were certainly laid in protohistory, but each region evolved from an individualized history rich in episodes of many kinds which sometimes resulted in the complete abandonment of earlier territorial divisions. Farming techniques, adapted to a barely changing climate and vegetation, provided a common infrastructure. Beyond this, the physiognomy of each region was shaped by socio-economic systems and modified under the influence of historical events.

The exploitation of raw materials

The exploitation of mineral resources, which had begun in the Neolithic period, took a decisive leap forward during the Bronze and Iron Ages. Long-distance trade was stimulated by the quest for metals and precious materials. Trade within northern Europe, and in particular between this region and the Mediterranean world, increased greatly. Gradually the objects of everyday life were modified and improved and became much more effective. Social structure was also affected by these new sources of power and wealth: some authors closely correlate the development of activities in the secondary and tertiary sectors with the gradual division of societies into complex hierarchies. Before turning to this problem it is necessary to survey the resources that were exploited in the Bronze and Iron Ages and the direct influence they may have exerted on the organization of settlements.

Three types of activity developed around non-agricultural production. First there was exchange, which at the beginning of our period was restricted to precious and lightweight materials. Then there is extraction, which passed from the stage of simple collecting to mining proper. Finally, there is the transformation of materials, which led to the appearance of specialist craftsmen. It has to be admitted that, despite all the efforts of archaeologists, the traces of these types of activity on settlement sites are difficult to interpret: enormous areas need to be excavated in order to evaluate effectively the changes that they brought about. In the interests of clarity, we shall deal with the different raw materials in turn.

The amber routes

Amber comes from the west coast of Jutland and from Poland. Around Gdansk it is collected on the coast whilst in Mazuria it is found in the hills of this inland region. It was above all the surface collection of amber in Poland which developed in protohistory. The demands of both the protohistoric peoples of the north and those of the Mediterranean resulted in the creation of commercial routes along which objects, techniques and new ideas were transmitted. One recollects the expedition of Pytheas to Britain, the island of Thule, and into the Baltic in the fourth century BC, and the place given in his story to the search for amber. One route started in Jutland and headed for the Elbe, the upper Danube, the upper Rhine and the British Isles. The most important route, however, linked Poland with the head of the Adriatic, via the Vistula, Moravia and Vienna. It was thanks to amber that Etruscan objects reached Poland. It was not by chance that new metal objects entered the northern lands along the amber routes, but in the opposite direction.

Graphite, sapropelite, lignite

The whole range of fossil materials from which bracelets could be made or which could be used for decorating pottery, the exact classification of which will not be discussed here, result in short- and medium-distance trade and the establishment of modest workshops. Hallstatt graphite-coated pottery, also known as *céramique à décor peint argenté*, is distributed throughout the Massif Central and northern and central-eastern France. The work of M.-J. Roulière has shown that the production centres were in the western part of the Massif Central. It was in this area also that C. Chevillot excavated a Hallstatt settlement that specialized in the manufacture of lignite bracelets.

These lignite bracelets were very popular in the second century BC. For Bohemia V. Kruta has shown how manufacture was spread over a series of small villages or hamlets, close to the mining area. They were then exported over the whole country, where they are to be found in many graves. In the Late La Tène they were gradually replaced in the south Bohemian *oppida* by glass bracelets. Their distribution was therefore confined to the north of the country, but in shape they imitated the glass ornaments of the *oppida* region.

Products like these, both relatively modest in value and easy to produce, serve to delimit these micro-regions; their distributions are contained within restricted areas. Their manufacture seems to have been grafted on to the agricultural production of the peoples concerned, without significantly changing settlement or social organization. The same applies to those stone quarries that produced quernstones (see above, p. 123). These items seem to have been exchanged through local networks within rural communities, and this was achieved without dislocating on traditional activities.

Salt

Salt played an important role among raw materials, but the archaeological traces are slight and do not do justice to that role. Salt deposits are rare, apart from in coastal regions, yet it is indispensable for preserving foodstuffs. The Celts made great use of it, if those Romans who appreciated their dried meats are to be believed.

Much evidence, in the form of briquetage, traces of the furnaces in which brine was heated in order to produce blocks of salt, is recorded along the coasts of the English Channel and the Atlantic. Archaeologists and ethnologists have recently been studying the development of this technology and the complex decision-making process which controlled the different stages of the process. There are very few material remains of settlements to put alongside the briquetage or the central European salt mines. Tessier has, however, been able to observe certain relationships between the coastal works of the bay of Bourgneuf and the settlements which produced remains of furnaces. During the Bronze Age these settlements were on the coast near the furnaces, but in the Iron Age they moved inland, occupying land between coastal streams, along a continuous line which corresponds with a route lying parallel to the sea.

There are not many salt deposits in continental Europe: Seille, near Nancy; Bad Nauheim, north of Frankfurt-am-Main; Halle in eastern Germany; and most likely also the mountains to the south of Krakow. The most famous is the Austrian Salzkammergut with its mines at Hallstatt and Hallein. They are renowned for the richness of their cemeteries, but the associated settlements remain virtually unknown. This has not prevented authors referring to industrial concentrations and going into detail about the allocation of duties and profits on the basis of the contents and distribution of graves! There were clearly groups of a hundred or so people, engaged on the same work, which was industrial in character. But, as with all ancient industries, this work brought only people together, whereas the word 'industrial' automatically evokes in the modern mind investment in machinery. No substantial agglomeration or sizeable fortified site is to be found near these mines. The grave goods show that part at least of this population was very wealthy. The men's weaponry comes from two distinct sources: south-eastern Germany and northern Yugoslavia. As in all historical periods, the exploitation of salt must have been controlled by a small group which supplied the areas to both the north and the south of the Alps.

Bronze routes

The relative rarity of copper and tin mines explains the birth of active trade across the whole of Europe. The metals needed to make bronze had to be assembled in order to be alloyed together, the resulting ingots being traded; or worn or broken artefacts had to be stockpiled for recasting as and when needed. These founders' hoards are in practice the main source of our information about Bronze Age cultures.

Copper was mainly exploited in the Tyrol and

Slovakia. It is estimated that 600 miners were working at Salzburg and 300 at Kitzbühl. Ore was already being mined in galleries 100m (328ft) deep. Unfortunately there are no traces of settlements and we know nothing of the miners themselves: were they farmers who worked the mines in their free time or were they specialists working for themselves, or perhaps slaves? Nothing is known about them.

Tin mining was concentrated, apart from some secondary sources, in north-western Spain, Brittany, Cornwall and Ireland. Current research is attempting to locate the mines, but up to the present we have only the evidence provided by ancient authors and the distribution of luxury objects along the routes on which the metal was transported. The discovery of groups of continental bronze objects from the Channel off the southern coast of England bears witness to imports from northern France during the Middle Bronze Age. These artefacts, intended for recasting, represent a regular supply of metal to English bronze-smiths.

The importance of metals in trade is already well known. Each village needed to have supplies, either of ore or scrap metal or of finished products, to meet its requirements. However, the role of this production in settlement organization is difficult to estimate. Although it might seem normal to find traces of metalworking on all the large sites, such as the Swiss lake villages, Fort-Harrouard (Eure-et-Loir), Hallunda (southern Sweden) or Rathgall (Ireland), it is surprising to find small bronze-casting workshops in much less important settlements such as Padnal (Grisons), consisting of three to six houses, occasionally nine. The art of the bronze worker seems to have been widely distributed and, even though this required a measure of specialization, it seems to have been part of the knowledge of at least one person in each village (unless we fall back on the itinerant bronze workers beloved of Gordon Childe, although the existence of local peculiarities in ornaments and some utilitarian artefacts leads to the contrary view). Only small amounts of metal would have been produced at one time, and the need to have access to ore resources did not lead to the establishment of settlements at the extraction sites. It is possible, however, that the existence of alluvial tin in the Dartmoor streams allowed the meagre agricultural resources there to be supplemented by working tin for trading purposes. The transition to the production of iron artefacts seems not to have changed this situation until the La Tène period, when the requirements of large-scale production led to the establishment of settlements on the mining sites themselves in Poland.

Iron

It may be suggested that the significance of the transition to iron-using had more to do with the adoption of a higher level of technology rather than with the introduction of a new metal. This took five centuries, and longer in some cases. Iron production developed first in those regions where there were large bronze-working establishments. By contrast, iron was very late in being introduced into those countries where bronze had only penetrated as an imported material. The proliferation of small forges and the generalized use of iron for tools and constructional purposes brought about profound changes in technology and the organization of production from the middle of the La Tène period.

Unlike the ores used to make bronze, iron ores are to be found almost everywhere in Europe, since in protohistory it was surface deposits that were being used, even if they were relatively poor. Haematite, limonite, and even outcrops of underground deposits ensured adequate supplies. British and Dutch iron-makers already knew how to use the bog ore deposits which coloured their waters red. New concentrations formed in the pits from which this bog ore was dug and these could be collected some forty years later.

There are spectacular remains in Poland of an iron industry which reached its apogee in the first century AD. The Holy Cross Mountains are riddled with batteries of low-shaft furnaces partly dug into the ground. At Biskupice, south-east of Warsaw, the ore from the river terraces was mined in trenches perpendicular to the river. The furnaces were grouped together in a separate part of the settlement here, but the work of forging took place in the houses themselves.

The successive phases of the development of iron metallurgy have been clearly defined for central Europe. Three have been identified: in the first, finished products were imported and the new metal was used essentially for decorating bronze artefacts. In the second phase iron artefacts were forged locally from imported ingots. It was only in the third phase that iron ore was extracted and smelted locally.

Romania, being directly influenced from Asia Minor, entered the first phase as early as the Hallstatt A period and the two others in Hallstatt B. An imported iron dagger has been found in a context dated to around 1500 BC in Czechoslovakia, but the second phase cannot be recognized until the end of Hallstatt B and the third in Hallstatt D. In the western provinces of the Lausitz Culture the same development can be observed as in the upper and middle

Danube areas, but the eastern provinces were importing iron ingots until Hallstatt D.

The first iron objects appeared in France during the eighth century BC. These were small artefacts, such as awls and arrowheads, although Lake Annecy has produced an ingot and several graves contain iron swords with bronze hilts and knives. At the confluence of the Oise and the Aisne J.-C. Blanchet discovered a settlement where the main function seems to have been metal manufacture. Iron furnaces appeared alongside the bronze furnaces in the seventh century, and these are the earliest known in the Paris basin.

Iron production was flourishing in western Europe at the beginning of the La Tène period. In the Hunsrück-Eifel bipyramidal ingots were being made, more than 700 examples of which have now been identified. This region was able to meet its own needs and export its products as far afield as Dorset. Several authors have pointed to the overlapping distributions of the princely graves of this period and those areas richest in iron ore in the middle Rhine region and in Lorraine. Unfortunately no mine of this period is known, and the handful of settlements that have been partly excavated have produced no unequivocal traces of iron working. This does not invalidate the theory that has been put forward but it still needs significant discoveries before it can be substantiated.

Iron spread very widely over the whole of Celtic Europe during the Middle La Tène period. It began to be used for nails in domestic buildings as well as for ordinary tools. Caesar notes, for example, that the anchors of the ships of the Veneti were attached with iron chains, whereas at that time the Romans were still using ropes. The fashion for using iron reached its peak when, probably at the beginning of the first century BC, rampart builders began to secure the timber framework beams with large iron spikes. Blacksmiths made tools which, as mentioned earlier, were specialized for working in wood, horn and bone or for making special types of artefact (see Fig. 20). The abundance of metal that characterizes the end of the Iron Age as well as the Gallo-Roman period contrasts with the High Middle Ages, when iron tools became much scarcer.

Evidence of metal working becomes increasingly widespread in the course of the La Tène period. The farm at Gussage All Saints (Dorset) produced evidence of a bronze workshop, with the remains of many moulds for casting bronze artefacts. Some graves contained tools, probably related to the dead man's occupation. At Danebury (Hants) the density of metal objects increased regularly throughout the second half of the first millennium BC. There was, however, no evidence of metalworking on the settlement. During this period metal manufacture was not greatly in evidence. Either it was temporary, leaving very few vestiges on site, or it was carried on outside and so left few traces that could be discovered or dated.

In the Late La Tène several large production centres developed, such as the Steinsburg in Thuringia, the Holy Cross Mountains of southern Poland or the Biskupice deposit. At Biskupice iron production represented an exceptionally important part of the community's activities. At the same time, the large villages of the late second century BC, such as the majority of the oppida, had forges where iron ingots were worked in those cases where ore was not being smelted on the site. Excavations have unfortunately not always been extensive enough to allow the identification of workshops or quarters of the settlement reserved for this activity. It is mainly the presence of tens of kilogrammes of slag which bears witness to metalworking.

The Polish example shows that various situations were possible: in the Holy Cross Mountains the rows of furnaces that were laid out and added to in the early first century AD demonstrate both the rigorous organization of the work and intensification of production. However, these workplaces, apparently located some distance from settlements, may correspond with seasonal working.

If the main trends in the development of the exploitation of raw materials during the Bronze and Iron Ages need to be summarized, the following schema might be proposed. Temperate Europe began with the exchange of raw materials. This was stimulated by increasing demands on the part of the Mediterranean lands. At first it was confined to high-value goods that were easy to transport; then the export of bulk ores required both organized trade routes as well as transport that was both regularly available and better equipped. Finished products obtained in return led to imitations, soon followed by local manufacture. Up to the mid first millennium BC these workshops left few traces in settlements; they did not significantly change peasant society. From the middle of the La Tène period, however, craftsmen began to specialize and increased in numbers. Industrial concentrations appeared and production diversified. Excavation hints at great diversity, and at the existence side-by-side of village blacksmiths, workshops exporting their products over a radius of a few hundred kilometres, and large production centres located on the main mining sites and participating in trade on an international level.

10 Settlement and society

Society

Although we now know a good deal about protohistoric architecture, the same does not hold good for the organization of settlements in the landscape or for the social system that it reflects. Few habitations or nucleated settlements lend themselves to analysis of this kind, and they are very unevenly distributed in time and space. Moreover, they only provide partial and indirect evidence about social distinctions. It is necessary to compare evidence of this kind with the overall picture derived from the entire range of surviving evidence from each protohistoric culture in order to create models of social organization; some aspects of this may be reflected in the arrangements of community layouts.

Celtic society in the eyes of ancient authors

The information provided by Greek and Roman authors always refers to a late period, from the first century BC onwards. At this time Celtic society appears to have been poised between an already complex traditional structure and the transfer of power to the wealthiest members of society, who took advantage of the new economic conditions. In Gaul power resided in certain *civitates* − a *civitas* is an area of land occupied by a tribe and generally covering between one and three modern *départements* − with an assembly of nobles, who delegated it to a magistrate, the *Vergobret*, for a specific period. This state of affairs, which corresponds with the period of occupation of the *oppida*, seems to have been the result of a process of evolution, traces of which can be found in the early Irish texts, even though these are more recent. Several clans or groups of related families, consisting of a number of branches claiming descent from a common ancestor, made up the tribe, which was ruled by a king (it is tempting to relate this social structure to that implied by the sixth century BC Hallstatt princely graves). There was a distinction between free men, who had the right to bear arms, to own livestock and to take part in the tribal assembly, and clients, who received animals from the free men as a concession and conceded their juridical status to them. The importance accorded among free men to the personal acquisition of prestige created a social dynamic: prestige and rank were obtained by means of the redistribution of goods, especially during ceremonial feasts in which everyone would participate according to his social status. This dynamic was also the cause of innumerable warlike conflicts and a measure of political instability.

According to Caesar there were only two classes that counted in Gaul: the nobles and the Druids. The latter were responsible for the most important religious activities, but also for the oral transmission of knowledge and religious and legal traditions (*De Bello Gallico*, 6, 13). Their noble origins in fact made them part of the aristocracy.

The interpretation of the texts suggests that there was a twofold or threefold division in Celtic society, according to whether it is considered that the only free men who took part in the assembly were the aristocracy or whether there was a true intermediate class. Information from cemeteries does not permit the latter interpretation earlier than the La Tène period. It was only from this time onwards that some large cemeteries included a group of graves of armed men which can be seen to be intermediate between rich and common graves.

The earliest models of protohistoric society

Archaeologists began early on to attempt to reconstruct protohistoric societies. Large grave-mounds were considered to be those of chiefs, and the social system postulated for the Bronze Age was one of tribal chiefdoms, whereas that of the Iron Age was of principalities with larger territories.

The first to go beyond these vague ideas was V. Gordon Childe, who considered the nature of prehistoric and protohistoric societies in terms of their technological and economic levels. In *Social Evolution* (1951) he showed self-governing Neolithic peasant groups becoming interdependent in the Bronze Age, as the privileged castes of warriors, entrepreneurs, craftsmen and merchants emerged. This hierarchical system disappeared in the Iron Age as metal became available to all, giving way to a system of 'republican' *civitates* with a large middle class. Like all his contemporaries, Childe assigned a decisive role in the diffusion of innovations from the Mediterranean and the Near East.

In eastern Europe the more or less rigid application of Marxist theory led a number of archaeologists to see military democracies in the Bronze Age and La Tène B societies of central Europe. In the schema for the evolution of societies constructed by Engels in *The Origin of the Family, Private Property and the State* (1884), 'military democracy' was an intermediate stage between tribal societies living in primitive communism and hierarchical societies that were feudal or based on slavery. Power was in the hands of warriors, who accumulated by war the wealth and prestige that distinguished them from other members of the clan. For F. Horst the appearance in central Europe of graves containing rich bronze weapons was evidence of metal objects becoming concentrated in the hands of warriors at the end of the Early Bronze Age in Saxony and Poland, and therefore of a military democracy. The existence of comparatively rich graves in greater numbers in the Late Bronze Age and the considerable increase in the production of metals shown by hoards in his view pointed to the emergence of a more complex society in which priests, 'civil servants' and craftsmen in metal formed privileged *gens* (clans of related individuals) between the elite and the peasants. In the same way, the rich Late Bronze Age I barrows of Slovakia were for Paulik proof of the existence of a military democracy. In the 1960s W. Kimmig and H. Härke proposed models of feudal society to explain the existence in the Hallstatt period of strongholds and chariot graves containing material imported from Greece or Italy. The 'princes' who occupied these fortified sites based their power not only on the control that they exercised over trade in precious objects with the Mediterranean but also on the possession of land and the agricultural surpluses that they derived from it.

Structuralist models

Whatever the merits of these early models, they had the demerit of not taking into account certain characteristics of the periods involved by leaving many of them out of the reckoning. More recent Anglo-American and Scandinavian models have tried to fit in more closely with the archaeological facts and to explain the main changes that affect settlement, funerary practices and material culture. They have been based on the one hand on the work of M. Sahlins and J. Friedman on tribal economy and of K. Polanyi and M.I. Finley on the economy of the classical empires, and on the other hand on the work of J. Friedman and M. Rowlands on the reproduction of social structures. They are characterized by being diachronic and based on an evolutionist perspective. Socio-economic systems evolved on a regional scale following alternate cycles of expansion and decline, the growth phase being accompanied by a more hierarchical society and the crisis phase by a return to a more egalitarian situation, although a different one from the original.

The ideas of Friedman and Rowlands can be summarized as follows: the power of 'big men' and chiefs in tribal systems is based on the prestige resulting from the acquisition and redistribution of valuable objects during feasts and religious ceremonies. Competition between lineage clan chiefs is shown by intensification of agricultural production in order to produce the surpluses needed to obtain prestige objects, by a strategy of exchanges of these goods, first at the local and then at the regional level, and by a strategy of alliances and marriages which gradually led to power becoming hereditary. Intensification of production and demographic pressure demanded greater social integration and stronger hierarchization of both men and settlements. Over-exploitation of land resulted in ecological imbalance and an economic crisis which destabilized the political system and fragmented society once again into smaller units.

The Danish model of Kristiansen

Kristiansen's model is based on the example of Zealand but it is applicable to the whole of Denmark and, even more widely, to northern Europe, with some variations. It is intended to explain the changes that occurred in these regions between the Neolithic and the end of the Bronze Age.

He sees the earliest chiefdoms appearing at the end of the fourth millennium BC, megalithic monuments and causewayed enclosures being the seasonal ceremonial sites where clans assembled. Collective tombs were those of chiefs and their families as well as sites of ancestor cults. Amber, copper and battle-axes were prestige objects used as interregional trade goods while polished stone axes were used for ordinary trade. Deforestation extended gradually over less fertile lands. An initial crisis, linked with shortening fallow periods and increasing deforestation, led to the collapse of chiefdoms, the end of interregional trade, and abandonment of the megaliths. Society restructured itself in segmentary tribes, consisting of several lineages (corresponding with Corded Ware groups) and was then further split into smaller units, the members of which were interred in individual graves beneath family barrows.

From the Late Neolithic animal husbandry became increasingly important and society was regrouped into segmented tribal groups ruled by non-hereditary 'big men'. Interregional trade developed in flint and later in bronze. The rise in agricultural production and in long-distance trade in metal objects once again brought about social hierarchization. In the Early Bronze Age (1900–1500 BC) power became concentrated in the hands of chiefs who drew their political and religious power from production surpluses and trade, and were organized in regional networks of alliances, identifiable from the distribution of luxury objects. They are characterized by their rich interments under barrows in oak coffins, their wooden stools and their unusually long houses. This system was at its height between 1500 and 1200 BC and again between 800 and 650 BC. In the intervening period a crisis connected with deterioration in arable soils, around 1000 BC, resulted in repatterning of settlement sites on the better agricultural land and a marked decrease in metal imports. While Jutland declined into smaller territorial bases, the eastern regions continued to expand.

Prestige goods no longer figured in the richest graves but were collected together in hoards after long use. After another period of ostentatious display, agricultural crisis recurred around 600 BC, leading to society being split up into small autonomous units which did not start to expand again until the introduction of iron, the clearance of new lands and the implementation of new farming practices. Kris

tiansen estimates the population in this last period to have been equal to that of the nineteenth century, on the basis of the density of graves and settlements. There is evidence of later crises, such as that which caused the Cimbri and Teutones to emigrate from Jutland towards the Celtic regions in the late second or early first century BC. According to Kristiansen, this model is also applicable to Great Britain, but the cycles there were shorter.

The prestige goods economy model of Rowlands and Frankenstein

This model lays stress on the fundamental role of long-distance trade and the stimulus exercised by the Mediterranean lands on western and central Europe. It distinguishes three main evolutionary phases: Early-Middle Neolithic; Late Neolithic-Early Bronze Age; and Late Bronze Age-Hallstatt. The power of tribal chiefs was essentially based on the control of external exchange and internal distribution of prestige goods. When economic prosperity allowed, a hierarchy was created among the chiefs, certain of them becoming suzerains of the others. This is what happened when the elites that were in power in Burgundy and southern Germany succeeded in controlling trade with Greece and Italy. Their chariot burials and hillforts such as Mont Lassois and the Heuneburg bear witness to their exceptional importance. Their decline is attributable to a change in direction of long-distance trade routes, which moved to the middle Rhine and Champagne, where the La Tène culture was born. In the Bronze Age and the Iron Age, the contrast between ascribed hereditary status and achieved status resulting from competition is illustrated by alternation between different burial practices: barrow interments accompanied by rich warrior equipment were replaced in the Late Bronze Age by cremations in flat graves or urns with poor grave goods; the former reappeared in the Hallstatt period and gave way once again in the Early La Tène. The transition periods are characterized by growing competition for the control of arable land, evidenced by the construction of territorial boundaries ('Celtic fields', ranch boundaries, etc.), by movement of settlements, and by a reduction in the number of fortified central places in the Iron Age.

Wells' industrial Iron Age

P. Wells pushes the consequences of relations between the Mediterranean world and Europe to the extreme. For him, barbarian Europe transformed its subsistence economy during the Iron Age into a commercial economy exporting to Greece and the Mediterranean through the Greek colonies. True industrial centres were created around mines, as at Hallstatt. The innovations and the social upheaval that resulted were the work of 'entrepreneurs', individuals motivated by their thirst for wealth and power, who developed mines, crafts and trade. This model has, quite rightly, been heavily criticized. The Greek and Phoenician colonies are not known to have organized imports of grain for their mother-cities, and nowhere in temperate Europe are there any traces of industrial towns. The salt-mines of Hallstatt and Hallein employed no more than a hundred miners at any given time and the settlements associated with them were small and probably occupied seasonally. He is, however, probably justified in highlighting the role of individuals in the La Tène period, since ancient authors describe how diversified Celtic society was and how much wealth and influence varied within the Celtic aristocracy and even within particular noble families in the first century BC. It should, however, be noted that it was at the moment when free enterprise had, once again, become the fashionable economic theory that this term appeared in the literature relating to protohistory.

Bintliff's chiefdoms

J. Bintliff offers a fundamental criticism of the two preceding models which seriously limits their application; he considers it to be impossible for the dependence of Europe on the Mediterranean lands to have been such as to control its development. Greek and Italian imports were always small in quantity. Because of the lack of roads and efficient means of transportation, the chief wealth of the continent – grain, hides, slaves – could not be exported in sufficient quantity. Moreover, countries such as Lausitz Poland, Britain and Scandinavia underwent the same developments as the rest of Europe without any significant trade with the Mediterranean. The creation in urban agglomerations of a specialist artisan class is a normal phenomenon which is not due solely to the requirements of an elite. Phases of expansion and crisis in protohistoric cultures, moreover, occurred at different dates and at different frequencies according to country, thereby showing that these were independent regional processes.

For this reason Bintliff proposes a model in which the seat of power is dependent on the ownership or control of farming lands: in the Late La Tène period an aristocrat's power was assessed in terms of ownership of land or animals, in numbers of slaves and clients. Control of trade in prestige goods is a manifestation of this power, not its cause, and the elite went along with, rather than bringing about economic growth. In the Bronze Age Europe was divided into small independent communities whose chiefs can be distinguished by their graves, their weapons and the ownership of prestige objects. In those cases where the territories of chiefdoms can be identified, they are seen to be 3–5 km (2–3 miles) in diameter – in southern Britain, western Bohemia or between the Oder and the Vistula, for example. A higher grade of overlord occurred only intermittently in the Bronze Age, and only in certain regions, such as Early Bronze Age Wessex or Bohemia at the beginning of the Late Bronze Age. Although evidence of this can be found in burials, there are still few traces of the corresponding settlements. A number of ecological, demographic and economic crises led to less land being cultivated, to social upheavals that are manifested in changes in burial ritual and to settlement migration, as for example in Hungary and Slovakia in the Middle Bronze Age or some regions of northern and western Europe in the Late Bronze Age.

From the Hallstatt period, the introduction of iron and new farming practices brought with them a rise in productivity and economic improvement, first in eastern and then in western Europe. The symbols of power were once again mound burials, weapons (this time inspired by those of the Scythians of eastern Europe) and prestige goods imported from the Mediterranean. In some favoured areas, such as Burgundy or southern Germany, a new three-tiered society of 'princes'/chiefs, peasants and slaves arose, for which the fortified central places have been recognized. A crisis that may have been more political than economic in origin came at the end of the Hallstatt period, marked by decline of trade with Greece. Further north, it was an ecological crisis which brought the Lausitz Culture of Poland and eastern Germany to an end, region by region; this is characterized by a reduction in cultivated land and settlement sizes, and by the abandonment of many fortified sites. A connection can also be made with Celtic raids and migrations to Italy in the fourth century BC, which are attributed by ancient writers to overpopulation and the search for land.

Other regions, including Champagne and the middle Rhine, became more prosperous again in the La Tène period. Cemeteries show that privileged intermediate classes emerged. Celtic society can be schematized, according to the economic situation, into two or three levels (aristocracy/people or aristocracy/lesser aristocracy/people). Bintliff recognized that the aristocracies occupied fortified sites and rural estates alternately; the latter, especially in La Tène II, have little to distinguish them from ordinary settlements. In the first century BC the aristocratic families regrouped in *oppida*, many of which retained a rural character with the inclusion of cultivated land.

Models as complex as these can only be summarized by schematizing them. They represent an indispensible step forward, even if it is already known that one of their weaknesses is the fact that they are based on concepts such as 'tribe' or 'chiefdom' which ethnologists criticize for the vagueness that surrounds them. They make it possible for the first time to obtain an overview of the fundamental changes that recurrently affected cultivated areas, burial rites, the circulation of objects and settlements, the field that interests us most. They offer convincing explanations for the abandonment, migration or reoccupation of settlements from one period to another, which can be integrated as well into economic processes as into historic events. They also explain the large variations between one region and another in settlement density or the distribution of major agglomerations.

The family

Ancient sources

Ancient texts provide a certain amount of information about Celtic families and society, but they lack precision and are strongly influenced by the conditions that prevailed in Mediterranean societies. Early medieval Welsh and Irish texts refer to a later reality that had already been considerably transformed. Nevertheless, one of the elements that is common to all these writings is an insistence upon the importance of extended families (consisting of several collateral lines) and of clans, based on patrilineal descent, and on the coming together of several clans within tribes ruled by a chief or a king. Women had rights that were very little different from those of men, they could inherit goods and sometimes even rule, as in the case of the queens Boudica and Cartimandua, who resisted the Roman legions in Britain; the existence of 'princely' tombs that obviously were those of women confirm this in archaeological terms. Concubinage seems to have been usual among the aristocracy. Fostering, whereby children were placed with adoptive parents from a higher social class, created additional alliances. From the La Tène period links with clients constituted a further network of

solidarity to strengthen the aristocracy and which gradually took over from clan solidarity.

We know even less about the Germans. Caesar and Tacitus laid stress on their bravery and the purity of their morals in order to contrast them with the Gauls. They gave no information, however, which would suggest that the structure of the family, or even of society, was really different from that of the Celts. Emphasis on the relationships between uncles and nephews probably relates to the extended family.

Archaeological data

Archaeology provides no clear evidence in this field. It is more than probable, however, that the long-houses of northern Europe, often larger than 100 sq.m (1076 sq.ft) in area, were occupied by extended families. The presence of several hearths in the houses at Emmerhout, Trappendal or Ristoft encourage this view. The rectangular houses of temperate Europe, which covered between 20 and 60 sq.m (215 and 646 sq.ft), would seem to have been for nuclear families of parents and children. These houses usually consisted of a single room and a single hearth. In Bronze Age Hungary, Romania and Slovakia, however, larger houses are found with two or three rooms, which may have housed extended families.

To restrict the distribution of extended family houses in northern Europe would therefore appear not to reflect the reality, which was much less clear-cut, and rich in regional diversity and adaptation. Two Swiss sites provide good examples of this. At Padnal-Savognin (Grisons) the small Early and Middle Bronze Age houses were replaced in the Late Bronze Age by long-houses covering 100–180 sq.m (1076–1937 sq.ft) and consisting of several rooms and hearths, built on the same sites. At Bavois-en-Raillon (Vaud) two buildings of over 100 sq.m (1076 sq.ft) replaced earlier houses of 30–50 sq.m (323–538 sq.ft). We have already seen that at Buchau in southern Germany, a little later in date, nine large farmhouses with U-shaped plans replaced some thirty earlier dwellings.

In Britain extended families are postulated for the ditched or palisaded settlements consisting of one to four houses. The furnishings inside the five roundhouses at Black Patch (Sussex) in the early first millennium BC testify to functional complementarity – in everyday chores, craft activities (by men?) and grain storage, in another cooking activities (by women?), in two smaller buildings ancillary activities (stabling for animals?), and in the last similar activities to those carried out in the first two (a building for young people, the elderly or relatives?).

In Glastonbury (Somerset) 89 buildings from the fourth to second centuries BC were divided into five to seven groups separated by paths and open spaces, and fulfilled different functions (dwellings, byres, workshops, storehouses).

All this information is very vague and it was only recently, with the excavations at the Grotte des Planches, near Arbois (Jura), that it became possible to take this analysis a stage further (Fig. 97). On the basis of the spatial organization of the cave and the distribution of material between the seven hearths, P. Pétrequin was able to show that layer D, dated to Late Bronze Age II, probably housed seven family units with identical domestic equipment. They were in two groups of four and three hearths respectively, distributed around two collective grain stores and they shared a communal stock enclosure. This spatial division into two was reflected in the pottery decoration, which varied slightly from one group to the other. Pétrequin saw in this the archaeological expression of two kindred groups or two extended families, each consisting of three or four nuclear families.

97

The Late Bronze Age cave occupation in the Grotte des Planches-près-Arbois (Jura). A refuge settlement in a cave, with installations around seven hearths. (P. Pétrequin, 1985. Redrawn by G. Searle.)

Extended family and nuclear family here articulate with one another clearly in an organization which could equally have been accommodated as easily in a large house with several hearths as in several smaller houses.

Populations

Demographic problems in antiquity can only be tackled indirectly, through cemeteries and settlements, and on the basis of comparisons with better known periods. There are two different questions: what was the population of any region or village at a given time, and how did it develop?

Taking a long-term view, it is the nature of population growth that is of interest. Variations in the number of houses, villages and graves and significant changes in the volume of material production make it possible to evaluate demographic trends. In the long term, protohistory is a period of population growth over the whole of Europe. Overall, there were many more settlements or cemeteries in the Late than in the Early Bronze Age, in the Late La Tène than in the Hallstatt period. Variations in this growth were long underestimated by attributing a lack of sites (in Early Bronze Age Hungary, for example, or the early first millennium BC in England) to deficiencies in archaeo-

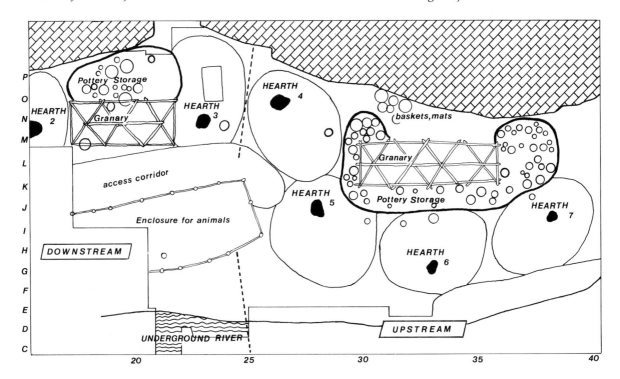

logical research. The parallels established between ecological crises and diminution in the amount of cultivated land attested by pollen analysis on the one hand and the marked decrease in settlement numbers at certain times on the other has now led to archaeological data being interpreted more literally. There are good reasons to argue for the existence of periods of rapid growth, some of which were followed by true demographic crises.

Fluctuations in population numbers can be observed in Hungary and Slovakia between the Middle and Late Bronze Ages. The Early and Middle Bronze Ages seem there to have been periods of strong growth, with village-scale occupation on tells continuing over several centuries. The tells were abandoned at the end of the Middle Bronze Age, to be succeeded by much more transient and dispersed settlement.

Another demographic crisis has been recorded by C. Burgess in Britain at the beginning of the first millennium BC, when the advance of peat-bogs made agriculture impossible over much of the Highlands, settlements returned to the valleys and the Lowlands and there was a marked lack of domestic artefacts in metal. This unfortunate period was framed by two phases of rapid population growth between the fifteenth and thirteenth and between the eighth and sixth centuries BC.

Although K. Kristiansen only dealt with the economic aspect of the crises that affected Jutland, he did not fail to notice the shrinkages of settlement at the end of the Neolithic period and again at the end of the second millennium BC and around 650 BC. Finally, it is difficult not to connect the end of the Lausitz culture in Poland and eastern Germany, which took place in different areas between the middle and the end of the fifth century BC, to a demographic crisis. Most of the large fortified sites were abandoned or replaced by small undefended villages, and for several centuries the total number of sites was decreasing. This perspective, which is more catastrophic than the slow growth previously accepted, accords well with the evolutionary models of society described above. It was less climatic deterioration that lay at the root of economic and demographic downturns than ecological imbalances resulting from over-exploitation of the land. Economic and political instability combined to bring in their wake periodical profound modifications to human groups and to the patterning and scale of their settlement in the landscape. Overpopulation and the quest for new land were the causes put forward by ancient authors to explain the Celtic and Germanic raids and migrations from the fourth to first centuries BC. And the obligatory virginity up to the age of 20

among the Germans described by Caesar may be evidence of birth control, since delaying the age of marriage has always been, along with infanticide, one of the most common methods of population control.

Identifying demographic trends and proceeding to numerical estimates of populations are at two different levels of difficulty: the latter is much more delicate and uncertain. British archaeologists have put forward figures for the Late La Tène period in Britain by comparing the number of sites and graves in cemeteries in this period and in the Middle Ages. B. Cunliffe and P.J. Fowler consider that the population of England in the first millennium BC may have been the same as or even greater than that recorded in the Domesday Book in 1086, i.e. 1.5 million inhabitants.

Other estimates have been made at house or village level. However, they diverge markedly, according to the number of inhabitants per house – 4–5 according to some scholars and 7–8 according to others. This results in great ambiguity, as C. Masset has shown in his palaeodemographic studies. Up to the nineteenth century, prior to Jenner's discovery of vaccination, 50 per cent of children died before the age of 12. It is therefore necessary to consider four people of more than 12 years of age per family, or units of six, including young children, in order to ensure generation renewal and a stable demographic situation. If the models that assume large population variations proposed earlier are adopted, it is necessary to assume family numbers that are higher or lower, according to the trend. Nevertheless, the addition of a fifth living person per family and per generation results over a century in a growth that exceeds 100 per cent. A more appropriate figure is 4/5 adults rather than 7/8.

Figures of 1000–1250 and 2500 inhabitants respectively have been proposed for the fortified settlements of Biskupin and Sobiejuchy in Poland at the beginning of the Iron Age. These figures seem to be exceptional, if not disproportionate. Other calculations have led to a proposed population of 700–750 inhabitants for Biskupin. For less densely occupied sites, figures of 200–400 inhabitants have often been calculated, as, for example, in the Late Bronze Age Swiss lake villages, English hillforts such as Danebury in the second century BC or the Iron Age villages of Jutland such as Hodde. The Hallstatt and Hallein cemeteries belonging to communities that were exploiting the rich salt-mines of the Austrian Salzkammergut represent populations of around 450 and 250 people respectively. The totality of these observations gives a picture of a relatively large overall protohistoric population, comparable with that in the Middle Ages. It was, however, less dense and more dispersed.

11 Development of settlement in the Bronze Age

a world of villages

Characteristics of protohistoric settlement

Dispersed and nucleated settlements

There is considerable regional diversity in protohistoric settlement. Dispersed settlement predominated in the British Isles and Scandinavia, whereas grouped units were the rule in continental Europe. There is a clear tendency for settlements to increase in size over time, but this operated discontinuously, and large villages may alternate with hamlets or isolated farmsteads in the succeeding period. Is it therefore legitimate in such circumstances to talk of proto-urbanism in respect of the large Bronze Age or Hallstatt agglomerations? The answer is in the affirmative if this is considered to be a phase with characteristics of its own, independent of what was to follow it, but it must be in the negative if it is seen as the stage immediately preceding urbanism proper.

In this respect, south-eastern Europe seems by the Bronze Age to have reached a more advanced stage of pre-urbanization before the rest of the continent. Large stable villages had been established as early as the Chalcolithic period, in the third millennium BC. They consisted of some dozens of houses that were rebuilt on the same site over several consecutive centuries. Rebuilding on top of the ruins of earlier houses led to the formation of tells, which rose several metres above the surrounding plain. This concentration of population, however, was interrupted at the end of the Middle Bronze Age and the tells were abandoned in favour of smaller sites that were fewer in number. The end of the Bronze Age in Germany saw the construction of large fortified sites which had no parallels in the Hallstatt Iron Age. The process of

population concentration was neither gradual nor uniform in operation but followed instead cycles that were often succeeded by regression for periods of varying duration.

Protohistoric Europe was an essentially rural world, with its economic and social organization based on villages.

The protohistoric village

In the Middle Ages the term 'village' had a precise meaning: it was situated at the centre of the territory that it exploited and consisted of houses grouped round a cemetery, a church and often a castle. It united a peasant community in a parish that had legal status. It provided the context for commercial and craft functions. It is impossible to be so precise for the protohistoric period in our present state of knowledge. Any settlements that encompassed several houses are termed villages, the words 'farmstead' or 'hamlet' being reserved for smaller groups of two or three buildings, regardless of their functions.

The reality of protohistory differs profoundly from later situations: the agglomerations that we know – hamlets and large or small villages – represent the highest degree of urbanization attained up to the Iron Age. They were thus the only places where all the functions necessary for economic and social life – farming, crafts, exchange with neighbouring communities of products from near and far, social life – had to be performed. This is confirmed by archaeology: the most specialized of activities, metal production, was carried out in most villages. The communities that lived in these villages seem nearer to the peasant communities studied by ethnologists than to those studied by historians. In the Bronze Age these were independent communities, closely connected internally by family and clan loyalties and externally by marriage alliances and by trade networks which may be traced in the archaeological record. In Gaulish society religion, with its great centres located outside the settlements, cemented tribal and intertribal relationships, at least up to the first century BC. The same may have been the case in the Bronze Age, where the few known sanctuaries also lay outside settlements.

Towards a settlement hierarchy

Anglo-American social models lay stress on the existence of central places, agglomerations that served as political and economic centres for tribal chiefs or aristocrats. In the absence of special buildings related to these functions, however, the archaeological data are singularly silent on this question. There are agglomerations that differ greatly in size, and some have monumental defences that are at times disproportionately large or contain richer metal objects than others. It is still very difficult to demonstrate archaeologically that the more outstanding settlements in fact controlled the lands around them. None the less, two types of study have thrown some light on this question: in Britain it has been shown that certain hillforts, such as Late Bronze Age Rams Hill or La Tène Danebury, possessed storage capacities that were ten to twenty times greater than those of neighbouring sites, and this corresponds well with what might be expected of settlements occupied by an elite that drew its power from the control of exchange and agricultural surpluses.

On the other hand, study of the distribution of contemporaneous fortified sites in certain regions that have been well surveyed shows that the larger sites are more or less equidistant from one another, and therefore may have controlled territories of roughly the same size. The size of such territories increased between the Bronze Age and the end of the Iron Age. It was 10–20km (6–12 miles) in diameter for regions such as western Bohemia in the Late Bronze Age or southern England and the land between the Oder and the Vistula in Poland at the beginning of the Iron Age. In southern Germany and England it had grown to 80–120km (50–76 miles) in diameter by the end of the La Tène period. This expansion, which can be connected with the concentration of power and services in increasingly large central places, which at the same time became fewer in number, seems to provide good confirmation of the existence of these centralized functions at places, even though at the moment it is still very difficult to identify the farmsteads and

villages that were dependent on them. On the eve of the Roman conquest, the hierarchy of settlements in Gaul varied from one *civitas* to another. I. Ralston has emphasized the opposition between those regions that tended to be archaic, with an enormous *oppidum* accompanied by relatively small settlements that were still rural in character, and the richest provinces, where a dozen proto-urban centres seem to have disputed economic control amongst themselves.

Developing villages

The study of agglomerated settlements is concerned with three aspects: layout, function, and the social organization that they reflect at the real as well as the symbolic level. The first difficulty in identifying the different types of agglomeration and the number of houses in them lies in the recording of the successive occupation phases in order to study only groups that are contemporaneous. In the past studies were based on the oldest and the most recent finds, which determined the *terminus ante quem* and the *terminus post quem* of the occupation; it was considered that a settlement would have been occupied continuously throughout the intervening period. Radiocarbon and dendrochronological dating of house posts has shown that occupation phases were shorter than had been supposed and that they were separated by periods of abandonment. The earliest Neolithic villages on Lake Clairvaux (Jura) lasted some twenty years, their successors around a century. At Cortaillod and Auvernier (Neuchâtel) the villages twice survived for fifty years and were rebuilt close to the original site. At Champréveyres (Neuchâtel) the occupation, which was marked by some thirty phases of tree-felling to provide structural timbers, spread over two hundred years and gave evidence of growth during several phases. It is equally highly unlikely that all the 24 houses that have been identified at Auvernier were in existence at the same time.

In other cases radiocarbon dates have shown that apparent great similarities in the structures that were erected mask successive occupations. At Green Knowe (Peeblesshire), despite a more or less regular layout of houses on the hill-slope, their dates range from the seventeenth to the ninth century BC and argue for multiple occupations separated by periods of abandonment. The impression of a settlement strung out along the hill-side given by the excavation plans is contradicted by the dates. By contrast, radiocarbon analysis has confirmed the contemporaneity of buildings at Black Patch (Sussex): platform 4 had four round-houses on it, the three pits of which were dated

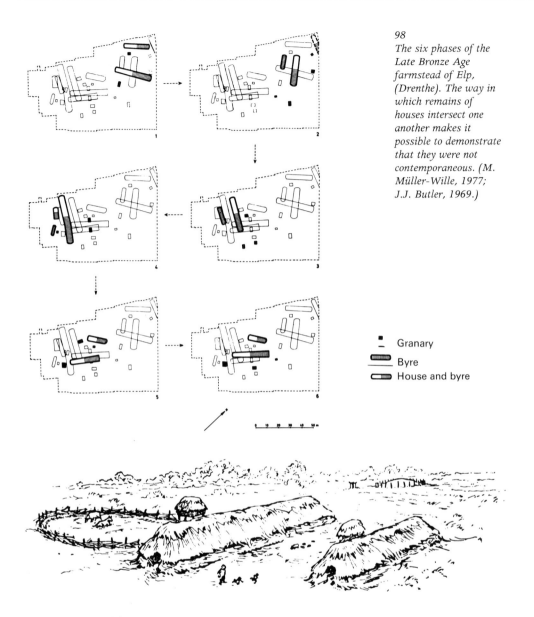

98
The six phases of the Late Bronze Age farmstead of Elp, (Drenthe). The way in which remains of houses intersect one another makes it possible to demonstrate that they were not contemporaneous. (M. Müller-Wille, 1977; J.J. Butler, 1969.)

■ Granary
▬
▭▭▭ Byre
◀▭▭ House and byre

to 830–830 bc (with single standard deviations of 30–80 years). They were thus most probably contemporaneous. The material found in them also suggests that they had complementary functions, one being used for cooking, another for general craft activities and storage, and the remaining two to activities that left no trace in the ground.

The evolutionary nature of settlement agglomerations makes any typological analysis a delicate matter when there are no absolute dates available. Some layouts do, however, contain within them evidence of a development which does not allow all the buildings to be treated as contemporaneous, especially when their emplacements overlap. The village of Elp in Drenthe (the Netherlands) attributable to the end of the second millennium BC provides a particularly clear example of this situation (Fig. 98). The superimposition of the different structures allowed H.T. Waterbolk to show that there was only a simple farmstead consisting of a long byre-house, either accompanied by a shorter example or by a shorter byre as well as barns and granaries. Five rebuildings in four centuries were evidenced with six plans distinguishable by the positioning and orientation of the structures.

In northern Europe long houses were often laid out on the same orientation and occupied selected topographical settings. Successive overlapping of buildings shows that villages developed in a linear way, either by being displaced longitudinally in successive phases (e.g. Bjerg or Spjald in Denmark) or laterally (Hijken in the Netherlands), and it may be inferred with a considerable degree of certainty that each village at any given period contained considerably fewer houses than may appear from first impressions. Even when this bias is taken into account, the tendency of villages in protohistory to grow remains a reality, albeit one that is subject to substantial regional variations.

The Bronze Age/Iron Age break is completely artificial in many regions. Continuity was maintained in both the British Isles and northern Europe. There was, however, a break due to the disappearance of the lake villages at the end of the Bronze Age. Changes in location introduce a major discontinuity in data and have led to the creation of independent *corpora* of data compiled from different points of view, the most recent being focused on the origins of towns. It is for this reason that the Bronze and Iron Ages are treated separately in the pages that follow.

Settlement in Britain

Isolated settlements

In the British Isles settlement was at first dispersed, most often a farmstead comprising a single round-house or a complex of between two and five buildings accompanied or not by granaries, pits and sheds. This form is to be found in all regions of Britain – for example, Amberley Mount (Sussex) in the south-east, Chalton (Hants) and Bishop Cannings Down (Wilts) in the south-west, and Gwithian (Cornwall) in the west. Gwithian, where several phases were characterized by a house set in the middle of a small system of rectangular fields, is fairly typical of settlements from the first half of the second millennium BC. Some settlements testify to remarkable stability, producing materials that span most of the second millennium BC, from beakers to Deverel-Rimbury urns, especially in the south-west. In the north and south-west of England the remains are particularly numerous because they are easily visible in the landscape owing to their having been built on platforms cut into

hillsides. In the uplands of Scotland and northern England several hundred houses of this type are now known, especially in the Cheviots.

From the mid second millennium and throughout the first millennium farmsteads often consisted of more than one building. Some of them continued to be built in open countryside, but most were enclosed from this time onwards. They were surrounded with a palisade, a bank or a ditch, the shape of which varies according to the region. The discovery of traces of palisades beneath some banks suggests that this may be the earliest form of enclosure. A. Ellison considers that the typical settlement of this period consisted of a main round-house, one or two subsidiary buildings and storage structures. The plains and hills of southern England have produced hundreds of settlements of this type. What we still need to know is the distance between these settlements and the extent of the agrarian zones they exploited. Study of the landscape and its resources led P. Drewett to calculate the land cultivated by the inhabitants of Black Patch (Sussex) to be about 2km ($1\frac{1}{4}$ miles) in diameter, i.e. *c.* 300ha (741 acres), an area that seems to be compatible with the known distribution of other sites of the same period. If the distribution of these farmsteads was regular, the South Downs between the Ouse and the Cuckmere would have been exploited by eleven farmsteads.

The defended farmsteads of Wessex and Sussex are best known, since they have been studied for nearly a century. On the chalk uplands of this region the typical settlement was a farmstead surrounded by a bank, whose sub-rectangular shape was often connected with the adjacent Celtic fields, with which they were integrated from the outset or later. These enclosures were often as much as 50m (164ft) across and could have one or more entrances in a corner. The Wessex enclosures, which are often larger than the Sussex examples, are both banked and ditched. They contain between one and five round-houses and most of them date from the middle and second half of the second millennium BC. They are sometimes associated with Deverel-Rimbury cemeteries, which correspond with extended families.

In Sussex the enclosures are usually in the form of a bank alone, as at Plumpton Plain A, New Barn Down, or Itford Hill (Fig. 99). Some of these sites have produced evidence of long continuity: Shearplace Hill and Poundbury, near Dorchester (Dorset), both lasted from the fifteenth to the tenth centuries BC, with three construction phases at the former.

All these settlements cover areas comparable with undefended settlements and must therefore have

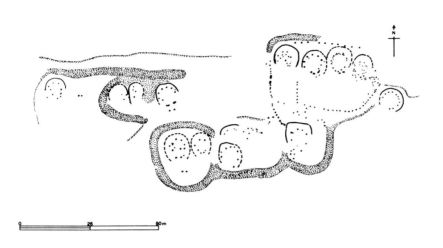

99
Middle-Late Bronze Age settlement on Itford Hill (Sussex). This palisaded settlement is typical of the Deverel-Rimbury group. It was rebuilt, probably four times, on sites that were very close to one another. In each unit there was a main house with a porch and ancillary buildings for cooking and storage, on a terrace. (B.W. Cunliffe, 1974.)

housed an equal number of inhabitants. They bear witness to a mixed agricultural economy devoted to the production of wheat and barley and the rearing of cattle, sheep and a few pigs. In addition, it should be borne in mind that in a number of cases they had storage capacities greater than those of open sites. Only Martin Down (Dorset) with its much larger dimensions is different: it may represent a higher grade of settlement. The same applies to Hook (Hants), the rectangular ditch of which is breached by a very large entrance edged with massive upright posts.

Isolated settlements must have been very important in Ireland, but there are few traces of them. The artificial platforms known as 'crannogs' rarely have more than one house on them. Ballinderry no. 2 (Co. Offaly), Knockalappa (Co. Clare), and Rathtinaun (Co. Sligo) are the only examples so far datable to the Bronze Age, but there can be little doubt that there were many more at this period. Irish archaeologists consider that temporary settlements of branches or even hides must have been common. Caves were also occupied on a seasonal basis, especially along the coast, as was also the case in England.

In Shetland and Orkney most of the settlements were scattered farmsteads accompanied by fields. Two 'villages', each of three houses, succeeded one another at Jarlshof in the Late Bronze Age (see Fig. 61). Liddle Farm I and Beaquoy in the Orkneys were also isolated settlements, characterized by the large dumps of burnt stones and the cooking pits inside or associated with the stone houses.

British archaeologists have for many years been uncertain about the dating of some of their protohistoric pottery, and as a result also of the sites in which

the pottery is found. For a long time they believed that they were unable to identify early first millennium settlements. C. Burgess has recently put forward a new theory, which attributes the marked decrease in sites from this period to a major economic and demographic crisis, similar to that which destroyed the later Roman Empire or fourteenth century Europe. This should be discernible not only in settlements but also in a dramatic fall in the production of workaday bronze objects.

The upland palisaded farmstead, in due course typical of the Iron Age, spread from the beginning of the first millennium BC. It consisted of two or three round-houses and granaries enclosed by a palisade. A typical example is Staple Howe (Yorks; Fig. 100). Some sixty sites of this kind are known in the Cheviots, dating to the first millennium BC.

Hamlets and villages

In south-western England (Devon and Cornwall), in Wales and in the uplands of northern England and Scotland, building was in unmortared stone (drystone) and walls replaced the banks of the chalk south. Open and enclosed settlements are to be found alongside one another, as in other regions, but the former can also be dated to an earlier period. It is very difficult to estimate their importance owing to the lack of absolute dates, since the gradual migration of buildings results in a scatter of neighbouring buildings after several centuries. Round-houses can be identified on hill-slopes by virtue of their levelled platforms: the number of such platforms on a single site can vary between one or two and a dozen, and in northern

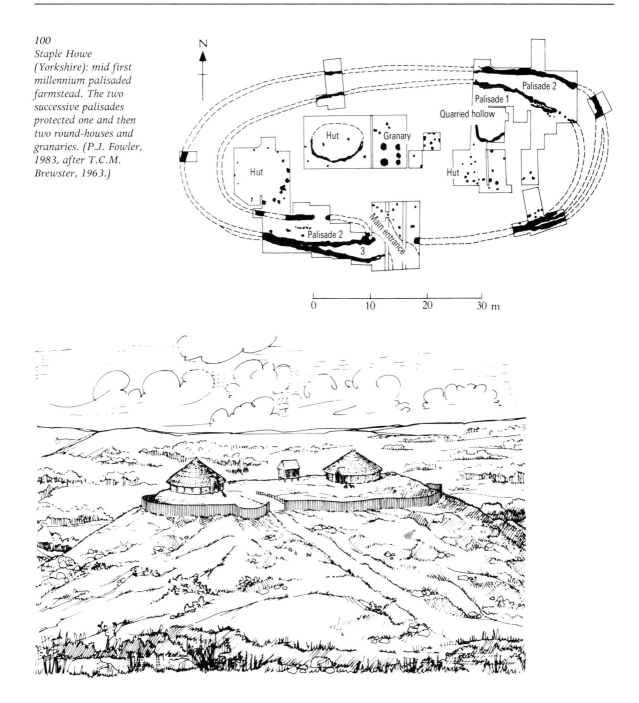

100
Staple Howe (Yorkshire): mid first millennium palisaded farmstead. The two successive palisades protected one and then two round-houses and granaries. (P.J. Fowler, 1983, after T.C.M. Brewster, 1963.)

England can occasionally be as many as thirty. Nine are known at Green Knowe (Peeblesshire), three of them of different dates and ranging from the seventeenth to the tenth century BC. They are associated with a system of banks and clearance cairns that is known over some 2.5ha (6 acres) but which must have been more extensive. The closest site is just on the other side of the stream on the slopes of White Knowe and consists of about eighteen platforms, which are unlikely to have been contemporaneous in view of the proximity of Green Knowe.

In the Dartmoor region, occupied intensively from

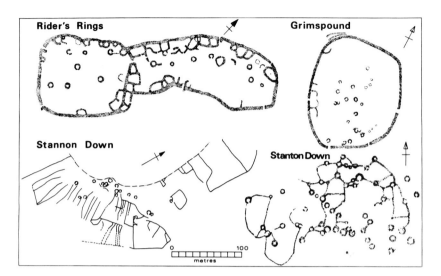

101
Bronze Age upland settlements in south-west England. The round-houses, built on platforms where the land slopes, are in some cases dispersed over the landscape (Stannon Down, Dartmoor), sometimes joined by walls (Stanton Down, Bodmin Moor), and sometimes grouped inside walled enclosures (Rider's Ring and Grimspound, Dartmoor). In each case the houses are not all contemporaneous and the villages are smaller than the archaeological remains suggest. All these villages are associated with 'Celtic fields'. (C. Burgess, 1980.)

the mid second millennium BC until the first third of the first millennium, unenclosed houses are less numerous than enclosed ones, and one-third of the buildings in the Plym valley belong to this category. The enclosure walls are, however, often later than some of the houses that they enclose. Open settlements contain a very variable number of buildings. Traditionally, a distinction is made between the farming establishments located on the drier eastern flanks of Dartmoor, which comprise between one and four houses and are at the heart of a small system of 'Celtic fields' (e.g. Rippon Tor, Horridge Common, Blissmoor), and the larger concentrations, more based on pastoralism, which may include several dozens of houses (Fig. 101). Stanton Down on Dartmoor consists of 68 buildings.

As in the previous case, these defended settlements may be true hamlets or villages (Fig. 102). Among these the 'pounds', which are always surrounded by a stone wall, are more or less irregular in shape, or at best subcircular. Grimspound and Rider's Ring contain around a score of round buildings that are not necessarily contemporary. Other enclosures bear witness to gradual enlargement with the successive incorporation of houses that are slowly linked by supplementary walls, whilst others are clearly excluded, as at Legis Tor or Lower Hentor. It is questionable whether these exclusions were made for functional reasons, to suit family groupings, or for reasons that we cannot comprehend.

Defended and open settlements seem to have been complementary in certain parts of Dartmoor: in the Plym valley, for example, most of the sites lie between 336 and 367m (1102 and 1204ft) above sea-level. There are, however, settlements that are generally open and contain smaller houses lying above the reaves which mark the limit between the valley and the upland communal pasture. These most likely correspond with seasonal transhumance occupation connected with animal husbandry, whereas the larger settlements in the valleys associate this activity with agriculture and exploitation of the resources of the river.

In northern England and Scotland isolated farmsteads are much more common than grouped settlements, whether enclosed or open. They appear in the Neolithic but were most highly developed during the Early and Middle Bronze Age. The house surrounded by an interrupted enclosure at Swine Sty (Derbyshire) dates from the beginning of the second millennium BC. Houseledge (Northumberland), where the undefended platforms are very similar to those at Green Knowe, goes back to the Early Bronze Age. Isolated houses and hamlets multiplied throughout the second millennium BC and part of the first millennium. Some had a linear layout, as at Corbury Hill (Lanarkshire), or were clustered, as at Craig Law (Peeblesshire).

In the northern isles of Orkney and Shetland, stone houses of the Skara Brae and the later Jarlshof type were, from the Late Neolithic to the Late Bronze Age, occasionally in groups. They were distributed in small hamlets or villages of between three and eight houses, as at Gruting, Mavis Grind or Stanydale. In the case of Stanydale and Whalsay, one more imposing house has traditionally been interpreted as a temple by reason of its affinities with the Shetland form of megalithic chambered cairn.

The first grouped settlements in Ireland were in the uplands: the oldest, Knockadoon on Lough Gur, consisted of rectangular Neolithic houses and also of later circular buildings, one of which was a Middle Bronze Age metal workshop.

A new type of site has recently been discovered in the Thames valley: excavations have revealed a large settlement on the river bank at Runnymede Bridge, Egham, to the west of London. It is dated to the Late Bronze Age (eighth century BC). It is located in a meander of the Thames cut by a Bronze Age channel

and consists of a strong double palisade running parallel to the river bed that has been revealed over some 50m (164ft). Excavations over an area running 80m (262ft) back have produced many post-holes, which suggest closely set buildings. Two interpretations have been put forward: the palisade was either consolidation work on the river bank by means of a post revetment or it was a meander fortified by a palisade. Whatever the true explanation, the richness of the material that excavation produced and the continental provenance of part of the artefacts show that this settlement played an important role in river-borne trade in the Thames valley and beyond. It is at

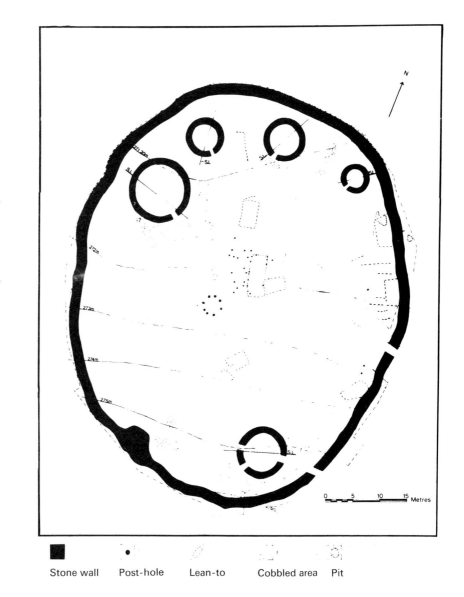

102
Enclosure 15, Shaugh Moor, Dartmoor, Devon (Bronze Age, late second millennium BC). The thick drystone wall encloses five round-houses, rectangular huts and two cobbled working areas. Radiocarbon dating shows that the houses, which were in most cases rebuilt twice over several centuries, were not all contemporaneous. In the main occupation phase, around 1650 BC, there must have been three or four houses. (G.J. Wainwright and K. Smith, 1980.)

Stone wall   Post-hole   Lean-to   Cobbled area   Pit

103

The Late Bronze Age hillfort of Mam Tor, Derbyshire. The ditch and bank follow the contours of the hilltop, which is closed to the south by a cross-bank. The remains of many round-houses can be distinguished in the interior of the fort. (Airviews M/cr Ltd, Manchester.)

the present time the oldest of a series of sites known from their piles, especially in the Trent valley.

Hillforts

Contrary to what used to be believed, hillforts, one of the most characteristic settlement forms in Iron Age Britain, did not first appear in this period but half a millennium earlier. The earliest defended upland sites date from the Late Bronze Age: Mam Tor (Derbyshire) was occupied around 1100 BC (Fig. 103). It is situated on a crest some 500m (1640ft) above sea-level and its 6ha (15 acres) are surrounded by a stone and earth rampart backing up a ditch. The dozen round-houses in the area that has been explored are sited for preference on the slopes inside the rampart and also a

short distance away from it.

From the Middle Bronze Age large enclosures are known in southern England alongside farmsteads. The enclosures are greatly outnumbered by the farmsteads and are often sited in a central location in relation to them. According to A. Ellison they are generally situated at the junction of two pottery stylistic regions. Rams Hill (Berkshire), one of the best known fortified sites in southern England, and Martin Down (Hants) lie on the edges of the distribution areas of different pottery types. Siting of this kind seems to emphasize control over trade, whilst the central positions of Iron Age hillforts correspond more with control of territories. Nevertheless, a number of these hillforts in fact began in the Bronze Age. This is the case at Rams Hill, where the Early Bronze Age inturned ditch was strengthened in the Middle Bronze Age by a box rampart, which was in turn reconstructed with a double palisade and several entrances around the eleventh century BC and was finally replaced in the Iron Age by an enclosure that was three times larger. The hectare occupied by the original fort contained few buildings at any given time

– no more than two or three, plus some ten four-post granaries. Other forts, such as Cow Down (Wiltshire) or Old Down (Hants, in the Test valley) contained only a single house. South Barrule (Isle of Man), with seventy houses, was an exception, or it may have anticipated later settlements of this kind.

The end of the Bronze Age saw the number of hillforts increasing from Wales to Scotland via the Midlands, but eastern England remained outside this development. In Ireland it appears that the hillfort phenomenon had already begun in the Late Bronze Age, since recent discoveries have revealed the existence of settlements of this kind on upland sites at this time. Later fortifications have in general prevented the identification of Bronze Age defences, but there is a strong presumption to this effect at Rathgall (Co. Wicklow), Navan (Co. Armagh) or Downpatrick (Co. Down).

English archaeologists have been discussing the origins of hillforts for many years. At the present time they are in agreement that they are in part connected with a reorganization of the landscape and the new division of territories represented by the systems of linear ditches. They have also observed that from the Bronze Age onwards many hillforts generally had storage capacities greater than those of open sites. When erosion rendered some of the land unsuitable for further cultivation, greater pressure was exercised over ownership or control of the remaining fertile land. The creation of fortified settlements at the centres of land-division systems and, later on, concentration of settlement on these better defended sites represented a response to the crisis.

If the regions of building in drystone are omitted (and this must be done cautiously, since by definition these are based on more durable archaeological evidence), Bronze Age settlement in the British Isles remained fundamentally rural in character, and even dispersed, but this does not preclude there having been a hierarchical society at that period, when the distribution of prestige metal objects is taken into account.

Farmsteads and villages in northern Europe

Despite the abundant documentation on this subject and the countless discussions about it, it remains difficult to evaluate the importance of protohistoric nucleated settlement in the Netherlands, northern Germany, and Scandinavia. The absence of enclosures or fortifications until late in the Iron Age made it possible for houses to be replaced gradually one after another, as shown by the lateral displacement of the settlement.

Farmsteads

A number of isolated three-aisled long-houses are known, accompanied by some ancillary buildings. The example of Elp (Drenthe) and its six successive farmsteads has already been mentioned. A number of other farmsteads with several buildings are known from the Low Countries. The site of Nijnsel (Brabant: Fig. 104) consisted of a single four-aisled long-house

104
The Middle Bronze Age farmstead at Nijnsel, Brabant. The four-aisled house is accompanied by barns, granaries, and a circular structure. (G. Beex and R.S. Hulst, 1968.)

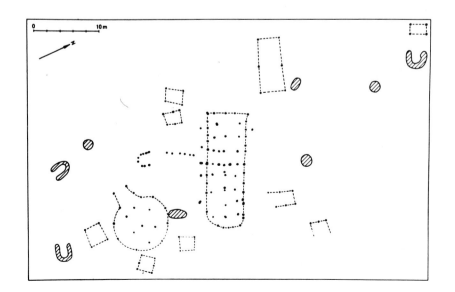

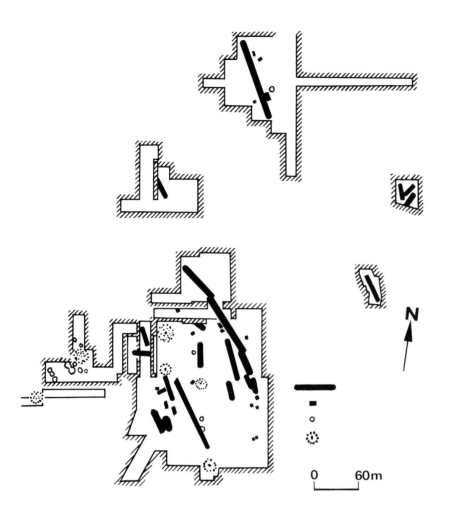

105
Angelsloo-Emmerhout,
Drenthe (Middle and
Late Bronze Age).
Several groups of
between two and six
contemporaneous
buildings succeed one
another, retaining the
same orientation. Very
long three-aisled byre-
houses, two of them, 80
and 65m (262 and
213ft) long
respectively, shorter
houses or barns and
granaries can be
distinguished. (T.
Postic, after J.J.
Butler, 1969.)

N

0   60m

with a shorter barn, a circular structure (enclosure or round-house?), seven four- or six-post granaries, and some pits. This association of a long-house with a circular structure can also be found at Dodewaard (Guelderland) and Lesdain, near Tournai. All these farmsteads date to the Middle Bronze Age with the exception of Elp, from the Late Bronze Age. Isolated houses are also known – two-aisled, like the successive buildings at Molenaarsgraf (Netherlands), dated to the turn of the second millennium BC, and Ripdorf (Saxony), or three-aisled, like those at Zijderveld (southern Netherlands) from the end of the Middle Bronze Age or Trappendal, north of Schleswig.

Isolated houses and farmsteads are also known from Denmark. At Hover (western Jutland) a house was built in the Late Bronze Age on top of an earlier one. In the same region, at Grøntoft, three sets of Bronze Age structures which may have been isolated farmsteads

with only one or two buildings, lie outside the Iron Age village.

Hamlets and villages in the Netherlands

Several hundred Bronze Age houses are known in northern Europe. Some sites contain as many as sixty, which in most cases do not belong to the same period. At least three periods have been identified at Middle and Late Bronze Age Andijk (western Friesland), where there was a succession of long-houses, shorter houses, and finally houses built on *terp* mounds. At Bovenkarspel, less than 10km (6 miles) away, it is possible to distinguish four phases of occupation with a total of 58 buildings between 1350 and 850 BC, and then three phases with no more than fifteen houses on *terps* between 850 and 750 BC – that is to say, if occupation was continuous, of the order of three houses every thirty years.

Dutch archaeologists agree that these Bronze Age villages contained between two and six byre-houses: at Angelsloo-Emmerhout, where all the buildings were aligned north-west/south-east and where the groundplans of certain buildings overlapped (Fig. 105), Van der Wals believed that he could make out groups of two or three farmsteads with ancillary buildings, as at Elp. At Hijken (Fig. 106), as at Bovenkarspel, there seem to have been no ancillary buildings. The houses were built near a morainic ridge in order to leave the freely-drained land for cultivation. The tree species selected for building at Bovenkarspel imply that structures there did not last very long. This hamlet did not consist of more than four houses in the earlier period and three in the later, when the houses were shorter, probably because the byre was reduced in size (confirmed in the eastern part by the contents of the boundary ditches).

Two settlement models are currently distinguished in the Netherlands: one consists of between one and three farmsteads made up of several buildings, one of which is substantially larger than the others, but is not necessarily the only dwelling, and the other is represented by between two and six farmsteads, each consisting of a single house of uniform size. The first

evidence of social differentiation may perhaps be observable at Elp and Angelsloo-Emmerhout, represented by the difference in size between the very large byre-houses and the shorter ones.

Scandinavian hamlets and villages

Most of the Scandinavian settlement sites have alignments of houses, all on the same orientation and some of them with intersecting groundplans. This clearly demonstrates the gradual migration of the settlement over time. These settlements are unfortunately for the most part rather poor in artefactual material and so it is as yet only possible to divide them into an early and a late phase. The best known examples come from Jutland.

The Early Bronze Age sites of Myrhøj and Egehøj have each produced three houses, but there may have been more. At least five houses were revealed at Jegstrup; there were only three at Fragtrup, one of them much smaller, which was clearly an outbuilding of the largest, but there was evidence of other house groups, 150m (492ft) to the east and 400m (1312ft) to the north.

The sites of Vadgård, Bjerg, and Spjald were occupied more intensively, or at all events repeatedly

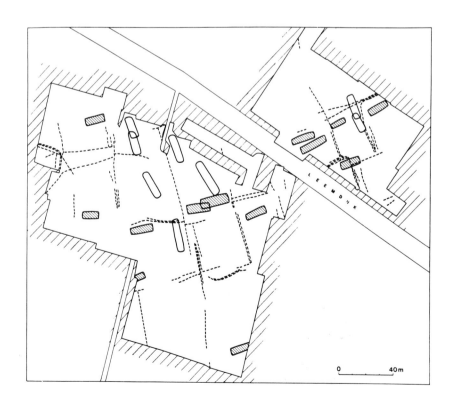

106
Bronze Age and Hallstatt period village and 'Celtic fields' at Hijken, Drenthe. The houses with rounded ends of the late second and early first millennium BC (unshaded) are all orientated NNW-SSE, whereas the rectangular Iron Age houses (shaded), which are wider and shorter, are all aligned on an ESE-WNW axis. The overlapping of buildings bears witness to the gradual movement of the settlement, the buildings of which remained integrated with the 'Celtic field' system. (D. Harsema, 1980.)

LEEN DIJK

0   40m

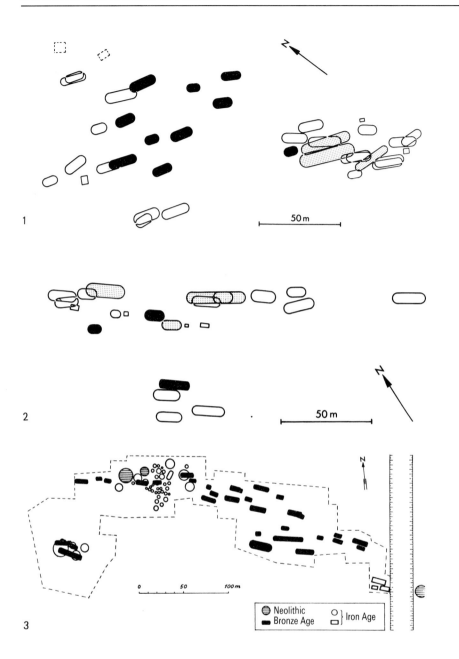

107
1,2: The villages of Bjerg A and B, Ringkøbing, Jutland. The numerous overlapping house plans show that village A (1) developed by moving from the SE towards the NW and that it became larger, the later types of house being more numerous than the earlier. In village B (2) it is the houses of the intermediate phase that are the most numerous, but the length of these phases is not known. Shaded: earlier Late Bronze Age houses; unshaded: later Late Bronze Age houses; black: Iron Age houses. 3: The village of Spjald, Jutland. (C.J. Becker, 1982.)

Neolithic
Bronze Age
Iron Age

(Fig. 107). Around 1350–1200 BC the Vadgård settlement moved some 160m (525ft) over a hundred years, and eight houses are assigned to each of two phases. At Bjerg A three long-houses, two of which overlapped, belong to the early phase of the Late Bronze Age; in the later phase the maximum number of contemporaneous houses was at most seven, six, or two, according to the group. The Iron Age village that succeeded it consisted of ten houses, which are considered to represent

two or three phases of a village of three or four houses. C.J. Becker distinguished three successive stages at Bjerg B, each of three independent houses separated from one another. At Spjald 33 Late Bronze Age houses were grouped along a crest in a area measuring 350m by 75m (1148 by 246ft). Becker attributed these remains to one or two isolated farmsteads that were periodically moved over four or five centuries. J. Jensen, on the other hand, sees the agglomerations as representing in fact true villages.

Certain coastal sites, such as Kirkebjerget at Vold-tofte (Fyen), produced no houses but the occupation layers there are several metres thick and indicate multiple or long periods of occupation. The Bronze Age settlements in Sweden, which are well known in Skåne, contain few houses – three at Ingelstorp, five at Istaby, ten at Fosie IV. Despite the vagueness of our knowledge, settlement in Scandinavia always seems to have been dispersed: there were few houses in the villages and the differences in social or economic status are only distinguishable in terms of house size. The small size of these settlements should be compared with those of the Middle Ages, when according to written sources they consisted of no more than three or four farmsteads.

Settlement in continental Europe

Continental Europe is characterized by the size of its nucleated settlements. As early as the Bronze Age there were agglomerations of a size unknown in northern Europe or the British Isles. Open sites on plains or in valleys existed alongside fortified upland settlements and other protected sites, such as the lake villages or the tells of south-eastern Europe. There was at one time a tendency to contrast these different settlement types with one another. Nowadays, how-ever, they are seen rather as complementary forms of settlement that could be occupied by the same peoples, sometimes by the same inhabitants, in response to the imperatives of security or economic opportunities. In parallel it now seems clear that from this time on cave dwellings were no more than refuges, additional temporary solutions that could occasionally replace the defended upland sites. Factors other than topographic setting, which was for too long given pride of place, also play an important role in the definition of settlements, such as the length and intensity of occupation, the respective functions of nucleated sites, and their positions within their territories.

Isolated settlements

Until the last few years, single farmsteads had hardly been recognized as a feature of continental Europe. Examples included the Early Bronze Age houses, accompanied by a number of pits, at Frouard in Lorraine and at Ripdorf in Lower Saxony. This situation has been completely changed over the last decade by the development of extensive rescue excavations in both France and Germany. It is only now that the importance of single farmsteads in Bronze Age continental Europe is becoming clear.

The rescue excavation project, organized by the Regional Antiquities Service at the new regional airport for Lorraine has revealed a suite of farms extending from the Early Bronze Age until the La Tène period; several buildings attributable to the Bronze Age are identifiable. The farms themselves shifted little by little across the landscape. In the Rhineland, excavations have equally produced indications of a scatter of Bronze Age isolated farm units, comparable with those known from the Iron Age.

Making use of such newly-available information, P. Brun has now proposed a settlement model in which, for certain regions, sets of such farms could have played the role of central places which elsewhere is attributed to more substantial settlements. This may have been the case, for example, in the zone around Aulnay-aux-Planches in Champagne: here, series of pits, which correspond to former settlements, are spaced fairly regularly through the landscape.

Much of the evidence suggestive of scattered small-scale settlements is indirect; it takes the form of chance finds of grain-storage and other pits. In France, for example, hundreds of pits have been identified either as single discoveries or grouped in small clusters. In the Ardennes, a site at Nanteuil-sur-Aisne consisted of four pits set close together; they included a rich assemblage belonging to the end of the Late Bronze Age. In comparison with the series of hundreds of pits known from central European Bronze Age sites, such small groups must correspond to more modest settle-ments, of a few houses at most.

This type of settlement, characterized by small units made up of one to three farms, has been recognized in numerous regions of the Continent. In the Liswarta valley of Poland, for example, there are numerous small units distributed every 300–500m (984–1640ft) along the river at both Dankow-Zbro-jewsko (Klobuck District) and Bodzanowice (Olenso District); these date to the Middle and Late Bronze Age. The recovery of scatters of pottery in field survey is another indication of such small-scale settlements. Hungarian archaeologists tend to refer to them as 'temporary sites', whereas their colleagues elsewhere, as in Germany, may simply identify them as 'finds-pots'. F. Horst has identified no fewer than 675 such sites in the Altmark and the Havel region in the Late Bronze Age.

Another component in the tissue of isolated settle-ments in the European Bronze Age consists of cave occupations, such as that at Planches in the Jura (for which see p. 125 and Fig. 97). It is only recently, as a result of excavations like that at Planches, that the use of caves as temporary refuge settlements has become evident; the subject of Bronze Age assemblages in caves is ripe for reassessment. Intermittent settlement during times of stress is unlikely to provide a satisfactory explanation on its own for the widespread use, in both southern France and the Alps, of caves as living-places. In these areas, there are no indications of the stalling of sheep in caves as has been frequently demonstrated for the Neolithic. Whilst such caves also include burial deposits of Bronze Age date, the settlement horizons are readily separable from funerary ones, and can attain impressive thicknesses: this suggests long-lasting, if only intermittent, occupation within them.

Nucleated settlements

In continental Europe, the dominant form of settlement recovered by archaeology consists of nucleated units. These include both unenclosed villages, as well as others that are fenced or protected by fortifications. Tell settlements form a distinctive group.

Unenclosed settlements

The great majority of known settlement sites in continental Europe consists of small unenclosed agglomerations, whether these are located on plains, within valleys or on the uplands; they are usually set centrally within the territories they exploited. One of the best indications of the population increase during the Bronze Age is the fact that they became both more common and increased in size.

Without the extremely detailed chronologies that would be necessary to enable distinctions to be drawn firmly, criteria to permit sites used on a seasonal basis to be distinguished from those occupied permanently – whether for long or short periods – remain rather tentative. A Polish attempt to achieve this distinction is ultimately founded on the quantity of material culture preserved and the presence or absence of hearths and other indications of houses. There are, however, too many criteria dependent on the degree of preservation of individual sites for us to have confidence in this approach at present.

Various distinctions can be drawn on the basis of the plans of villages; such an approach has been widely applied in Germany. For the Bronze Age, the principal distinction is between a *Haufendorf*, in which

no apparent order is visible in the positioning and orientation of individual structures, and a *Runddorf*, where they are disposed around a central unencumbered space. Villages consisting of several rows of houses or those where the buildings are arranged along streets do not develop fully until the Hallstatt Iron Age. A final pattern that can be identified is where houses are strung out in a single row.

Some protohistoric villages have layouts that were obviously planned. They are characterized by parallel rows of houses. The most famous is Iron Age Biskupin (see Fig. 70). Mediterranean influences have been discussed in this connection, but they differ from Near Eastern agglomerations and Hippodamian town plans in one essential particular: the streets or open spaces between houses are only aligned in one direction and the houses are contiguous within each row. Even at the *oppidum* of Nages (Gard), which belongs to the Mediterranean south that was under Greek influence, cross-streets did not exist.

Even though this cannot be proved, for lack of accurate dating, study of available settlement plans leads to the conclusion that layouts were closely connected with the initial space available for building and with the possibilities for enlargement. Preserving an empty space in the centre is evidence of an act of will. Behind these essentially material considerations lie others that are social or symbolic in nature, which we cannot appreciate. Consider, for example, those Baltic villages with two rows of houses whose layout is strictly hierarchical with respect to the rising sun, the houses lying furthest east having the highest prestige.

The number of settlements grew considerably during the second millennium BC, and ten times more Late Bronze Age sites are known than Early Bronze Age. Certain regions do, however, yield more information than others about the early stages of the Bronze Age, by virtue of the development of cultural groups that were both dynamic and wealthy. This is the case with the Nagyrév and Hatvan cultures in Hungary. Undefended settlements are the more numerous category there, but it has been the fortified tells that have held the interest of archaeologists, as a result of which nothing is known about the spatial organization of the open settlements.

Another region of expansion in the Early Bronze Age was Bohemia, cradle of the Únětice culture, whose influence reached as far as the Rhône valley. More than a hundred settlements are known but few have been extensively excavated. At Postoloprty (Žatce) B. Soudský has revealed sixteen 4–10m (13–33ft) long sub-rectangular structures belonging to the early and late phases of the Únětice culture, without any

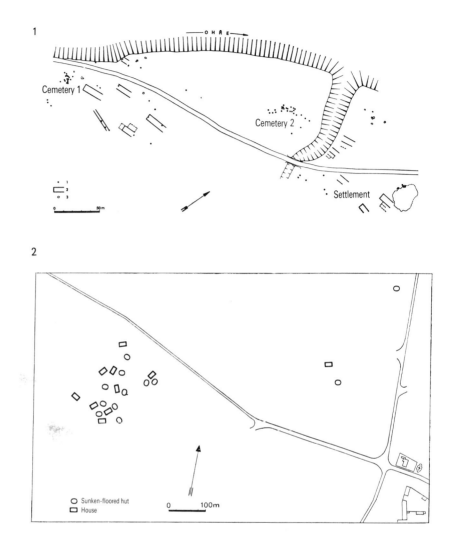

108

1: Early Bronze Age settlement at Březno o. Louný, Bohemia. The two hamlets of four or five large houses are associated with two cemeteries, each with about twenty graves. They may be interpreted as the settlement over time of some eighty people. (R. Pleiner, 1978.)

2: Late Bronze Age settlement at Vikletice, Bohemia. The rectangular houses are accompanied by oval houses used for craft purposes. Their layout reflects neither order nor preferential orientation. (R. Pleiner, 1978.)

preferred orientation or special layout. On the basis of the total area of the settlement and the distances between houses, he believes that there may have been as many as 40 houses on the site and that the early Únětice village may have contained 20–30 houses (not necessarily contemporaneously). This figure now seems a little high by comparison with other settlements. At Březno o. Louný, much longer houses (c. 20m or 66ft) were in two distinct groups some 150m (492ft) apart (Fig. 108). Each consisted of 5–6 houses orientated east-west and sited a score of metres apart from one another. Immediately to the west of each of these hamlets there was a cemetery of 15–20 graves that was contemporaneous with it.

Outside these regions only Switzerland has produced a number of Early Bronze Age settlements. They contained a very small number of modestly sized rectangular houses. These were built in wood (as at Muota, Fellers) or with foundations partly in stone, as at Cresta, Cazis (Grisons), where they were laid out in an extended line. The village of Padnal, near Savognin (Grisons), gives a much more accurate picture of the mountain-valley villages, and in particular of the evolution from Early to Late Bronze Age (Fig. 109). Occupation began around 1700 BC with a clearing in a wooded area. The settlement was created in a hollow, the bottom of which was filled up on the down slope and excavated out above. The first village of at least five or six post-built and stone-foundation houses formed a single alignment running north-south. An open space or alleyway separated the northern from the southern group. Only one of the houses had no

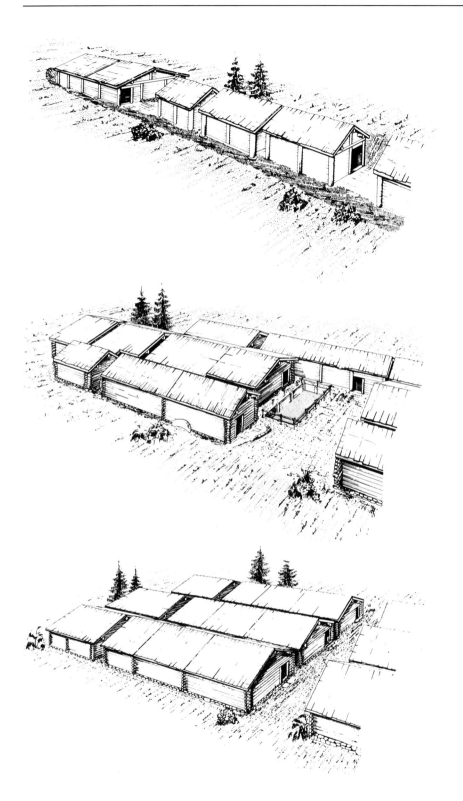

109
Reconstruction of
successive stages of the
hamlet of Padnal,
Savognin, Grisons,
from the end of the
Early Bronze Age to
the beginning of the
Late Bronze Age. (J.
Rageth, 1986.)

hearth and all had experienced between three and five rebuildings or refloorings.

The fourteenth century BC settlement extended further along the sides of the hollow, which had been terraced. It consisted of eight or nine houses in three north-south rows. The rows were bisected at one-third of the way along their long axis from the north end by the now widened alleyway. The houses in the southern group were larger, up to 9m (29ft) long. They were not all built at the same time and almost all contained hearths. Earlier a wooden cistern had been set into the bottom of a pit, beyond the last house on the south, no doubt to drain the hollow.

After an imperfectly understood intermediate phase in the thirteenth century BC, the Late Bronze Age village consisted of nine houses split into three parallel rows, still with a separation between the northern and southern groups. The settlement still had three houses in the eighth century.

The village of Padnal – or at least that part which we know – thus experienced many episodes of recon-struction, and we do not know whether there were any discontinuities, although they may be assumed from the thickness of the archaeological layers – 3–4m (10–13ft) maximum for more than a thousand years. The development of the settlement shows a growth in population, revealed by an increase in the number of houses and by their having been rebuilt on a grander scale. A traditional spatial organization survived in the collective memory of the inhabitants: houses occupied the same sites from one village to the next, and the division into northern and southern groups survived right through to the penultimate village. New building techniques did, however, gradually appear. The use of stone wall footings was not standardly adopted until the Middle Bronze Age and corresponded with the adoption of the *Blockbau* technique with walls of morticed planks and uprights.

The lengthening of certain houses, their division into rooms equivalent in area to the preceding houses and the presence of hearths seem to indicate that they housed the various units of an extended family. In relation to the model of the Grotte des Planches, it is equally tempting to interpret the north-south div-ision, which was carried on from village to village, as the spatial expression of the distinction between two lineages or clans, but could such a division have lasted for several centuries? Alongside dwelling houses, identified by their hearths, there were byres and barns. A metal workshop was rebuilt several times on the same spot: this permanence suggests that this activity was a hereditary one, handed down from generation to generation.

The village of Bavois-en-Raillon (Vaud) provides another example of development on the same site. It was set up in a small valley and seven phases of occupation succeeded one another, from the Beaker period to Late Bronze Age II, 1900–1000 BC. The clay of the ruined houses makes up a good portion of the fill of the valley, which reaches some 4m (13ft) thick. This exceptional degree of silting makes it possible to read the alternate phases of occupation and abandonment in the stratification and to record how the settlement gradually changed from the archaeological layers. In the first phase the houses were laid out irregularly, then they were aligned in rows, and finally in a single row. Trapezoidal house plans were replaced by rectangular ones, which then alternated with square plans. In the middle of Late Bronze Age II the houses suddenly increased in size from 40–50 to 80 and finally 100 sq.m (430–538 to 1076 sq.ft). The built area varied between 150 and 300 sq.m (1615 and 3229 sq.ft) overall but intermediate episodes show that the settlement contracted.

J.-L. Voruz and J. Vital suggest that the variations in overall surface area were not haphazard but cyclic, and that three periods of enlargement were inter-rupted by two returns to less extensive roofed areas. Dating shows that the average length of occupation phases was 22 years, or a generation. This is a period of the same order as that of the lakeside houses dated by dendrochronology (15–20 years).

Undefended settlements are much more numerous from the Late Bronze Age onwards and several have been completely excavated, showing that unordered layouts predominated over layouts in rows over the whole of Europe. At Künzing (Bavaria), where A. Zippelius recognized the first large houses built without internal roof supports, the ten houses are spread over a very large area, but the four that lie closest together are on the same orientation. At Buch, near Berlin, so many houses are superimposed upon one another that it is impossible to draw up a coherent plan of the settlement layout. About a hundred houses appear to have been on the site, and one row of eight houses can be discerned. The nine houses and ancillary buildings at Viesecke, also near Berlin, formed three parallel rows.

Dispersion was not always completely haphazard in these settlements where successive buildings were scattered in space rather than built on top of one another. At the Perleberg, Prignitz, P. Pétrequin distinguished expansion in a series of roughly concen-tric bands from the orientations of the houses. The sixteen houses were in four groups (Fig. 110). The first group of seven, the entrances of which faced south/

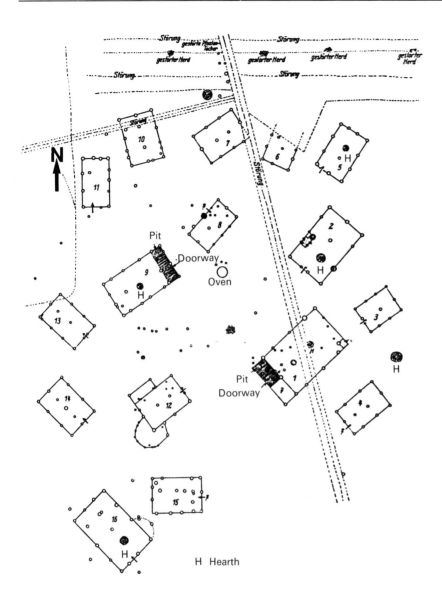

110
The Perleberg, eastern Germany. The houses can be divided into three groups according to their orientation and to the position of the doorway, located on the SW in the group of houses on the right, on the NE and E in those in the central strip, and on the SE and S in those on the left. These semi-circles may, according to P. Pétrequin, represent successive phases of construction. A larger house in the centre of the village with a vestibule is often considered to be the house of the 'chief'. (W. Böhm, 1937.)

H Hearth

south-east, had in its centre a furnace and a house with a porch that was clearly larger than the others. The second group consisted of four houses orientated to the south-west, the third three houses orientated north-west and the fourth two houses facing south. Fairly regular spacing between houses can be observed within each group.

Differentiation between buildings within individual settlements appears in the Late Bronze Age. Lovčičky (Bohemia) produced 48 rectangular houses and 295 pits from the beginning of the Late Bronze Age. The layout suggests that this was a 'round' village (Fig. 111). A measure of overlapping and very

variable spacings between houses shows that they were not all contemporaneous. Several types of building are found to be grouped together and probably relate to different functions: these are small houses with two rows of large posts (granaries?) or with three rows of small posts as well as large structures with three rows of widely spaced posts, some of which must have had hipped roofs. Two buildings were exceptionally large, and one of them, sited on a platform in the open space in the centre of the village, had additional intermediate uprights which may have supported a loft.

The diversity in house shapes and sizes shows that

there must have been complex interrelationships that elude us: what role was played in selecting between one type and another by the function of the building or the social status or size of the family that lived in it? What was the population of the community represented by these structures?

The nature and the favoured position of the central building seems to mark it out as the residence of the most important man or family in the village. This is one of the earliest indicators of the insertion of social hierarchy into the organization of the built-up space. Grain storage and other pits are scattered throughout the settlement whereas they were in general sited on the edges of the house zone in contemporary settlements of the Knoviz culture. At Prague-Cakovice, for example, two houses at the edge of the built-up area

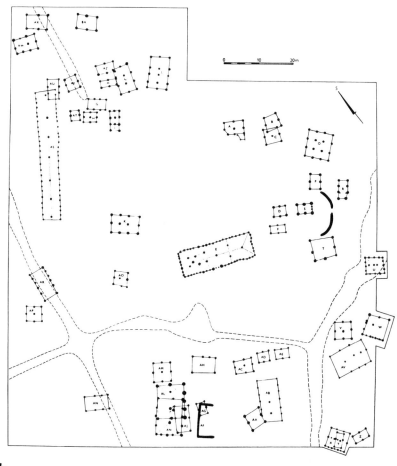

111
Lovčičky, Vyškov, Moravia: plan of Late Bronze Age village and reconstruction of the large central building. The variety of plans certainly relates to buildings with different functions and which are not all contemporary, since some of the remains cut into one another. The house in the middle of the central open space can be distinguished from the others by virtue of its position and dimensions and by the supplementary internal posts over one-third of its length. This structure may belong to an earlier phase (Únětice culture). (J. Ríhovský, 1982.)

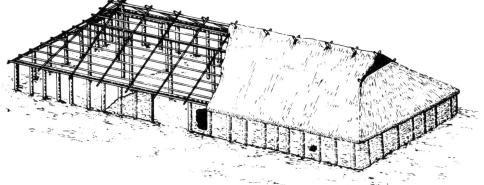

were sited alongside an area containing more than 150 pits and five double-chambered furnaces, most likely pottery kilns. A circular enclosure, in which a sandstone stele was found and whose entrance faced away from the settlement, is considered by B. Soudský to have been a sun sanctuary.

Nucleated unenclosed settlement is also well known in Poland from the Late Bronze Age and in eastern Germany in the territories of the Lausitz culture. More than 400 open settlements and 100–200 defended settlements have been recorded, but there is a considerable gap between these figures and the 3500 Late Bronze Age and Iron Age cemeteries that have been identified.

Up to the end of Late Bronze Age III open settlements were relatively short-lived, of the order of a single generation (15–25 years) in the opinion of Z. Bukowski. They often developed through gradual lateral migration as shown by the occupation layers which form a narrow band extending several hundreds of metres, or even several kilometres. All the different types of plan are known: *Haufendorf* ('heaped') villages at Konin (Great Poland) or Lutomiersk (Little Poland); *Runddorf* ('round') villages at Turbia (Tarnobrzeg District), where a central open space 35m (115ft) in diameter is surrounded by houses; and a layout in rows, as at Dębnica, which contains some thirty houses of 10–28 sq.m (108–301 sq.ft) sunken-floored huts, several hundred pits and hearths.

Settlements occupied for longer periods have overlapping structures which make it impossible to identify houses, but they are characterized by very large numbers of pits: more than 200 were excavated at Brześć Kujawski (Kujavia). A cemetery that was in use over a longer period than the buildings is often found near a settlement, occupying a median position in relation to the successive positions of the groups of houses. At Bodzanowice (Olesno District) eleven settlements spread along the Liswarta over some 5km (3 miles); the common cemetery lies between the fifth and sixth.

Very small settlement units also exist alongside these villages in both Poland and Germany. Hamburg-Boberg and Berlin-Lichterfelde have a small number of houses alongside hundreds of pits, although further houses may have escaped notice during excavation.

In France settlement studies are a decade or two behind other European countries and little is known about undefended settlements. Only one village in a valley-bottom setting has been completely excavated. At Dampierre-sur-le-Doubs P. Pétrequin found two successive villages from Late Bronze Age IIb and IIIb near the river. In the first of these, the indecipherable scatter of post-holes included evidence of successive rebuildings. It was covered by alluvial deposits attributable to flooding that explained its abandonment. A cremation cemetery, a rare occurrence, adjoined the village but beyond the palisade. The second village consisted of 28 rectangular houses in groups of two, three, or four (Fig. 112). Most of them contained a hearth and may be considered to be dwellings. Pétrequin saw these groupings of houses as representing the nuclear families that made up extended families. Three of the houses had wooden floors. One larger house with an apsidal end may have had a function similar to the central buildings at the Perleberg or Lovčičky.

Other villages are only partially known: the many post-holes at Perthes (Marne) imply rectangular houses surrounded by a ditch 100m (328ft) long. At Coulon (Deux-Sèvres) several houses, 6–10m (20–33ft) long, set parallel with each other, were associated with more modest apsidal structures, granaries and roasting pits for small-scale craft production. According to J.-P. Pautreau the village was divided into quarters and each group of houses was enclosed by a rectangular ditch interrupted by a gateway. The buildings lay on either side of a central open space where the roasting pits were grouped. At Montagnieu (Ain) at least four buildings of Late Bronze Age IIIb, between 6 and 9m (20 and 30ft) long, replaced an early Late Bronze Age settlement of two or three houses and a granary. In Burgundy and the centre of France, traces of settlements, houses or sunken-floored huts are all that have been recovered of small settlements, such as Champaux-Bœufs, Vallery, Les Glaciers, Saint-Martin-du-Tertre (both Yonne), Vauvretins, Épervans (Saône) and Le Brezet III, Clermont-Ferrand.

Elements of settlements have also recently come to light in southern France, such as the two rectangular houses at Saint-Dionisy, La Roque de Viou (Gard), or the probable hut at Gandus, Saint-Ferréol-Trente-Pas (Drôme), which formed part of a much larger settlement. It seems certain that these open villages, the normal settlements of the Bronze Age peoples of southern France, will increasingly come to light in the years to come.

Tells

Tells are settlements formed by the successive reconstruction of buildings in the same place over several centuries which gradually raises them above the level of the valley or plain and so they are evidence of long and intensive occupation. They are typical of south-eastern Europe and their distribution extends as far as Romania, eastern and southern Hungary, and eastern Slovakia. They first appeared in the Late Neolithic period but were then replaced for five centuries by less permanent settlements during the cultural changes and population movements that affected the Danube and the Hungarian plain in the late third millennium BC. They reached their apogee between 2000 and 1300 bc (uncalibrated dates) before the region once again experienced times of trouble and influences from south-eastern Europe were replaced by those of central Europe.

Tells, which are to be found on both plains and uplands, are characteristic of the Nagyrév, Hatvan and Füzesabony cultures which in turn occupied the Hungarian plain, and of the Otomaní culture which developed in the border region between Romania, Hungary and Slovakia. Their occupation layers built up to thicknesses of several metres – 6.5m (21ft) at Tószeg – and within them are preserved the frequently renewed floors of successive houses. They take the form of mounds that tend to be circular or oval in plan. From the mid second millennium onwards they were increasingly often defended by one or two ditches and sometimes by an earthen rampart. Quite frequently the ditches enclosed only part of the settlement, often described as the 'citadel' (*Burg*) by Hungarian and Slovak archaeologists.

At Tiszalúc-Dankadomb the village lies along the Tisza river. A 25m- (81ft-) wide semi-circular ditch connected with the river defends the central part of the settlement (100 sq.m or 1076 sq.ft). Houses were built on either side of the ditch. At Emöd-Nagyhalom the central portion of the settlement, which occupies some 300m (984ft) of a hillside, is surrounded by a circular ditch. Beyond this houses spread over other hillsides. At Jászdózsa-Kápolnahalom, the 6m (20ft) high tell is sited in the middle of a meander of the Nyavalyka river. A rampart and ditch protect the central tell, measuring 120m by 60m (394 by 197ft). A second rampart and ditch enclose the entire settlement. This tell rises 2.4m (8ft) above the plain in six successive levels of the Hatvan culture (Early and Middle Bronze Age). These levels are made up of parallel rows of large houses separated by alleys, 1.8m (6ft) wide rebuilt six times. The ditch round the tell, probably originally accompanied by a palisade, was dug 6m (20ft) from the houses. The occupied zone outside the tell, which has grain pits to the north and houses to the south, was abandoned in the following period, belonging to the Füzesabony culture.

The Tószeg tell originally covered 7ha (17 acres) and was surrounded by an internal and external ditch, the intermediate zone of which was not excavated. Large houses with several rooms and sometimes several hearths were excavated in the centre of the site and were generally arranged in parallel rows. If the entire settlement was occupied at the same density as the excavated area it must have included at least forty houses.

The special layout of these settlements, with their fortified centres, has caused much ink to flow among

112
The later phase of the Late Bronze Age village of Dampierre-sur-le-Doubs. The shaded areas are wooden floors and the black dots are pits. (P. Pétrequin, J.-P. Urlacher, and D. Vuaillat, 1969.)

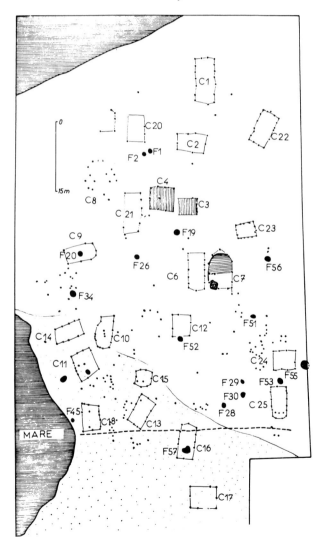

central European archaeologists. This layout, reminiscent of the upper towns (*villes hautes*) of the Middle Ages, has been considered to be the first indication of an inegalitarian society where the work of all (during the construction of the fortifications) was annexed to the profit of a few. The archaeological facts thus conform with the schema for the origins of the state put forward by Engels in *The Origin of the Family, Private Property and the State*. Whilst different structural patterns and the presence or absence of defensive architecture clearly distinguish the two sectors of this site, the meaning of this difference in functional terms is not as clear as was asserted in the 1950s. At Jászdózsa, for example, the outer village, which was only in existence during the period of greatest extent of the settlement, contained the grain-storage pits. Thus, in spatial terms at least, the inhabitants of the *ville haute* could not have exercised direct control over the grain stocks. Could the boundaries between the *ville haute* and the surrounding areas have moved, as was the case in medieval towns, as the population of the settlement expanded or contracted? This is not impossible, but does not exclude the possibility of there being a category of privileged inhabitants. In fact, the fortified centres of settlements have often produced hoards of high-value objects: jewellery or bronze weapons associated with houses, as, for example, at Jászdózsa.

Tells are found in regions where settlement density was high, but their irregular distribution does not appear to give them the status of regional centres. Some are very close to one another. Their long periods of existence, evidence of a completely sedentary way of life, might have enabled them to develop towards urbanization or at least pre-urbanization. However, as in Greece, the economic and cultural turmoil of the thirteenth century BC brought this process to a halt, if indeed it ever existed, and it was on a completely different basis that the Late La Tène towns developed.

Lake villages

The establishment of large villages in marshland or on the shores of lakes is one of the characteristics of the Alpine Neolithic and Bronze Age. These settlements have long been the subject of controversy: were they true lake villages built over water on raised platforms, as F. Keller proposed in the 1860s, or were they villages built on the shores of the lakes, as E. Vogt would have it in the 1950s? This dispute has now been resolved by the ethnoarchaeological work of P. Pétrequin on the contemporary lake settlements of Benin. Some villages are certainly built on the lake shore and are only very occasionally touched by exceptional flooding. Others, on dry land at times of low water level, are raised on piles to protect them against high water levels. The expansion of these villages was always extended in the direction of the lake and it is common to find different constructional techniques used according to the siting of the houses – landfill, caissons (or log-built substructures) or piling. The survival of banding within the remains, best preserved when underwater, permits the identification of the contemporary shoreline. True lake settlements in open water are very rare: they consist of houses built on individual platforms.

All these villages developed as enclosed settlements, occupying a restricted area, even when the defensive palisade on the landward side was added after the houses. The zone where building was possible between the shore and deep water is in fact very limited. This results in a spatial organization which is to be found in all lake villages. It is based on communal consensus, and in some cases deliberate planning, and results in the houses being built in parallel rows separated by alleys. This is obviously the most economic layout. This form of layout appears as early as the Neolithic period. Building houses in rows is a constant at this period, whether a single row on the edge of the marsh, as at Clairvaux II, or 30–35 closely set houses in several rows, as at Ehrenstein in the Swabian Jura, but this did not prevent the later development of regional differences.

In the Early Bronze Age, at Auvernier-Port on Lake Neuchâtel and La Motte aux Magnins on Lake Clairvaux, more modest settlements succeeded those of the Late Neolithic: they consisted of a row of houses arranged in an arc behind a palisade. This variation resulted in the houses being more dispersed, but it seems to have been introduced at a time when the settlements were contracting in size.

Lake settlements increased in number in northern Italy during the Early and Middle Bronze Ages. They include the only true lake villages in open water whose existence can be demonstrated archaeologically. Unfortunately, conditions for excavation have up to the present not allowed the houses themselves or the settlement plans to be identified, only the piles and the raft foundations on which they were set. Some of these villages certainly contained several dozen houses, to judge from the amount of foundations and the wealth of material recovered from Ledro, Mercurago, Barche di Solferino, Lavagnone and, later, Peschiera in the province of Verona. At Fiave one of the three settlements was in open water and required the use of many 7–9m- (23–30ft-) long piles.

113

1 The Late Bronze Age lake villages of Cortaillod-les-Esserts (left) and Cortaillod-Est, Lake Neuchâtel. In the air photograph taken on 22 April 1927 the palisades, parallel rows of piles, and streets are clearly visible. (M. Egloff, 1981.) 2: Interpretive plan of the village of Cortaillod-Est (research as in 1984). The numbers shown on the houses refer to the succesive phases of demolition. (B. Arnold, 1986.)

1

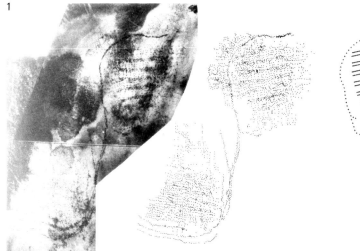

2

The few Swiss settlements known from the Early Bronze Age are laid out in rows: at the Mozartstrasse site in Zürich the inhabitants installed themselves on a low knoll, islet or peninsula, jutting out into the lake. In the earliest village there were six houses in three parallel rows lengthwise, a seventh house perhaps belonging to a fourth row, along with two small buildings which do not conform with the alignment. At Baldegg (Lucerne) the reconstruction is still hypothetical: seven buildings lying east-west and two north-south, which would have belonged to east-west rows, facing a corridor entrance in the enclosing palisade, are proposed.

The Late Bronze Age villages of Lake Neuchâtel show a stricter plan: the houses were aligned on their long axes in parallel rows separated by alleys that were roughly the same width. The eight rows of parallel houses at Cortaillod-Est lay inside a strong palisade. They were built in five successive phases over 25 years and thus conformed with a predetermined plan or a strong tradition. The site was abandoned after some fifty years and reoccupied a century later by a new village, nearer the shore and on a layout similar to the preceding one (Fig. 113).

Bevaix-Sud, less than 3km (2 miles) away, also consisted of parallel rows of three-aisled houses, spreading over 70m (230ft). At Concise V, further south on the same lake shore, two villages were superimposed: the smaller was surrounded by a circular palisade, but the second spread much further, protected on the landward side by a long palisade that had seventeen rows of houses aligned behind it.

The houses at Auvernier were laid out in a similar way, but less regularly within the rows (Fig. 114). The alleys were also narrower and less straight. The village, contemporaneous with that at Cortaillod-les-Esserts, was occupied between 807 and 779 BC. The 25 houses that made it up represent roughly one-fifth of

the area inhabited in the Late Bronze Age, but this phase of occupation possibly did not extend any further, since its abandonment was due neither to flooding nor to fire. B. Arnold believes that its inhabitants moved to a site some tens of metres away that was better protected against waves, after first having removed all their valuables. It is true that the palisade at Auvernier-Nord did not separate the village from dry land but served as a breakwater between the settlement and the open lake.

Despite their varying lengths, the houses in these villages are very similar and produced identical artefactual material. The only open space lay along the palisade and gave no evidence of special use. There is some evidence of domestic cults, but none of a sanctuary beyond the open space. Community life, the intensity of which is expressed in the settlement layouts, was not based on such elements, essential in later periods.

The villages of Lakes Zürich, Constance and Geneva

114
Plan of the excavated part of Auvernier-Nord, Lake Neuchâtel (Late Bronze Age). The second palisade could not have been erected until after houses 5 and 8 had been abandoned. (B. Arnold, 1983.)

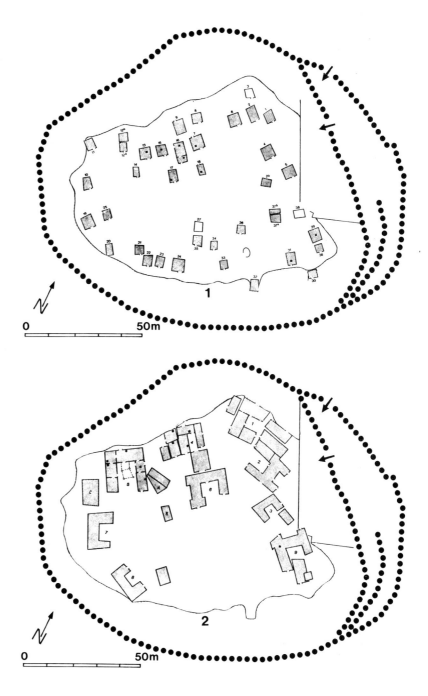

115
The Wasserburg, Buchau, Baden-Württemberg (Late Bronze Age). 1: The earlier village (c. 1100 BC) comprised 39 Blockbau houses and five post-built houses with wattle walls. 2: The later village was built on top of the earlier and consisted of nine large two-winged houses and several ancillary structures. The open space had moved southwards in relation to that in the earlier village. (W. Kimmig, 1981.)

are less well known. There are some indications that their internal organization was less strict. Around 1000 BC the small houses of the Nussbaumersee and Greifensee-Böschen were built in less regular rows and, in the case of the latter, more widely spaced. In these sites, as at Zug, foundations of very small structures (2.5–3m (8–10ft) sides) have been found.

They may be ancillary buildings or may have been constructed platforms that extended beyond the surviving elements, as shown in the Val Camonica engravings.

The best known of these settlements, the Wasserburg at Buchau on the Feddersee (Bavaria), is completely different from the Swiss lake villages. Two successive villages existed between 1100 and 800 BC (Fig. 115). They were situated in an area that stood slightly above the level of the marsh and were completely enclosed by palisades consisting of several rows of posts. The 'heaped' (*Hauendorf*) layout of the houses recalls that of undefended villages.

In the older of the two villages, the 39 houses were all orientated on a NNW-SSE or N-S axis, with their entrances to the south, such that only those houses on the north opened on to the irregular open space formed by the absence of structures in the centre. These buildings do not seem to be systematically aligned on the same axis, but they seem to adhere to a minimum distance between them. The houses to the south had a common north-south axis which distinguished them from the others. O. Paret, who believed that this was a marsh, not a lake, settlement, calculated that there must have been around fifty houses in the first village. However, what is now known about protohistoric villages does not allow us to be wholly satisfied with the plans of the Wasserburg that Reinerth produced.

The later village had the same completely enclosed appearance and the 'heaped' layout of the houses. The nine farmsteads with two projecting wings occupied the east, north and west of the area of dry land, leaving a large open space to the south. Ancillary buildings overlapped or butted up against them, whilst the general layout of the principal farmsteads respected a minimum spacing between them. It is not clear whether they were contemporaneous. As at the Perleberg, Lovčicky or Dampierre-sur-le-Doubs, the largest house is in the middle of the village. Can it be deduced from this that it was the house of the chief, as Reinerth proposed?

The Wasserburg produced much more pottery and many more metal artefacts than the land-based settlements in its vicinity. As in the defended sites of central Europe, the inhabitants had on several occasions hidden valuable objects in the ground – hoards of bracelets, chains and pendants, and a wooden jewellery box.

Work recently begun on the neighbouring site of Forschner, also on the Feddersee, gives the impression of a land-based settlement, measuring 150m (492ft) by 100m (328ft) and enclosed by a double and triple palisade. This site is older (Middle Bronze Age). Two main phases of clearance to provide structural timbers have been distinguished, around 1760 and 1727/1726 BC. The excavations were undertaken to resolve the current dispute between supporters of island settlements and marsh settlements. The present state of understanding is that the Feddersee settlements were established on flat ground rather than on rises in the ground.

In the Bronze Age there were also riverbank settlements, related to the lake villages by their use of piles. River dredging in the nineteenth century has largely destroyed or severely damaged these settlements. They are only known indirectly through the very abundant finds produced by the dredgers, at Villeneuve-Saint-Georges on the Seine, for example, or the Île Saint-Jean near Mâcon on the Saône. Excavations at Ouroux on the Saône have produced very fine organic finds, but the structures from which they came have been irretrievably destroyed. At the Gué des Piles at Chalon-sur-Saône, however, a palisade of staggered piles and two rows of structures have been identified at a depth of 5m (16ft).

The date of construction of lake villages varies from one region to another. In Switzerland and Franche-Comté, Late Neolithic occupation continued into the Early Bronze Age. The main period in Italy went from the Early Bronze Age to the end of the Middle Bronze Age and such settlements disappeared after Late Bronze Age I. In southern Germany the first occupation took place in the Middle Bronze Age, when the Swiss and French lake shores had been deserted. They were reoccupied sporadically in eastern Switzerland from the thirteenth century BC, and more intensively after 1100 BC, to be abandoned again around 1000 BC. In western Switzerland reoccupation was later, but it went on a little longer, until 850 BC. The settlements on Lakes du Bourget and Annecy were also abandoned in the last third of the ninth century BC.

Despite their large size, the rather numerous populations that they must have housed and the prosperity to which they bear witness, the lake villages do not seem to have acted as central places; there are no smaller settlements around them as dependencies. More significantly, however, some of these villages were contemporaneous, even though they were very close to one another and must have been obliged to exploit limited territories, between lake and mountains. This was the case with Cortaillod-Est and Champréveyres or Cortaillod-les-Esserts and Auvernier-Nord, the first pair of which are about 12km (7 miles) apart and the latter are less than 5km (3 miles).

A marsh platform dating to 1000 BC has recently been discovered in the Fens of eastern England. Flag Fen is unique in two ways: it was built in an area of shallows on a marsh island revetted with superimposed tree trunks, beams and branches; and it contains at least one three-aisled rectangular building of continental type. Were these immigrants from the

Low Countries or was a continental building technique that was better adapted to a wet environment being applied?

The development of lake villages is comparable with that of all Bronze Age sites, with a marked increase in occupied area and number of houses between the Early and Late Bronze Age. Until contemporary dry-land villages in their vicinity are known, however, it is not possible to appreciate the way in which they fitted into the overall regional picture. In relation to such they do seem to represent settlements that are substitutes for, rather than complementary to, the dry-land sites. All that can be said at the present time is that they were a form of defended nucleated settlement, used by different communities over one or more generations and then abandoned in favour of other settlement types, perhaps of a more dispersed character.

Fortified settlements

It is fortified settlements that are best known. However, in spite of their conspicuous positions in the landscape, with their ramparts often still visible, very few of them have been exhaustively excavated. They can be divided into two groups, according to the intensity and length of occupation. Some were used only occasionally, as places of refuge, whilst others were permanently inhabited, just like the open and lake villages. This distinction seems to have no straightforward correlation with the nature or size of the fortifications, but it does reflect variations in the organization of the built area and the functions of the settlement.

When they were only used for short periods the traces of occupation are sparse and the remains of houses are found only along the ramparts. The promontory fort of La Roche Maldru at Marnay (Jura) and Mont Bert at Bavans (Doubs) belong to this category. Often these are sites that had already been fortified in the Middle or Late Neolithic and where the fortifications were put in order or heightened. The sites of Saint-André at Bracon (Jura), La Groutte at Drevant (Cher) and Le Châtelet at Etaules (Côte-d'Or) are good examples. In southern France the tradition of Chalcolithic fortified enclosures with solid towers

116
The Early Bronze Age settlement at Barca, near Košice, Slovakia. The fortified village (level 2) consisted of three rows of two- and three-roomed houses. (J. Vladár, 1973.)

along their walls survived into the Early Bronze Age at the Camp de Laure at Rove (Bouches-du-Rhône).

It was in central Europe, however, that permanently occupied fortified settlements developed in the Early Bronze Age, in parallel with tells. As with the lake settlements, the restricted internal space soon led to buildings being arranged on a regular layout of parallel rows of houses. The best example is Barca, near Košice (Slovakia), which belongs to the Otomaní culture (Fig. 116) It is situated on a promontory 12m (39ft) above the confluence of two rivers and protected on the plateau side by a rampart surmounted by a palisade and a wide ditch. In the interior there were at least three successive Early Bronze Age villages. The houses were arranged in closely spaced parallel rows.

At Spišský Štvrtok (Slovakia) a row of 26 two-room houses were aligned north-south and delineated,

along with the rampart, an open space paved with stones.

Some of these fortified settlements had valley settlements beneath them, a phenomenon that was doubtless analogous to the double settlements on some

117
Relief models of Bronze Age fortified settlements in Slovakia and central Hungary. 1: Malé Kosihy-Torökdomb: the upland settlement alongside the river is surrounded by a bank and ditch; it was occupied in the Early and Middle Bronze Age. The nearby lowland settlement of Papföld, which was also surrounded by a ditch, seems to have replaced it in the Middle Bronze Age. (A. Točik, 1981.) 2: Vál-Pogányvár and 3: Sárbogard-Bolondvár: Double fortified Middle Bronze Age settlements. (T. Kovács, 1982.)

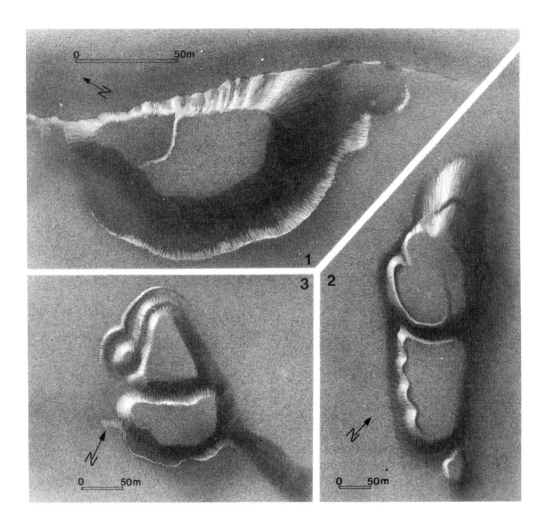

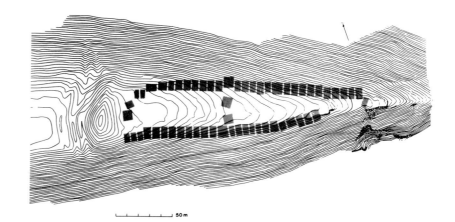

118

The Late Bronze Age fortified promontory settlement of the Wittnauer Horn, Argau. The promontory is fortified by a 10m-(33ft-) high rampart. There was no water on the site. House positions are shaded. (R. Wyss, 1971.)

50 m

tells. At Early and Middle Bronze Age Malé Kosihy the upland settlement perched on a promontory and defended by a wide ditch overlooked a settlement that contained some forty pits surrounded by an oval ditch. Analysis of the material shows that settlement migrated between the Early and Middle Bronze Age from the heights down into the plain.

The distribution of settlements of the Vatya group, which occupied the middle Danube in Hungary during the Middle Bronze Age, is well known. So far 58 open settlements have been recorded, along with 28 upland fortified settlements on the outer margins of the lowland distribution and along the Danube. The group gives the impression of a territory that was fortified at its strategic points (Fig. 117). These upland settlements were set on hills directly overlooking the plain, with one or two natural saddles used to divide the settlements into either two (as at Lovasberény, Val, or Alcsut) or three parts (Pákozd). The theory that this division was based on the existence of different social classes was adhered to for many years. However, the only extensive excavation, at Lovasberény-Mihály-vár, did not find evidence of two separate areas: the one area found contained storage pits and a metal-founder's workshop and was devoted to farming and craft activities, whilst another, no doubt, contained houses, although only trial excavations took place there. It is by no means certain that a ditch that extended the natural depression was defensive in function, since hearths were set up on its fill. All the excavated ramparts were built later than the settlement that they defended. Fortification of the best sited settlements at the end of the Early Bronze Age is evidence of an increase in the threats from, in particular, the westernmost peoples (connected with the Tumulus cultures) and those in the eastern

Carpathian basin. These threats must have been grave since in the fourteenth century BC occupation was interrupted for several centuries, or even came to an end, in almost all the Vatya settlements.

All these upland villages had metal workshops and evidence of substantial domestic and craft activities. Occupation extending over several centuries made them long-term settlements, just like the tells of eastern Hungary. They may have been local centres in relation to the small undefended settlements on the plains around them, but it seems very unlikely that they functioned as a group for defence organized on a regional level. The simultaneous late fortification of certain settlements seems rather to have been a reaction to common danger.

P. Pétrequin has recently shown that detailed regional studies reveal chronological differences in the periods of occupation or construction of fortified sites. Thus in Franche-Comté the cave refuges north of the Doubs were used as refuges mainly in Late Bronze Age IIb, whereas those south of the Doubs were in use later, in Late Bronze Age IIIa.

In general terms, fortified sites in all regions of Europe increased in number at some time in the Late Bronze Age: this trend becomes evident at the beginning of the period, first in the Lausitz settlements of southern Poland that were in contact with peoples further to the south and then extending to other regions. It was a later development in Germany and Switzerland, where the defended settlements, like the lake villages, for the most part date to Late Bronze Age IIb-IIIb/Early Hallstatt.

It was in this period that fortified settlements such as the Senftenberg (eastern Germany), the Dünsberg (Hesse), the Wittnauer Horn and the Kestenberg (Aargau), the Hohlandsberg at Witzenheim (Haut-

Rhin), the Camp du Château at Salins (Doubs), the Camp du Myard at Vitteaux (Côte-d'Or), and Catenoy (Oise) were built.

The organization of built-up space in these settlements shows two different layouts: in one the houses were in rows up against the ramparts or along the upper margins of the steep natural limits of the promontories on which they were set, leaving the central area open; and in the other the houses were laid out in parallel rows, but leaving an open space, at least on one side. The Wittnauer Horn is the best example of the former. It was built at the end of the Late Bronze Age on a long narrow spur some 230m (755ft) in length, closed on its only accessible side by a strong rampart of stone and timber (Fig. 118). The houses were in two parallel rows along the edges of the plateau, apart from four that were built in the central open space, on the same orientation. Most of the structures contained a hearth and were used as dwellings. In the early phase they were all roughly the same size and contained similar material. In the later phase some of them were larger, sometimes occupying two of the earlier platforms: this was the case with the four inner houses. This settlement was abandoned in

the Early Hallstatt Iron Age and was reoccupied at the end of the period.

The Camp de César at Catenoy (Picardy) was also of this type. It was a promontory, fortified in the Middle Neolithic period with a rampart and ditch. In Late Bronze Age IIIa the rampart was strengthened and the southern side of the spur was protected by a drystone wall. A few rectangular houses, orientated north-south along the edge of the plateau, constituted a small village that was short-lived but prosperous, judging from the abundance of finds.

The best known example of the second type, with rows of houses, is the Alte Schloss at the Senftenberg in eastern Germany, from the seventh century BC (Fig. 119). The circular rampart, which had a staggered entrance, enclosed a sub-circular area some 100m (328ft) in diameter. Two-thirds of the interior were occupied by houses laid out in parallel rows. A road ran parallel with the inner face of the rampart. In its second phase, in the Iron Age, the scatter of post-holes was so dense that interpretation is not possible. Unlike the Wittnauer Horn, water supply was assured by a well. But here, as in all the fortified upland sites in southern Germany, no 'chief's house' or cult centre

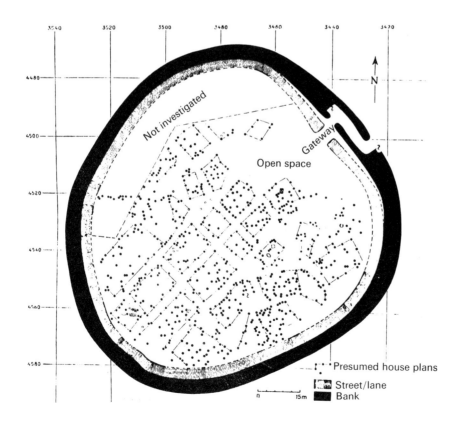

119
The Late Bronze Age 'Alte Schloss' on the Senftenberg, eastern Germany, early phase. Hypothetical reconstruction of the layout of the early phase structures. A large open space containing several wells faced the gateway. The houses are laid out in rows aligned NE-SW. (J. Herrmann, 1969.)

Presumed house plans
Street/lane
Bank

could be identified. Traces of metallurgical activities were, however, abundant.

Some fortified settlements have layouts that are intermediate between the two types. At Velem-Szent-Vid, in the Alpine foothills of western Hungary, the 10ha (25 acres) plateau is arranged in terraces 6–10m (20–33ft) wide. Excavations carried out by G. Bandi on the upper and lower terraces have revealed houses in closely set parallel rows. The earliest date from the beginning of the Late Bronze Age and had been repeatedly remodelled. Occupation, whether continuous or discontinuous, lasted many years, as shown by the thick archaeological layers. Velem-Szent-Vid was a large village that was probably heavily populated and it was also a metal-producing centre whose output far exceeded local demand.

The Hohlandsberg at Witzenheim (Alsace, previously Haut-Rhin) demonstrates different types of spatial organization within the same defences, but in an agricultural and stock-raising context. It is a rocky promontory of 4–5ha (10–12 acres) encircled by a drystone rampart (Fig. 120). Three details have been observed: at the top, the isolated house and kiln of a potter; at the south-eastern extremity (Linsenbrunnen I) houses set against the rampart; and in the centre, where the slope is rather steep, houses ranged along several terraces, following the contours (Linsenbrunnen II and III). The different areas are not contemporaneous and consist of between one and four houses. At Linsenbrunnen III the pottery kiln is integrated into the houses, as at Auvernier.

The promontory fort of Fort-Harrouard (Eure-et-Loir), by contrast, was the site of intensive metallurgical activities from the end of the Middle Bronze Age, with a new phase of substantial production in Late Bronze Age IIb and IIIa. The old excavations unfortunately do not give a clear idea of the organization of the internal space. There seems to have been an open space in the middle of the village (of the *Runddorf* type) and the residential zone seems to be distinct from the craft zone, which was characterized by semi-subterranean structures. By reason of its geographical situation, Fort-Harrouard belongs to an Atlantic cultural group, the settlements of which are poorly understood outside the British Isles.

Fortified settlements are very variable and occupy greatly varying surface areas, often as low as 1–2ha (2½–5 acres). In some rare cases they are as large as 5, 10 and even 30ha (12, 25 and 74 acres) in area, as in the case of the Büllenheimer Berg (Lower Franconia), and in such cases it may be assumed that fields and pastures existed inside the ramparts. Some settlements, at first open, were later fortified, as, for example, Lübbenau (Kr. Calau) or Burg (Kr. Cottbus) in eastern Germany, whereas others, such as the Wittnauer Horn in Switzerland, were fortified from the outset. Finally, there are others which developed into open settlements.

Villages with small or large populations?

The size of the populations living in all these settlements remains a subject of discussion. Some estimates have been attempted: at Padnal, J. Rageth suggests four or five people per house, or per room in the case of long-houses. He estimates that between one-third and one-half of the settlement has been excavated, which gives a figure of 36–90 villagers in the Middle Bronze Age and 40–120 in the Late Bronze Age.

According to Z. Bukowski, house timbers last around 25 years. He proposes therefore that the number of houses found on a site should be divided by the number of 25-year periods corresponding with the total period of occupation. In these circumstances large settlements with 8–15 houses each inhabited by 6–8 people would have had an average of 100–120 inhabitants. Similar results can be obtained using such calculations applied to groups of graves in cemeteries. At Březno, on the basis of two hamlets of five or six large houses and on the cemetery with 15–20 graves, I. Pleinerova estimates that they lasted around fifteen years and 80 people lived in them. R. Wyss has estimated five people per house in the Middle Neolithic period on the evidence of Elgozwill 5 and the Lenzbourg cemetery in the Aargau.

Because of the population increase that probably took place in the Bronze Age, a figure of 6–8 people (12–16 for larger houses) might be more plausible and would lead, for example, to a population of 60–200 at Padnal and 150–200 in the Polish Lausitz villages. Villages of the Auvernier or Cortaillod type may have had populations of 400 using the lower hypothesis and 500–600 according to the other.

Open and fortified settlements: complementary or interchangeable?

Historical models for urbanism tend to place fortified sites at a high level in the hierarchy of settlements, as the seats of civil power. Were the Bronze Age fortified

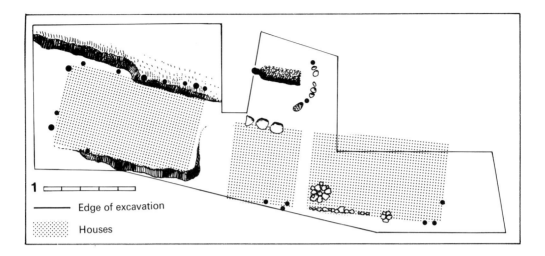

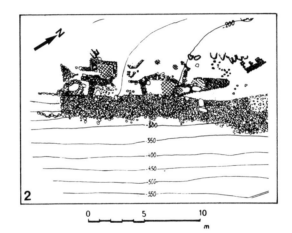

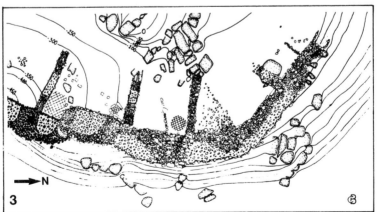

1

Edge of excavation

Houses

120

The Late Bronze Age fortified settlement of the Hohlandsberg, Haut-Rhin. The hilltop is surrounded by a strong stone wall, except on the steep N and NE sides. It contains several Late Bronze Age elements including at the top of the hill-slope the house of the potter; in the mid-slope the Linsenbrunnen II and III houses (1); and below those at Amont-route (2 and 3). The houses were built with stone walls and butted up to the rampart (2 and 3) or post-built with walls of wattle-and-daub and erected on terraces (1). The hearths, often protected by stone walls, are shown by cross-hatching. (C. Bonnet, 1973, and drawing by G. Tosello after C. Bonnet et al., 1985.)

settlements complementary to the open settlements and did they operate as regional centres within a hierarchy of sites; or were they interchangeable with unenclosed settlements and occupied only in periods of insecurity?

In order to focus on this question more clearly, it is necessary first to distinguish those fortified settlements that were only occupied sparsely or for very short periods, from those with multiple phases or intensive occupation (the one often goes with the other). The former may be considered to have been refuges, used in the same way as caves. The latter are similar to the lake villages in the probable size of their populations and the metallurgical activities carried on in them. However, like the lake villages, they were primarily farming settlements, concentrating on agricultural and pastoral activities. The probable territories of the strongholds rarely exceeded 20km (12 miles) in diameter on the basis of the known examples, that is to say, no more than a day's march from the centre. In such restricted territories there was assuredly no place for large satellite villages, only for small villages, farmsteads or hamlets.

These central settlements did, however, have functions which went beyond domestic production. The metallurgical activities carried out at many of them exceeded local requirements and the range of products was often wider than in open settlements. A proportion of the bronze output was retained on the site. Archaeologists in eastern Europe see this stockpiling as becoming possible in the Bronze Age due to improvements in productivity, a result of progress in

technology, but this, admittedly necessary, condition is not enough. Hoarding is associated characteristically with fortified settlements and was common in periods immediately preceding major cultural discontinuities, such as the end of the Early Bronze Age in eastern Europe or Late Bronze Age IIb/IIIa in western Europe. It is more likely to have been connected with intensification of competition among the elites for prestige, than motivated by reasons of security. It has nothing at all to do with the recovery of disused tools and weapons for remelting, since it is associated with precious metal objects and prized artefacts such as metal vessels or weapons.

Hoards of gold jewellery have been found at Barca or Spišský Štvrtok (Slovakia) in developed Otomaní levels or in Koszider-type hoards in upland sites in Transdanubia at the end of the Vatya culture. In the Late Bronze Age most of the fortified sites in Germany and Poland contained several hoards of metal objects. In the later periods they seem to occur on the favoured routes for trade in 'exotic' objects. The flow of objects was more or less continuous – cargoes of bronze objects from the Tumulus culture going to Britain at the end of the Middle Bronze Age, for example – but it was interrupted whenever there was a period of cultural upheaval. New circulation routes were then set up. In this way objects from the lake villages arrived in small quantities in the Carpathian basin in Late Bronze Age III when imports from eastern Europe had ceased. It was, however, also by a system of exchange that metal ores and ingots and foundry scrap reached the workshops of metal founders or smiths in most settlements.

In the present state of knowledge we still barely understand how small independent territorial units fitted together so as to form homogeneous cultural regions. We can only observe that certain settlements belong to one exchange network for prestige objects from which others are excluded. Settlements seem to be more often interchangeable rather than arranged in hierarchies, and affirmation of the existence of open settlements as dependencies of fortified settlements, although certain, owes more to historical logic than the archaeological facts at our disposal. Despite all these lacunae, however, the pattern of Bronze Age settlement testifies to an active and expanding rural world over the centuries.

12

The Iron Age

———— from village to town ————

Today we can distinguish many regional variations in the cultures of the Early Iron Age, and the Hallstatt culture itself is characterized by numerous facies. The gradual introduction of iron and intensification in the exploitation of land did not result in basic changes in the organization of settlements, which remained fundamentally agricultural – isolated farmsteads and hamlets were only rarely grouped together and in many regions upland fortified sites played complementary roles that are difficult to define: refuges, storage areas, temporary settlements, or settlements reserved for a small group. Let us first look at the region where structural changes manifested themselves most clearly: the north-west fringe of the curve of the Alps.

The Hallstatt period: a hierarchical society

W. Kimmig in 1969 summarized the main results of research carried out in southern Germany and eastern France. Very characteristic groupings emerged in the Late Hallstatt period, each consisting of a relatively small upland fortified site associated with a group of rich burial mounds. The hillforts were sometimes extended by means of undefended settlements, making them resemble the citadels of larger agglomerations. Within the enclosures settlement was dense and permanent. The presence of luxury goods, in particular imported material, bears witness to the wealth and power of the inhabitants. Small groups of burial mounds are characterized by their luxury grave goods and the presence of wheeled vehicles. The richest of these are located on axes of communication – the valleys of the Doubs, the Rhine and the Danube.

The most typical examples are at Vix (Burgundy) and the Heuneburg (Baden-Württemberg).

Mont Lassois rises up from the upper Seine valley as a completely isolated hill (Fig. 121). A bank fronted by a ditch runs round the base of the hill and takes in the lowland adjacent to the river – an area of some 40ha (99 acres). Settlement evidence is only preserved on terraces cut into the hillslopes. R. Joffroy recorded beaten earth floors, wattle-and-daub walls and post-holes. Only one building plan has been published, apparently that of a granary. The great abundance and richness of the artefactual material, both local and imported, however, attests to the density of occupation and the impressive life-style of the inhabitants. The population reached a peak at the end of the Hallstatt period, when the site was suddenly abandoned until the Late La Tène period. Three chariot burials can be related directly to this settlement; the most famous is that at Vix, but the mounds at Sainte-Colombe have also produced remarkable grave-goods, in particular a bronze Greek tripod and gold jewellery.

As at Mont Lassois, the Heuneburg hillfort stands on a small hill alongside the Danube. In this case it was only the summit, some 3ha (7½ acres), that was fortified, at the point where there was a break of slope of the hillside (Fig. 122). A settlement defended by a wooden box rampart of *Kastenbau* form was established as early as the Middle Bronze Age. It was reconstructed on several occasions from then until Reinecke's Hallstatt A period, but the Hallstatt B is marked by a very clear break in the record at this site. A new series of successive occupations began with the following period, continuing without interruption until the beginning of the La Tène period.

Nearly half the site has been excavated. The whole of the central area had been damaged by erosion and,

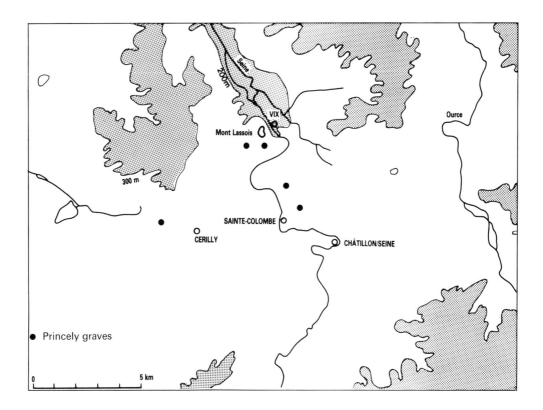

121
The Mont Lassois region (Côte-d'Or). (T. Postic.)

in the present state of publication, detailed plans are available only for the south-eastern corner of the hill, an area of 50 by 60 m (164 by 197ft). The foundations of the buildings were well preserved and detailed excavation revealed the successive occupation layers. Relationships between the buildings and the defences, which turn a sharp corner here and contain an entrance, have been very closely established for all the periods. Several construction techniques were used: buildings on lateral load-bearing uprights, with two aisles, or on horizontal sleepers. The excavators distinguished two different functions essentially on the grounds of the presence either of a hearth, signifying dwellings, or a furnace and metal waste for smiths' workshops. Square structures and a large three-aisled timber-framed building were identified as granaries. These hypotheses have to be accepted, at least until the full report is published.

In the Hallstatt C period the site was surrounded by strong defences, built in *Kastenbau* style, two caissons

wide. Rectangular buildings on frameworks of wooden beams, each surrounded by a palisade, were associated with granaries. They were all built on the same north-south orientation and covered an area of some 80 sq.m (861 sq.ft). The main period of the Late Hallstatt (Hallstatt D1) began with the building of the famous Greek-style wall of unfired bricks, with close-set projecting bastions.

The buildings from these periods were still in the local tradition. Workshops and dwelling houses replaced granaries. They were tightly packed together in the south-eastern area of the site. Rather than interpreting this as evidence of organized planning it is more appropriate in our opinion to talk of the rational use of a restricted space. The network of drains taking rainwater away into a channel that ran through the ramparts is a better indicator of the careful planned organization of this settlement.

In Hallstatt D2 a traditional timber and earth rampart replaced the Greek-style one. The more recent buildings were not well enough preserved to allow the overall plan of this part of the settlement to be traced. If the site continued to be occupied until the end of the fifth century BC, as W. Kimmig maintains, it was latterly occupied by a conservative group, whose

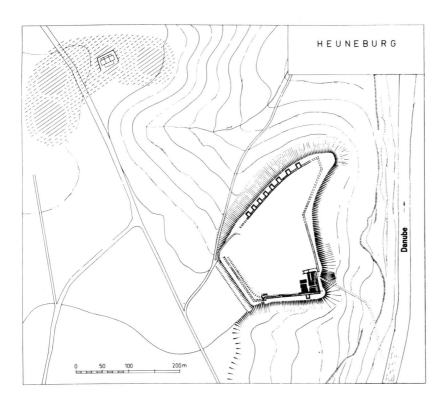

HEUNEBURG

Danube

0 50 100 200 m

122
The Heuneburg, Baden-Württemberg, in the Late Hallstatt period. The Talhau house is built 500m (1640ft) from the defences, facing the Greek-style rampart with its mud-brick foundations and projecting bastions. (W. Kimmig, 1975.)

ornaments remained typically Hallstatt in character, although their pottery was already influenced by La Tène types.

The presence some 400m (1312ft), from the hillfort of the houses at Talhau, miraculously preserved beneath burial mounds, is worthy of remark. By comparison with the houses on the hilltop these were veritable palaces, large in size and divided into several rooms. As a result the question arises of where the people who were buried with such pomp in the nearby Hochmichele mounds lived – at Talhau or on the Heuneburg? At present it is difficult to answer that question. It is evident, however, that these people controlled on the one hand the stores of basic foodstuffs, all imports from and relations with, the Mediterranean peoples, and on the other the crafts-men who worked for them in the hilltop citadel.

The study of other south German settlements in the same region also leads to the conclusion of not overstating the role of fortified sites. The inhabitants of the Kyberg (Bavaria) must also have belonged to a privileged social class; the small crest on which they lived had five occupation phases between Hallstatt C and the beginning of the Early La Tène period. It began as a small undefended hamlet 4000 sq.m (43,060 sq.ft) in area which was then enclosed with a palisade

and ditch pierced by a monumental gateway. A house from the last phase of occupation overlies this entrance, which suggests that the fortifications were no longer in use in the final period.

The Goldberg, which rises above the rich plain of the Ries, makes use of the natural escarpments of an isolated hill. A detailed interpretation of the 46 house plans excavated by G. Bersu (Fig. 123) has been carried out by A. Zippelius. He considers the two-aisled buildings with hearths to be dwelling houses, the long single-aisled buildings to be byres; and the three-aisled structures to be barns. From these data he has distinguished twelve 'farmsteads', each comprising at least one byre and one dwelling house. He postulates that the three barns were used collectively by the whole community, although in fact their siting allows them to be associated with the farmsteads nearest to them. The siting of structures in each unit is in fact very irregular and permits several interpretations.

In contrast, the buildings in the north-eastern corner of this settlement, isolated from the rest of the settlement by a system of ditches and palisades reminiscent of those round the Kyberg (Bavaria), are clearly differentiated from the others by their large-diameter uprights, which must have supported a heavy frame, perhaps even an upper storey. This group has always been interpreted as the residence of an individual who dominated the rest of the settlement by means of his authority, which is an acceptable hypothesis. Zippelius sees building 41 as a communal structure (*Gemeinschafthaus*) since it is the only one with a porch and because it stands alone opposite the entrance to the north-eastern enclosure. By comparing it with the Kyberg, K. Schwarz, like Zippelius, has emphasized the rural character of this site, which distinguishes it from other hillforts of this period. We do, however, know much larger fortifications of the period, so far unexplored, such as the Ipf, near the Goldberg, which may have served as major central places.

We have seen earlier that scholars nowadays see Hallstatt society developing within an economic system based on the exchange of prestige goods. Examination of known settlements does not contradict this model in its broad outlines. The information available to us is, however, generally inadequate to permit the classification of these sites in a rigorous hierarchy. H. Härke has attempted to make a distinction between *Fürstensitze* (princely seats); *Herrensitze* (aristocratic residences); upland fortified sites with

123

The Goldberg, Baden-Württemberg. The dotted lines group together buildings which constitute farmsteads according to Zippelius. (A. Zippelius, 1956.)

continuous but only partial occupation; complex upland fortified sites; refuges; upland fortified sites without special features; unfortified upland sites; and palisaded sites on hill-slopes. The available documentation is, however, too limited to take analysis any further. Härke himself has provided a good example of the complex course of local development between Hallstatt B and La Tène A, particularly in southern Germany: the Hallstatt B upland settlements, whether fortified or not, were in many cases abandoned in Hallstatt C in favour of other similar sites, some 10–15km (6–9 miles) distant. On the other hand, the Hallstatt D-La Tène A *Fürstensitze* were often built on sites that had already been in use in Hallstatt B.

Recent studies have revealed the existence of many Hallstatt settlements. Few of these have been excavated, especially over large areas, but the identification of large series of sites of similar type has completely revised our view of this period. Aerial photography has shown up rectangular enclosures with rounded corners, delineated by one or more rows of ditches and palisades and covering 1500–4000 sq.m (16,147–43,060 sq.ft). The best known is that at Landshut-Hascherkeller which was excavated over a long period by R. Christlein and P. Wells (Fig. 124.4). This consisted of four square enclosures, each of 2500 sq.m (26,910 sq.ft) lying on the north-western edge of the main branch of the River Isar. Enclosure A was defined by a palisade and the others by double ditches, the inner of which partly enclosed each unit.

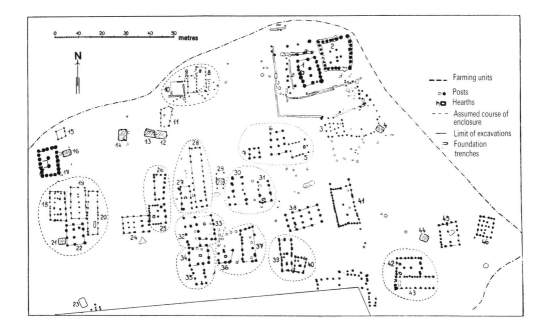

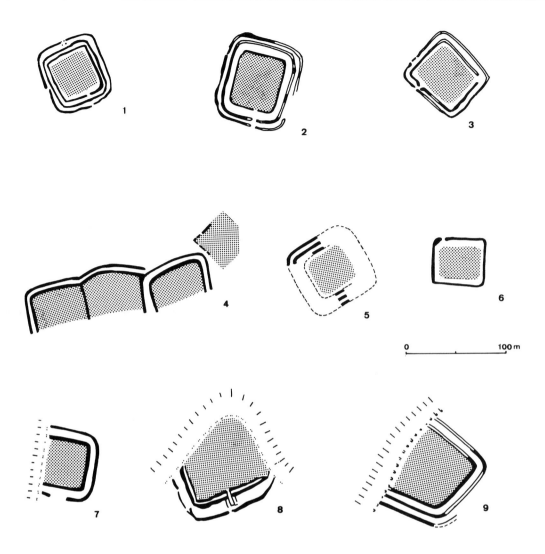

124
*Hallstatt period farmsteads in the Landshut region, Bavaria.
No.4 is Landshut-Hascherkeller. (O. Braasch and R.
Christlein, 1982.)*

The external ditch, which ran along the upper part of
the slope, enveloped two of the enclosures. Excavation revealed several single-aisled post-built structures in enclosures A and B. Preliminary examination
of the finds suggests that there were agricultural and
pastoral activities being carried out, along with
metallurgical activities. This set of sites was in use
from the end of the Urnfield period up to the middle of
the Hallstatt.

A fifth-century BC village has been recorded

occupying some 13ha (32 acres) at Kirchheim
(Bavaria). The 2ha (5 acres) excavated produced the
foundations of fifty buildings. A little apart was found
an enclosure containing an enormous single-aisled
structure. The latter was interpreted by the excavators as the residence of a family that was higher in
status than the rest of the villagers.

These farmsteads, whether isolated in the Bavarian
countryside or set near to small settlements of houses
orientated roughly north-south though without any
regular layout, were considered by R. Christlein to
represent the same culture as the *Bürger* or hillforts of
Baden-Württemberg in the late Hallstatt period. In
Bavaria however, the nobles contented themselves
with palisaded farmsteads lying some distance from

the hamlets. The Goldberg (see p. 215), which is on the border between the two regions, has the settlements both of the 'lord' and of the peasants on the same site.

This hypothesis remains rather tentative since the rare farmsteads that have been excavated have produced very little in the way of finds. However, the presence of a settlement of this type in the immediate vicinity of the central zone of princely fortifications is revealing. We have seen that at the Heuneburg itself the large house at Talhau at the base of the defences may well have been the family residence of the 'prince'. Thus we should not be too quick, even in the Hallstatt period, to associate the seat of power with the fortified upland site; this is also the case in Celtic civilization.

Moving away from the north-western fringes of the Alps, we can see that the pattern of Hallstatt settlement is made up essentially of isolated farm-steads and hamlets. The concentration of population or wealth in large fortified settlements is exceptional, and seems generally to be limited both geographically

and in time. Research is at the same time fascinated by these brilliant manifestations and incapable of explaining either their origins or their sudden disappearance.

The series of fortified villages in the Biskupin region (Poland) is typical in this respect. Despite the excellent conditions of preservation due to a waterlogged context, we are unable to explain the reasons for either their being established or their abandonment a few centuries later. How should the strict planning of Biskupin, with its houses that are all alike and fill the whole of the available space, be explained (see Figs. 70 and 71)? Why did the inhabitants of this region systematically occupy the islands and the peninsulas of its lakes, only to abandon them later? The political events which may explain this phenomenon are unknown to us. Throughout the Iron Age the family production unit is exemplified archaeologically by the form of the farmstead with its ancillary buildings. The agglomerated settlements of the La Tène period, both villages and *oppida*, are in one sense no more than

125
Grøntoft, Denmark.
Settlement of the
Bronze Age (unshaded)
and Iron Age (black);
the circles represent
burials. (C.J. Becker,
1982.)

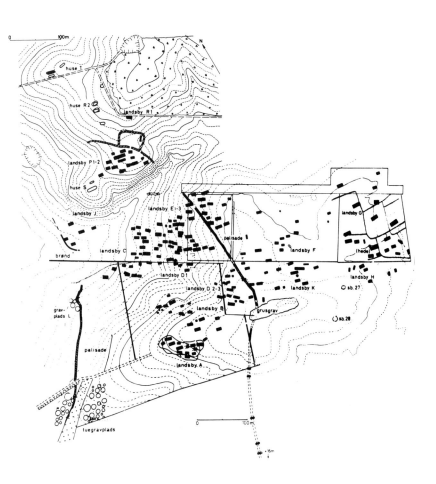

collections of farmsteads. It is rather the problem of the disappearance of hierarchical cultures during the Hallstatt period that needs to be considered. Rises in lake water levels or the disappearance of the threats that led men to fortify their settlements may have resulted in a return to better drained land, where the conditions for preservation of archaeological remains are much less favourable.

Outside those regions that we have been discussing, there is no question of talking of discontinuity in the middle of the first millennium BC, and if the La Tène culture gradually replaced the Hallstatt, settlement continuity reveals the limitations of invasion hypotheses. We thus prefer to consider the development of settlement from its origins until the end of the Iron Age region by region, not returning to look at the whole of Europe until it becomes necessary to tackle the phenomenon of the *oppida*.

Dispersed settlement in northern Europe

In the current state of knowledge abrupt transformations such as that in the Late Hallstatt period or even the advent of the oppidum civilization cannot be observed in northern Europe. Extensive excavations of settlements that are poor in finds but rich in structural remains have demonstrated slow, constant development from the Bronze Age until the end of the period under review. We can follow in the long term the gradual grouping of farmsteads into hamlets and then villages, the emergence of specialized buildings centred on byre-houses, and finally the emergence of non-farming activities and of social differentiation within the village. In this region the traditional divisions of protohistory have no meaning.

In Denmark the grouping of houses becomes more apparent from Iron Age 2 (i.e. the fourth and third centuries BC). The site of Grøntoft, where excavation is still in progress, shows how gradual the trend towards settlement concentration was (Fig. 125). Dating evidence is not always adequate to allow the phases to be separated and the excavators have found it difficult to distinguish the early hamlets from the village or villages that replaced them. A collective organizational will is well illustrated by the palisade which envelops the settlement but the buildings inside are laid out without any discernible system.

The grouping of structures is even looser on some sites, such as Drengsted or Sarrup where the houses are 15–60m (49–197ft) apart and the excavators are unsure whether to describe them as villages or 'isolated farmsteads'. The village of Hodde is the earliest organized agglomeration in Jutland (Fig. 126). This settlement, which covered 1.5ha (4 acres) at its greatest extent, admirably summarizes the paradox of settlement evidence in temperate Europe: a boundary palisade and an empty central area represent the spaces common to the entire group. At the same time, however, the enclosure round the buildings of each farmstead and the gateway in the external palisade

126
The village of Hodde,
Denmark: third phase.
The shading indicates
the position of the byre
in the houses. (S.
Hvass, 1975; M.
Müller-Wille, 1977.)

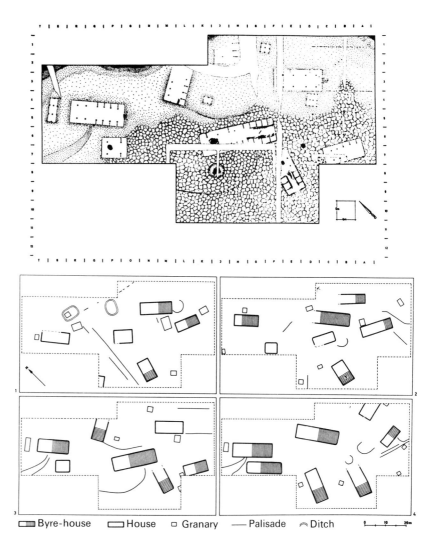

127
Boomborg-Hatzum,
Lower Saxony: a
Hallstatt period
hamlet. Shading
indicates the position of
the byre in the houses.
(W. Haarnagel, 1969;
M. Müller-Wille,
1977.)

🔲 Byre-house ▭ House ▫ Granary — Palisade ⌒ Ditch

which allows each of them access to the surrounding countryside shows that each production unit was independent within the group. Here, at the start of the Christian era, it is the organization of the settlement, the presence of substantial craftsmanship in metal, and growing differentiation between social groups that makes it possible to speak of a true village.

Man and the sea on the southern littoral of the North Sea basin

The low-lying coastal region known as the Marsch, recently emerged as the result of a drop in sea-level, was for the most part colonized in the seventh and sixth centuries BC, and many farmsteads have been recorded or excavated from the northern Netherlands to the mouth of the Weser. Both at Ezinge and Jemgum the earliest phases correspond with relatively developed but isolated farmsteads. At the Boomborg site, on the other hand, where there are ten superimposed phases from the sixth century BC onwards, some ten farmsteads are grouped together (Fig. 127). The simultaneous presence of byre-houses and granaries suggests an economy where both animal husbandry and agriculture played important roles.

In the sandy lands of the hinterland occupation density was lower than in the Late Bronze Age. Current research suggests that the farmers were struggling against poor soils by using 'Celtic fields', but also by moving their settlements when soil fertility became exhausted. When a rise in water-level drove men out of the Marsch, their migration back inland made it necessary to delineate land-holdings more precisely and to make stronger rules in relation to land occupation. The first agglomerated settlements appear in Drenthe in the second century BC at a time when 'Celtic fields' were still in use. P. Schmid has stressed the role of technological developments, such as the appearance of the mouldboard plough, in settlement stabilization and population growth. H.T. Waterbolk has shown that the landholdings laid down in Drenthe at this time form the basis for the modern system of land division.

The *Wurten* at Feddersen Wierde and Ezinge (Fig.

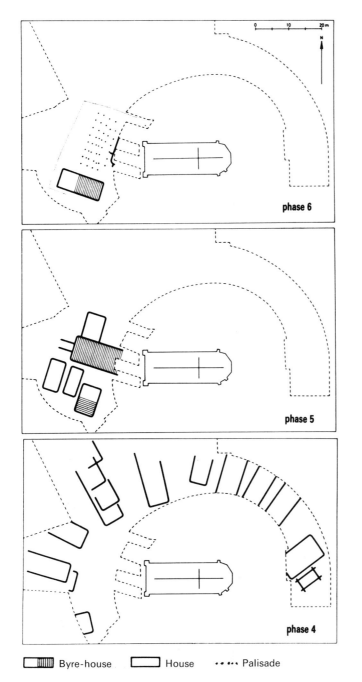

128
Development of the Wurt *at Ezinge, Drenthe. The dotted line indicates the area excavated; the position of the church is shown. (A.E. van Giffen, 1936; M. Müller-Wille, 1977.)*

phase 6

phase 5

phase 4

▭▥ Byre-house   ▭ House   •••• Palisade

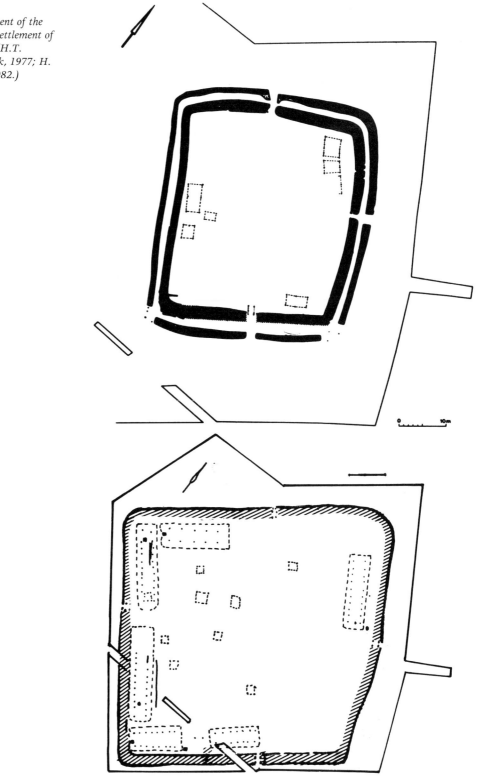

129
Development of the
fortified settlement of
Zeijen I. (H.T.
Waterbolk, 1977; H.
Steuer, 1982.)

128) show how hamlets were slowly transformed into villages at the end of the first millennium BC. The houses were first laid out in parallel lines but then were orientated end on to a central open space which became the summit of the artificial hill on which the whole settlement was raised against the rise in sealevel. The buildings began to show differences in size, and craft workshops were assigned a fixed place inside the buildings, and at length a larger unit developed, isolated from the others by a palisade and containing more imported objects. Social differentiation became apparent in this way, but by this time we are well into the first millennium AD.

One final type of settlement still resists interpretation, whilst at the same time providing a link between structures in this region and those of the rest of the continent. These are settlements enclosed by a rectangular fortification, which occur singly in the region around Bremen (Heidenschanze, near Sievern) or at the mouth of the Ems (Bentumersiel) or as a group of three within a 5km (3 mile) radius in Drenthe (Zeijen 1 [Figure 129] and 2 and Vries, Vries district). The earliest dates back to the third century BC. Comparisons with the middle Rhine or southern England are apparent: a capacity for storage together with defence concentrated in one place, under the control of one section of society about which we know little, owing to the absence of rich burials in northern Europe. Danish and Dutch scholars have noted the persistence of isolated farmsteads alongside hamlets and the earliest villages.

The lower Rhine groups

There are few settlement plans for the southern borders of the great North European plain. The Münster region and the whole of the Netherlands, however, seem to have undergone the same development as the coastal regions. Although the settlement remains are much less well preserved, there has been no discovery which would enable a model to be put forward that differs from that for the more northerly regions.

Around the Westphalian Gate, on the heights of the Teutoburger Wald which dominates the upper basins of the Ems and the Lippe, recent research has drawn attention to a series of medium-sized hillforts. They cover 3–15ha (7½–37 acres) and their ramparts in earth, stone and timber are always carefully constructed. They were occupied mainly from the Late Hallstatt to the Middle La Tène period, in some cases continuing into the Late La Tène. Preliminary spatial analyses

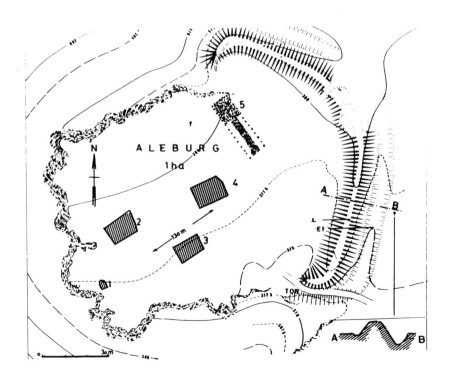

130
The Hallstatt promontory fort at Aleburg, Befort, Duchy of Luxembourg. Five structures were identified in this 1ha (2½ acres), enclosure. Of these, three were built on earthfast posts: two structures, both irregular in plan, each covered c 100 sq.m (1076 sq.ft), and a very large three-aisled house, some 30m- (98ft-) long, which is reminiscent of the byre-houses of northern Europe. (G. Thill, 1977).

have shown that settlement on lower-lying ground is associated with these enclosures. Naturally attempts have been made to relate these fortifications to the frontier between Celts and Germans. This hypothesis is, however, no longer tenable since it has been shown that their destruction in no instance coincides with the appearance of Germanic materials in the adjacent cemeteries. The reasons for their existence is to be sought in the structure of local society. K. Günther readily places the *principes* referred to by Ptolemy in these settlements.

Still on the Celtic-German frontier, the peoples of the left bank of the middle Rhine, from Belgium to Mainz, are closer in terms of settlement element to the group that has been discussed above than to those of the North European plain. A great deal of research has been carried out over the past forty years by Belgian and German scholars and by the English scholar working in Canada, the late Edith Wightman, for the end of the period. The picture remains a complex one and many questions are still to be answered, but there is no doubt that this region provides the most

131
One phase of the La Tène fortified settlement of the Altburg-bei-Bundenbach, Hunsrück. (R. Schindler, 1975.)

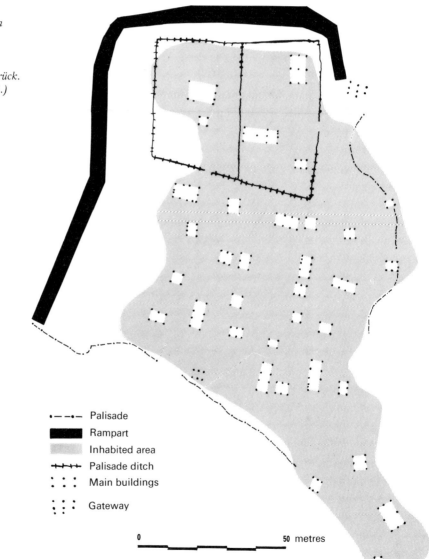

- •— —•— Palisade
- ▮ Rampart
- ▓ Inhabited area
- ++++ Palisade ditch
- ⦙ ⦙ ⦙ Main buildings
- ⦙ ⦙ ⦙ Gateway

0   50 metres

complete view of settlement development in the La Tène period (second Iron Age).

Among the fortified settlements that have been almost completely excavated, some differ very little, in terms of the number of buildings that they comprise, from the isolated farmsteads of the plains. The Hallstatt settlement of Befort (Luxembourg) is situated on a small promontory defended by means of a curved rampart (Fig. 130). The Altburg-bei-Bundenbach is on a spur which overlooks a small river in the Hunsrück from its schist cliffs (Fig. 131) and was occupied from the Middle La Tène period. The interpretation of its settlements as either storage areas, military emplacements or the seat of a minor lord with his entourage is rendered difficult by the unfortunate scarcity of finds.

Alongside major excavations there have been trial excavations in the Belgian Ardennes, the Saarland and the Palatinate (Pfalz) which demonstrate development in the construction of defences employed in the many enclosures dominating the steep valleys of the tributaries of the Moselle and the Meuse. They have aspects in common with the settlements of both the upper Rhine Valley and of Britain. They increased in number throughout the whole period of the Hunsrück-Eifel culture. In the Belgian Ardennes (Fig. 132) there are few traces of occupation and there has been no major excavation because trial excavations have produced little evidence of occupation. Befort and Bundenbach are still the only two 'models' available. Settlements from the earlier phase are sometimes identified as *Herrensitze*, small castles occupied by overlords. In the later phase these fortresses would rather have served instead as refuges for the inhabitants of the farmsteads that are scattered in the neighbourhood. None of the enclosures in the Belgian Ardennes has up to the present produced any evidence of occupation in the Middle La Tène period. Excavations at Bundenbach in the Palatinate suggest that there were fortified settlements which brought together larger numbers of people than the earlier lowland settlement. As mentioned above, excavation has not made it possible to decide unequivocally between several hypotheses: should the military aspect be stressed, for instance, or the division of this form of settlement into two contrasting sectors? As so often happens, excavation poses new questions which divert attention away from the original question. Recent work by H.-E.

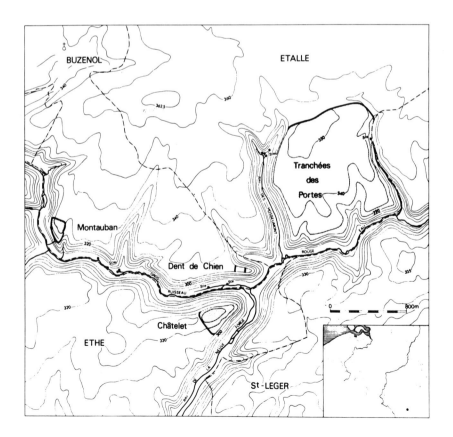

132
The fortifications of the Buzenol region, Belgian Ardennes. (A. Cahen-Delhaye, 1982.)

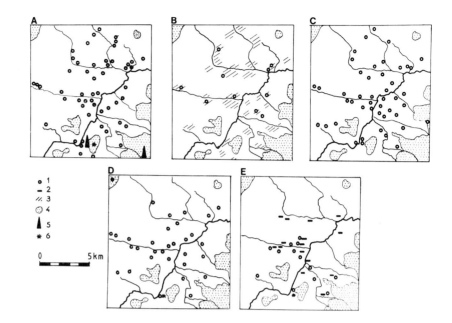

133
Evolution of settlement
pattern in northern
Bohemia from
Hallstatt D to La Tène
D2. A: Hallstatt D to
La Tène A. B: La Tène
A and B1. C: La Tène
B1. D: La Tène B2–C1.
E: La Tène C2–D2.
1: Celtic settlement.
2: Germanic settlement.
3: Occupation by an
older group linked with
Celtic incursions.
4: Land over 350m
(1148ft).
5: Fortifications.
6: Cult centres. (J.
Waldhauser, 1981.)

Joachim in the Aachen area has revealed the existence of nucleated settlements in the Middle and Late La Tène. The largest is that at Eschweiler Laurenzberg, where 68 buildings were identified in an excavated area of 12,000 sq.m. (129,171 sq.ft). As at Bundenbach they were small in size, and all the nine-post structures, thought by Joachim to be dwelling houses, could also be interpreted as granaries. Whatever they may have been, this was unquestionably a nucleated settlement with, among its structures, a number that were used for storage.

The cemeteries in this region show an uneven distribution of wealth and a very marked social hierarchy, although less so than in Hallstatt society. Local resources, and iron ore in particular, underpinned the growth of a leisured class among the indigenous population. As in much of Europe, in the earlier phase here there can be seen a dispersed form of settlement from which small 'seigneurial' fortresses emerged, followed by the development of modest agglomerations, and finally the appearance of a small number of very large enclosures each surrounded by a *murus gallicus*.

Early La Tène farmsteads and villages

In distancing ourselves from the central sector of the Hallstatt culture, we have moved into regions where settlement developed without any abrupt discontinuity between the two Iron Ages. Storage of foodstuffs became so important that special structures, easily visible on settlement plans, were designed for them. The existence of such stores both presupposes that there were surpluses and caused settlements to become fixed in space. The general impression from the various regional analyses that have been carried out seems to indicate that the hamlets of the beginning of the period, apparently used for only a few generations, were replaced by small agglomerated settlements occupied over several centuries.

This locational stability is also demonstrated by the cemeteries, which have been studied much more closely than the settlements themselves. Generally speaking they correspond with small communities that buried their dead in the same place for several centuries.

In northern Bohemia large areas have come to light due to the opencast mining of lignite (Fig. 133). The land was occupied discontinuously, the land-holdings being separated by uncultivated land, as we have seen earlier. At the level of communities' lands, continuity was absolute throughout the whole Iron Age, from Hallstatt C to La Tène D. The settlements themselves remained unorganized and relatively mobile in the Early La Tène period. Although a dozen of them continued throughout the periods of greatest change, between La Tène A and La Tène B, eight were abandoned and seven new ones appeared at what is conventionally termed the Celtic horizon, namely that represented by cemeteries of flat graves which lasted for several centuries. At the same time fortified settlements, occupied in Hallstatt D-La Tène A, disappeared and were not reoccupied until La Tène C. According to J. Waldhauser, these farmsteads or hamlets, the positions of which were restricted solely by ecological constraints, could easily move their locations according to need. It was when new activities, such as metalworking, appeared that settlements began to be located more permanently and workshops and other manufacturing facilities began to cluster.

On the Swiss plateau, in southern Germany or in the Marne valley little is known of the settlements that logically must correspond with the cemeteries. Current research, particularly in northern and eastern France, is producing evidence of many sites dating from the Hallstatt to the Late La Tène, but in almost every case this comes from relatively small-scale excavations. Isolated farmsteads and hamlets certainly existed, not only in the valleys but also in intervening regions where they are more difficult to detect. At the present time no large agglomeration which might qualify as a village has yet been published. We have a provisional impression of a settlement pattern that was dense but dispersed, the stability of which is demonstrated by the associated cemeteries, especially in the Aisne and Marne valleys.

The British Isles

It is necessary to turn to the British Isles for usable data on settlement organization in this period. This was an exceptional region, if only because of its characteristic round-houses; but in the broad lines of its development settlement was not very different from what can be observed on the continent. We have already seen that the conditions for the preservation of buildings were good in this region, even though their dating is often difficult to determine.

As in the Bronze Age, isolated farmsteads were here the fundamental settlement unit. They existed, in slightly differing forms, over the whole region and no other type succeeded in supplanting them completely throughout the whole Iron Age. The most famous is that at Little Woodbury (Wiltshire), which remained the basic reference point until quite recently (Fig. 134). G. Bersu excavated more than half the total area of approximately 1ha (2½ acres). It was surrounded by a palisade and ditch, the extensions or antennae of which enclosed a gateway. There was a round-house,

which had been rebuilt several times, near the centre of the enclosure. To the east lay the remains of four granaries. In addition to several quarries, the site contained some 190 pits in the excavated area alone. These were classified variously as grain-storage pits, wells, and working hollows and were roughly grouped by type. Bersu believed that the pits were only used for short periods, no more than five or six being in use at any one time. The settlement was occupied between 300 BC and the beginning of the first century AD.

This dating has recently been subject to criticism, and J.R. Collis suggests that the establishment of the settlement should be dated as early as the sixth, or even the seventh, century BC. Others have queried whether there may not have been other buildings within the enclosure. Whatever the precise details, it is important to put Little Woodbury into its immediate context, that is to say along with the other remains detected by aerial reconnaissance within a radius of several hundreds of metres. In addition to ditch complexes, there are two small rectangular enclosures which may have contained smaller houses, whilst the neighbouring enclosure of Great Woodbury is surprisingly large: it is three times as large as Little Woodbury and appears to be enclosed within a bank and wide ditch, so that it is reminiscent of a small hillfort.

Excavation of the farmstead at Gussage All Saints, recently investigated with the intention of complementing Bersu's observations, produced some surprising results. The absence of any apparent trace of a large house provided the first difficulty, and the dating evidence, which allowed the occupation to be extended from the sixth to the first century BC, was also questionable. We do not go along with G.J. Wainwright's interpretation of the four-post structures as dwelling units: for us these are indisputably granaries of the kind found everywhere in Britain, where they can without difficulty be distinguished from round-houses. J.R. Collis has cogently remarked that the grouping of four-post structures in the early phase opposite a peripheral empty space near the site's perimeter is reminiscent of the hillfort of Danebury, which lies on a hill some kilometres to the north-east: the houses may have been on the periphery of the site, as suggested by some remains that survived in phase 2. He goes on to propose two phases in the evolution of these farmsteads: an early phase characterized by the large houses from Pimperne (see Fig. 37) and Little Woodbury and a late phase exemplified by Gussage All Saints, where the houses were smaller but more numerous within a single enclosure.

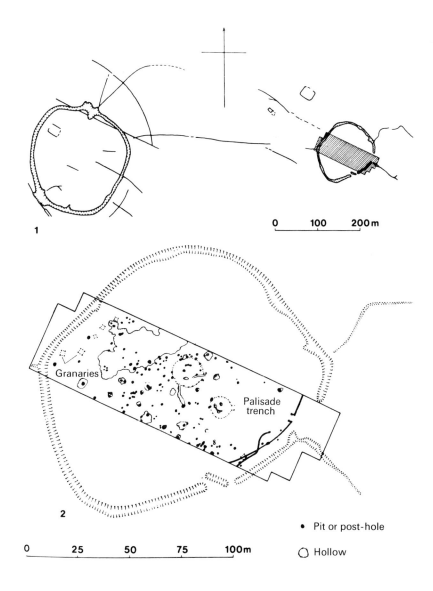

134
The Little Woodbury
farmstead (1, right,
and 2) and the Great
Woodbury enclosure,
Wiltshire, (1 left). (G.
Bersu, 1940; J.V.S.
Megaw and D.D.A.
Simpson, 1979.)

0   100   200 m

Granaries

Palisade
trench

1

2

0   25   50   75   100 m

● Pit or post-hole

○ Hollow

It should not be overlooked that at both Gussage and Little Woodbury other enclosures and ditch systems are known in the immediate vicinity. It is still difficult, even for this extremely well-studied region, to say whether these structures are characteristic of a particular period within the Iron Age or of a particular function in settlement hierarchy. Following the latter hypothesis, is it the social status of the owner of the land or the specific type of land exploitation within the local economy that is represented by these structures in the archaeological record? In this respect the presence of remains of a bronze workshop producing luxury horse trappings at Gussage All Saints offers a very interesting avenue to explore.

Isolated farmsteads or groups of a few dwellings remained the norm in the Iron Age over the whole lowland part of Britain. In the upper Thames valley the variety of remains reveals intensive occupation of the land and specialized activities according to the potential of each territory or zone. Settlements changed rapidly, seemingly in response to modifications in the methods of exploiting the land. In the south-east houses were often surrounded by rectangular enclosures, which could be as large as 20–30 m (66–98ft). There were also undefended settlements without ditches, but their less regulated layouts, often

227

locked into fossil field networks, makes them difficult to identify. Whenever these settlements are excavated they are seen to have complicated histories, with phases when the farmstead was undefended and others when it was fortified.

North-eastern England and south-eastern Scotland show independent development, the main trends of which are now becoming understood, even if there are numerous local variations. Settlements of the mid-first millennium BC are characterized by ring-ditch houses, which may have housed both men and animals. These settlements may contain several houses, and their economy was based on a combination of agriculture and animal husbandry. The land seems to have been exploited intensively and the herds were closely associated with the settlements. A new system developed in about the fifth and fourth centuries BC which combined hillforts and farmsteads of another type, consisting usually of fewer than three houses, often associated with extensive ditch systems. Some scholars believe that animal husbandry was practised in a different way: the animals were less closely controlled, being spread over distant pastures. The chronological succession from undefended to palisaded to banked-and-ditched settlement is a system that comes under heavy attack nowadays, even though there is no evidence for an alternative system. The choice between these different methods of protection may depend on other factors – the availability of wood, for example, or the wish to provide better defence against fire. Account also has to be taken of regional variations, and also a possible relationship between altitude and site type. It is still an open question.

At the end of the Iron Age settlements were once again undefended, but the main changes belong to the Roman period, with the appearance of stone-walled houses, set within small enclosures, which were usually rectangular. North-eastern Scotland has recently been the subject of intensive studies into settlements other than the famous vitrified forts, which had hitherto been the only ones investigated. Undefended settlements and many small enclosures, very diversified in form, are widespread in the region, extending from the isolated and harsh highlands down to the coast. An idea of the evolution of this settlement pattern must await the dating and excavation of those that have been identified. In the interim, however, it can be recorded that isolated family farmsteads developed widely during the Iron Age. Agriculture played a not insignificant role and here, as in the south, the rotary quern had been introduced before the arrival of the Romans. Between the coastal plain,

the foothills, and the mountains with their hillforts, which could not have housed permanent populations, there must unquestionably have been distinct forms of settlement organization, probably with complementary economies and exchange between one another which can no longer be distinguished.

In the Iron Age the whole of the west of the British Isles, from Scotland to Cornwall, presented a picture totally different from that in the east. Stone buildings straightaway give a different appearance to settlement remains, but the differences go much deeper. Here fortifications and farming settlements are not easy to separate and the scarcity of remains of human activities discourages attempts at dating or constructing historical sequences. Researchers have to be content with architectural analysis, sometimes backed up by radiocarbon dates. In the northern part of this region the development of fortified sites – such as the duns and brochs of Atlantic Scotland, the latter recently radiocarbon-dated to the fifth century BC – well illustrate the very scattered nature of settlement. Small fortified settlements are also the rule in Wales, although there are some large enclosures like Tre'r Ceiri which contain several dozen round-houses. The Cornish rounds, which can cover as much as 1ha (2½ acres), usually contain one or two houses. These date largely to the end of the Iron Age, but are mostly of Roman date.

Glastonbury (Somerset), lying on the boundary between the Atlantic and southern zones, is exceptional, like so many wetland sites. D.L. Clarke has proposed an interpretive model for this village which, although based on slight data, compels us to focus on the nature of the settlement record at a level that is much closer to the reality experienced by Iron Age societies (Clarke 1972). He distinguishes four main occupation phases and five settlement clusters, or groups of buildings, distributed around a central open space (Fig. 135).

The archaeological structures can be grouped in units, each consisting of a certain number of basic elements: one or two main houses, on one side or the other of a small courtyard, accompanied by workshops for crafts such as metalworking, an ancillary building for domestic activities surrounded by granaries, sheds for animals, furnaces and working areas. The successive phases consist of (1) four units, or twelve houses for some 60 people; (2) five units and fifteen houses; (3) seven units and 21 houses; and (4) seven units and fifteen houses, this last representing around 120 people. Thus in theory the population doubled over the roughly one hundred years of the village's existence, which straddled the turn of the

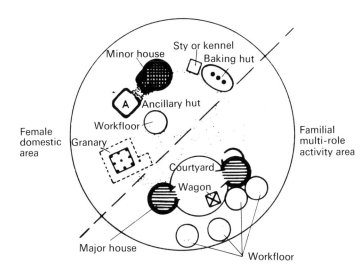

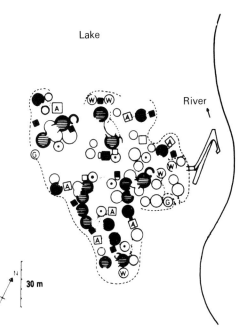

second and first centuries BC. He postulates that the community dispersed once it reached a critical threshold, in this case double its initial level.

The units are virtually identical, with the exception of house 42, which produced more metal objects. This model does not contradict what we know of Celtic societies from Irish literary sources. It highlights the existence of a structured organization and the identical nature of the units which made up the settlement. The hypothesis of the break-up of the settlement when its population doubled remains theoretical: it assumes that neither society nor economy changed over time, the successive generations reproducing themselves identically like amoebae. Dynamic systems are now being sought which attempt to take account of changes in environment and population. This example may be taken to represent, in size terms, the transition with hillforts which in some cases contain as many circular platforms or house foundations as Glastonbury.

We have already seen that in the British Isles the distribution of these fortified sites is very uneven: they are small and very numerous over the whole of the western coastal region, varied in size but relatively large and dense in the central part of the country, while there are almost no settlements of this type in the east. Their fortifications generally evolved from simple to complex, and the later centuries in particular are characterized by large enclosures with double or triple ramparts, some of them with monumental entrances. The presence of guard chambers adjacent to gateways in some instances emphasizes the true

function of these entrances, suggesting permanent defence or monitoring of the movement of people or goods.

Analysis of the ditched ranch boundary systems, which sometimes run for several kilometres, often ending at an enclosure, shows that hillforts played a part in the exploitation of the surrounding landscape. Although there is no direct proof, it is likely that they had a role in stock rearing, the pasturing of animals and the provision of fodder. The results of the Danebury excavations (Fig. 136) provide an example of evolution throughout the entire Iron Age. This enclosure in Hampshire covers an area of 5.3ha (13 acres) on the top of a low rounded hill. It is situated within a system of wide ditches and 'Celtic fields'. Its territory, possibly delimited by the river network and by neighbouring hillforts, spreads over about 60km

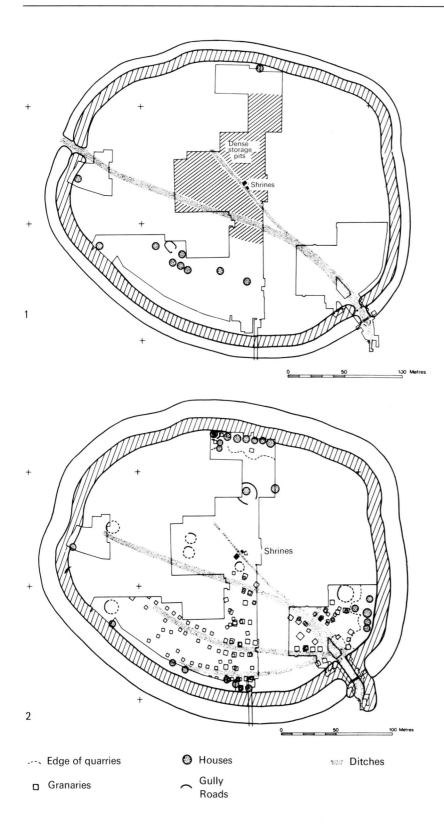

136
Danebury hillfort. 1:
early phase; 2: late
phase. The southern
residential area gives
way in the later phase
to an area of granaries.
(B.W. Cunliffe, 1983.)

Dense storage pits

Shrines

1

0   50   100 Metres

Shrines

2

0   50   100 Metres

.·-. Edge of quarries   ⊛ Houses   ⚞ Ditches

▫ Granaries   ⌒ Gully
                       Roads

(37 miles). Some twenty undefended isolated settlements are distributed evenly along the river valley slopes.

Excavation between 1970 and 1982 resulted in the examination of nearly half the interior of the hillfort. The chalk subsoil is riddled with cylindrical pits used for storing grain. A roadway linking the entrances lying on the south-west and the east was respected by the dwelling houses throughout the entire life of the settlement.

The hilltop was occupied from about 1000 BC. B. Cunliffe attributes a ritual function to the wells that he excavated immediately in front of the south-eastern gateway. In the early phase four-post granaries, soon replaced by storage pits, filled the whole of the centre of the enclosure north of the main roadway. The southern part was occupied by round-houses, each with several storage pits. At the end of this phase houses were built along the internal face of the rampart in a quarry which had supplied material for strengthening the defences. The excavator assumed that the northern part was used for storing the products of the surrounding territory whilst the southern part served to house the permanent inhabitants of the hillfort. Around the end of the fifth century BC two additional roadways were laid out in the southern part, where many four- or six-post granaries covered almost the entire area. Storage pits were laid out in small groups whilst the round-houses continued to hug the internal face of the rampart. The central and northern parts were cleared and several rectangular buildings, probably sanctuaries, were erected in place of the storage pits of the earlier phase. This layout continued until the first century BC. In this period various changes were made to the fortifications: the rampart was strengthened; the outer rampart was added, thereby creating what was doubtless a kraal for livestock; and the eastern gateway was made more elaborate. During the following two centuries the site was much less densely occupied, and limited to the central and southern parts of the enclosure. Cunliffe estimates that the population may have reached 300–350 people. The storage capacity greatly exceeded the needs of the residents, since the average of 850 cubic m (30,017 cubic ft) in storage pits and granaries would have been capable of feeding four times as many people. Danebury may have received the produce of a score of farmsteads.

There is evidence of craft production, weaving and above all of iron working, especially in the later periods, but the settlement remained basically a farming community. Cunliffe has commented that the peak period of Danebury, beginning in the fifth century BC, corresponds in the whole region to a period when the overall number of hillforts decreased whilst the survivors increased in size. At the same time that these central places were developing, their functions as permanent storage centres were confirmed. In the preceding period hillforts were not occupied intensively: it is suggested that they were used for penning animals or for periodic meetings of a religious or military nature, the details of which remain virtually unknown to us. The Danebury site and its region show that the situation changed around the middle of the first millennium BC: those hillforts that survived were densely and permanently settled and storage capacity greatly exceeded the requirements of the inhabitants. Another example is known at Moel-y-Gaer.

Moel-y-Gaer is on Halkyn Mountain in north-eastern Wales. Excavation has revealed two types of structure in the second occupation phase of the site: round-houses in the central and northern parts of the excavated area and four-post granaries in the southern part (see Fig. 78). Those elements that were closely associated with one another on isolated farmsteads were here spatially separated. Sectors reserved for storage or as living quarters replaced family production units. This does not necessarily mean that the family production structure disappeared. However, the fact that the storage pits or granaries were physically separated from the residential area means that the former had assumed a new significance for the community as a whole, even if ownership of crops remained with family units.

Villages and craftsmen in the Middle and Late La Tène period

During the second century BC an important change in production and economy became apparent over the whole of continental Celtic Europe which had clear consequences for the organization of settlement. Marseilles and Rome, which created the province of Narbonensis in 121 BC, developed trade on a completely different scale from earlier periods: the most obvious archaeological evidence is in the form of wine amphorae. From the late second century BC they are to be found throughout Gaul and up as far as Britain. We do not know exactly what northern Europe was supplying in exchange, but we can see that its economy made substantial progress: we have already referred to stocks of food surpluses, craftsmanship in iron, the production of rotary querns and above all the appearance of silver and bronze coinage.

This economic context goes a long way towards explaining, in our opinion, the development of a new form of settlement in the second century, during the Middle La Tène period II in France (C in central Europe). Several excavations have revealed the existence of relatively large agglomerations, usually covering 5–10ha (12–25 acres), the function of which was obviously no longer exclusively agricultural.

Alongside the remains of animal husbandry and grain storage can be seen evidence of craft production and long-distance trade, the proportion varying from site to site. This takes the form of weaving, the working of bone, metal and glass; the manufacture and use of coins; and in the case of trade imports of wine amphorae and Campanian wares.

The available examples are, as has already been

137
Oppida and lowland villages. 1: Levroux; 2: Basle; 3: Hochstetten. (T. Postic.)

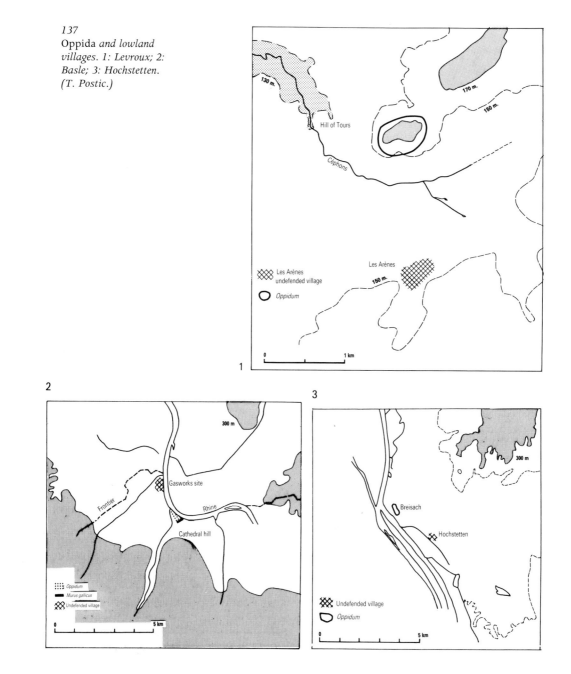

stressed, not very satisfactory: the large-area excavations are lacking which would make it possible to understand how these settlements were organized. Destruction of occupation layers often creates almost insurmountable difficulties in establishing site stratigraphies. On the other hand, the extraordinary abundance of rubbish 'trapped' in pits makes reliable statistical analysis possible, since material of this kind is found in assemblages of tens of thousands of items.

Site plans are rare, but they hint at the existence of streets; there are fences defining dwellings and their ancillary structures. These sites are usually on low-lying ground and are not fortified. The buildings have left very few traces, either because the top 30cm (12in) of the ancient ground surface have been disturbed, or because the improved constructional techniques used did not require the uprights to be set deep into the earth. Hundreds of iron nails are collected from these sites: for the first time they were being extensively used for everyday purposes.

At Les Pichelots, 25km (15 miles) south-east of Angers, Dr Gruet is excavating a lowland settlement which, if the excavated stretch of palisade is extrapolated, covered 7ha (17 acres). More than two hundred Dressel 1A amphorae have been found. Weaving seems to have been an important activity in the village. The presence of Nauheim brooches dates the main occupation to around 80–50 BC.

The Hochstetten settlement in the Rhine valley occupied a gravel terrace at the foot of the volcanic hill of the Münsterberg, where the town of Breisach is situated (Fig. 137.1). The settlement appears to have covered 8ha (20 acres). The surviving structures consist of pits, wells and palisade trenches. The site has produced evidence of glass, brooch and coin production. A large quantity of La Tène 2 brooches alongside a few of Nauheim type dates the site to the end of the second century BC.

The site near the Basle gasworks, where almost all the brooches were of Nauheim type, is dated to 80–50 BC (Fig. 137.2). Here again the archaeological evidence consisted largely of pits and palisade trenches. In addition to farming, metalworking played a major role, and the presence of amphorae is easily explained by the situation of the settlement on a major trade route.

The settlements at Aulnat, near Clermont-Ferrand, and Levroux (Indre) follow the same pattern: the structures, activities and imports are similar. It is this resemblance which leads us to assert that the ten or so villages known to date seem to be representative of a general phenomenon. It only needs to be noted that, in the case of Aulnat, the current state of knowledge

suggests that there were hamlets from the end of the Early La Tène which gradually increased in size. At Levroux it is the recovery of workshops for metal, bone and coins that is the novel element resulting from the continuing excavations. Like Hochstetten, these two villages seem to have been occupied from the end of the second century BC.

In Britain the settlement on Hengistbury Head, to the west of Portsmouth, seems to belong to the same chronological horizon. Its role appears, however, to have been commercial in nature: most of the finds consisted of imports and its location on the south coast certainly emphasizes its role as a port.

No settlement of this type is known in central Europe from such an early date. They might be expected at the ends of Alpine passes, as, for example, on the Swiss plateau. It is, however, the Rhône-Saône-Rhine corridor which seems once again to have experienced the earliest innovations under the stimulus of Mediterranean imports. Some decades later the accounts of Roman merchants scratched on the walls of houses at the Magdalensberg, in south-eastern Austria, are evidence of massive trade in metal objects destined for Italy.

Manching (Bavaria) is the most easterly settlement in this category of craft villages, although it presages the succeeding phase (Fig. 138). It appears that at the centre of this famous *oppidum* there was initially an undefended village similar in every aspect to those described above. The defences, which enclose 380ha (939 acres), were built well beyond the outskirts of the settled area, even during its period of greatest extension. Like the other villages Manching is situated in the plain alongside a river. The construction of an *oppidum* around an earlier settlement is a somewhat rare occurrence.

'La civilisation des *oppida*'

The plan and scale of the Manching defences are typical of a completely new and sudden phenomenon, the foundation of *oppida*. In a recent, fascinating book on this period, J.R. Collis rejects the idea of the deliberate foundation of *oppida* as was the case with certain medieval towns. But how can Manching be analysed otherwise, even though the earlier village was in the same place as the *oppidum*? At a certain moment the inhabitants, or their chiefs, who did not necessarily live in the settlement, designed and carried out a comprehensive, ambitious project: to enclose an area much larger than the the original village with continuous defences on an imposing scale. Thousands

The following legends appear within and below the figures:

— Limit of excavation ⌐ Post-holes ▬ Small ditch ○ Pit ▰ Dried-up river bed

0 6 12 18 24 30m

1

▤ Dense occupation   ▭ Sparse occupation

100 0 100 200 300 400 500 m

2

138

The Manching oppidum. 1: Excavated area 2: general plan.   *(W. Krämer, 1962, 1975; F. Maier, 1985.)*

of nails were forged in order to build a *murus gallicus* in western style; and elaborate entranceways surmounted by gatetowers were erected.

How could such major projects be carried out without a well worked out plan? Why should they deliberately choose to occupy 380ha (939 acres) when neither the size of the existing settlement nor the topographical constraints required such an enormous area? As Collis suggests, it would be better to look for a model in catastrophe theory than among evolutionary approaches to account for the rise of the 'civilisation des oppida'.

With the exception of Manching, Lutetia, Besançon, and a few other villages that were transformed into *oppida* without being relocated, most *oppida*, by taking advantage of a geographical situation that was favourable both for trade and defence, were created in locations that were situated elsewhere. Farming flatlands or the neighbourhood of land or water routes, where villages developed quite naturally, were abandoned, though settlements did not move far, only a few kilometres. *Oppida* were sited in less accessible places, where it can easily be shown that the settlement was closely linked with major trade routes or rich grain-producing plains.

In fact, the founders of the *oppida* were clearly seeking to re-establish the tradition of fortified upland settlements, which had been somewhat abandoned in the La Tène period in those regions where craft production and farming had made the greatest progress. It should be recalled at this point that during the two millennia that cover the Bronze and Iron Ages it was the upland defended sites, the hillforts, that represented the acme of construction and symbolized the power of social groups. In order to give material expression to the development of their way of life, the inhabitants of second-century BC villages returned to the traditional model of the hillfort.

This model was, however, superseded and transformed in order to conform with the inclinations of the time. With new technological aids – the general use of metal, for example – and with pretensions to urban life, inspired no doubt by the cities of the Mediterranean, enormous undertakings were set in train. In 1965 W. Dehn produced a definition of *oppida* (based primarily on German examples) that stresses admirably how they can be distinguished from earlier hillforts:

> The following characteristics can be considered to be typical of *oppida* in general: they were almost always fairly spacious settlements, whether built on high ground or in more or less

flat terrain, whilst the plan of the enclosure shows a preference for straight lines that join at obtuse angles. Valleys and depressions were crossed without regard to the loss in height; a berm or wide ditch ran in front of the rampart; the fortification sometimes conceals a *murus gallicus*, more frequently there was a wall reinforced with wooden posts set upright on the outer face. In both cases there was an earthen dump in the form of an inclined ramp at the back of the fortifications which often made them very thick. What is also very typical is the fact that rampart ends were turned back at right-angles into the interior to edge the entranceways (*Zangentore*). In the large settlements that are indubitably Celtic (Finsterlohr, Heidengraben, etc), this layout is very accentuated.

It is by their size that *oppida* can be distinguished from earlier defended enclosures: an area of 20–30ha (49–74 acres) is common in continental Europe, and a score of them range between 90 and 600ha (222 and 1483 acres), even exceptionally 1500ha (3706 acres) at the Heidengraben in the Swabian Jura. It should be recalled, for comparison, that the Paris of Philippe-Auguste in 1210 covered 253ha (625 acres) and that with Charles V's extension in 1370 Paris became the largest town in France at 438ha (1082 acres). Such enlargement led the *oppidum* builders to enclose several hilltops and the valleys between them in a single defensive work, as at Závist in Bohemia (Fig. 139), the Heidetränk near Frankfurt-am-Main (see Fig. 47), or Mont Beuvray in Burgundy (Fig. 140), in such a way that the ramparts ran down the hillsides, which made them more vulnerable.

Contrary to earlier traditions, the defences were in fact no longer confined to natural features in those regions where steep slopes or a river did not afford natural protection: they ran right round the site, as if they had to indicate the physical separation between interior and exterior. The choice of the technique using internal wooden frameworks was also significant: this was in part a return to traditional techniques that had been updated to suit current taste. The use of thousands of iron clamps within the *murus gallicus* was probably of symbolic value rather than of defensive benefit and likewise the development of stone cladding would certainly have given the walls a more monumental appearance when confronted by assailants, although such facings would in fact have been extremely fragile. Caesar's testimony is there to show that the Gauls paid dearly in the struggle against Roman siege engines for this choice of ornamental

139
The Závist oppidum. Several parallel ramparts protect the hilltop settlement. (K. Motyková, P. Drda, and A. Rybová, 1982.)

walls rather than the massive earthen ramparts that better withstood the effects of fire or battering rams.

The gateways, their considerable widths flanked by the inturned rampart ends, were in effect triumphal arches. At the same time the marked separation between entry and exit roads and the means of closing them with gates presumes that there was regular monitoring of people and goods.

The evidence of settlement inside the enclosures corresponds with permanent occupation. Here are to be found the structures and the activities associated with the villages of the previous generation: organized farming, storage and craft activities, grouped in their own compounds or along the streets. Cult places, which are clearly identified in some of the settlements despite the slightness of their remains, seem also to have been important elements in the occupation of *oppida*. Craft-production increased in scale with specialists mass-producing items, as is attested by the hundreds of artefacts – such as small bronzes,

140
Plan of the oppidum *of Bibracte (Mont Beuvray), Burgundy, France. The heavy line indicates the principal fortification and gates. Water provision on the site is shown by the various springs (fontaines) and streams (ruisseaux). The workshop quarter at la Come-Chaudron and the upper class residential area on the saddle at the Parc aux Chevaux are identified. (J. Bertin.)*

engraved bone objects and glass bracelets – which are characteristic of all the European *oppida*. Bronze coins and accurate weighing balances, amphorae and Campanian wares testify to active long-distance trade and exchange.

It is probably through the spatial distribution of activities rather than their nature that it is possible to discern a difference between villages and *oppida*.

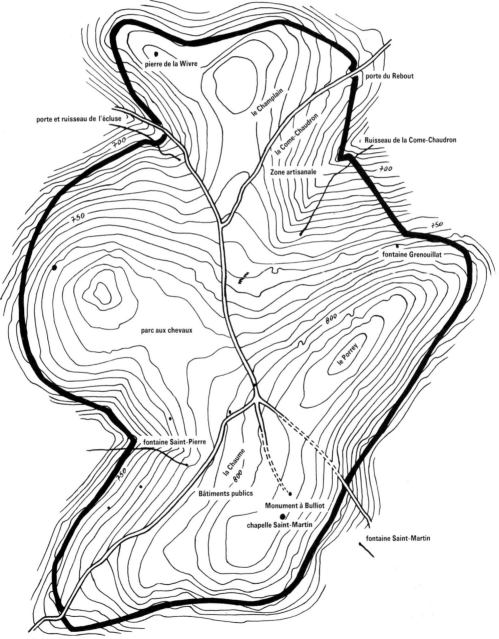

There seem to have been specialized areas in the latter (Fig. 140), with one reserved for religious activities and another for communal meetings, craftsmen's areas along the roads and near the gateways, more traditional dwellings (i.e. with characteristics similar to those of farmsteads) and richer ones, away from the traffic axes. This conception is based on sparse data: the results, only partly published, of the Manching excavations, which are difficult to use in this context, and above all the work of J.-G. Bulliot and J. Déchelette on Mont Beuvray (Burgundy). One of the main reasons for starting excavations again on this site is to analyse the distribution of activities within the settlement against the background of more accurate dating techniques now available. Several sites contribute useful information about the internal organization of *oppida*, such as Staré Hradisko in Moravia and Hrazany and Třísov in Bohemia. In all these cases, however, the data are just enough to sustain the theories, but they do not provide convincing proofs.

In the shelter of a meander of the Aisne, some kilometres to the east of Soissons, the defended settlement of Villeneuve-Saint-Germain, which is still being excavated, may provide some interesting answers. Well defined enclosures link dwellings and storage structures (Fig. 141). They are distributed regularly along the rectilinear road network. There is a craftmen's quarter that is separated from this zone by a double palisade in which the buildings, although more difficult to identify, have nothing in common with those in the first zone. It should be noted, however, that this settlement belongs to the third quarter of the first century BC and its position in the valley, below the fortresses of Pommiers and Le Vieux Laon, makes one hesitate to include it with the classic *oppida*.

Several cases are known where an undefended village is succeeded by an *oppidum* on the same site, demonstrating a deliberate intention to create a new elevated and fortified settlement immediately alongside its predecessor. This phenomenon can be observed clearly at Levroux (Indre: Fig. 137.3). The village of Arènes was abandoned around 80–70 BC at the latest in favour of the hill of Tours, the last foothill of the Boischaut, which rises only 1500m (4921ft) from the earlier settlement. A *murus gallicus* encircled the 20ha (49 acres) of this low summit, and was quickly strengthened in places by a massive bank. The earliest traces of occupation here are masked, as is so often the case in the Paris Basin, by an extraordinarily rich Augustan level. Finally the Roman settlement, dating from the beginning of the Christian era, was established once again in the plain.

The same sequence can be observed at Hochstetten, which was abandoned in favour of the neighbouring hill on which Breisach sits (see Fig. 137.1). At Basle, too, the promontory crowned by the cathedral (the Münsterberg) is protected by a *murus gallicus* whilst the settlement on the site of the gasworks was abandoned in the 60s BC (see Fig. 137.2). The villages of Aulnat in Limagne were deserted in favour of several hillfort settlements, the *oppida* of Côtes de Clermont and the plateaux of Corent and Merdogne, one of which must be the historic site of Gergovia. There is therefore a distinctive trend for settlement to migrate towards higher ground, a phenomenon which is to be found in many other regions and periods. What is surprising about the *oppidum* phenomenon is that it corresponds with simultaneous development of craftsmanship and trade. The political imperatives must have been strong to be able to uproot the social groups involved in these activities from their natural milieu on the plains, at road junctions, and at ports.

Regional groups

Several regional groupings can be distinguished among the *oppida*, and so the homogeneous picture presented above needs modification. The group of sites in western Germany offers a very diverse array, due to the relatively large number of excavations that have been carried out. The northern part of the country was not affected by the *oppidum* phenomenon. Altburg-Niedenstein, near Kassel, marks the northernmost limit of the Celtic world. The Pipinsburg in the Harz produced Late La Tène material, but in view of its mere 10ha (25 acre) area and its modest rampart it is on the edge of the *oppidum* region. A homogeneous group of sites can be recognized in central Germany, between Kassel and Frankfurt-am-Main: some earlier fortified sites were reused in the Late La Tène period and adapted to meet the new criteria. These settlements were not clustered in the rich Wetterau plain but on the lower slopes of the Taunus range and the neighbouring hills. The Dünsberg, whose lofty silhouette can be seen from afar and which had already been fortified, was encircled by a rampart at the base of its slopes. The hillforts on the tops of the Goldgrube and the Altenhöfe, which probably date back to the Early La Tène period, were connected by means of a bank which crossed the valley separating them, to enclose 130ha (321 acres).

In the same way the Donnersberg, in the Palatinate, already occupied in the Late Hallstatt period, was surrounded with an enormous fortification, bringing its enclosed area to 240ha (593 acres). In this region,

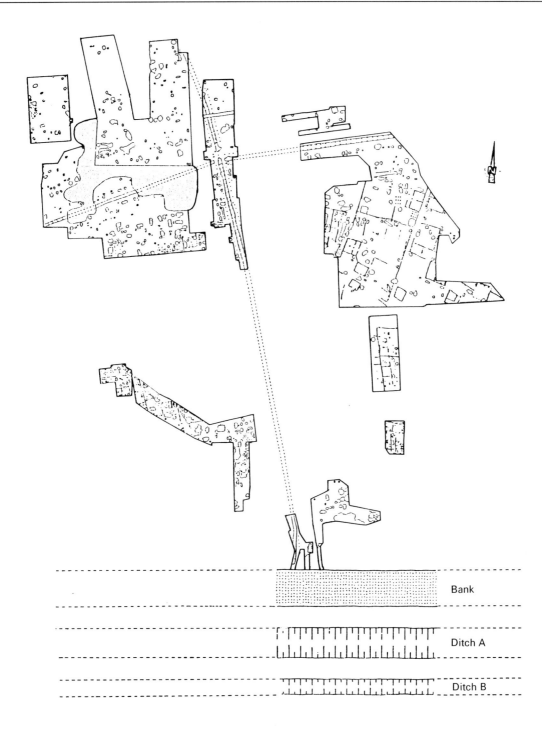

Bank

Ditch A

Ditch B

which remained somewhat marginal – it was not, for example, affected by the wine trade – the *oppidum* phenomenon manifested itelf by the occupation and enlargement of older fortifications.

The *oppida* of southern Germany were for the most

141
Undefended settlement of Villeneuve-Saint-Germain. On the east is the artisans' quarter and on the west the residential area, with its parallel streets and houses built within rectangular courtyards. (J. Debord and URA No 12.)

part entirely new foundations, and they enclosed vast areas: 316ha (781 acres) at Altenburg-Rheinau, 630ha (1557 acres) at Kelheim, 1500ha (3706 acres) at Heidengraben. They controlled the Rhine and Danube routes, and were situated either close to the rivers themselves, where natural possibilities for fortification allowed this, or further back, as at Zarten, on the edge of the Black Forest, which defended the passage between the Alsatian plain and the sources of the Danube. They were protected by the most highly developed defences of the period: nailed *muri gallici*, walls incorporating vertical timbers of the Preist or Kelheim type, or a combination of the two, with earthen ramp backing on to their inner faces. They contributed to the substantial trade with Gaul and the Mediterranean world: bronze coins, amphorae and painted pottery have been collected in large quantities at these settlements. It is obvious, despite Caesar's assertions to the contrary, that the Rhine was not a frontier for the *oppidum* civilization.

The Germans are to be found further north, whilst the Celts were involved in the same phenomenon of proto-urbanization in Bohemia. Since the time of Déchelette, commentators have related the finds from Stradonice with those from Mont Beuvray: it is true that the similarities are striking, suggesting continuous contacts between the peoples of two widely separated areas. The presence of amphorae and imported Italian bronze vessels at Stradonice demonstrates the importance of the Vltava trade route, closely controlled by the *oppida* of Třísov, Hrazany and Závist. The last-named recalls Heidetränk, since it, too, developed around a Hallstatt defended site, enclosing a valley within its large area of 170ha (420 acres). The other *oppida* seem to have been more recent foundations.

In Moravia the *oppida* were established a little back from the plains, but still controlling the trade routes of the Danube and its tributaries; further east, in Slovakia and Hungary, the settlements have slightly different characteristics. A fortified citadel or acropolis was associated with undefended areas in which craft activities seem to have been concentrated. This is Collis's Zemplin type.

What, finally, of Gaul, where we might anticipate a special concentration of data, in view of its position near Narbonensis and of Caesar's account?

The *oppidum* phenomenon spread over the whole land (Fig. 142), with variations in the already Romanized south or north of the Somme valley, which provides a link with the British Isles. It has already been shown that craft activities and the amphora trade developed in the second century associated with undefended settlements, before the creation of the *oppida*. Most regions took part in this economic expansion, either as a result of their agricultural wealth, like the Paris basin or the plains of the southwest, or because of their location on trade routes, such as Brittany or the Morvan.

The most interesting hypotheses stem from study of the size and or the spatial distribution of *oppida*. I. Ralston in particular has carried out work in this field, using several techniques borrowed from geography. It already appears that certain regions, such as Limousin, were organized around a large central *oppidum*, which ruled over many smaller enclosures. In more developed provinces such as Berry or the Aisne region, it is difficult to identify a central *oppidum* from ten or more medium-sized settlements, covering 20–30ha (49–74 acres), which may have controlled the equivalent of two or three contemporary cantons. In Gaul it is difficult to define a list of criteria necessary in order to differentiate *oppida* from other categories of hillforts. In some cases it is clear that certain trading villages did not follow the movement towards higher ground, although they received the same imported materials and produced the same artefacts as the *oppida*. In others, however, the major settlement of a canton some distance from the main axes of communication witnessed the enclosure of some hectares with a *murus gallicus* and imported amphaorae at great expense, but remained fundamentally agricultural.

Finally, the post-conquest period, which saw rapid Romanization of building techniques, is difficult to distinguish from its immediate predecessor. Although it is clear that the *oppida* were abandoned in the last quarter of the first century BC in favour of the Gallo-Roman *civitas* capitals, we know little of this process beyond certain individual cases.

Documentary evidence

The evidence of Caesar, the earliest detailed account of the peoples of temperate Europe, has to be taken into account when considering Gaul. This text must, however, be used with caution, since it was primarily a military report to the Senate, and at the same time a highly skilled piece of propaganda intended for the Roman public. To use *De Bello Gallico* to fix a site on the ground is a gamble, and to take an isolated sentence at its face value is to adopt the logic of the conqueror. Nevertheless a systematic analysis of the text reveals some interesting information.

The word *oppidum* is one of the nouns most used by Caesar in *The Gallic War*: it appears 133 times, whilst the most common noun, *hostis* (the enemy), occurs 286

142
Surface areas of
fortified settlements in
France. 1: Early La
Tène period; 2: Late La
Tène period. (O.
Büchsenschütz, 1984.)

times, underlining the military character of the text. Some twenty names of *oppida* are quoted, most of them in the eastern central region of Gaul. Caesar is specific that the Germans had no *oppida*, and he only uses the word once in connection with Britain, attributing the precise definition in this case to the local people: 'The Britons describe as an *oppidum* a forest that is difficult of access which they have surrounded with a bank and ditch and which they use as their normal place of refuge in the face of enemy invasions' (5,21). This has nothing to do with the *oppida* of Gaul, which he describes, exclusively in Book 7, as towns (*urbs*). As we have been able to show along with I. Ralston, this is a matter of exaggeration, which affects a number of the words Caesar uses in Book 7, the last he wrote after Alésia, in order to ensure that he was granted a triumph on his return to Rome. In the earlier books, in fact, the word *urbs* was reserved exclusively for Rome. If this exaggeration was possible in respect of Gaul, however, and if the conquest did not finally succeed until Caesar had gained control of these settlements, it was because the process of urbanization was widely under way.

Several scholars have correlated the word *castellum* with the smaller enclosures that co-existed with the *oppida*, but in fact Caesar's evidence on this score is limited. The only interesting reference (*De Bello Gallico*, 2,29) concerns the Atuatuci, a tribe from the Namur area, abandoning their *castella* and *oppida* to take refuge in a single *oppidum*, which had better natural defences.

Reference has already been made to the description of the settlements of the Helvetii (1,5), which according to Caesar included twelve *oppida*, around 400 villages (*vici*) and an indeterminate number of isolated farmsteads (*aedificia privata*). We believe that these figures, along with the triple classification, faithfully reflect what he observed. In this instance there is no reason for Caesar to have modified the truth, of which he was perfectly aware, having seized tablets indicating the number and origins of those who had attempted to emigrate in the enemy camp (1,29). *Vici* and *aedificia* are almost always used in a formula which appears seventeen times in the text and which, in its complete form, ran: 'They [or: we] burned the corn, the fodder, the isolated farms, the villages and the *oppida*'. The three types of habitat were therefore consistent for Caesar, a template which typified Gaul at the time of the conquest, distinguishing it from Germany and Britain. Caesar was (or pretended to be) unaware of what archaeology has shown us: the whole of southern Germany, Bohemia and parts of Moravia, southern Poland and Austria had reached the same

stage of development at this time.

When discussing the phenomenon of urbanization in the first century BC it is therefore necessary to bear in mind the written evidence. Several authors have taken up positions on the origin, the reality and meaning of this phenomenon, and Anglo-American scholars have proposed models derived from the social sciences to explain the underlying reasons. We will leave on one side the blandishments of P. Wells, who sees no fundamental difference between Late Hallstatt settlements and *oppida*: this is to disregard all the new factors which distinguish the latter. In many articles summarized in a work of synthesis, J.R. Collis has explored in great detail the different systems that can be put forward to explain the phenomenon of urbanization. The main functions of *oppida* were for him craft activities, mass-producing artefacts, trade and administration of the surrounding territory. He accepts that the creation of *oppida* constitutes a discontinuity in settlement evolution. For him it is the need for defence that was 'ultimately' the decisive factor in this transformation. He goes on to add, however, that this phenomenon should not be linked with historically attested wars or invasions. There is no direct relationship between these exceptional threats and the fortification of settlements, which should be related rather to endemic conflicts between neighbouring tribes.

In fact the problem is one of explaining why second-century BC villages, which had already adopted many innovations that had long been attributed by scholars to the *oppida*, should have been abruptly abandoned in favour of the latter. The choice of naturally defended sites and the construction of immense ramparts shows, of course, that concern to protect the wealth accumulated in settlements of this type was not lacking in the minds of the Gauls. However, we believe that we can distinguish in the characteristics of the *oppida* the signs of motivations that go beyond the need for defence. By going back to earlier hillforts or installing themselves in similar upland locations the Gauls resumed an older tradition. Timber-laced ramparts, albeit modified, were also in the direct building tradition of two thousand years of development. Extending them right round the settlements regardless of topographic necessity, however, and the immense areas enclosed indicate a wish to delineate an urban space, separated from the countryside. Historians have identified the intentions of Philippe-Auguste who, in building a wall round Paris, wanted the houses to be built right up to the ramparts, whereas his successors tried to enclose within successive ramparts the houses that continued to overflow them. The latter wanted to contain the population, for defensive reasons, whereas the former's objective was the encouragement of urbanization, by giving priority to the ascendancy of the town over the countryside.

Excavations have neither been extensive nor numerous enough to allow us to know the patterning of specialized areas within the *oppida*. The model proposed by Collis is, however, an acceptable hypothesis. The hierarchical organization of *oppida* within *civitates* is also difficult to understand. The external signs of *oppidum*-based civilization seem to have affected almost all the Celtic lands. In the less developed *civitates*, however, an immense central *oppidum* is found in association with many small defended settlements, often enclosed by a *murus gallicus* and rich in imported amphorae, but still belonging to an essentially farming environment. In the more developed regions it is difficult to distinguish a capital among a dozen or so medium-sized *oppida* which have produced on excavation traces of extensive craft activity and coin production. Whatever the regional differences may be, however, the whole of continental Celtic Europe was influenced by the phenomenon of urbanization. Even if the traditional power of the aristocracy was still rooted in the countryside, the vital forces of the *civitates* were concentrated in the *oppida*. J. Werner has emphasized the fact that the Roman conquest was limited to the region of *oppida*, whose inhabitants, after a legitimate reaction of resistance, quickly found common interests with their invaders. Northern Europe, which was wholly orientated towards farming, vigorously repulsed a civilization that was too different from its own. For its part, the Roman army could establish no hold over a population that was spread over such a vast territory.

The abandonment of *oppida* in Gaul in the closing decades of the first century BC is also a relatively abrupt phenomenon, but it is a complex one. The political will of the Roman administrators is not adequate to explain the foundation of new towns in lowland settings below *oppida*. The pressures of trade, the development of a way of life acquired from Italy and the gradual disappearance of conflicts between Gaulish *civitates* meant that the main reasons for the *oppida* coming into being disappeared. Only their traditional roles, for religious festivals and the fairs that accompanied them allowed them to continue to function in a reduced way. Productive forces and administration reoccupied their natural place, in the centre of the territory and at the crossing points of trade routes. The Roman conquest took place in three stages: first, commercial penetration, which coincided with the development of *oppida*; then military conquest, which took advantage of the concentration of the vital forces of the Celtic peoples in these settlements; and finally the adoption of a new way of life with the foundation of Gallo-Roman towns, which led to the desertion of the *oppida*. Hillforts, which had played a primary role throughout the Bronze and Iron Ages, were henceforth, like megalithic monuments, to become part of the domain of legend and religion.

Conclusion

A rapid survey of our contemporaries would undoubtedly show that the two thousand years of the Bronze and Iron Ages do not greatly clutter their memories. The nineteenth century resuscitated Vercingetorix, but proper history began with the Roman conquest. The absence in France of a university tradition of studying protohistory left the field open for fantasies of all kinds; even the most eminent historians, when dealing with allegedly 'obscure' periods, are not always capable of either critical comment or displaying their sources. It is nowadays possible, however, to define the place of the Bronze and Iron Age cultures in the history of Europe on the basis of available data. We shall endeavour to summarize the essential points.

The inheritance

The wide range of techniques developed during the Bronze and Iron Ages continued to be of great importance in rural life until relatively recently. If the towns and the ruling classes followed Mediterranean models to the point of pastiche, the countryside, in which until the nineteenth century the overwhelming majority of the population lived, retained a way of life inherited directly from the Celts. Thatched wooden houses, nowadays as rare as castles, did not begin to lose their predominance until the last century, when the *préfectures* insisted upon tile roofs for safety reasons. The village forge, which has been changed before our eyes into an engineering workshop, was born in the La Tène period and for two thousand years played a central role in the farming economy. Certainly the Middle Ages and recent times saw the introduction of many important improvements. We must render unto the protohistoric peoples, however,

those things which are not Caesar's: metalworking; the development of what finally became the plough; the crafts necessary for building carts and vehicles; crop rotation and soil improvement, which developed in a zone that stretches from the Balkans to Britain and from southern Italy to Scandinavia. Latin authors wrote treatises on farming, but it was the 'barbarians' who put them into practice and who exported corn, salted meat and iron implements to the Mediterranean.

Only archaeology can recreate this rural world where knowledge and traditions were dependent upon a purely oral culture. We can see the results of this intensive activity in the improvement of the standard of living in the countryside and, above all, in the growth of towns. Europe was characterized by the juxtaposition of small territorial units. They were independent in so far as they produced all their own food and the primary requirements of life. At the same time, however, they were engaged in all kinds of trade amongst themselves, exporting or importing clothing, salt, metals and other products, both everyday and luxury. We understand contemporary trade of this kind very well. We should, however, be correct in supposing that it began to develop thousands of years earlier, with flint from Grand-Pressigny and amber, and later trade in metals and salt.

The countryside developed more in the two thousand years that preceded the Christian era than in the following nineteen-hundred years. After the disappearance of the last hunter-gatherers and nomadic peoples, temperate Europe became above all else a land of farming, where intensively cultivated landscapes reduced the area of scrub and woodland, much earlier than is usually thought. For various reasons nucleated settlements emerged from this mosaic: places of refuge protected by landscape advantages or by marshes, markets, craft centres and finally centres of power. Caesar was struck by the hierarchy of settlements that characterized Gaul: isolated farms, villages, *oppida*. We now know that the roots of this organization lie far back in the Bronze Age, if not earlier. The functions of the medieval village, as defined by J. Chapelot and R. Fossier, are not very different from those that we have been able to observe, at least from the La Tène period. Despite the absence of the major stone buildings that have been indissolubly linked with towns, from Vitruvius to Peter the Great, *oppida* performed the same functions as latter-day metropolises. They can be differentiated from the cities of antiquity in one vital respect: they were not the obligatory centres of political organization. Whilst archaeology has revealed the success and the central role of *oppida* in the organization of territories, Latin texts hint at rivalry between the traditional centres of political control spread throughout the countryside and the inhabitants of the *oppida*, whose influence on society became increasingly important.

The weight of words

It should not be forgotten that the real differences between temperate European and Mediterranean cultures have been exaggerated by the nature of our sources and by the specialization of the historians who have studied them. In his last work, F. Braudel stressed the reluctance of historians to accord the status of towns to the Celtic *oppida*, before developing arguments that led him to come down in favour of this view. Other historians are, however, readier to concede a degree of equivalence; we know that most provincial capitals in Gaul are nothing more than *oppida* that came down from their hilltops and clad themselves in stone in Roman fashion. However, the traditional historian feels that he is out of his depth when dealing with civilizations without writing. Even though he may be interested in them, he does not dare to exercise the critical judgment that he habitually employs in his own special field, and Braudel, for example, used very uneven documentation in this area. This attitude allows these 'origins' to be presented as 'mysterious', idyllic or squalid according to the requirements of the occasion; such periods are not in fact described for their own value but only as introductions to what is to follow. Thus, in order to enhance the brilliance of Gallo-Roman civilization or the classic Middle Ages it is necessary to reduce earlier periods to the lowest possible level. When describing

the High Middle Ages, R. Fossier talks of 'ephemeral villages' or 'unstructured countryside'; he describes '. . . the huts, the even more exiguous sunken huts, hovels for weavers or slaves, all thrown together without any other foundations than beam slots . . . In addition, occupation was short-lived . . . because of soil exhaustion, which they were incapable of remedying . . .' As for R. Delort, he talks of the development of the adze and the axe in the eleventh century 'to combat the ever-invasive scrub and to clear undergrowth': these are tools that were already more than a thousand years old and woods that had been overexploited for centuries. People clearing woodland always believe that it is the primeval forest that they are attacking; thus it was the discovery of Roman ruins in woodland in the eighteenth century that contributed to the birth of the Sleeping Beauty story. These somewhat subjective reflections would be no more than an interesting aside, were it not for the fact that historical approaches of this kind repeatedly insist upon the precarious nature of this so-called 'primitive' way of life.

In addition to a vocabulary which may perhaps be unconsciously pessimistic, interpretations such as this are in direct opposition to the much more optimistic perspectives offered by prehistorians. In fact, with villages that migrated from time to time, semisubterranean craft workshops, a limited range of metal tools, and a pre-monetary economy, protohistoric peoples faced an environment very comparable with that of the first millennium AD, and with equivalent means at their disposal. Protohistorians speak of technological and economic progress, growth of production and trade, increased numbers of villages and population growth. In the British Isles it was even a question of clearance of the uplands in order to mitigate the shortage of lower-lying land, and the effects of deforestation and ecological imbalance. Is this simply a difference of viewpoint or, more realistically, a question of two thousand years of prosperity followed by nearly a thousand years of crisis? It is necessary to begin by emphasizing the differences in terminology, the semantic weight of which is by no means negligible. Whereas historians can allow themselves to speak of invasions, wars and changing alliances, protohistorians must confine themselves to population movements, to the widespread abandonment of villages and to the recognition of cultural discontinuities, normally expressed in terms that are as vague as they are cautious.

Much more important than the words themselves, however, the nature of the data collected by the two groups also result in different types of information.

The archaeological approach is based on long-term developments and general trends. Historical events are usually beyond the grasp of archaeologists. The historical approach, by contrast, first seeks out accounts of important events from ancient chroniclers: these are more often catastrophes, famines and wars than 'unrecorded' years of prosperity. Long-term trends only become apparent after detailed studies of records or account books which hardly exist even in the High Middle Ages.

A second distinction has to be made between the discourses of historians and of protohistorians, since it is a matter of knowing which kind of history is involved. The history of towns consists of extraordinary periods of rapid progress – fifth-century BC Athens or Augustan Rome, for example – separated by long periods of stagnation, or even recession. The history of the countryside, by contrast, progressed steadily, slowly digesting the most radical of disturbances. The whole of protohistory is essentially the history of the countryside, with a few outstanding exceptions, and in this above all it differs from conventional history. The absence of documentation about political events, people, or connections between individuals compels us to give prominence to the slow development of technology and standards of living. The nature of agriculture, trade and craftsmanship slowly emerge in the archaeological record and lead inevitably, as it were, to the circumstances of our own time. Anglo-American archaeologists of the 1960s rejected invasion and conquest scenarios, refusing to accept that there was any conflict or political event that interrupted this steady development: rural communities developed side-by-side, in an atmosphere of serenity, undisturbed by the quest for power.

This idyllic vision is no more satisfactory than the previous one. If protohistory gives the impression of development that was steady and positive overall, that is because the poor quality of our data only permits long-term evolution to be appreciated. It is for this reason that prehistorians such as K. Kristiansen, J. Bintliff and M. Rowlands have reintroduced economic and political crises into their models as necessary stages in the evolution of the Bronze and Iron Ages. It is now certain that there were crises, advances and recessions: climatic changes, which have long-term effects, played an important role in antiquity; destruction of the environment by man himself, followed by crises that were political in origin, influenced the history of Europe well before documents begin to make us aware of them. We are still unable to identify or explain these crises. We can only observe advances and recessions followed by fresh advances in the exploitation of a farming region or in the patterning of settlements. Demographic crises such as that which Europe underwent in the fourteenth century give us cause for thought. What would we know about this disaster if there were no written records?

The events which marked this long period, the epics and the defeats, the crises and the times of plenty, are only now beginning to become known. However, the evolution of Europe during protohistory should not simply be an introduction to history proper. The Gauls are not 'the latest geological stratum in France'. These two millennia, some aspects of which we have outlined, forged the distinctive appearance of the countryside of temperate Europe and laid the foundations for its wealth.

Bibliography

General Works

BECKER C. J., SCHMID P., JOACHIM H.-E., REICHMANN Ch., KOSSACK G., HVASS S. (1982), 'Ländliches Siedlungswesen in vor- und frühgeschichtlicher Zeit', *Offa*, 39, Neumünster.

BURGESS C. (1980), *The Age of Stonehenge*, Dent, London.

FURMÁNEK V. and HORST F. (1982), *Beiträge zum Bronzezeitlichen Burgenbau in Mitteleuropa*, Academies of Science of DDR and Slovakia, Berlin-Nitra.

JANKUHN H., SCHÜTZEICHEL R. and SCHWIND F. (1977) éd., *Das Dorf der Eisenzeit und des frühen Mittelalters*, Göttingen.

PÉTREQUIN P. (1984), *Gens de l'eau, gens de la terre*, Hachette, Paris.

Foreword

BLOCH M. (1929), *Les Caractères originaux de l'histoire rurale française*, Oslo-Paris.

CHAPELOT J. and FOSSIER R. (1980), *The Village and House in the Middle Ages*, trans. Henry Cleere, Batsford, London.

DION R. (1934), *Essai sur la formation du paysage rural français*, Paris.

DUBY G. and WALLON A. (1975), *Histoire de la France rurale, des origines à 1340*, vol. 1, Seuil, Paris.

FINLEY M. I. (1975), *The Ancient Economy*, Hogarth Press, London.

HUBERT H. (1932), *Les Celtes et l'Expansion celtique jusqu'à l'époque de La Tène*, L'évolution de l'humanité, 21, Albin Michel, Paris.

ROUPNEL G. (1932), *Histoire de la campagne française*, 1955, Club des libraires, Paris.

VITRUVIUS (1956), *De Architectura*, trans. F. Granger, Heinemann, London, 2 vol.

1 From primitive society to the birth of the European countryside

BITTEL K., KIMMIG W. and SCHIEK S. (1981), *Die Kelten in Baden-Württemberg*, Konrad Theiss Verlag, Stuttgart.

BRUN P. (1987), *Princes et princesses de la Celtique*, Les Hespérides, Paris.

BRUNAUX J.-L. (1986), *Les Gaulois, sanctuaires et rites*, Les Hespérides, Paris.

BUTLER J. (1969), *Nederland in de Bronstijd*, Van Dishoek, Bussum.

CHAMPION T., GAMBLE C., SHENNAN S., WHITTLE A. (1984), *Prehistoric Europe*, Academic Press, London.

COLES J. M. and HARDING A. F. (1979), *The Bronze Age in Europe*, Methuen, London.

COLLIS J. R. (1984), *Oppida, Earliest Towns North of the Alps*, University of Sheffield, Sheffield.

DRACK W. *et. al.* (1971), *Ur- und Frühgeschichtliche Archäologie der Schweiz*, vol. 3, *Die Bronzezeit*, Schweiz. Gesell. für Ur- und Frühges., Basle.
(1974), vol. 4, *Die Eisenzeit*.

DUVAL P.-M. (1971), *La Gaule jusqu'au milieu du Ve siècle*, Les sources de l'histoire de France, Picard, Paris, 2 vol.

DUVAL P.-M. (1977), *Les Celtes*, l'Univers des formes, Gallimard, Paris.

GAUCHER G. (1988), *Peuples du Bronze*, Hachette, Paris.

GIOT R., BRIARD J., PAPE L. (1979), *Protohistoire de la Bretagne*, Ouest-France, Rennes.

GLOB P. V. (1969, 1977), *The Bog People*, Faber and Faber, London.

GLOB P. V. (1983), *The Mound People*, Paladin, London.

GUILAINE J. (1980), *La France d'avant la France*, Hachette, Paris.

JENSEN J., MUNKSGAARD E., RAMSKOU T. (1978), *Prehistoric Denmark*, National Museum, Copenhagen.

JENSEN J. (1982), *The Prehistory of Denmark*, Methuen, London.

KRUTA V. (1976), *Les Celtes*, Que sais-je?, P.U.F., Paris.

LIVY, *Histories*

MEGAW J. V. S. et SIMPSON D. D. A. (1979), *Introduction to British Prehistory*, Leicester University Press, Leicester.

PEYRE C. (1979), Butser *La Cisalpine gauloise du IIIe au Ier siècle avant J.-C.*, Presses de l'École Normale Supérieure, Paris.

REYNOLDS P. J. (1979), Butser *Iron Age Farm*, British Museum Publications, London.

SZABÓ M. (1971), *Sur les traces des Celtes en Hongrie*, Corvina, Budapest.

2 The history of protohistoric studies

BERSU G. et GOESSLER P. (1924), 'Der Lochenstein bei Balingen', *Fundberichte aus Schwaben*, Neue Folge 2, 73–103.

BERSU G. (1930), 'Der Goldberg bei Nördlingen und die moderne Siedlungsarchäologie', *Deutsches archäologisches Institut, Ber. über die 100. Jahr. Feier*, 313–18.

BERSU G. (1930), 'Vorgeschichtliche Siedlungen auf dem Goldberg', *Neue deutsche Ausgrabungen*, 130–43.

BERSU G. (1934), 'Zur Frage der Hüttenbewurfes', *Germania*, 18, 134–5.

BERSU G. (1940), 'Excavations at Little Woodbury (Wiltshire), the settlement revealed by excavation', *Proceedings of the Prehistoric Society*, 6, 30–111.

BERSU G. (1945), *Das Wittnauer Horn*, Monographie zur Ur und Frühgeschichte der Schweitz, 4, Basle.

BERSU G. (1977), *Three Iron Age Round Houses of the Isle of Man*, Douglas, Isle of Man.

BUCHSENSCHUTZ O. (1984), '150 ans de recherches sur les fortifications en terre en Europe tempérée', *Les Celtes en Belgique et dans le Nord de la France, Revue du Nord*, special number, 217–75.

BULLEID A. and GRAY H. St. G. (1911, 1917) *The Glastonbury Lake Village*, 2 vol., Glastonbury.

BULLEID A. and GRAY H. St. G. (1948, 1953), *Meare Lake Village*, 2 vol., Glastonbury.

BULLIOT J.-G. (1899), *Fouilles du Mont Beuvray*, Autun, 2 vol.

DÉCHELETTE J. (1914), *Manuel d'archéologie préhistorique, celtique et gallo-romaine*, tome 4, Le Second Âge du fer, Paris.

GIFFEN A. VAN (1936), 'Der Warf in Ezinge, Prov. Gröningen, und seine westgermanischen Häuser', *Germania*, 20, 100–47.

KIEKEBUSCH A. (1923), *Die Ausgrabung des bronzezeitlichen Dorfes Buch bei Berlin*, D. Reimer, Berlin.

NAPOLÉON III (1865–1866), *L'Histoire de Jules César*, Paris.

TRIER B. (1969), *Das Haus im Nordwesten der Germania Libera*, Münster, 2 vol., 28 pl.

SPECK J. (1981), 'Schloss und Schlüssel zur späten Pfahlbauzeit', *Helvetia Archaeologica*, 12, 45/48, p. 230–41.

ZIPPELIUS A. (1948), *Der Hausbau der Hallstatt- und Latènezeit im Südlichen Mitteleuropa*, typed thesis, Göttingen.

3 Methods of research

BERTIN J. (1967), *Sémiologie graphique*, Gauthier-Villard, Paris.

CUNLIFFE B. (1983), *Danebury, Anatomy of an Iron Age Hill Fort*, Batsford, London.

CASTAGNÉ E. (1868), *Mémoire sur la découverte d'un oppidum avec murailles et emplacements d'habitations gauloises à Murcens, commune de Cras*, Cahors.

GASSMANN P. (1984), 'Dendrochronologie: 100 000 cernes sur Cortaillod-Est', *Archäologie der Schweiz*, 7, 2, 63–8.

HAMPL F. (1970), *Das Museum für Urgeschichte des Landes Niederösterreich mit urgeschichtlichem Freilichtmuseum in Asparn-an-der-Zaya*, Vienna.

HANSEN H. (1977), *The Prehistoric Village at Lejre*, Historical Archaeological Research Center, Lejre.

HARDING D. W. (1976) ed., *Hillforts: Later Prehistoric Earthworks in Britain and Ireland*, Academic Press, London.

KOSSACK G., BEHRE K.-E., SCHMID P. (1984), *Archäologische und Naturwissenschaftliche Untersuchungen an Siedlungen im deutschen Küstengebiet*, Acta Humanoria, DFG, Bonn, 2 vol.

KOSTRZEWSKI J. (1950), *Compte rendu des fouilles de Biskupin en 1938–39 et 1946–48*, Poznan.

MOBERG C.-A. (1981), *Similar finds? similar interpretations?*, Göteborg.

PÉTREQUIN P. et al. (1986), *Les Sites littoraux de Clairvaux, Problématique générale, l'example de la station III*, Maison des sciences de l'Homme, Paris.

RUOFF U. (1981), 'Die Ufersiedlungen an Zürich- und Greifensee', *Helvetia Archaeologica*, 12, 45/48, 19–61.

SCHWARZ K. (1959), *Atlas der spätkeltischen Viereckschanzen Bayerns*, Munich.

4 Raw materials and building techniques

ARCELIN P., BÜCHSENSCHÜTZ O. (1985), 'Les données de la protohistoire', in *Architectures de terre et de bois*, Actes du colloque de Lyon 1983, Documents d'Archéologie Française, 15–28.

ARNOLD B. (1982), 'The architectural woodwork of the late Bronze Age Village Auvernier-Nord', Greenwich Symposium 1980, *Woodworking techniques before AD 1500*, British Archaeological Reports, 129, Oxford, 111–28.

ARNOLD B. (1983), 'Les 24 maisons d'Auvernier (Bronze final)', *Jahrbuch der Schweizerischen Gesellschaft für Ur- und Frühgeschichte*, 66, 87–104.

ARNOLD B. (1984), 'A propos de Cortaillod-Est (Bronze final): le pilotis, une source d'information trop souvent méconnue', *Archäologie der Schweiz*, 7, 2, 54–62.

ARNOLD B. (1986), *Cortaillod-Est, un village du Bronze final. 1. Fouilles subaquatiques et photographie aérienne*, Éd. du Ruau, Saint-Blaise (Archéologie neuchâteloise, 1).

BLANCHET J.-C. (1984), *Les Premiers Métallurgistes en Picardie et dans le Nord de la France*, Paris, Mémoires de la Société préhistorique française, 17.

BOCQUET A. et coll. (1982), 'Charavines, un village au bord d'un lac il y a 5000 ans', *Histoire et archéologie, Les dossiers*, no. 64, June 1982.

BREN J. (1966), *Třísov, oppidum celtique en Bohéme*, Prague.

CRUDEN S. (1951), *The Brochs of Mousa and Clickhimin, Shetland*, HMSO, Edinburgh.

GUILLAUMET J.-P. (1982), 'Le matériel du tumulus de Celles (Cantal)', *Le Deuxième Âge du fer en Auvergne et en Forez*, Saint-Etienne, 189–213.

JACOBI G. (1968), *Werkzeug und Geräte aus dem Keltischen oppidum von Manching*, Die Ausgrabungen in Manching, 5, Wiesbaden.

PY M. (1978), *L'oppidum des Castels à Nages (Gard)*, 35e suppl. à *Gallia*, CNRS, Paris.

REYNOLDS P.J. (1979), op. cit.

REINERTH H. (1928), 'Die Wasserburg Buchau', *Führer zur Urgeschichte* No. 6, Augsburg.

RIETH A. (1969), *Führer durch das Federseemuseum*, Bad Buchau.

ROUDIL J.-L. (1981), *Cambous, village préhistorique, Viol-en-Laval*, Soc. languedocienne de Préhistoire, Montpellier.

RUOFF U. (1984), 'Zug "Im Sumpf" und Greifensee- "Böschen": zwei Siedlungen mit Blockbaukonstruktionen', *Helvetia Archaeologica*, 57/60, 76–82.

SCHWEINGRUBER H. (1975), 'Das Holz als Rohstoff in der Urgeschichte', *Helvetia Archaeologica*, 6–21, 2–15.

WINIGER J. (1981), 'Ein Beitrag zur Geschichte des Beils', *Helvetia Archaeologica*, 12, 45/48, 161–88.

ZIPPELIUS A. (1954), 'Vormittelalterliche Zimmerungstechnik im Mitteleuropa', *Rheinisches Jahrbuch für Volkskunde*, 5, 7–32.

5 House architecture

BALAAM N. D., SMITH K. and WAINWRIGHT G. J. (1982), The Shaugh Moor Project: Fourth report – Environment, Context and Conclusion, *Procs. of the Prehist. Society*, 48, 203–78.

BANNER J., BÓNA I. and MÁRTON L. (1957), 'Die Ausgrabungen von L. Márton in Tószeg', *Acta Archaeologica*, 10, 1–140.

BANNER J. et BONA I. (1974), *Mittelbronzezeitliche Tell-Siedlung bei Békés*, Akad. Kiadó, Budapest.

BECKER C. J. (1982) 'Siedlungen der Bronzezeit und der vorrömischen Eisenzeit in Dänemark', *Offa*, 39, 53–71.

BLANCHET J.-C., BÜCHSENSCHÜTZ O., MENIEL P. (1983), 'La maison de La Tène moyenne de Verberie (Oise)', *Revue archéologique de Picardie*, actes du colloque 'Les Celtes dans le Nord du Bassin parisien', 96–126.

BONNET C. (1973), 'Une station d'altitude de l'époque des Champs d'Urnes au sommet du Hohlandsberg', *Bulletin de la Société préhistorique française*, 70, Études et Travaux, 455–78.

BOUREUX M., ROWLETT R. M. and E. S. J. (1969), 'A rectangular Early La Tène Marnian house at Chassemy (Aisne)', *World Archaeology*, 1,1, 106–35.

BRIARD J. and NICOLARDOT J.-P. (1985), 'Un habitat de hauteur côtier de l'âge du bronze en Bretagne, la grosse Roche à Saint-Jacut-de-la-mer', D. SPRATT and C. BURGESS eds. *Upland Settlement in Britain, the second Millennium BC and After*, British Archaeological Reports 143, Oxford, 365–75.

FREI B. (1958/59), 'Die Ausgrabung auf der Mottata bei Ramosch', *Jahrbuch der schweizerischen Gesellschaft für Ur- und Frühgeschichte*, 47, 34–43.

GUILBERT G. (1981), 'Double-ring Roundhouses, Probable and Possible, in Prehistoric Britain', *Procs. of the Prehist. Society*, 47, 299–317.

HAARNAGEL W. (1969), 'Die Ergebnisse der Grabung auf der ältereisenzeitlichen Siedlung Boomborg/Hatzum, Kr. Leer, in den Jahren 1965 bis 1967', *Neue Ausgrabungen und Forschungen in Niedersachsen*, 4, 58–97.

HAMILTON J. (1953), *Jarslshof*, Official Guide, Edinburgh.

HARSEMA D. (1982), 'Structural Reconstruction of Iron Age Houses in the northern Netherlands', DRURY P. ed., *Structural Reconstruction*, British Archaeological Reports, 110, Oxford, 199–221.

HERRMANN F. R. (1975), 'Hausgrundrisse aus einer Urnenfelderzeitlichen Siedlung von Künzing (Niederbayern)', *Ausgrabungen in Deutschland*, 1, 155–70.

HULST R. S. (1973), 'A contribution to the study of Bronze Age and Iron Age House-Plans: Zijderveld', *Berichten van de Rijksdienst voor het Oudheidkundig Bodemonderzoek*, 23, 103–7.

MOOSLEITNER F. and PENINGER E. (1965), 'Ein keltischer Blockwandbau vom Dürrnberg bei Hallein', *Mitteilungen der Gesellschaft für Salzburger Landeskunde*, 105, 47–88.

MUSSON C. (1970), 'House-Plans and Prehistory', *Current Archaeology*, 21 July, 267–73.

PAUTREAU J.-P. (1984), 'Éléments pour la datation du grand bâtiment d'Antran', *Bulletin de la Société Préhistorique Française*, C.R.S.M., 2, 81, 40–2.

PÉTREQUIN P. *et al.* (1978), *Le Gisement néolithique et protohistorique de Besançon-Saint-Paul*, Archéologie 30, Les Belles Lettres, Paris.

PÉTREQUIN P. and MAGNY M. (1979), 'Les fondations en milieu lacustre: aspects techniques et culturels au néolithique et à l'âge du bronze', *Dialogues d'histoire ancienne*, 5, 7–15.

PÉTREQUIN P. (1983), 'Sablières basses et semelles de pieux dans l'architecture lacustre: l'exemple de Clairvaux-les-Lacs (Jura)', *Bulletin de la Société préhistorique française*, 80, 10–12, 361–74.

PÉTREQUIN P. (1983). 'Etat actuel des connaissances sur le problème archéologique', *L'Habitat lacustre préhistorique*, Actes du colloque de Genève 1982, Archives des sciences, 36, 2, 215–32.

PÉTREQUIN P. (1984), *Gens de l'eau, gens de la terre*, Hachette, Paris.

RUOFF U. (1984), op. cit.

TRIER B. (1969), op. cit.

SCHINDLER R. (1969), 'Die Aleburg von Befort in Luxemburg', *Hemecht*, 21, 37–50.

SCHINDLER R. (1977), *Die Altburg von Bundenbach, eine befestigte Höhensiedlung des 2/1. Jahrhunderts v. Chr. im Hunsrück*, Trierer Grabungen und Forschungen 10, Mainz.

STRABO (1966), *Geography*, vol. II, book 3 (Spain) and book 4 (Gaul), trans. H. L. Jones, Heinemann, London.

ZIPPELIUS A. (1953), 'Das vormittelalterliche dreischiffige Hallenhaus im Mitteleuropa', *Bonner Jahrbücher*, 153, 13–45.

ZIPPELIUS A. (1955), 'Frühformen mitteleuropäischer Hofanlagen', *Rheinisches Jahrbuch für Volkskunde*, 6, 1–49.

ZIPPELIUS A. (1975), 'Zur Rekonstruktion der Urnenfelderzeitlichen Holzbauten von Künzing', *Ausgrabungen in Deutschland*, Mayence, 164–8.

ZÜRCHER A. (1972), 'Funde der Bronzezeit von St. Moritz', *Helvetia Archaeologica*, 9, 3, p. 21–28.

6 Fortifications

BERSU G. (1946), 'A Hill-fort in Switzerland', *Antiquity*, 20, 4–8.

BÜCHSENSCHÜTZ O. (1981) ed., *Les Structures d'habitat à l'âge du fer en Europe tempérée, l'évolution de l'habitat en Berry*, Colloque de Levroux, 1978, Maison des sciences de l'Homme, Paris.

BÜCHSENSCHÜTZ O. (1984), *Structures d'habitats et fortifications de l'âge due Fer en France septentrionale (Mémoires de la Société préhistorique française*, tome 18), Paris.

COLLIS J. R. (1975), *Defended Sites of the Late La Tène in Central and Western Europe*, British Archaeological Reports, Suppl. Series 2, Oxford.

COLLIS J. R. (1984), op. cit.

COURTIN J. (1975), Un habitat fortifié du Bronze ancien en basse-Provence: le camp de Laure, commune du Rove, Bouches-du-Rhône', *Bulletin du Museum d'histoire naturelle de Marseille*, 35, 217–40.

FORDE-JOHNSTON J. L. (1976), *Hill-forts of the Iron Age in England and Wales*, Liverpool.

HAMILTON J. (1968), *Excavations at Clickhimin, Shetland*, Ministry of Public Buildings and Works, Edinburgh.

HERRMANN J. and OTTO K. H. (1969), *Siedlung, Burg und Stadt*, Deutsche Akademie der Wissenschaft zu Berlin, Schriften der Sektion für Ur- und Frühgeschichte, 25, Berlin.

HILL D. and JESSON M. ed. (1971), *The Iron Age and its Hill-forts, Essays presented to Sir Mortimer Wheeler*, Southampton.

HOGG A. H. A. (1975), *Hill-forts of Britain*, London.

NICOLARDOT J.-P. (1974) 'Structures d'habitats de hauteur à caractères défensifs dans le Centre-Est de la France', *Antiquités Nationales*, 6, 32–45.

PAUTREAU J.-P. (1978), 'L'habitat protohistorique du coteau de Montigné à Coulon (Deux-Sèvres), travaux 1978', *Bulletin de la Société historique et scientifique des Deux-Sèvres*, 2ᵉ série, 11, 2–3, 191–226.

PY M. (1978), op. cit.

TOČIK A. (1978 et 1981), *Nitriansky Hrádok-Zámeček*, Materiala Archaeologica Slovaca, Nitra, 3 vol.

WHEELER R. E. M. (1943), *Maiden Castle, Dorset*, Reports of the Research Committee of the Society of Antiquaries of London, 12, Oxford.

WHEELER R. E. M. and RICHARDSON K. (1957), *Hill-forts of Northern France*, Society of Antiquaries of London, Report 19, London.

Various authors (1969–1987), *Die Ausgrabungen in Manching*, 10 volumes pub., F. Steiner, Wiesbaden.

7 Houses and daily life: the organization of settlements

BANNER J. (1957), op. cit.

CLARKE D. L. (1972), 'A provisional model of an Iron Age society and its settlement system', in D. L. CLARKE ed., *Models in Archaeology*, London, 801–69.

DRAIBY B. (1984), 'Fragtrup, en boplads fra yngre bronzealder i Vesthimmerland', *Aarbøger for Nordisk Old Kyndighed og Historie*, 127–216.

DREWETT P. (1982), 'Later Bronze Age Downland Economy and Excavations at Black Patch, East Sussex', *Procs. of the Prehist. Society*, 48, 321–400.

HAARNAGEL W. (1979), *Die Grabung Feddersen Wierde, Methode, Hausbau, Siedlungs- und Wirtschaftsformen sowie Sozialstruktur*, 2 vol., 221 pl., Franz Steiner, Wiesbaden.

HAMILTON J. (1956), *Excavations at Jarlshof, Shetland*, Ancient Monuments and Historic Buildings, Edinburgh.

KALICZ N. (1968), Die Frühbronzezeit in Nordostungarn, Akad. Kiadó. (Archaeologia Hungarica, 45).

KOVÁCS T. (1977), *L'Age du bronze en Hongrie*, Corvina, Budapest.

RAGETH J. (1979), 'Die bronzezeitliche Siedlung auf dem Padnal bei Savognin, Oberhalbstein, GR, Grabung 1975', *Jahrbuch der schweizerischen Gesellschaft für Ur- und Frühgeschichte*, 62, 30–76.

(1985), 'Grabungen 1981–82', ibid, 68, 65–122.

(1986), 'Die wichtigsten Resultate der Ausgrabungen in der bronzezeitlichen Siedlung auf dem Padnal bei Savognin (Oberhalbstein, GR)', ibid, 69, 63–103.

ŘÍHOVSKÝ J. (1982), 'Das Wirtschafts-und Gesellschaftsleben den Velaticer Siedlung in Lovčičky', *Památky archeologické*, 73, 5–56.

STJERNQUIST B. (1967), 'Das Problem der Grubenhäuser in Südschweden', *Jahrbuch der römisch-germanischen Kommission zu Mainz*, 14, 144–52.

8 Activity areas and social spaces

FOX A. (1973), *South West England*, David and Charles, Newton Abbot.

HORST F. (1985), *Zedau*, Akademie Verlag, Berlin (Schriften zur Ur- und Frühgeschichte no. 36).

IJZEREEF G. F. (1981), 'Bronze Age Animal Bones from Bovenkarspel, the Excavation at Het Valkje', *Berichten van de Rijksdienst voor het Oudheidkundig Bodemonderzoek*, 31, 1–228.

JAANUSSON H. (1981), *Hallunda, a Study of pottery from a late Bronze Age Settlement in Central Sweden*, Statens Historiska Museum, Stockholm.

JANKUHN H. (1970), *Vorgeschichtliche Heiligtümer und Opferplätze im Mittel- und Nordeuropa, Symposium in Reinhausen bei Göttingen* 1968, Göttingen.

LAGRAND C. and THALMANN J.-P. (1973), *Les Habitats protohistoriques du Pègue (Drôme)*, Centre de documentation de la préhistoire alpine, Grenoble.

LAMBOT B. (1988), *Acy-Romance, les sanctuaires du Bronze final et du Premier Âge du Fer en France septentrionale*, Mémoire de diplôme de l'EHESS sous la direction de J. Guilaine, Toulouse.

MÜLLER A. von (1964), *Die Jungbronzezeitliche Siedlung von Berlin-Lichterfelde*, B. Hessling Verlag, Berlin (Berliner Beiträge zur Vor- und Frühgeschichte, no. 9).

O'KELLY M. (1954), 'Excavations and experiments in ancient Irish cooking places', *Journal of the Royal Society of Antiquaries of Ireland*, 84, 105–55.

PAUTREAU J.-P. and MATARO I PLADELASALA M. (1988). 'Temples et/ou cimetières: les enclos', in *Avant les Celtes. L'Europe à l'Age du Bronze, 2500–800 avant J.-C.*, catalogue of an exhibition held at the Abbey of Daoulas, Daoulas, 112–13.

PÉTREQUIN P. (1985), 'Les habitats néolithiques et l'expansion agricole dans la Combe d'Ain', *Néolithique Chalains-Clairvaux, Fouilles anciennes*, Presentation of the collections of Musée de Lons-le-Saunier, 1, 23–39.

RENFREW C. (1985), *The Prehistory of the Orkneys*, Edinburgh University Press.

ROUDIL J.-L. (1972), *L'Age du Bronze en Languedoc oriental*, Klincksieck, Paris.

RAGETH J. (1980), 'Die bronzezeitliche Siedlung auf dem Padnal bei Savognin (Oberhalbstein), Die Grabungskampagne 1976', *Jahrbuch der schweizerischen Gesellschaft für Ur- und Frühgeschichte*, 63, 21–75.

RYCHNER V. (1984), 'La matière première des bronziers lacustres', *Archäologie des Schweiz*, 7, 2, 73–78.

SIGAUT F. (1985), *L'Evolution technique des agricultures européennes avant l'époque industrielle*, E.H.S.S., Centre de recherches historiques, type written.

WATERBOLK H. T. and VAN ZEIST W. (1961), 'A Bronze Age sanctuary in the raised bog at Bargeroosterveld (Dr.)', *Helinium*, 1, 1, 5–19.

WATERBOLK H. T. (1975), 'Evidence of cattle stalling in excavated pre- and protohistoric houses', in A. T. CLASON ed., *Archaeozoological studies*, conference at Groningen (1974), Elsevier, Amsterdam, 386–94.

WHIMSTER R. (1981) *Burial Practices in Iron Age Britain*, 2 vol. British Archaeological Reports no. 90, Oxford.

9 Settlements in the landscape

BALKVILL C. J., CLAYTON N., BENSON D. and MILES D. (1974), *The Upper Thames Valley, an Archaeological Survey of the Rives Gravels*, Oxfordshire Archaeological Unit, no. 2.

BOWEN H. and FOWLER P. eds. (1978), *Early Land Allotment in the British Isles*, British Archaeological Reports, 48, Oxford.

BRADLEY R. (1978), *The Prehistoric Settlement of Britain*, Routledge and Kegan Paul, London.

BRONGERS J. A. (1976), *Air Photography and Celtic Field Research in the Nederland*, Rijksdienst voor het Oudheidkundig Bodemonderzoek, Nederlandse Oudheden 6.

BURGESS C. and MIKET R. (1976), *Settlement and Economy in the Third and Second Millennia BC*, British Archaeological Reports, 33, Oxford.

BURGESS C. (1985), 'Population, climate and Upland Settlement', in D. SPRATT and C. BURGESS eds. *Upland Settlement in Britain, the second millennium BC and after*, British Archaeological Reports, 143, Oxford, 195–230.

FLEMING A. (1978), 'The Prehistoric Landscape of Dartmoor: part 1, South Dartmoor', *Procs. of the Prehist. Society*, 44, 97–123.

(1983), part 2, North and East Dartmoor, *ibidem*, 49, p. 195–241.

FOWLER P. (1983), *The Farming of Prehistoric Britain*,

Cambridge University Press, Cambridge.

HULST R. S. (1973), 'Reflections on Dutch Prehistoric Settlements', *Berichten van de Rijksdienst voor het Oudheidkundig Bodemonderzoek*, 23, 65–76.

JANKUHN H. (1969), 'Vor- und Frühgeschichte von Neolitikum bis zur Völkerwan-derungzeit', in *Deutsche Agrargeschichte*, vol. 1, Stuttgart.

10 Settlement and society

BINTLIFF J. ed. (1984), *European Social Evolution: Archaeological Perspectives*, Bradford.

BRADLEY R. (1984), *The social foundations of prehistoric Britain*, Longman, London and New York (Longman Archaeological Series).

CUNLIFFE B. and ROWLEY T. (1978), *Lowland Iron Age Communities in Europe*, British Archaeological Reports, 48, Oxford.

FOWLER P. (1983), op. cit.

FRANKENSTEIN S. and ROWLANDS M. (1978), 'The internal structure and regional context of Early Iron Age society in south-western Germany', *Bulletin of the Institute of Archaeology*, University of London, 15, 73–112.

FURMÁNEK V. and HORST F. (1982), *Beiträge zum bronzezeitliche Burgenbau in Mitteleuropa*, Academies of Sciences of DDR and of Slovakia, Berlin-Nitra.

KHRISTIANSEN K. (1982), 'Information of tribal system in later European prehistory: Northern Europe, 4000–500 BC', *Theory and Explanation in Archaeology, Southampton Conference*, ed. RENFREW C., ROWLANDS M.; ABBOTT P., SEGRAVES, Academic Press, London, 241–79.

PÉTREQUIN P. (1985), *La grotte des Planches-près-Arbois (Jura)*, Maison des sciences de l'Homme, Paris.

STEUER H. (1982), *Frühgeschichtliche Sozialstrukturen in Mitteleuropa*, Göttingen.

WATERBOLK H. T. (1964), 'The Bronze Age settlement of Elp', *Helinium*, 4, 97–131.

11 and 12 Development of settlement in the Bronze and Iron Ages

AVERY M., SUTTON J. E. and BANKS J. W. (1967), 'Rainsborough, Northants, England, excavations: 1961–1965', *Procs. of the Prehist. Society*, 33, 207–306.

BARRET J. and BRADLEY R. ed. (1980), *The British Later Bronze Age*, British Archaeological Reports 83, Oxford, 2 vol.

BECKER H., CHRISTLEIN R., WELLS P. (1979), 'Die hallstattzeitliche Siedlung von Landshut-Hascherkeller', *Archäologisches Korrespondanzblatt*, 9, 3, 288–302.

BÖHM W. (1937), *Die Vorgeschichte des Kreises Westprignitz*, Leipzig, Curt Rabiksch Verlag.

BRAASCH O. and CHRISTLEIN R. (1982), *Das unterirdische Bayern*, Stuttgart.

BRADLEY R. and ELLISON A. (1975), *Rams Hill*, British Archaeological Reports 19, Oxford.

COBLENZ W. and HORST F. (1981), *Mitteleuropäische Bronzezeit*, Berlin 1978, Akademie Verlag.

COOMBS D. G. and THOMPSON F. H. (1979), 'Excavation of the Hill Fort of Mam Tor, Derbyshire 1965–1969', *Derbyshire Archaeological Journal*, 99, 7–51.

CUNLIFFE B. (1991), *Iron Age Communities in Britain*, 3rd ed. Routledge, London.

DRACK W. (1968 to 1974), *Archäologie der Schweiz*, Verlag der schweizerischen Gesellschaft für Ur- und Frühgeschichte, Basle, 4 vol.

EBERSCHWEILER B., RIETHMANN P., RUOFF U. (1987), 'Greifensee-Böschen ZH: ein spätbronzezeitliches Dorf, ein Vorbericht', *Jahrbuch der schweizerischen Gesellschaft für Ur- und Frühgeschichte*, 70, 77–100.

FILIP J. (1966), *Investigations archéologiques en Tchécoslovaquie*, Academia, Prague.

FILIP J. (1971), Symposium 'Keltische oppida in Mitteleuropa und im Karpatenbecken', Prague-Liblice, 1970, *Archeologické rozhledy*, 23, 3, 4, 5.

FURMÁNEK V. et HORST F. (1982), op. cit.

GUILBERT G. (1975), 'Planned Hillfort Interiors', *Procs. of the Prehist. Society*, 41, 203–21.

HÄRKE H. G. H. (1979), *Settlement Types and Patterns in the West Hallstatt Province*, British Archaeological Reports, International Series, 57 Oxford.

HNÍZDOVÁ I. et PLEINEROVÁ I. (1953), 'Hameaux et cabanes du peuple uneticien en Bohême', *Archeologické rozhledy*, 5, 380–92.

HULST R. S. (1973), 'A contribution to the study of Bronze Age and Iron Age House-plans, Zijderveld', *Berichten van de Rijksdienst voor het Oudheidkundig Bodemonderzoek*, 23, 103–7.

KIMMIG W. (1981), 'Buchau', *Reallexikon der Germanischen Altertumskunde*, 4, 1–2, 37–44.

KIMMIG W. (1983), *Die Heuneburg an der oberen Donau*, Führer zu archäologischen Denkmälern in Baden-Württemberg, 1, Konrad Theiss, Stuttgart.

JENSEN J. (1982), *The Prehistory of Denmark*, Methuen, London.

KEEFER E. (1984), 'Die Bronzezeitliche "Siedlung Forschaner" bei Bad Buchau, Kr. Biberach, 1. Vorbericht', *Berichte zu Ufer- und Moorsiedlungen Südwest-deutschland*, 1, 37–52.

MEDUNA J. (1970), 'Das Keltische oppidum Staré Hradisko in Mähren', *Germania*, 48, 34–59.

MOHEN J.-P. and BAILLOUD G. (1987), *La Vie quotidienne, les fouilles du Fort-Harrouard*, L'Age du Bronze en France, 4, Picard, Paris.

MÜLLER-WILLE M. (1977), 'Bäuerliche Siedlungen der Bronze- und Eisenzeit in den Nordseegebieten', in JANKUHN H., SCHÜTZEICHEL R. et SCHWIND F. eds. *Das Dorf der Eisenzeit und des frühen Mittelalters*, Göttingen, 153–218.

NEEDHAM S. P. (1985), 'Neolithic and Bronze Age settlement on the buried floodplains of Runnymede', *Oxford Journal of Archaeology*, 4.2, 125–37.

PATZOLD J. (1963), 'Ein späthallstattzeitlicher Herrensitz im Alpenvorland bei Müchen', *Germania*, 41, p. 101–3.

PAUTREAU J.-P. (1987), 'Les habitats poitevins à la fin de l'âge du Bronze atlantique', in *Les Relations entre le Continent et les îles Britanniques à l'Age du Bronze, Actes du Colloque de Lille, 2–7 septembre 1984*, Revue archéologique de Picardie-Société préhistorique française, Amiens, 239–53.

PÉTREQUIN P., URLACHER J.-P. and VUAILLAT D. (1969), 'Habitat et sépultures de l'Age du Bronze final à Dampierre-sur-le-Doubs', *Gallia Préhistoire*, XII, 1, 1–36.

PRYOR F., FRENCH C., TAYLOR M. (1986) 'Flag Fen, Peterborough I: Discovery, Reconnaissance and Initial Excavation (1982–85)', *Procs. of the Prehist. Society*, 52, 1–24.

RAGETH J. (1978), 'Die bronzezeitliche Siedlung auf dem Padnal bei Savognin', *Jahrbuch der schweizerischen Gesellschaft für Ur- und Frühgeschichte*, 61, 7–64.

RAGETH J. (1986), op. cit.

RÍHOVSKÝ J. (1982), 'Das Wirtschafts- und Gesellschaftsleben der Velaticer Siedlung in Lovčičky', *Památky archeologické*, 73, 5–56.

RUOFF U. (1981), 'Altersbestimmung mit Hilfe der Dendrochronologie', *Helvetia Archaeologica*, 12, 45/48, 89–97.

SCHINDLER R. (1977), *Die Altburg von Bundenbach*, Trierer Grabungen und Forschungen, 10, Mayence.

SCHINDLER R. (1969), 'Die Aleburg von Befort', *Hemecht*, 21, 37–50.

SCHWAB H. (1973), *Le Passé du Seeland sous un jour nouveau: les niveaux des lacs du Jura*, Editions universitaires, Fribourg.

Settlements in Scotland, 1000 BC-AD 1000, Scottish Archaeological Forum 10, Edinburgh University Press, Edinburgh.

VITAL J. and VORUZ J.-L. (1984), *L'Habitat protohistorique de Bavois-en-Raillon (Vaud)*, Bibliothèque historique vaudoise, Cahiers d'Archéologie romande, 28, Lausanne.

VLADÁR J. (1973), 'Osteuropäische und Mediterrane Einflüsse im Gebiet der Slowakei während der Bronzezeit', *Slovenská Archaeológia*, 21, 2, 253–357.

WIDHOLM D. (1980), 'Problems concerning Bronze Age settlements in Southern Sweden', *Meddelanden från Lunds universitets historiska museum, (1979–1980) Papers of the Archaeological Institute, University of Lund, 1979–1980)*, New series 3, 29–48.

252

Index